Exclusive Revolutionaries

Social History, Popular Culture, and Politics in Germany
Geoff Eley, Series Editor

A History of Foreign Labor in Germany, 1880–1980: Seasonal Workers/Forced Laborers/Guest Workers
Ulrich Herbert, translated by William Templer

Reshaping the German Right: Radical Nationalism and Political Change after Bismarck
Geoff Eley

The Stigma of Names: Antisemitism in German Daily Life, 1812–1933
Dietz Bering

Forbidden Laughter: Popular Humor and the Limits of Repression in Nineteenth-Century Prussia
Mary Lee Townsend

From Bundesrepublik *to* Deutschland: *German Politics after Unification*
Michael G. Huelshoff, Andrei S. Markovits, and Simon Reich, editors

The People Speak! Anti-Semitism and Emancipation in Nineteenth-Century Bavaria
James F. Harris

The Origins of the Authoritarian Welfare State in Prussia: Conservatives, Bureaucracy, and the Social Question, 1815–70
Hermann Beck

Technological Democracy: Bureaucracy and Citizenry in the German Energy Debate
Carol J. Hager

Society, Culture, and the State in Germany, 1870–1930
Geoff Eley, editor

Paradoxes of Peace: German Peace Movements since 1945
Alice Holmes Cooper

Jews, Germans, Memory: Reconstruction of Jewish Life in Germany
Y. Michal Bodemann, editor

Exclusive Revolutionaries: Liberal Politics, Social Experience, and National Identity in the Austrian Empire, 1848–1914
Pieter M. Judson

Exclusive Revolutionaries

Liberal Politics, Social Experience, and National Identity in the Austrian Empire, 1848–1914

Pieter M. Judson

Ann Arbor

THE UNIVERSITY OF MICHIGAN PRESS

Published in the United States of America by
The University of Michigan Press
Manufactured in the United States of America
∞ Printed on acid-free paper

1999 1998 1997 1996 4 3 2 1

A CIP catalog record for this book is available from the British Library.

Library of Congress Cataloging-in-Publication Data

Judson, Pieter M.
Exclusive revolutionaries : liberal politics, social experience, and national identity in the Austrian Empire, 1848–1914 / Pieter M. Judson.
p. cm. — (Social history, popular culture, and politics in Germany)
Includes bibliographical references (p.) and index.
ISBN 0-472-10740-2 (cloth : acid-free paper)
1. Austria—Politics and government—1848–1918. 2. Liberalism—Austria—History. 3. Nationalism—Austria—History. 4. State, The. 5. Austria—Social conditions. 6. Antisemitism—Austria—History. I. Title. II. Series.
DB85.J8 1996 96-29423
943.604'4—dc20 CIP

For Doug, K., and T.

Contents

Acknowledgments

This book takes the position that when nineteenth-century Austrian liberals resorted to illiberal measures they did not betray their ideals. To the contrary, they fulfilled the demands of a worldview meant to help them overcome the social conflict they experienced in everyday life. Despite the compelling emancipatory power of its universalist rhetoric, liberalism was marked by a profound—yet barely acknowledged—sense of hierarchy that distinguished between the enlightened and the dependent individual. That this recognition underlies my approach to liberalism should not surprise historians in related fields where liberalism has long been the subject of careful scrutiny. In Austrian history, however, nineteenth-century liberalism is still viewed primarily as a rootless ideology, and a foreign one at that: a rational and secular idealism adopted by a fragile middle class.

Until now, nineteenth-century liberalism has been of interest to students of Austrian history only to the extent that it constitutes the necessary antecedent to the cultural and political explosions of the Viennese fin-de-siècle. According to most scholars, the normalization of radical nationalism and anti-Semitism in Austrian political culture around 1900 marked a decisive rejection of all things liberal and a middle-class retreat from politics. These developments supposedly prevented liberalism from leaving any but the most insignificant mark on Central European society. *Exclusive Revolutionaries* tells a different story: one that makes visible the social power of the liberal Austrian middle classes, and the critical cultural legacies of their hierarchic worldview.

This story can be told thanks largely to generous support I received for two years of research in Vienna from the Fulbright Commission in Austria. Fulbright directors Dr. Anton Porhansel and Dr. Georg Frühwirth, along with their friendly and able assistant Frau Eva Schussek, did everything in their power to make my forays into the complex world of archival bureaucracies as painless as humanly possible. They also shared with me bits of arcane information critical to survival in Vienna, including, most memorably, the secret of how to obtain a telephone hookup there. Grants from the National Endowment for the Humanities, from Pitzer College, and from Swarthmore College funded subsequent research trips to archives and libraries in Graz, Linz, Vienna, and the Czech Republic. A Whiting Fellowship provided release from teaching at an early stage in the writing of the book.

Twenty-five years ago Wolfgang and Jutta Fischer introduced me to the paradoxical challenges of Austrian culture, history, and politics. More recently, several hospitable Austrian scholars, among them: Wolfgang Häusler, Hugo Portisch, Hannes Stekl, Gerald Stourzh, Waltraud Heindl, Elizabeth Springer, Harald Troch, Peter Urbanitsch, and Christian Witt-Döring have helped me to navigate both the pitfalls of Habsburg history and the peculiarities of Austrian research institutions. The staffs of the Allgemeines Verwaltungsarchiv, the Haus- Hof- und Staatsarchiv, the historisches Museum der Stadt Wien, the Museum für angewandte Kunst, the österreichische Nationalbibliothek, the Niederösterreichisches Landesarchiv, the Oberösterreiches Landesarchiv, the Parlamentsarchiv, the Steierisches Landesarchiv, the Wiener Stadt und Landesarchiv, the Wienerstadtbibliothek, and the Leo Baeck Institute in New York City also provided me with friendly and valuable assistance. I am especially grateful to Prince Heinrich Auersperg for granting me access to the Auersperg family archive.

I have been fortunate to have enjoyed the benefits of wise and judicious guidance liberally bestowed on me by Istvan Deak at every stage of the writing of this book. His is a rare example of personal generosity and humanist values in an academic world where neither is sufficiently cherished. Gary B. Cohen, Herman Lebovics, Harry Liebersohn, Harry Ritter, Scott Spector, and Robert Weinberg read and commented on the entire manuscript, helping me to strengthen the individual arguments throughout. William Bowman, Matti Bunzl, Jane Caplan, Stacey Freeman, Richard Handler, Lothar Höbelt, Young Sun Hong, Sarah Judson, Klemens von Klemperer, Rudy Koshar, Stuart McConnell, Robert Paxton, Miranda Pollard, Marsha Rozenblit, Jonathan Sperber, Sharon Ullman, Jacqueline Vansant, Solomon Wank, and Lora Wildenthal gave generously of their time to advise me on particular sections. While writing most of the book I was greatly privileged to work closely with anthropologist Daniel Segal. Dan's intellectual comradeship consistently challenged me to devise new ways of thinking about nationalism in both its global and Central European contexts. Douglas McKeown has tolerated the Austrian liberals for many years now, always giving unstintingly of his time, support, and editorial acumen to improve the quality of my writing about them.

In Vienna Milan Hornak, Lars Larson, Peter Matzka, Stanislav Rakusan, and Christian and Ursula Hübner provided me with unmatched hospitality, friendship, musical, artistic, and culinary insights, in short, with sustenance of every kind. And of course the book could never have been written (nor would it have its title) without the inspired insights and emotional support afforded me over the years by my dear friends Diane Shooman and Laura Lee Downs.

I want to thank Geoff Eley for his determination to expand the boundaries of German studies by including my book in a series on social history, popular culture, and politics in Germany. Several editors pay lip service to the diversity of cultures in Central Europe, but Eley is truly committed to reimagining the field in thoughtful and intellectually stimulating ways. Margaret Lourie did a superb job with the copyediting. My editor Susan Whitlock kept a first-time author in good humor during the normal trials of publication. David Good, executive editor of the *Austrian History Yearbook*, graciously permitted me to include materials in chapters seven and eight that had previously appeared in two articles for the journal.

Since I began my inquiry into Austrian Liberalism, AIDS has claimed the lives of many dear comrades and mentors. I want to acknowledge three individuals in particular who died during the writing of the book: Austrian friends Klaus Kühbacher and Ferdinand Lehman, and my teacher Eugene M. Weber.

Note on Place Names

For places that have names in common English such as Vienna, Prague, Bohemia or Silesia, I have retained this usage. In case of places with no English name and that had ethnically mixed populations I have used the German names. In many cases those names are no longer in use, and their use was contested in the nineteenth century. A list of these German place names with their Czech (C), Italian (I), Polish (P), Rumanian (R), Slovene (S), or Ukrainian (U) counterparts follows.

German Name	
Aussig	Ústí C
Böhmisch Leipa	Česká Lipa C
Brünn	Brno C
Budweis	České Budějovice C
Cilli	Celje S
Czernowitz	Czerniwci U, Cernauti R
Eger	Cheb C
Gablonz	Jablonec C
Gottschee	Gocej S
Iglau	Jihlava C
Karlsbad	Karlovy Vary C

German Name	
Königgrätz	Hradec Králové
Kremsier	Kroměříž C
Laibach	Ljubljana S
Lemberg	Lwow P Lviv U
Leitmeritz	Litoměřice C
Marburg	Maribor S
Olmütz	Olomouc C
Pilsen	Plzeň C
Reichenberg	Liberec C
Saaz	Žatec C
Teplitz	Teplice C
Trient	Trento I
Znaim	Znojmo C

Introduction

This book traces the emergence and transformation of a German liberal movement in the Habsburg monarchy. In mid-nineteenth-century Austria men and women, largely of Bürger social origins, forged a political movement that challenged the legitimacy of the reigning systems of government. Calling themselves "liberals," they mounted a revolutionary campaign in 1848 to establish their own rule over Austrian society. The ensuing struggles between liberalism and its various opponents were political in the broadest sense of the word. They were as much about establishing an alternative system of values and cultural practices in Austrian society as they were about mastering specific political institutions.

The liberals fought their battles using two strategies. The first of these produced an interregional political culture meant to serve as an alternative to the stifling rule of bureaucratic absolutism during the *Vormärz*. Organized through independent voluntary associations, this political culture became a means for building, coordinating, and controlling participation in politics by the *Volk*. The other strategy involved the deployment of a powerful public rhetoric developed by liberals to justify their revolution. Starting in 1848 with an explosion in print culture and the proliferation of voluntary associations, the values and perceptions associated with liberalism gradually came to dominate public discourse in the Habsburg monarchy. They remained a cultural force to be reckoned with long after the official liberal parties had declined in the 1890s.

Despite severe setbacks in the years following 1848, their strategies paid off in the 1860s as Austrian liberals enjoyed some success in their efforts to transform social and government institutions. In 1867 they imposed a constitution largely of their own making on an unwilling emperor, thereby ending the historic dominance of local politics by the bureaucracy, the nobility, and the Catholic Church. They established a system of compulsory education for Austrian youth, substantially reducing the influence of the church over curriculum and instruction. Already in the 1870s it was apparent that these victories had brought enormous changes to Austrian social and political life. Liberal political parties came to dominate local and state institutions in many parts of the monarchy, while their economic and social reform projects often transformed sleepy provincial landscapes into booming centers of industrial production.

At the same time, liberal cultural values gradually gained broad acceptance in urban Austrian society. Most of these—ideas about market competition, individual self-improvement, personal respectability, and a confident rationalism—rested on the fundamental belief that the economically independent individual was the productive cornerstone of public life. It was this individual's financial and intellectual independence that gained for him the rights of active citizenship. The logic behind this concept of active public citizenship implied the existence of a complementary realm as well, however, one inhabited by passive, dependent individuals who lacked the vision that supposedly derived from intellectual maturity and financial independence. Despite the equal status assigned to all people by a liberal rhetoric of universal citizenship, active citizens maintained implicitly hierarchic relationships with the women and children, as well as racial and class inferiors. The presumed inability of the latter to use reason consigned them to passive rights of citizenship. The ideological and juridical distance separating the denizens of these two spheres was simultaneously profound and insignificant, according to the liberal worldview. It was profound because passive citizens could never, as such, enjoy active rights of participation. Yet this gulf was also insignificant since basic human nature gave at least some of these passive citizens the tools for eventually earning the rights of active citizenship.

Starting with revolutionary events in 1848, liberal rhetoric about society reconciled any apparent contradiction between fundamental human equality and the political necessity of retaining distinctions between active and passive forms of citizenship. The success of this rhetoric reflected the liberals' ability to connect the social practices with the beliefs of a politically frustrated urban Bürgertum inside their new political organizational structures. Common practice in local voluntary associations shaped the new liberal rhetoric, thereby ensuring the increasing popularity of such rhetoric throughout much of the socially and regionally diverse Habsburg monarchy. The combination of liberal ideology with an emerging liberal political culture provided both rhetorical and real spaces for the mediation of liberalism's two powerful yet often contradictory urges in nineteenth-century Austria: between egalitarian demands for individual empowerment and the property owner's desire to prevent potentially dangerous social change.

Another enduring legacy of liberal discourse about society, one that continues to dominate the political cultures of Central Europe today, was the creation of a nationalist identity politics among German bourgeois activists.[1]

1. I do not wish to imply here that German nationalism developed outside the context of other earlier and aggressive forms of nationalism like that of the Czechs. Nevertheless, I want to

Since its appearance, scholars have framed German nationalism in nineteenth-century Austria, particularly its more radical varieties, as fundamentally opposed to liberal principles and practices. Contemporary observers and later historians alike attributed the very decline of political liberalism in the 1880s to the simultaneous political mobilization brought about by German nationalist activism. This book challenges that view, arguing that liberal rhetoric and organizational practice actually determined the shape and content of nationalist mass politics well into the twentieth century. The liberals themselves created a powerful new politics organized around nationalist identity in order to repulse the growing threats to their local hegemony, threats that were increasingly couched in nation-based (the Czechs), class-based (socialism), or race-based (anti-Semitism) discourse. Liberal rhetoric about society provided a crucial ideological foundation for the later explosion of German nationalist politics at the end of the nineteenth century, as activists transformed their ideas about the social differences that separated the spheres of active and passive citizenship into beliefs about national differences. The liberal belief in separate spheres of active and passive citizenship itself was transformed by 1900 into a discourse about cultural and, later, often racial difference. Even the German radical and anti-Semitic groups that challenged liberal hegemony in the 1880s and 1890s simply promised to carry out liberal nationalist commitments more effectively.

Historians have generally ignored these proofs of liberalism's underlying vitality to focus more narrowly on the Liberal Party's apparent inability to survive in an age of mass-based suffrage and political mobilization. Dwelling on Austrian liberalism's brief parliamentary history, they have treated liberalism largely as an unchanging ideological phenomenon with few natural constituents beyond an elitist upper bourgeoisie. Certainly the liberal parties faltered at the parliamentary level after 1880, and the uncritical acceptance of several traditional liberal values declined. A decade of harsh economic depression and the growing perceptions of a corrupt opportunism within the liberal parties weakened popular belief in liberalism's utopian promises and suggested that liberal rhetoric did not always match liberal actions. By 1900, the once powerful liberal movement seemed curiously spent as a political force in Austria. The liberal parties, once the largest bloc in parliament, all but disappeared, to be replaced by regional and nationalist interest groups. Unlike other liberal parties in Europe that managed to maintain some parliamentary presence well into the twentieth century, the Austrian liberals seem to have been completely eclipsed by the rise of mass socialist, Catholic, and nationalist populist parties on the left and right of the political spectrum.

---

stress the ways in which liberal and radical forms of German nationalism derived both their organizational style and their ideological content from liberalism and its traditions.

This parliamentary decline, however, represents only a small part of the story and one that was played out primarily in the imperial metropole Vienna.[2] If one approaches liberalism from the perspective of the regional political cultures it created, the narrative looks very different. Liberal political culture seems to have reinvented itself frequently, adapting its influential social rhetoric and organizational practices to dramatically changing circumstances as it tried to maintain its power to order local society. From this viewpoint, the central drama of Austrian liberalism becomes the challenge to alter its practices in order to maintain its social hegemony, not its parliamentary defeat at the hands of the populist parties. Outside Vienna it was the liberals, not their populist opponents, who politicized ethnic and gender differences most successfully in the 1880s by forging a new mass politics organized around nationalism. In Austria, German nationalism came to serve a political function closely resembling that of early liberalism, namely to consolidate Bürger hegemony in local politics by demanding social unity at all costs. Nationalism helped to mediate an attempted *trasformismo* from traditionally elite liberal politics to a controlled form of mass politics under the watchful eye of Bürger elites. By the late nineteenth century, German nationalism often augmented liberalism as a worldview that promoted social harmony and the protection of property among a Bürgertum whose social parameters were increasingly more broadly defined.

Starting in the 1880s the few historians who wrote about Austrian liberalism approached it from the vantage point of its spectacular parliamentary decline. Reacting with bitterness to their loss of parliamentary power, nineteenth-century liberal observers criticized the apparent short-sightedness of their leaders, citing factionalism as the major reason for the movement's downfall. These accounts dwelt on the excessive personal pride and greed displayed by party leaders, as well as their noticeable want of political acumen.[3]

---

2. This is one problem, for example, with John Boyer's observations about liberalism in *Political Radicalism in Late Imperial Vienna: Origins of the Christian Social Movement, 1848–1897* (Chicago, 1981).

3. Harry Ritter, "Austro-German Liberalism and the Modern Liberal Tradition," *German Studies Review* 7 (1984): 227–47. Ritter points out that "the terms and metaphors which control present-day discourse about nineteenth-century [Austrian] liberalism are, to a great extent, taken over directly from the figurative language of pathology invented in some cases . . . by insecure or disillusioned turn-of-the-century liberals themselves." Journalist historians who wrote from this point of view include Heinrich Friedjung, Heinrich Pollak, Ferdinand von Krones, and Richard Charmatz. Charmatz's *Deutsch-Österreichische Politik: Studien über den Liberalismus und über die Auswärtige Politik Österreichs* (Leipzig, 1907) is one of the best of the early surveys. In the 1950s, Georg Franz published an exhaustive work on liberalism in the 1860s, *Liberalismus. Die deutschliberale Bewegung in der habsburgischen Monarchie* (Munich, 1955). Although sympathetic in tone, the book combines the tragic self-diagnosis of turn-of-the-century liberal authors with a more nationalist and occasionally anti-Semitic viewpoint. Karl Eder's *Der Liberalismus in*

Other historians with liberal sympathies blamed the movement's decline on the rapid rise of political nationalism at the end of the century. These observers believed that the rise of nationalism in the ethnically diverse monarchy eventually robbed political liberalism of its core urban constituencies. In both the First and Second Republics, the handful of nationalist voters who refused to support either the socialist or Catholic parties are still viewed as the missing constituents of liberalism.[4]

After the Second World War and particularly in the 1960s, Austrian liberalism fell victim to another powerful historical interpretation, the *Sonderweg*, or "exceptional route," theory of German development.[5] Although this interpretation has been adequately criticized on both theoretical and empirical grounds by several historians of Germany, it is worth briefly pointing out how it has come to influence Austrian historiography. In the 1960s, several historians of Germany began looking explicitly to nineteenth-century political culture for keys to understanding the rise of authoritarianism in the 1930s. The "exceptional route" model explained twentieth-century fascism by charting the ways in which so-called preindustrial social and cultural patterns of behavior in the spheres of society and politics survived well into the "modern" era. An unusually weak bourgeoisie, unable to promote its own "modern" ways of doing business against the force of traditional elites, supposedly adapted itself to the ruling, "semifeudal" structures of public life.[6] Historians who promoted this view based it on several kinds of decontextualized sociological evidence, such as, for example, the authoritarian behavior of German industrial employers

---

Altösterreich: Geisteshaltung, Politik, und Kultur (Munich: 1955) takes an unsympathetic, Catholic political approach.

4. This interpretation accorded well with a larger theory of political continuity that has served, since the 1950s, as the privileged explanation for past and present conflict in Austrian political life. That theory views the Austrian electorate as historically divided into three, generally unchanging voting blocs: Catholic, socialist and liberal/nationalist. Adam Wandruszka, "Österreichs politische Struktur; die Entwicklung der Parteien und politischen Bewegungen," *Geschichte der Republik Österreich,* ed. Heinrich Benedikt (Vienna, 1954), 291–485. It is important to note that while this theory appears to describe political behavior in the first and second Austrian Republics adequately, it completely ignores the political behavior of German speakers in other parts of the monarchy such as Bohemia and Moravia, which had been important centers of Liberal Party strength.

5. David Blackbourn and Geoff Eley, *The Peculiarities of German History* (Oxford, 1984); Eley, "What Produces Fascism: Pre-Industrial Traditions or a Crisis of the Capitalist State?" in his *From Unification to Nazism: Reinterpreting the German Past* (Boston, 1986), 254–82; Richard J. Evans, *Rethinking German History: Nineteenth-Century Germany and the Origins of the Third Reich* (London, 1987), 23–92; Robert G. Moeller, "The Kaiserreich Recast?" *Journal of Social History,* 1984, 655–83.

6. The most influential work to develop this approach is Ralf Dahrendorf's *Society and Democracy in Germany* (London, 1968). See also Barrington Moore, *The Social Origins of Dictatorship and Democracy* (London, 1967).

toward their workers, which they attributed to the survival of feudal traditions. In this example as with so many others, historians overlooked the possibility that such workplace behaviors may have had quite modern origins and may have suited the particular needs of German capital, particularly given the strength of organized labor in Germany.[7]

Sonderweg historians also held up the achievement of fully democratic parliamentary political institutions as a critical standard by which the success or failure of nineteenth-century liberal movements ought to be measured. This anachronistic reading misrepresented the political philosophy and social goals of nineteenth-century liberals and misunderstood the critical distinction between public civic equality and private hierarchy that underlay liberal beliefs about political democratization. Few liberals, whether British, French, German, or Austrian, felt comfortable enough with the idea of political democracy to support the immediate extension of unrestricted suffrage to the working classes. Liberals could not even agree on extending the suffrage to middle-class women. And as several historians have repeatedly pointed out, Britain, that paragon of liberal development, introduced universal manhood suffrage long after Germany had done so.[8]

Comparative analysis in the last decade has at least relativized the more ahistorical claims of the *Sonderweg* approach. Yet troublesome questions remain regarding the assumed links between twentieth-century authoritarianism and earlier forms of social organization. Those links may be well worth pursuing precisely because they indicate phenomena too complex to be explained away simply in terms of the survival of traditional elites. If elements of Austrian corporatism or fascism developed from nineteenth-century antecedents, those antecedents may reflect modern responses to nineteenth-century conditions and not the remnants of feudal culture. Blind to this possibility, however, most *Sonderweg* historians attributed fascism's appeal to the survival in Central Europe of traditional authoritarian social elites who had supposedly vanquished a weak nascent liberalism in the nineteenth century. Often taking fascism at its own word, they stressed its conservative ideological critique of liberal, individualist capitalism while playing down its strong anti–trade unionist policies and its obsession with the protection of individual property rights and bourgeois family norms. The label totalitarianism, popularized during the 1950s, aided this fiction by lumping German fascism together with Soviet communism in a general category clearly opposed to the more advanced liberal individualism upheld by

7. For an elaboration of this point, see, for example, Dick Geary, "The Industrial Bourgeoisie and Labour Relations in Germany 1871–1933," in *The German Bourgeoisie: Essays on the Social History of the German Middle Class from the Late Eighteenth to the Early Twentieth Century*, ed. David Blackbourn and Richard Evans (London and New York, 1991).

8. Geoff Eley, "Liberalism, Europe, and the Bourgeoisie 1860–1914," in *The German Bourgeoisie*, ed. Blackbourn and Evans, 296–7, 299–300.

the United States and Western Europe. Both fascism and communism, it was claimed, developed in backward societies with politically weak middle classes and surviving traditions of authoritarian rule.[9]

Most historians located liberalism's specific failure in its inability to forge democratic change from the revolutions that raged across Central Europe in 1848–49. This was the critical moment at which, in the words of A. J. P. Taylor, history reached its turning point and then, in Germany and Austria, "failed to turn."[10] The liberals ought to have destroyed the power of the traditional elites (or at least badly damaged it), as had their British and French counterparts. Instead, the story goes, their failure to impose more democratic political institutions on the Austrian monarchy proved that they lacked the robust dynamism of their British or French counterparts. This apparent failure and the resilience of the dynasty, aristocracy and army held serious consequences for Austria's later development. Small wonder that Austrian liberalism, beset by nationalist and class conflict and with little apparent popular support, failed in the tasks historians (if not history) set for it.[11]

The picture of a backward and doomed Habsburg monarchy has been reinforced by a teleological view of national conflict in Austria-Hungary. In its final years, nationalist strife appears to have overwhelmed the empire and posed a serious obstacle to the kind of reasoned political discourse favored by liberal middle-class groups. The sheer inevitability of ethnic conflagration, it is argued, made the question of liberal options or achievements largely irrelevant. Noting the power of this line of thought, one historian has recently observed that "Ideas of what was possible for nineteenth-century Austrian liberalism are colored by conventional ideas about what was possible for the old empire. If we believe the empire was 'destined' to collapse, this is likely to affect our approach to liberalism and its *fate*."[12]

The fact that so many national groups seem to have coexisted uneasily in a single state makes the monarchy appear qualitatively different from its neighbors to the north and west. Nationalist conflict, it is imagined, had to ex-

---

9. Alexander Gerschenkron, *Economic Backwardness in Historical Perspective* (New York, 1965) and *An Economic Spurt that Failed* (Princeton, 1977); David F. Good, *The Economic Rise of the Habsburg Empire 1750–1914* (Berkeley and Los Angeles, 1984), 1–10, 237–56; Walter Rostow, *The Stages of Economic Growth* (Cambridge, MA, 1965). Good includes a useful, critical survey of this literature with special emphasis on economic arguments.

10. A. J. P. Taylor, *The Course of German History: A Survey of the Development of German History since 1815* (London, 1945), 68; Blackbourn and Eley, *The Peculiarities of German History*, 159.

11. The pervasive influence of Carl Schorske's brilliant *Fin de siècle Vienna: Politics and Culture* (New York, 1980), which relies on several of these assumptions about Austrian liberalism, testifies to their continuing ability to persuade.

12. Ritter, "Austro-German Liberalism," 232. Despite the laudable efforts of several historians to challenge this approach, it remains powerful, partially due to the contemporary importance

plode because this state was not a true nation state organized around a single national group. Yet if anything, recent scholarship has taught us to view the traditional nationalist claims of France, Germany, or Italy with some skepticism and to ask how nineteenth-century state policy actually created national citizens out of radically diverse local populations. Is it not finally time to see the Habsburg monarchy in the same terms as those other states?

In the last fifteen years, new historical work on state, economy, and society in Austria and Germany has helped substantially to modify these rather extreme views. Studies of regional economies and markets have revealed the underlying strength of capitalist transformation and industrial development in many parts of the monarchy, placing regions like Bohemia and Lower Austria within the context of Western European trends. Comparative analyses have also demonstrated the rather obvious point that capitalist economic systems do not necessarily require a British or American political model in order to flourish. Ironically, some historians now suggest that the survival of traditional elites was stronger in Britain than usually admitted, while in Central Europe a thriving bourgeois class exercised a variety of powers in unexpected ways. Scholarship on Austria has especially benefited from new approaches to the study of social groups loosely defined as Bürger and their often hidden but nonetheless effective means of defining their interests and exerting influence. Regional social histories have revealed the complex associational networks that structured middle-class social life in the nineteenth century. Traditionally viewed as a source of social division in Central Europe, the voluntary association actually helped middle-class Austrians to formulate and disseminate common social and cultural norms. The associations constituted a middle-class public sphere where interregional issues could be recast in terms of local identities and struggles.

Austrian scholars themselves have recently initiated a series of ambitious international projects designed to study the social origins and developing cultures of various Bürger and Mittelstand groups in all parts of the former monarchy. Yet relatively little of this excellent new work has yielded a discussion of Bürger political culture. Instead, most historians of this highly variegated Bürgertum focus on regional class formation without class politics. The student of the period is left with carefully nuanced insights into an emerging bourgeois world, insights that coexist uncomfortably with more rudi-

of ethnic identity in Central and Eastern European politics. Some of the more thoughtful revisionist work on the issue of nationalism in the monarchy includes Gary B. Cohen, *The Politics of Ethnic Survival: Germans in Prague, 1861–1914* (Princeton, 1981); Istvan Deak, *Beyond Nationalism: A Social and Political History of the Habsburg Officer Corps 1848–1918* (New York and Oxford, 1990); Katherine Verdery, *Transylvanian Villagers: Three Centuries of Political, Economic and Ethnic Change* (Berkeley, 1983).

mentary knowledge of that world's various means of political expression.[13] It is not as if good models were not available for the kind of work that would connect class formation to class politics. Fifteen years ago, groundbreaking books by American scholars Gary B. Cohen and John W. Boyer had already presented superb local studies of Bürger political culture in Prague and Vienna.

My own approach challenges several common interpretations of liberalism in Central Europe, particularly the importance it assigns to the culture of the voluntary association. This focus should redress the exaggerated orientation of the literature toward the atypical experience of liberals in Vienna and develop a more nuanced view of liberalism's relation to German political nationalism in the late nineteenth century. A standard explanation for the apparent political failure of Austrian liberalism is that it lacked indigenous roots and was established by a socially isolated group of intellectuals and ideologues who imported it from France and Britain.[14] Austrian liberals were never such dry theorists whose ideas had no practical application to Austrian conditions. On the contrary, and this is perhaps the most important point, their liberalism expressed the powerful yearnings of Austrian Bürger for institutional legitimation of their contributions to society, for control over their local polity, and for the security necessary to pursue their economic goals. An examination of the political culture that emerged from associational life demonstrates the ways in which the liberals' worldview originated largely in their particular organizational experience.

This book's focus on political culture also helps to address larger questions about the extent of the collective social and political power exercised by the Bürgertum in the nineteenth-century Habsburg monarchy. The urban middle-class battle to legitimate and institutionalize its hitherto informal influence in local social relations constituted the most successful element of an ongoing bourgeois revolution in Austrian society in the 1860s and 1870s. Liberals of all varieties, from conservative to radical, may have suffered political defeat in 1848, but their particular notions of public virtue, their myths of community, their visions of economic development gradually came to dominate Austrian public life, even in the darkest years of the post-1848 reaction. Historians of Austrian liberalism have typically pointed to the success or failure of specific political reforms as a standard by which to evaluate this revolution. Rather than view the bourgeois revolution in such narrow terms, however, I

---

13. Ernst Bruckmüller, Ulrike Döcker, Hannes Stekl, Peter Urbanitsch, eds., *Bürgertum in der Habsburgermonarchie* (Vienna, 1990); Hannes Stekl, Peter Urbanitsch, Ernst Bruckmüller, Hans Heiss, eds., *"Durch Arbeit, Besitz, Wissen und Gerechtigkeit." Bürgertum in der Habsburgermonarchie II* (Vienna, 1992).

14. Franz, *Liberalismus*. Throughout his book, Franz treats liberalism's emphasis on individualism as a Western import alien to Central European thought and conditions.

believe it makes far more sense to approach nineteenth-century European societies in terms of ongoing contested relations of political and social power fought at several different levels.[15] In Austria as elsewhere in Europe, few of the struggles that pitted the middle classes against the crown, nobility, military, and bureaucracy were limited to the arena of formal politics, and very few of these struggles resulted in absolute victory or defeat for any one group. Nevertheless, if the particular strengths or weaknesses of the Austro-German Bürgertum must be understood in a context of unresolved struggles for mastery in nineteenth-century Austrian society, it was a liberal discourse about society that persistently set the terms for these contests.

15. David Blackbourn, "The Discrete Charm of the German Bourgeoisie," in his *Populists and Patricians: Essays in Modern German History* (London, 1987), 73. For an extreme and problematic statement of bourgeois weakness throughout Europe, which nevertheless helps to correct ideas about Central European exceptionalism, see Arno Mayer's provocative *The Persistence of the Old Regime. Europe to the Great War* (New York, 1981). David Blackbourn has noted with regard to the German example, "one should be wary of assuming that the bourgeoisie simply succumbed to the aristocratic embrace. What matters is the terms on which this symbiosis of old and new took place. This is not easy to determine. But at least we should not confuse the form with the substance: much of its behavior illustrated the buoyancy as much as the capitulation of the German bourgeoisie."

CHAPTER 1

Bürger, State, and Civil Society in *Vormärz* Austria

Throughout the nineteenth century, European liberalism constituted both a collection of visions about the organization of society and a series of movements dedicated to their realization. Austrian liberalism, much like its counterparts elsewhere in Central Europe, emerged from two different kinds of social experience. One of these was the relatively narrow tradition of urban citizenship, or *Bürgerrecht*, which prized the corporate privileges granted to free members of a municipality by fellow citizens, often vis-à-vis the legal powers of the state or local nobility. The Bürgertum comprised a special community of citizens, and membership in its ranks did not follow from city residence or tax payment alone. The *Bürgerrecht* might be inherited, but it could not easily be bought or given up. And its conferral often depended on the candidate's perceived ability both to maintain an independent livelihood and to uphold standards of community honor through personal behavior.[1] In particular, the *Bürgerrecht* carried with it certain social and moral obligations toward the urban community, holding its owner to a high standard of charity toward fellow city dwellers.[2] By 1848 in most Austrian cities, the privileges of the *Bürgerrecht* had been reduced to membership in a largely ceremonial Bürger militia and to certain economic privileges granted to those engaged in some traditional industries. They no longer included much political autonomy, and local administrative

1. For an excellent discussion of the concepts of Central European *Bürgerrecht*, see Mack Walker, *German Home Towns. Community, State and General Estate 1648–1871* (Ithaca, NY, 1971), especially 26–33, 102–7, 137–42.

2. For meanings of the term *Bürgertum* before 1848, see Ernst Bruckmüller, "Wiener Bürger: Selbstverständnis und Kultur des Wiener Bürgertums vom Vormärz bis zum fin de siècle" in *"Durch Arbeit, Besitz, Wissen und Gerechtigkeit." Bürgertum in der Habsburgermonarchie II*, ed. Hannes Stekl, Peter Urbanitsch, Ernst Bruckmüller, and Hans Heiss (Vienna, 1992), 43–68; James Sheehan, *German History 1770–1866* (Oxford, 1989), 132–43.

freedom from state intrusion (*Vielzuvielregieren*) was a frequently heard demand in the years leading up to 1848.[3]

A different kind of social experience that contributed to Austrian liberalism was that of the new bourgeois, the entrepreneur active in commerce and industry who sought to foster the development of capitalist production under the old regime.[4] In *German Home Towns* Mack Walker referred to such individuals existing outside the confines of guild regulation as "movers and doers." The local Bürger, however, referred to them more often as: "disturbers, *Störer* . . . purveyors of alien production . . . raiders of the hometown economy." In the eighteenth century these men might create dynamic new industries outside the traditional restrictions on trade and manufacture exercised by city guilds, industries that tended to undermine what little survived of the world of the *Bürgerrecht*.

Yet if the traditional Bürger and the new bourgeois disagreed potentially on economic policy, by the end of the eighteenth century both saw their interests primarily in political terms, sharing a common antipathy to the state bureaucracy. When liberalism made its public debut as a political movement in 1848, the urban Bürger tradition of civic autonomy had already become closely linked in the public mind to the value placed on economic freedom, independence, and productivity by the commercial and industrial bourgeoisie. In the late eighteenth century an emerging bourgeois ideology, which promoted a theoretical economic liberty, converged with what remained of the world of *Bürgerrecht* to create the independent urban citizen, the man who formed the productive cornerstone of society. The combination of these visions produced a powerful and distinctive liberal rhetoric about society as well as a distinctive political culture in the Austrian half of the Habsburg monarchy.[5]

As a movement, liberalism worked broadly to shape both state and society to satisfy the needs of its twin visions, to empower urban capitalist society's so-

---

3. Karl Ucakar and Manfred Welan, "Kommunale Selbstverwaltung und konstitutioneller Rechtsstaat," in *Wien in der liberalen Ära*, ed. Felix Czeike (Vienna, 1978), 5–30.

4. Walker, *German Home Towns*, 120.

5. By 1900 the terms *Bürger* and *bourgeois* in Austria had come to describe often interchangeable groups that shared larger political attitudes. What Charles Maier argued for the use of the term *bourgeois* in the 1920s could in fact have been argued for the Austrians who invoked the term *Bürger* fifty years earlier: "It really did evoke the basic social divisions of a market economy and industrial social order," and "Frequent recourse to the term revealed a nagging preoccupation with inequality and class antagonism." Charles Maier, *Recasting Bourgeois Europe: Stabilization in France, Germany, and Italy in the Decade after World War I* (Princeton, 1975), 7. Austrian liberal rhetoric distinguished itself from British liberalism in its preoccupation with civic autonomy, its acceptance of the state as a useful instrument to accomplish its goals, and its idealization, from a distance, of the economy.

called productive individuals as fully as possible and to confer upon them the political power that their newly improved social status demanded. The men and women who sought to replace existing social and political hierarchies with something new in 1848 outlined a system of values that bestowed the traditional privileges of Bürger freedom and autonomy on those bourgeois whose economic success demonstrated their productivity and therefore their right to participate in political rule. In fact, by 1848 liberalism appealed to a much wider social spectrum than simply those who held traditional Bürger privileges or those active in commerce and finance. Membership in this Bürgertum was extended to other social groups as well, particularly to educated professionals. Austrians whose occupations demanded a significant commitment to education (civil servants, teachers, lawyers, physicians) gradually gained the status of comembers in an expanded Bürger class. According to the early liberals, a complex society required more for its healthy development than simply a number of economically productive independent citizens. It required, for example, an educated citizenry, one able to look beyond the narrow horizons of local provincialism to understand the interests of the community in global terms. The value placed on the abstract idea of education reflects the common equation of economic with cultural achievement by liberals throughout Central Europe.

This growing Bürger class looked quite different depending where one traveled in mid-century Austria. The spread of capitalist relations in the Habsburg monarchy, as elsewhere in Europe, varied significantly by region and locality. Different scales of production throughout the monarchy created contradictory needs among different types of producers and, consequently, differing economic demands made on the state.[6] In the early nineteenth century some parts of the empire had developed strong interregional markets and industrial production as sophisticated as any in continental Europe. In Bohemia, Moravia, Lower Austria, and Styria, urban merchants, artisans, elements of the aristocracy, and immigrants from Western Europe who could raise the capital had founded textile or mining industries. Here the growth of large-scale capitalist firms in the eighteenth century challenged the prevailing legal and customary concepts of property ownership, commerce, banking practices, labor organization, and technological development. In other regions to the east and south (Bukowina, Dalmatia, Galicia), however, production remained relatively isolated from interregional trade and overwhelmingly agricultural until well into the twentieth century. Legal limits on credit and the absence of a banking network hampered industrial expansion and the creation of new firms, while a maze of local tariffs and commercial restrictions often made even neighboring markets inaccessible to each other. And in the more economically

6. Good, *Economic Rise*, 14–73.

advanced regions industrialists frequently sought protective tariffs from the government even as they demanded an end to traditional internal restraints on production.[7]

Immigrant and local capitalist producers in the more developed crownlands were not alone in their desires to lift several of the burdens imposed by traditional restrictions on production. During the latter half of the eighteenth century, the imperial state administration had become increasingly committed to shaping more coherent economic policies for the monarchy as a whole. This was not easy, since the monarchy itself consisted of a collection of territories that enjoyed different rights and privileges in relation to the central government in Vienna and little relation to one another. In the second half of the eighteenth century Austria's rulers steadily introduced programs of political centralization, economic rationalization, regional specialization, and enhanced growth, often against serious political opposition from provincial nobles, who saw in the reforms a direct challenge to their own local powers. The rulers' goals were both political and economic. By linking regional markets in a viable, territorial economic unit, they hoped to accomplish a greater integration of their politically and geographically decentralized monarchy. Political and economic centralization in turn would help to revive Austria's international fortunes.[8]

Austria's so-called reforming monarchs, Maria Theresa (1740–80) and her sons Joseph II (1780–90) and Leopold II (1790–92), laid much of the groundwork for further capitalist expansion and an industrial revolution in Austria. They interfered in legal relations between peasants and lords, hoping to establish a class of smaller-scale agricultural producers. They made it easier for non-nobles in many regions to buy debt-ridden aristocratic estates, often offering titles of nobility as an incentive.[9] At the same time, the rulers gradually stripped the provincial diets of key administrative powers, handing these over to a burgeoning central bureaucracy. As the instrument through which the Habsburgs tried to shape society, the growing imperial bureaucracy was meant

7. Hermann Freudenberger, "Industrialization in Bohemia and Moravia in the Eighteenth Century," in *Journal of Central European Affairs* 19 (1960): 493–509; Freudenberger and Gerhard Mensch, *Von der Provinzstadt zur Industrieregion* (Göttingen, 1975); Good, *Economic Rise*, 23, 53–55; Hubert Weitensfelder, *Interessen und Konflikte in der Frühindustrialisierung. Dornbirn als Beispiel* (Frankfurt/M, 1991). By 1790 the empire, excluding Galicia and the Tirol, had 280 manufacturing firms. Of these, half could be found in Lower Austria and a third in Bohemia. Bohemia and Moravia became important textile centers, and Brünn gained a reputation as the "Manchester of Central Europe" after 1765. Styria was an important producer of iron and iron products.

8. Good, *Economic Rise*, 27–34.

9. Ernst Bruckmüller, *Landwirtschaftliche Organisationen und gesellschaftliche Modernisierung. Vereine, Genossenschaften und politische Mobilisierung der Landwirtschaft Österreichs vom Vormärz bis 1914* (Salzburg, 1977), 24–27; Paul Ghelardoni, "Die feudalen Elemente in der österreichischen bürgerlichen Gesellschaft von 1803 bis 1914" (Ph.D. diss., University of

The Austrian Crownlands, 1867-1914

to offer expert opinion, to formulate policy, and to administer it ruthlessly. The bureaucrats themselves developed a consciousness of their special role in the accelerating process of state building in the late eighteenth century, generally identifying their interests with those of the reforming state from which they derived their mandate to interfere in society.[10]

This era of reform came abruptly to a close after the untimely death of Leopold II in 1792. Threatened by the specter of social unrest unleashed by revolution in France, Leopold's son Francis II/I made peace with the nobility. He did so, however, not by renouncing the centralist achievements of his predecessors but by using their formidable bureaucratic machinery for more socially conservative ends. For the next fifty years the bureaucracy assumed the unfamiliar and often uncomfortable role of preserving a conservative status quo. This change gradually filled the entrepreneurial bourgeoisie with ambivalence toward its former champion, the state bureaucracy, bringing it closer to the complaints of the traditional urban Bürgertum against government interference in local affairs. On the positive side for the economic bourgeoisie, the bureaucracy had encouraged a liberalization of local and interregional economies. In addition, the rapidly expanding state administration continued to offer new career opportunities and social advancement to the educated sons of both the Bürgertum and the bourgeoisie. Waltraud Heindl's recent study of the world of imperial officialdom brilliantly documents how this bourgeois invasion of a previously noble preserve transformed the administration. Despite an aristocratic monopoly on the highest positions, the bureaucracy as a whole gradually came to embody bourgeois virtues of thrift, hard work, and regular hours during the *Vormärz*. Nevertheless, after 1800, Bürger and bourgeois society chafed under the increasing restrictions imposed by an intrusive and conservative state on a developing civil society. As the bureaucracy became a tool for the preservation of the economic and social status quo under

---

Vienna, 1961); Good, *Economic Rise*, 27–37; C. A. Macartney, *The Habsburg Empire 1790–1918* (London, 1969), 199–233; Heidemarie Ortner, "Das Eindringen des wiener Bürgertums in den landtäflichen Grundbesitz Niederösterreichs, 1815–1895" (Ph.D. diss., University of Vienna, 1968), 143–48, 194–201. By 1848 almost a third of the noble estates in the province of Lower Austria had passed into the hands of bourgeois owners. Their owners pioneered capitalist methods in farming and a system of large-scale commercial production. In the late eighteenth century Maria Theresa, Joseph II, and Leopold II had already diminished most internal customs barriers substantially while raising tariffs against foreign-made goods. They promoted an improved transportation infrastructure and supported technological innovation in industry, encouraging the immigration of skilled artisans and offering privileges to entrepreneurs who introduced innovative industrial processes. In some industries the law subverted guild powers by requiring artisans to use new methods and technologies or risk losing their licenses.

10. Waltraud Heindl, *Gehorsame Rebellen. Bürokratie und Beamte in Österreich 1780 bis 1848* (Vienna, 1990), 21–89.

Francis II/I, many in the Bürgertum blamed it specifically for impeding social and economic progress.[11]

If Bürger society resented the incursions of the bureaucracy (its "*Vielzuvielregieren*" and "*Durchregieren*"), it nevertheless appreciated the potential uses of state institutions. Like their counterparts in other parts of Central Europe, Austrian liberals supported the existence of a powerfully centralized state, not because, as many have argued, they were themselves officials who feared reform from below and not simply because their minds had been colonized by the traditions of a powerful state. Rather, the state offered them a ready instrument with which to impose their own vision on Austrian society. In their hands the central state gave liberals an unparalleled opportunity to apply the law equally to all Austrians, regardless of corporate allegiance or provincial privilege, and thereby create a society peopled by responsible citizens. By elaborating a system of consistent rules for all to live by, Austrian liberals sought to remake the state into a powerful guarantor of individual rights. They would accomplish this not by limiting or even destroying the power of the state but rather by purging it of abuses and directing its power toward liberal aims, by creating the *Rechtsstaat*, the "state of law." In this they appear to differ from their British counterparts, who, despite their reliance on the state for support of commercial ventures, preferred to focus on local initiative as the source of reform. They resemble far more their nineteenth-century French counterparts, for whom the central state also served as an instrument to create citizens from a confusion of corporate and local identities.[12]

During the period 1780 to 1848 the urban Bürgertum seems to have developed a strongly independent cultural identity, one that increasingly distinguished it from the social and cultural standards set by aristocratic society. While their emerging social world included some emulation of the nobility's cultural standards, the bourgeois just as frequently displayed a self-conscious moral superiority toward the second estate. Ulrike Döcker has shown in her suggestive studies of late eighteenth-century manners and morals in Austria how uncertainty regarding the creation of new public standards of behavior

---

11. Waltraud Heindl, "Bürokratisierung und Verbürgerlichung: Das Beispiel der Wiener Zentralbürokratie seit 1780," in *Bürgertum in der Habsburgermonarchie II*, ed. Stekl et al., 193–202; Heindl, *Gehorsame Rebellen*, 179–200, 225–43; Josef Polišenský, *Aristocrats and the Crowd in the Revolutionary Year 1848, a Contribution to the History of Revolution and Counterrevolution in Austria*, trans. Frederick Snider (Albany, NY, 1980) 45–46. The majority of Bürger administrators functioned at the middle and lower levels of the state bureaucracy, accounting for half of all lower court administrators in the *Vormärz*. By 1848 their share of positions had declined.

12. Leonard Krieger, *The German Idea of Freedom* (Chicago, 1972), 252–61; James J. Sheehan, *German Liberalism in the Nineteenth Century* (Chicago, 1978), 45–46.

plagued the emerging Bürgertum. Nevertheless, guides to public manners published in the 1780s and 1790s praised the independence and hard-working ethos of the Bürgertum, often contrasting these virtues with the imagined idleness of the aristocracy.[13] By the 1830s these attitudes had become standard fare in urban middle-class society. Referring to his father's ennoblement in 1836, for example, Leopold von Hasner of Prague felt compelled to note that neither he nor his young sisters were in the least impressed by their family's new title: "we disdained anything not founded on independent accomplishment and believed we could dispense with the pretence associated with such social differences for which we had, in reality, no respect."[14]

The spread of these values and attitudes occurred largely in the context of the independent voluntary associations created by Bürger and bourgeois Austrians in the eighteenth and early nineteenth centuries. In an overlapping network of professional, philanthropic, and social organizations, different occupational groups learned about their social and political commonalities, quickly creating a sense of larger group or class interest. If not completely free from direct state interference, the voluntary association nevertheless offered the Bürgertum an independent social space for the development of alternative social visions. It assumed a vital role in the creation of a civil society in *Vormärz* Austria.[15]

Starting in the mid-eighteenth century, several consecutive statutes governed the creation and existence of voluntary associations. A law of 1764 shows that the Vienna government had already established a concession system for regulating such organizations. Those who wished to found an association had to apply to the provincial bureaucracy for permission and provide membership lists, statutes, and a list of club purposes and goals.[16] Also starting in the 1760s, several decrees either forbade or regulated membership in Free-

13. Ulrike Döcker, "Bürgerlichkeit und Kultur—Bürgerlichkeit als Kultur. Eine Einführung" and Döcker "Jeder Mensch gilt in dieser Welt nur so viel, als wozu er sich selbst macht'— Adolph Freiherr von Knigge und die bürgerliche Höflichkeit im 19. Jahrhundert," in *Bürgertum in der Habsburgermonarchie*, ed. Bruckmüller, et al., 95–104, 115–25.

14. Leopold von Hasner, *Denkwürdigkeiten. Autobiographisches und Aphorismen* (Stuttgart, 1892), 18.

15. On middle-class voluntary associations in Central Europe, see, in particular, Blackbourn and Eley, *The Peculiarities of German History*, 190–205; Blackbourn "The Discrete Charm of the German Bourgeoisie," in his *Populists and Patricians*, 67–83; Rudy Koshar, *Social Life, Local Politics and Nazism, Marburg 1880–1938*, (Chapel Hill and London, 1986); Thomas Nipperdey, "Verein als soziale Struktur in Deutschland im späten 18. und frühen 19. Jahrhundert. Eine Fallstudie zur Modernisierung I," in *Gesellschaft, Kultur, Theorie: Gesammelte Aufsätze zur neueren Geschichte*, ed. Nipperdey (Göttingen, 1976); Peter Urbanitsch, "Bürgertum und Politik in der Habsburgermonarchie. Eine Einführung," in *Bürgertum in der Habsburgermonarchie*, ed. Bruckmüller et al., 165–75.

16. M. von Stubenrauch, *Statistische Darstellung des Vereinswesens im Kaiserthume Österreich* (Vienna, 1857), 2.

mason lodges. With the radicalization of the revolution in France, the government began to see a potential for sedition in every voluntary association. In 1791 administrators were admonished to keep strict watch over all "suspicious and dangerous meetings, clubs, or secret organizations."[17] And indeed, government investigations culminated in the trial and execution of several Austrian Jacobins in 1794 and 1795. Seditious political clubs and conspiracies were not limited to Vienna—if the police reports are to be believed—surfacing as well in Hungary, Carinthia, Styria, the Tirol, and Upper Austria.[18] Finally, an 1801 law forced bureaucrats to swear an oath that they had not joined any secret societies, a policy designed to terminate the existence of the Freemasons in Austria.[19] Following the Napoleonic wars, however, bad economic conditions contributed to a thaw in official attitudes toward associations and their usefulness. Now the government encouraged organizations that, through their charitable or self-help activities, would either assume some of the government's social obligations or work to stimulate an economic revival.[20] Nevertheless, Metternich remained vigorously opposed to all voluntary associations in principle, even those founded for charitable purposes. They were, he is reported to have said, "a German plague."[21]

Within the associations, members developed new ways of interacting and communicating. Dues-paying members elected an executive board that administered the association in the members' interests. Controversial issues were ideally put to a vote after an open, public discussion of possible alternatives. The experience gained from these procedures served the formation of general interests within a diverse new bourgeois class. Discussion, voting, and forging compromise in this privileged yet public space helped members to build alliances and general consensus by making visible just where various group interests intersected. And as associational life helped to fashion and spread an

17. Irmgard Helperstorfer, "Die Entwicklung des Vereinswesens im Vormärz," in *Bürgersinn und Aufbegehren. Biedermeier und Vormärz in Wien 1815–1848* (Vienna, 1988), 320.

18. Helmut Reinalter, "Die Französische Revolution und Österreich. Ein Überblick," in *Freiheit, Gleichheit, Brüderlichkeit auch in Österreich? Auswirkungen der französischen Revolution auf Wien und Tirol* (Vienna, 1989), 180–95; Reinalter, "Aufklärung, Freimauerei und Jakobinertum in der Habsburgermonarchie," in *Jakobiner in Mitteleuropa*, ed. Reinalter (Innsbruck, 1977), 243ff.

19. Heindl, *Gehorsame Rebellen*, 286–87; Kuess-Scheichelbauer, *200 Jahre Freimauerei in Österreich* (Vienna, 1959). Government bureaucrats had constituted most of the membership of Freemason lodges in the late eighteenth century.

20. Helperstorfer, "Entwicklung des Vereinswesens," 324; Stubenrauch *Statistische Darstellung*, 2. The government vigorously opposed student organizations like the Burschenschaften. Although one or two existed for a short time in the 1840s, this kind of association, so important to the revival of public life elsewhere in Central Europe, was uncommon in Austria.

21. L. A. Frankl, *Erinnerungen von Ludwig August Frankl* (Prague, 1910), 292; H. Obrovski, "Die Entwicklung des Vereinswesens im Vormärz" (Ph.D. diss., University of Vienna, 1970), 33.

array of new middle-class values, it also tended to undermine the power of traditional corporate social categories. Membership and leadership positions in associations conferred social status on their holders. "If one wanted to reach a certain degree of honor," noted one historian of the Vienna Bürgertum in the *Vormärz*, "then social engagement was unavoidable."[22]

By 1848, voluntary associations constituted semipublic settings where people otherwise deprived of a voice in policy formulation joined to articulate shared concerns about the community and the state. They did so using a rhetoric that avoided discussing issues in political terms. The government's injunction against open political activity thus had the unintended effect of casting reform discussions in general, moral terms. Members of the voluntary associations adopted a rhetoric that defined their interests against both the intrusive state and all so-called selfish interest groups. As in other parts of Central Europe, club members believed that in their organizations they constituted an alternative moral and social order to the state's, one that better reflected the universal concerns of the entire community. Clothing their political ideals in an idealistic rhetoric of virtue, they came to view political reform as a moral imperative rather than as a tactical attempt to achieve a limited aim. This orientation is clear from the ways in which associational statutes suggested the rules of a different kind of society, one, for example, in which each citizen, through engagement in the organization, took active responsibility for maintaining the good of the entire community.[23]

Among the most important *Vormärz* associations in terms of molding urban public opinion on issues were the reading associations and the industrial associations. Both groups defined themselves independently of the government and the church, something less true of the charitable organizations that also proliferated during the *Vormärz*. Both also understood their purpose in terms of public obligation, whether it meant educating themselves and the public, working to improve the business environment, or setting up self-help programs to aid and regulate the poor or unemployed.

Of the many *Vormärz* reading associations, historians have devoted particular attention to the Vienna Legal-Political Reading Association, partly because its membership reads like a "Who's Who" of post-1848 cabinets and ministries and partly because its location in Vienna put it at the center of several political conflicts. Founded in 1841 as a discussion club, the association counted over 200 dues-paying members by the end of 1847. Lawyers and bureaucrats made up the largest occupational groups among the members, followed by lawyers' assistants, university professors, physicians, industrialists, businessmen, and a few aristocrats. The annual membership fee of more than

22. Bruckmüller, "Wiener Bürger," 47.

23. Heindl, *Gehorsame Rebellen*, 286–90; Sheehan, *German Liberalism*, 14–18.

ten gulden did not restrict the membership simply to the wealthiest, and those who could not afford it, mostly students, applied for an associate membership at a reduced rate.[24]

The Legal-Political Reading Association provided its members with a library of almost 700 books and periodicals. Every year the association haggled with the censors over its subscriptions to foreign journals. In 1841, for example, the censors struck twelve newspapers from the club's proposed list of fifty-six, including all political and literary journals. In 1843 the police granted the association permission for the *Leipziger Zeitung*, the leading liberal paper of eastern Germany, as well as Ignaz Kuranda's left-leaning *Grenzboten*. In the following year the association was also granted the right to obtain two moderate French journals, *Le Constitutionel* and *Le Siècle*. Interestingly, the association seems to have displayed no interest in obtaining any journals, political or otherwise, from England. In later years other liberal journals from the Rheinland and Italy were added to the list, although permission previously granted for some journals was frequently reversed. As a result, both members and foreign guests often smuggled in copies of forbidden journals and volumes from France, Switzerland, and the other German states. According to the police, who staged periodic raids on the club's library, it housed over sixty officially forbidden titles.[25]

The association tried regularly to hold public lectures on contemporary issues, often disguising the subjects in order to gain police permission for its events. This modification became necessary because the police tended to cancel the association's planned lectures on the slightest pretense. In 1844 the police allowed a lecture on reform of penal institutions, for example, but canceled a lecture on phrenology, claiming that the topic had little to do with the club's stated purpose. When a popular professor of law at the university, Baron Anton Hye, announced a series of lectures on the history of Austrian criminal law, the police informed the association that the frequent holding of lectures was antithetical to the association's statutes. The association then petitioned to make lectures a regular part of its official program, pointing to the successful examples of reading associations in Graz and Innsbruck, where lectures were a

24. Friedrich Engel-Janosi, "Der Wiener juridisch-politische Leseverein; seine Geschichte bis zur Märzrevolution," *Mitteilungen des Vereines für Geschichte der Stadt Wien* 4 (1923): 58–66; Heinrich Reschauer, "Der juridisch-politische Leseverein in Monat März, 1848," DZ, March 28–29, April 4, 1888. Among the association's members, twenty-six would later serve as deputies to the Frankfurt Parliament in 1848, twenty-three would serve in the Austrian Parliament of 1848–49, and sixteen would serve as cabinet ministers. Five of these latter served in the Bürger Ministry of 1867: Johann N. Berger, Rudolf Brestel, Carl Giskra, Leopold von Hasner, and Eduard Herbst, who, because of his post at the University of Lemberg, was a corresponding member of the association.

25. Engel-Janosi, "Der wiener juridisch-politische Leseverein."

recognized part of club activities. The government did not relent and from this point on, lectures and discussions had to be held informally and in private. Still, even government censorship had its limits. Despite the repeated attempts by the Viennese police to close it down, the association remained open, thanks ironically to the efforts of those members who themselves occupied prominent posts in the government.[26]

Reading clubs in Graz and Innsbruck fulfilled a function for local Bürger society similar to that of the Legal Political Association in Vienna. They too had emerged from informal discussion circles, serving as focal points for debate of local, provincial, and national affairs, and they too had their own problems with the police. In 1846 the government intensified its censorship efforts, reporting "irregularities" at the traditionally better-behaved *Joanneum* in Graz. In Innsbruck the police actually confiscated several forbidden journals from the city's *Lesekasino*.[27]

Just as important as the reading groups in the development of an activist liberal political culture were the commercial or industrial associations: the Bohemian Industrial Association founded in 1828 in Prague, the Inner Austrian Industrial Association founded in 1837 in Graz (with branches in Klagenfurt and Laibach), and the Lower Austrian Industrial Association founded in 1838–39 in Vienna.[28] Each of the industrial associations grew out of local initiatives to force the central government to support business interests more actively and effectively. By the 1840s they brought together a broad coalition of manufacturers, merchants, artisans, and industrialists, which demanded a comprehensive reform of banking, credit, and tariff laws.

The industrial associations were hardly unanimous in their demands regarding tariffs and the possible merits of free international trade. In the years leading up to 1848 the growing complaints of industrialists and merchants about state economic policy did not imply that they held a unified position on trade policy. Far from it. Their unity lay in their common demands for instituting a system of political representation that would guarantee them a voice in policy formation. When in the first third of the nineteenth century a critical literature developed to champion new forms of social organization and economic production, it tended to demand general political reform rather than specific economic policy changes. Their lack of consensus on economic policy was

---

26. Engel-Janosi, "Der wiener juridisch-politische Leseverein," 62; R. John Rath, *The Viennese Revolution of 1848* (Austin, 1958), 30–31.

27. Engel-Janosi, "Der wiener juridisch-politische Leseverein," 64; Gerhard Pfeisinger, "Die Revolution von 1848 in Graz" (Ph.D. diss., University of Salzburg, 1985), 16, 25–28. Pfeisinger suggests that discussions in the local *Bürgerliche Ressource*, in coffee houses, and at the theater were far more openly political than those in the *Joanneum.*

28. Otto Hwaletz, "Zur ökonomischen, sozialen und ideologisch-politischen Formierung des industriell-gewerblichen Bürgertums. Das Beispiel der Industrieverein," in *Bürgertum in der Habsburgermonarchie,* ed. Bruckmüller et al., 177–204.

typical of continental liberals throughout much of the nineteenth century, particularly in Central Europe. The demands for free trade and unfettered resources that characterized liberal rhetoric reflected more a theoretical commitment to ideal liberties than anything else.[29] Support for free trade in Austria generally came from owners of larger industrialist concerns and from state bureaucrats who saw in it the necessary basis for their ambitious foreign policy objectives in Central Europe. Artisans and industrialists who feared competition opposed free trade and membership in the *Zollverein* (German Customs Union), as did most textile manufacturers. On the related issues of a free labor market and internal market restrictions, however, producers of all scales generally agreed on the necessity of liberalizing the complex local laws that restricted entrepreneurs from establishing new businesses and workers from moving to different employment.

The industrial associations produced a rhetoric of common group interest against what they perceived to be a do-nothing state and a bureaucracy that blocked any potentially progressive economic developments. These associations worked hard to raise public concern over Austria's relative economic backwardness. Such public concerns increased dramatically in the second quarter of the nineteenth century and became acute in response to a debate over Austria's possible entry into the *Zollverein* in the 1830s and 1840s.[30] Following an 1845 exhibition sponsored by the Lower Austrian Industrial Association in Vienna, one frustrated economist expressed the hope that this event would "finally awaken an awareness by the state that industry is useful" and an appreciation "of the value of private enterprise in terms of the state's interests."[31] The industrial associations initiated these industrial exhibitions not simply to influence the government but as part of a larger strategy of self-help, designed to acquaint potential foreign buyers with Austrian products and to teach members in turn about foreign markets and technologies. The Graz Association, which in 1847 claimed a membership of 2,391, helped individual members to expand their economic resources in ways that they could not have afforded themselves, by making credit or new technologies available to them at lower rates.[32]

The industrial organizations also debated the merits of various labor management techniques designed to promote increased discipline (or "harmony," as they put it) among the working classes. This echoes a second important

29. Sheehan, *German Liberalism*, 28–32.

30. Wolfgang Häusler, *Von der Massenarmut zur Arbeiterbewegung; Demokratie und soziale Frage in der Wiener Revolution von 1848* (Vienna, 1979), 51–68, 124–27; Rath, *Viennese Revolution*, 32. For a critical view of the government from the point of view of artisanal industry, see Karl Beidtel, *Die Geldangelegenheiten Österreichs* (Leipzig, 1847).

31. Anton von Kraus-Elislago, *Bericht über die dritte allgemeine Gewerbeaustellung* (Vienna, 1846); Häusler, *Massenarmut*, 68.

32. Hwaletz, "Industrieverein," 183–89.

complaint against the regime heard frequently in middle-class circles: that the government was unwilling to address the dangerous social volatility of the under classes. Fear of some kind of attack on property often motivated members' complaints against the government and led them to take up a limited agenda of social improvement in their own clubs. Several economic, philanthropic, and charitable associations worked, as one club stated, "to raise the welfare and the moral sensibility of the under classes" and to teach the virtues of "thrift and hard work" as a way to improve those classes.[33] In this way associations not only provided a space for the development of new, broad-based middle-class values; they also worked hard to spread those values to other social groups.

Association membership lists confirm an important point made at the outset of this chapter: that the social boundaries of this emerging middle, Bürger, or bourgeois class were not simply fixed rigidly by occupation or economic status but were constructed in terms of local perceptions about social relations. By the mid-nineteenth century property ownership of many scales and some degree of education defined this common Bürger culture far more than did traditional corporate allegiances. Individual membership regulations, club dues, or education requirements provide concrete examples of the different degrees of exclusivity used to define local Bürger identity. Professionals like journalists, lawyers, physicians and notaries, shopkeepers, small or large businessmen, civil servants, and local landowners generally made up the majority of club members. Yet the specific boundaries of this class of participants depended more on local conditions than on any set quality inherent to the individual. And in the end, Bürger might support or oppose free trade, membership in the German *Zollverein*, or the lifting of restrictions on labor, but Bürger understood their identity mostly in terms of the value of productive ownership. Production created property, and this more than anything else made education, individual reflection on the world, and self-cultivation possible. Reflection and education in turn produced an awareness of a greater community good, one that supposedly transcended all other sectarian interests.

In his important history of nineteenth-century German liberalism, James J. Sheehan characterized the last third of the eighteenth century in Central Europe as a time when one could locate the beginnings of a "political public," that is, "a small but significant group of men who tried to establish ties outside of the existing administrative, ecclesiastical, and corporate establishments."[34] By the 1840s in Austria, this "political public" had grown considerably from its modest beginnings in eighteenth-century urban sociability and the first voluntary associations. "Without our having ever heard much about freedom,"

33. Hwaletz, "Industrieverein," 190; Pfeisinger, "1848 in Graz," 231.
34. Sheehan, *German Liberalism*, 7.

recalled Leopold Hasner of this period in Prague, "a spirit of freedom took root in us."[35] Police censorship and bureaucratic rule notwithstanding, a growing intellectual vitality and economic dynamism characterized social life in Austria's largest cities. Writing in 1842, diarist Eduard Bauernfeld observed the change in his fellow Viennese, calling them "more serious" and noting that, "There is almost no important trend . . . in which the Viennese middle class does not take part. More is being read in Vienna in recent years. The masses of books and pamphlets that the capital city consumes, especially those dealing with politics and *belles lettres*, is astounding. There is no dearth of opportunities to obtain every contemporary literary work of any interest here, and everyone seems to be helping himself." In short, Bauernfeld concluded that "no new idea in Vienna can remain unknown or undiscussed among the educated classes for long."[36]

While public policy came under increasing scrutiny among the monarchy's urban middle classes in the 1830s and 1840s, it also became the focus of a revived opposition to the government in several of the provincial diets. Although each diet focused its demands on local issues, the growing chorus of opposition in the 1840s contained common elements, which will be briefly surveyed below. In addition, the appearance of several anonymous reform manifestos in the 1840s combined with the *Grenzboten*'s publication of documents and protocols obtained from both the Bohemian and Lower Austrian diets in 1846 heightened the sense of a coordinated interregional liberal opposition.[37]

Most reform programs, whether published by individuals or developed in regional diets, sought an end to the manorial system and the *Robot* in the countryside and a relaxation of censorship in the cities. Some also demanded more influence on tax issues for the local diets and a greater representation of the urban and rural Bürgertum in those institutions. As early as 1833 the Lower

35. Hasner, *Denkwürdigkeiten*, 17.

36. [Eduard von Bauernfeld], *Pia Desideria eines österreichischen Schriftstellers* (Leipzig: 1843), 15, 50; Bruckmüller, "Wiener Bürger," 48. "The Viennese," added Bauernfeld, "have, without a doubt, become more serious. Industry has set up its throne here, as it has everywhere else. A people who found industrial associations and build railroads has little time for grilled hens, vaudeville, and Strauss. . . . Still, the excited interest of this new Viennese in the arts, the sciences, and in public life has not yet been given its due."

37. Victor von Andrian-Werburg, *Österreich und dessen Zukunft*, 2 vols. (Hamburg, 1843–47); Rath, *Viennese Revolution*, 20–27; Francis Schusselka, *Österreich über Alles wenn es nur will* (Vienna,1848). Substantial differences actually separated these reform visions, all of which were considered "liberal" at the time. Andrian-Werburg, a high state official, criticized bureaucratic misrule and urged that the provincial nobility be given greater power as a step toward reforming the manorial system, developing greater local self-government, and improving education. Schusselka rejected the notion of the nobility as a force for change and urged the emperor to rely on the people and become a "citizen king."

Austrian Diet (where bourgeois agrarian interests were strong) had petitioned the government to replace the burdensome responsibilities of the manorial system with some form of state-paid administration. By the mid 1840s, bourgeois and noble landowners, bureaucrats, and representatives of the towns demanded an end to the *Robot* and to tithes, demanded tax reform, the right to review the budget, the institution of an imperial parliament in Vienna, and the addition of greater representation for Bürger classes. In an 1845 petition the Lower Austrian Diet strongly condemned state censorship. A year later the same diet proposed an agricultural credit bank, municipal reforms, an income tax, a reduction of indirect consumer taxes, publication of the state budget, and the right to approve new taxes. Finally, the diet warned against the deplorable condition of wage laborers and the peasantry, implying that a government failure to act on these demands would inflame an already volatile situation. Using the same reform rhetoric, the Styrian Diet also petitioned for an end to agrarian feudalism. In 1845 the Bohemian and Moravian diets likewise claimed their right to approve government budgets, and in 1847 they rejected the government's demand for an increase in the land tax. In 1838 the mayor of Vienna, Ignaz Czapka, a conservative bureaucrat himself, suggested that property owners and manufacturers elect a Bürger Committee, which would be allowed some limited role in setting the city's economic policy.[38]

In the 1840s, frustration with conditions for economic growth and fears of social unrest generated concern among bureaucrats, industrialists, professionals, artisans, and landowners alike. Several groups outside the diets criticized the government's inability to deal effectively with unrest, urging timely reform to stave off further uprisings. Common awareness of a social problem was heightened by several incidents in the mid 1840s. In 1842, for example, poor harvests and inflation led to outbreaks of violence among peasants and laborers all over the monarchy. Bloody peasant uprisings in 1846 terrorized Polish landlords in Galicia, arousing fears of similar agrarian violence elsewhere in the monarchy. In Brünn, Eger, Prague, Pilsen, and Reicheberg, riots by unemployed textile and construction workers, like those in Lyon or Silesia, underlined the dangerous social implications of worsening economic conditions. Critics complained of the government's refusal to address the fundamental economic issues that caused such revolts in the first place. And although the military intervened forcefully on the side of employers in Bohemia and Moravia in 1844 and 1846, those same employers were quick to

38. Viktor Bibl, *Die niederösterreichischen Stände im Vormärz. Ein Beitrag zur Vorgeschichte der Revolution des Jahres 1848* (Vienna, 1911), 63–136; 205–23, 294–334; Istvan Deak, *The Lawful Revolution: Louis Kossuth and the Hungarians* (New York, 1979), 24–62; Franz von Krones, *Moritz von Kaiserfeld. Sein Leben und Wirken* (Leipzig, 1888), 45–46; Polišenský *Revolutionary Year*, 1–93; Anton Ritter von Schmerling and Gotthard, Freiherr von Buschmann,

blame governmental policies of neglect for the original outbreak of violence.[39] Commenting on the Prague riots of 1844, the opposition *Grenzboten* maintained that the government under Joseph II had been far better equipped to deal with such social problems. The paper criticized the present regime particularly for not halting inflationary food prices.[40]

By the end of 1847, the imperial government in Vienna faced a social and financial crisis, which threatened to become a political crisis as well. Not only did another bad harvest and hard winter increase the likelihood of rural and urban violence, but growing fiscal problems left the state without the means to maintain social control. In the cities the numbers of unemployed, homeless, and destitute grew at an alarming and quite visible rate. Property owners watched helpless as the state's ability to maintain order collapsed. Throughout 1847 waves of jobless textile workers descended on Vienna from Bohemia and Moravia with their families, hoping to find work in the railway industry. Fully one-third of the population of industrial Linz depended on some form of charity for its survival. Reports of urban criminality and drunkenness multiplied at an exponential rate, according to many observers. Even the court suppliers were the targets of attacks on their way from the city to the palace at Schönbrunn.[41]

The government seems to have been well aware by 1848 that middle-class and provincial diet forces might take advantage of social violence to extract political concessions rather than support state suppression of an uprising. Coalitions of liberal landowners and reform-minded bureaucrats in some provincial diets that tried to alleviate both general and specific economic problems in 1847 found the government deaf to their suggestions. In response, they escalated their demands for more power to legislate, leading the government to voice its own suspicions that a liberal conspiracy was coordinating efforts to sabotage the government in the separate diets. On March 4, 1848, the official government newspaper openly warned Vienna's citizens against initiating any illegal political action. Reminding readers of the dangers of socialism and the threat that the example of the first French Revolution posed to all owners of private property, the *Wiener Zeitung* conjured up the name of Baboeuf and his Conspiracy of Equals, warning that "under the circumstances, there is only

---

Die niederösterreichischen Landstände und die Genesis der Revolution in Österreich im Jahre 1848 (Vienna, 1850); Karl Ucakar, "Demokratie und Wahlrecht in Österreich. Zur Entwicklung von politischer Partizipation und staatliche Legitimationspolitik" (Habilitationschrift, University of Vienna, 1984), 67–68.

39. Polišenský, *Revolutionary Year*, 52–61.

40. See editorials on this subject in *Die Grenzboten* in June and July 1844.

41. *Die Grenzboten* 1 (1847): 200, 282–85; Häusler, *Massenarmut*, 95—135; Ernst Violand, *Die soziale Geschichte der Revolution* (Vienna, 1850), 42–51.

one way to guarantee security: the governed of every social class, whatever their point of view, must be at one with their rulers and fulfill their duties loyally and honestly in the hour of danger."[42]

Such fears of opposition by the government were not unfounded. Middle-class and provincial diet circles in Vienna, Graz, Prague, and elsewhere monitored Austria's precarious financial position closely for any political opportunity it might give them. In addition to sponsoring a charity to distribute food and firewood to the poor, for example, members of the Legal-Political Association in Vienna organized private banquets where they openly debated political reform proposals. Most members expected that a combination of state bankruptcy and social unrest would soon bring down the absolutist system. Late in 1847, one member returned from a trip to Paris predicting both the impending fall of the July Monarchy and the drastic political consequences that event would unleash in Austrian public life.[43]

---

42. WZ, March 4, 1848.

43. Ernst K. Sieber, *Ludwig von Löhner: Ein Vorkämpfer des Deutschtums in Böhmen, Mähren und Schlesien im Jahre 1848/1849* (Munich, 1965), 17.

CHAPTER 2

1848: The Transformation of Public Life

In 1848 Austrian liberals fought to revolutionize their society. They established a model of responsible, activist citizenship and proposed a political framework to harmonize the monarchy's culturally diverse population. They transformed the voluntary association from a private initiative of individuals into a paradigmatic society of citizens, a society that could serve as both the inspiration and the instrument for social change. From March to October, Austria's urban Bürger forged a political culture in which different social groups struggled to realize their own social visions and to block the rearguard actions of their various opponents. Revolutionary governments came and went in 1848, but the creation of public spaces where citizens might gather to influence state policy—this revolution persisted, profoundly transforming middle-class social relations. The proliferation of local political clubs, of election organizations and parties, of a citizen's militia, and of a politicized press created new visions of citizenship for Austrians of all classes, including, on occasion, women, day laborers, and factory workers. Along with this political culture, Austrian Bürger produced a rhetoric for understanding and explaining their changing social relations, a discourse that served as the ideological foundation for liberal and German nationalist politics for the remainder of the century.

A New Political Culture

In most Austrian cities, new public spaces for political discourse and activism originated in town squares, those traditional foci for public complaint. In Vienna, the March revolution emerged from informal discussions during the preceding months, antigovernmental posters, petitions organized by prominent voluntary associations, and finally a demonstration in the square where the Lower Austrian Estates met. News of a revolution in France had already reached Vienna in February, bringing a stockmarket panic in its wake. In early March, public discussion among educated and property-owning Viennese about their own political future seems to have dominated social life. Several cultural and professional organizations in Vienna hosted informal political discussions and strategy sessions. Most saw in the government's hesitation an opportunity to submit grievance petitions. During the week leading up to March 13 the Austrian Commercial Association, the Booksellers' Association, and the Legal-Political Reading Association each demanded Metternich's resignation and an end to censorship. Soon larger groups of citizens organized by prominent members of these associations submitted more far-reaching demands.[1]

Ludwig von Löhner meanwhile invited the more radical members of the Legal-Political Reading Club to take matters into their own hands and transform the association into a political party. At a meeting on March 1, Löhner urged open revolt on his colleagues, reminding them that they had as yet no legal means to alter the present intolerable circumstances. Members who agreed founded the Reading Association Party. They published the most sweeping reform program of all in a Leipzig newspaper on March 4. Entitled "Suggestions of Austrian Citizens for a Reform of the State Administration in the Direction of Legal Progress," this document was the first to convey a specific political program that grew out of a consistent bourgeois worldview. Its authors, unlike the more cautious Bach and Bauernfeld, called for an overhaul of the entire system of government and administration. They demanded that the government arm the citizenry, curtail the broad powers of the police, abolish censorship, and concede the principle of Bürger representation to the Lower Austrian Diet. In addition, the petition called for judicial reform, religious tolerance, educational reform, institutionalization of the right to petition, and the creation of a central parliament in Vienna for the whole monarchy.[2]

Löhner also conceived a revolutionary strategy to complement these radical demands. He urged the leaders of the reform movement in the diet—many of them members of the Legal-Political Reading Association—to seize the initiative. Upon assembling for its next session, the diet should declare itself a permanent body, the fatherland in danger, and Metternich an enemy of the state. Simultaneously, thousands of pamphlets would inform the populace of this initiative, which had been carried out on its behalf. If necessary, a universal uprising of the people would follow to support the liberals' revolt.[3]

---

1. For the texts of the petitions, see Heinrich Reschauer and Moritz Smets, *Das Jahr 1848. Geschichte der Wiener Revolution* (Vienna, 1872), 1:135–147. For the Legal-Political Reading Association petition see Reschauer, *Der juridisch-politische Leseverein im Monat Maerz, 1848*, (Vienna, 1888), 13–14. Both Bach and Bauernfeld were members of the Legal-Political Association.

2. Reschauer and Smets, *Das Jahr 1848*, 1:126; Sieber, *Löhner*, 17–18.

3. Sieber, *Löhner*, 20–22.

Opposition leaders in the Lower Austrian Diet had developed their own strategy, however. Reform-minded bureaucrats Baron Anton Doblhoff-Dier and Anton von Schmerling hoped to broaden the diet's constitutional powers by wringing budget concessions and legislative rights from a paralyzed government.[4] Noting the potential for violence to property, the diet leaders also intended to keep the reform movement out of the streets. Given the desperate economic situation of day laborers employed in the suburban industries, the leaders feared they could not keep a popular demonstration under control. In a telling development, Löhner himself soon backed away from his earlier strategy of raising a universal revolt. After unemployed textile and machine workers rioted in the suburbs on March 10 and 11, Löhner decided that a violent uprising by the people might serve only its own short-term economic interests and not the universal cause of liberty. He now warned a gathering of the university's medical faculty of the consequences of allowing the so-called proletariat to become master of the city. "The most horrifying examples of plundering and arson would be the consequence" of such an uprising.[5]

The diet's refusal to lead an open revolt and the reluctance of Bürger to resort to violence did little to diffuse the atmosphere of expectation in Vienna. Anonymous posters appeared prophesying Metternich's imminent downfall and calling for a constitutional Austria. Contemporaries remarked on the expectant sense of opportunity that seemed to inform all classes.[6] On the morning of March 13, a diverse group of Bürger and workers gathered as curious onlookers in the narrow streets surrounding the *Landhaus*, where the Lower Austrian Diet was to meet. When a large band of students arrived from the University of Vienna to present its petition, the restless crowd had already blocked the neighboring streets. A young physician, Adolf Fischhof, rose to address the crowd while it waited impatiently for the diet members to emerge. Calling for freedom of the press, freedom of instruction, and an unspecified form of parity among the monarchy's national groups, Fischhof gave some coherence to the confused demands of the crowd. Events followed this signal thick and fast.[7]

Alarmed by the crowds, the diet sent a deputation to the palace, and during the rest of the day the government found itself in an increasingly desperate position. By the afternoon, the imperial government had called in the troops and closed the gates to prevent suburban workers from joining the growing crowds in the old city. In the confusion following the army's attempts to clear the streets, five people were shot and many more wounded. Far from regaining control, the authorities now lost it completely. Bands of workers attacked

---

4. Bibl, *Die niederösterreichischen Stände im Vormärz*; Rath, *Viennese Revolution*, 29–37.
5. Sieber, *Löhner*, 20–22; Häusler, *Massenarmut*, 148; WZ, March 10, 1848.
6. Reschauer and Smets, *Das Jahr 1848*, 1:106.
7. Rath, *Viennese Revolution*, 57–89; Reschauer and Smets, *Das Jahr 1848*, 1:173–96.

soldiers, and in the suburbs this was a signal for precisely the machine breaking and looting that the middle-class revolutionaries themselves had feared. This turn of events gave some direction to a hitherto unfocused uprising by forcing Vienna's prominent Bürger to take action against both the troops and the workers. The Bürger interpreted the day's events as an opportunity, however unwished for, to take over the twin functions of administering and maintaining order in the city. Reluctant to entrust their fate to the reactionary army and unable to rely on an ineffective state, Austrian property owners of all kinds took matters into their own hands.[8]

Vienna's mayor, himself an appointed official, apparently spoke for property owners when he begged the government to expand and arm the largely ceremonial civic guard (*Bürgergarde*) that very afternoon so that it might take over the task of pacifying Vienna from the unpopular army. The beleaguered government hesitated before agreeing to this step, recognizing that a reinforced civic guard might just as easily become the arm of a spreading revolution. In a few hours' time, these fears turned out to be completely justified. As the situation within the city worsened, and after some of its own members had been fired upon from a government building, the civic guard did indeed refuse to side with the military against the crowds.[9]

University students demanded arms for themselves that afternoon, calling for the creation of an academic legion to supplement the civic guard and preserve order in the city. Hours later, the government capitulated long enough to allow both the establishment of a large-scale national guard in Vienna and an armed academic legion. These concessions, combined with the removal of the army from the city, held extraordinary revolutionary implications. On the night of March 13 Bürger and students rushed to the *Am Hof* square to arm themselves. By March 15 over 30,000 men had joined either the civic guard or the academic legion and received arms.[10] Contemporary accounts confirm that socially conservative property-owning and professional elements made up a majority of the civic guard. The first guards were generally older, well-to-do men: lawyers, physicians, bureaucrats, bankers, merchants, and even some nobles. Their banners and slogans juxtaposed calls for "freedom" with demands for "order and security." These and other mottos reflected the Viennese guards' perception of their dual functions: to protect revolutionary concessions won from the government while maintaining order.[11]

A month later, statutes for the national or civic guard published throughout Austria by the new government revealed even more about the self-

8. Häusler, *Massenarmut*, 139–44; Rath, *Viennese Revolution*, 65–73.

9. Rath, *Viennese Revolution*, 68–70.

10. Rath, *Viennese Revolution*, 68–73, 124; Häusler, *Massenarmut*, 173–78. Some wage laborers also managed to pick up weapons in the general confusion.

11. OL, Flugschriftenversammlung B, vol. 10, "Kundmachung vom 10.4.1848."

identification of the revolutionary Bürgertum and its social boundaries. Only individuals "who do not belong to the class of journeymen, servants, and all those who live from daily or weekly wages" might join the guard.[12] In singling out journeymen and servants for particular mention, the new liberalized government confirmed the prevailing belief among the Bürgertum that economic independence was a more reliable measure of political maturity even than income. In fact, as we shall see, liberals treated independence as the most reliable external measure of one's internal ability to use reason in public affairs. Independence or reasonableness would become the most important requirement for participation in public life in 1848.[13]

Bürger groups had not initiated the revolution, and in fact the more prominent associations had actually refused to lead the revolt in its earliest moments.[14] Now, however, the associations stepped forward to provide the revolution with direction. This development is clear both from the initiative that created the national guard and from Bürger efforts in subsequent days to take over municipal government. Fifty self-defined Viennese Bürger met with Mayor Czapka on March 15 for the purpose of electing a provisional citizens' committee, which might run municipal affairs until a new city council could be elected. These notables elected a solidly bourgeois executive committee whose narrow social composition did not necessarily reflect the diverse interests of Vienna's independent producers. If somewhat conservative in its economic orientation, this new committee nonetheless asserted a radical political independence from the earlier regime. Its first action was to demand Mayor Czapka's immediate resignation because of his longstanding association with the Metternich regime.[15]

---

12. OL, "Kundmachung vom 10.4.1848."

13. Häusler, *Massenarmut*, 173–78. This particular ethos differed from that of the Viennese academic legion, many of whose members lived in impoverished circumstances and tended to sympathize far more with the economic demands of wage laborers and the unemployed in 1848. For this reason, the liberal-dominated Vienna city council viewed the Viennese academic legion with some suspicion and frequently attempted to have it dissolved.

14. Reschauer, *Leseverein*, 18–20; "Der juridisch-politisch Leseverein," in *Die Constitution*, March 20, 1848. On March 14, the Legal-Political Reading Association had hung a white banner emblazoned with the words "Freedom of the Press" from its balcony while Ludwig August Frankl read Vienna's first uncensored publication, a poem entitled "The University." On March 15 crowds had repeatedly gathered at the association looking for some direction. Although members addressed the crowd no fewer than seventeen times that evening, the organization refused to take an active role in the revolution.

15. Rudolf Till, "Die Mitglieder der ersten Wiener Gemeinde-Vertretung im Jahre 1848," *Wiener Geschichtsblätter* 4 (1950): 61–72.

First twenty-six Members of the Viennese Provisional Citizen's Committee, March 15–17, 1848

Occupation	%	(no.)
Commerce, Small	30.7%	(8)
Factory Owner	23.0%	(6)

In March 1848 Bürger in several Austrian cities attempted to seize local and regional administrative powers for themselves. In Graz, an impending meeting of the Styrian Diet provided a focus for petitions and demonstrations similar to the March 13 meeting of the Lower Austrian Diet in Vienna. Students at the University of Graz demanded a constitution guaranteeing freedom of instruction, an end to censorship, and the right to arm citizens and to found political associations. A performance of Schiller's *Don Carlos* on March 14 elicited a thunderous demonstration from a largely bourgeois audience at the moment when the Marquis of Posa begs Philip II to grant his subjects freedom of expression. On March 15, as hundreds massed outside the Styrian *Landhaus*, the citizens of Graz presented yet another petition with 600 signatures to the leaders of the diet.[16]

The Bürger clearly intended any reforms to empower themselves in almost every aspect of public life at the expense of the imperial bureaucracy: a city government to be freely elected "by all Bürger from the business and industry communities," participation in determining tax policy, the right to appoint and to dismiss public officials, the right to remove judicial functions from the police, the right to set education policy, freedom of speech, thought, and conscience, an end to censorship and corporal punishment, a popular militia to replace the police, and banishment for the Jesuits.[17] At this same meeting the Graz Bürger also decided to organize their own civic guard and academic legion. Already on the morning of March 16 the commander of the ceremonial *Bürgergarde* encouraged all citizens to put on red armbands and proceed to the city center to show their support for the town government. The municipal government decided to distribute 500 guns and 300 sabers to "those worthy of the general trust." As in Vienna, a number of journeymen and wage laborers also managed to obtain weapons, and this lapse increased the watchfulness of the new Styrian civic guards over their armed working-class comrades.[18]

Commerce, Large	7.7%	(2)
University Professor	7.7%	(2)
Medical Faculty	7.7%	(2)
Legal Faculty	7.7%	(2)
Nobility/Gentry	7.7%	(2)
Artisan	3.8%	(1)
Jewish Community	3.8%	(1)

16. Krones, *Kaiserfeld*, 44–47; Pfeisinger, "1848 in Graz," 38–54; Hans Pirchegger, *Geschichte der Steiermark 1740–1919* (Graz, Vienna, Leipzig, 1934), 377–78.

17. OL, Flugschriftenversammlung B, vol. 9, "Petition der Bürgerschaft der Hauptstadt Graz an Se. Majestät," March 15, 1848. The petition also demanded that the military swear an oath of loyalty to the new Austrian constitution.

18. Pfeisinger, "1848 in Graz," 55–56.

In the following days, the Graz Bürgertum indulged in a festive celebration of its victory, with observers pointing proudly to the way in which members of the aristocracy rubbed shoulders with Bürger and lesser civil servants in the civic guard.[19] Events in Graz had produced far less violence than those in Vienna, although the potential for food riots and social conflict was no less immediate. The Styrian bourgeoisie had profited from the imperial government's loss of control and from a fear that the type of violence that had erupted in Vienna could easily break out in other cities. For the moment, the general promise of a constitution, coupled with the news of Metternich's resignation, provided a universal panacea in Graz and removed the threat of violence.

In Linz, a city with significant industry and working-class population, the leading Bürger seem to have kept tight control over the course of the revolution. Although they would later impose a reformist agenda on the Upper Austrian Diet, the Linz Bürger did not lead a significant petition drive at this point. Instead, they organized a series of demonstrations in support of the emperor after learning on March 14 of his capitulation. The next day, "Bürger and civil servants drove their carriages to meet the long-awaited mail coach from Vienna," which brought copies of the emperor's proclamation. A celebration at the provincial theater that evening was followed by a torchlight parade organized by the local Association of Industrialists. Bürger and students both flocked to join the new national guard, which in turn "watched over the city." A local observer noted with satisfaction the absence of any excess of the kind experienced by the Viennese, emphasizing the fact that local business had not been interrupted by the revolution.[20]

In Prague, the complex issue of political nationalism rapidly undermined revolutionary Bürger unity, giving the events of March 1848 a significantly different character than in Vienna. The most politically active Bohemian Bürger were recruited from the Czech-speaking intelligentsia, largely because the formation of a strong Bürger class consciousness in Prague had proceeded in tandem with the active creation of a Czech nationalist consciousness.[21] A radical group of Czech-identified bourgeois intellectuals with some German participation took the revolutionary initiative by organizing a public meeting for March 11. The group planned to present a petition that demanded, in addition to municipal autonomy and the abolition of censorship: the unification of Bohemia with Moravia and Silesia under a central administration in Prague;

19. Pfeisinger, "1848 in Graz," 66.

20. "Brief aus Linz," *Wiener Zeitschrift für Kunst, Literatur, Theater und Mode* 59 (1848): 236.

21. Otto Urban, "Zur Frage der Voraussetzungen der politischen Tätigkeit des tschechischen Bürgertums in den Jahren 1848/1849," in *Bürgertum in der Habsburgermonarchie*, ed. Bruckmüller et al., 205–10.

the introduction of the Czech language into schools; and the abolition of the peasant *Robot*. In perhaps the most interesting clause of all, the petition called for "the regulation of work and wages" for day laborers.[22] This draft was presented for editing to the liberal Czech lawyer August Brauner. A bourgeois member of the growing Czech nationalist movement, Brauner expurgated the social demands from the petition and strengthened its nationalist and bourgeois character. Backing down from the original concern for the regulation of work, this draft called instead for the institution of a Bürger militia to protect society from the dangers of "proletarian [*sic*] disorder."

A number of prominent German-identified citizens, including wealthy members of the Merchants' Casino, signed the first petition despite its Czech nationalist overtones. Most of them feared some kind of popular uprising in Prague and hoped that by joining the constitutional movement they might exert some influence over it. For the moment, the mood in Prague was jubilant at the news of Metternich's fall and the abolition of censorship. Bourgeois activists and students of both nationalities rushed to form a civic guard and an academic legion on the Viennese model.

The full implications of the Czech nationalist demands may not also have been completely apparent to German-identified Bürger who worried more at this juncture about their property than their national position as Germans.[23] After the March revolution, however, nationalist differences soon divided Czech and German property owners in Prague into different bourgeois factions. Each group subsequently fought the other as much as it opposed both the Vienna government and the wage laborers.[24]

As elsewhere in Central Europe, national guardsmen now patrolled troubled neighborhoods and maintained order in Austrian cities threatened with worker unrest. Yet plenty of towns in the monarchy that were not threatened by social strife also formed civic or national guard units. The guard companies in small provincial towns proclaimed their intention to "protect the newly gained

22. Stanley Z. Pech, *The Czech Revolution of 1848* (Chapel Hill, 1969), 47–62; Polisensky, *Revolutionary Year*, 110; Wolfgang Rudolf, "Fürst Karl Auersperg (1814–1890); ein liberaler österreichischer Staatsman und Politiker" (Ph.D. diss; University of Vienna, 1974), 16–19. Unlike the situation in those provinces where the diets provided a focus for popular demands, the Bohemian Diet was not scheduled to meet in March 1848.

23. Pech, *Czech Revolution*, 47–79; Polišenský, *Revolutionary Year*, 110–12. Some German speakers preferred to consider themselves Bohemians rather than identify politically with either ethnic group.

24. Pech, *Czech Revolution*, 72–78; Polišenský, *Revolutionary Year*, 113–15. In April, however, when the news arrived that the government had assented only to parts of the Prague petition and had postponed consideration of the most controversial nationalist points, Czech activists rioted in the streets. A more radical petition was drawn up and sent, but no German-identified Bürger signed it.

freedoms" while "enforcing peace, security, and order," although against what enemy remained unclear.[25] Membership in citizens' guards proved popular, symbolizing as it did the individual's active participation in the March revolution. In many Austrian towns the guard embodied the pride of a middle class that had taken over responsibility for municipal government and public property. This pride was not limited to the citizen guard members alone. In the spring and summer of 1848 middle-class women frequently organized auxiliary associations to raise money and to create flags for local guard companies. Elaborate ceremonies across the monarchy grew up around these donations of the colors.[26]

The new institutions played a pivotal role in the construction of a new middle-class political culture. Civic guard units or provisional city councils served as new public spaces where ideology and strategy might be discussed, where the Bürger classes gained a legitimate voice in determining policy and in maintaining order. During the next months, the German middle classes created other organizations for political activism based on the most familiar of their social traditions—the voluntary association. The rise of specifically political clubs represented a new institutional development for the urban German-speaking bourgeoisie in 1848. Despite their small numbers and limited memberships in 1848, the political clubs contributed significantly to the creation of liberal discourse and traditions in Austria. Based on organizational skills honed by activists during the ostensibly apolitical *Vormärz,* the new clubs combined urban cultural traditions with newer liberal ideologies.

The citizens of Vienna, Graz, Brünn, or Prague may have been neophytes in politics, but they certainly knew how to organize a voluntary association. They demonstrated this particular talent repeatedly by the speed with which they founded political clubs during the spring and summer of 1848. Personal accounts and items published in newspapers indicate that groups of like-minded men and women began meeting regularly in certain Viennese hotels within days of the March revolution. Their immediate goal was to gain some control over the direction taken by the revolutionary events of those weeks.[27] This was especially true for political radicals, who were least satis-

25. OL, Flugschriftenversammlung B, vol. 10, "An die National-Garde Gmundens"; Bruno König, "Von der Nationalgarde (1848–1851)" *Zeitschrift für die Geschichte und Kulturgeschichte österreichisch-Schlesiens* (Troppau, 1906), 141–45. For a useful comparison with Bavarian examples from 1848, see James F. Harris, "Arms and the People: The *Bürgerwehr* of Lower Franconia in 1848 and 1849," in *In Search of a Liberal Germany*, ed. Konrad H. Jarausch and Larry Eugene Jones (New York, 1990).

26. NBF, 1848, "Aufruf eines Mädchens an ihre konstitutionellen Schwestern der königlichen Stadt Olmütz."

27. For a comparative view of the role of the political club in mid-century Europe, see Peter Amann, *Revolution and Mass Democracy: The Paris Club Movement in 1848* (Princeton, 1975)

fied with the victory of moderate reform. They now took the lead in organizing political clubs. Calling themselves democrats, they used speeches, petitions, and pamphlets to prod the government to carry out its constitutional promises, to take sterner measures against counterrevolutionaries, to give the franchise to a greater number of people, and to intervene on behalf of economically suffering artisans and workers. These activities set off a second wave of revolutionary outbursts in May, at which point political moderates began to organize themselves against what they perceived to be a new threat to property and status.

The best known of the early so-called democratic clubs in Vienna, the Society of Friends of the People, was founded at the beginning of April 1848 by a group that met at the Empress of Austria Hotel. According to its statutes, the society's purpose was to unite the supporters of progress in order to protect the revolution from both internal and external enemies. In their rules on procedure the founders conveyed an ideal form of behavior that contrasted markedly to the perceived arbitrariness of the old regime. Anyone could join who supported a constitutional monarchy, paid a "small monthly fee, and agreed to attend meetings at least twice a week." Debates were to be run according to parliamentary procedure. Members had to register their desire to speak beforehand with the secretary, who then recognized them at the appropriate moment. All who wished to join the debate had to be recognized by the president, and it was forbidden "to interrupt any speaker in his discourse." A stenographer recorded the association's debates, after which a committee would edit them and publish them as minutes. Issues requiring specific decisions by the club would be decided by ballot. The club's activities included sponsoring petitions to the government and publishing pamphlets and posters when it considered that the *Volk* required warning or political guidance. Most importantly, the society saw itself as a school to develop in its members the ability to participate effectively in civic affairs.[28]

If the democrats organized themselves to obtain further reforms, political moderates soon organized to blunt the influence of the democrats. On May 15, 1848, a second uprising of students and workers forced the Vienna government to concede a more democratic franchise for elections to the Austrian Parliament. On that very day a group of moderates published a program for a

---

and Häusler, *Massenarmut*, 197–216. Both scholars view the political club in 1848 as an intermediate stage of political development, falling between traditional forms of collective protest and the more sophisticated mass political organizations of the twentieth century. This view tends to minimize the degree to which nonpolitical associations, through their structures and membership practices, had already anticipated the phase of class building usually identified with later and more sophisticated forms of organization.

28. The statutes of the association are reproduced in *Vorträge des Dr. Schütte und politische Debatten der Gesellschaft der Volksfreunde*, ed. Adolf Chaises (Vienna, 1848), 7–8.

new association, the Friends of Constitutional Order and True Freedom. The Friends demanded the immediate establishment of constitutional government, the cessation of all so-called communist, republican activities—which they defined as "all public demonstrations"—and they petitioned the government to create a healthier environment for business and industry. These goals not only reflected disquiet among property owners over the power of the revolutionary mob; they also conveyed frustration with the steady deterioration of business conditions in the capital, particularly after the removal of the court to Innsbruck in May.[29]

Yet these moderates also vehemently opposed any return to the old order, and their program expressed disapproval of the former government's use of "inquisitorial methods." The association promised "to keep a careful watch that all sectors of the bureaucracy . . . behave in a truly constitutional fashion." Furthermore, the Friends offered an olive branch of sorts to the working classes, promising to try "to clarify misunderstandings among those less informed about their new constitutional rights and duties." Both radicals and moderates alike felt a strong responsibility to foster a sense of civic duty among the lower classes. After all, the fact that the revolution had triumphed thanks to the threat of violence might have conveyed the wrong impression of constitutional life to the masses. The association emphasized that under a constitutional regime, "one can gain legal redress to one's complaints" rather than resorting to violent demonstrations, which themselves only undermine economic stability.[30]

The membership of the Friends was divided hierarchically among a group of founders who contributed at least seventeen florins each, regular members who paid six florins annually, and corresponding members who paid a florin per month. Founders and regular members might serve as club officers. Although the group explicitly rejected the idea of a new aristocracy based on money, this membership division nonetheless illustrated a growing belief among liberals that wealth, education, and social achievement did reflect a citizen's relative capability for public service.[31]

Two other moderate Viennese organizations worthy of note were the Austrian Patriots' Association and the Constitutional Association. The former hoped to stabilize the precarious financial situation of the monarchy by convincing every citizen to donate at least one florin to the state treasury.[32] The

---

29. J. S. Hohenblum, *Statuten zur Bildung des Vereines der Freunde der constitutionellen Ordnung und wahren Freiheit* (Vienna, 1848), 3–4.

30. Hohenblum, *Statuten*, 3–5.

31. Hohenblum, *Statuten*, 6.

32. NBF, 1848, "Der österreichische Patriotenverein," September 23, 1848. The contributing members, whose names appear on a pamphlet from early September 1848, included the banker Georg Sina and the industrialist Rudolf Arthaber. Little more is known about this group than the fact that it managed to raise some 28,000 florins by the end of September.

Constitutional Association championed the most pressing concern of the Viennese Bürgertum by September of 1848: the reestablishment of public order.[33] Still another generally moderate organization, the First Viennese Democratic Women's Association, was founded by Baroness Caroline von Perin in August of 1848, after pay cuts for women workers had caused public riots. An anonymous invitation addressed to "noble German women" from "a German woman" invited all concerned women to wear the German cockade on the left breast and to attend a meeting in the *Volksgarten*. "We do not want to appear as amazons," claimed the organizer, "but rather to follow our calling and to heal wherever there are wounds: we are not judges but mediators!"[34]

The First Viennese Democratic Women's Association sought to educate women and young girls of all classes to love freedom, democracy, and German national heritage. It claimed that women could only achieve a higher social status if the government founded a public school system for women, changed the existing curriculum for girls, and elevated the miserable economic lot of poorer young girls. The association also worked to improve general conditions for local women by collecting money for the families of those wounded in recent uprisings and for women workers whose wages had fallen victim to recent government welfare cuts. Not immune to the tensions common in the liberal movement between moderate liberals and radical democrats, the Women's Association had its own share of controversy. At a meeting in September 1848, for example, democratic members wanted to condemn the recent refusal by Viennese landlords to postpone the collection of rents from artisans hard hit by economic crisis, while Perin considered any rent postponement to be an assault on the private property of the landlords.[35]

The Women's Association faced considerable hostility from men who opposed women's participation in politics. Male hecklers attempted to disrupt the very first meeting of the association on August 28, while the press caricatured the association, alternately ridiculing it and portraying its members as somehow dangerously unfeminine in dress and habit. In September of 1848 an anti-Semitic pamphlet deplored the recent election of Zortele Wertheimer, "pearl of Judaism," as president of the association, condemning all women who had adopted roles that "true Germanness could never ac-

33. NBF, 1848, "Programm des konstitutionellen Vereins," Vienna, September 8, 1848. The club membership grew rapidly to 25,000, yet it failed to develop the kind of organizational structure and common activities it needed to become an effective instrument, and it soon collapsed.

34. NBF, 1848, "Edle deutsche Frauen," August 1848. On women's 1848 activism in Bohemia and Moravia, see Pech, *Czech Revolution*, 319–29.

35. Häusler, *Massenarmut*, 363–64. One democratic woman accused the moderates of callous indifference to the poor, saying, "You all pull the bedclothes over your heads and pretend to sleep whenever the poor are starving."

cept."[36] Nevertheless, the association continued to publicize specific women's issues for the rest of its brief existence.[37]

The size of the membership in these Viennese political clubs is difficult to estimate since they fluctuated widely on a daily basis, depending on the current political atmosphere. The Viennese Democratic Women, for example, counted a consistent membership of around forty people. The democratic Society of Friends of the People in Vienna was capable of attracting a crowd of 6,000 to a public meeting on April 14, 1848, where it petitioned the government to call a constituent assembly to be elected by universal manhood suffrage. Furthermore, the society managed to collect over 20,000 signatures for this petition within a day of its announcement. This and other Viennese democratic clubs mobilized an impressive number of followers for certain issues at specific revolutionary moments in 1848. Yet these incidents convey little about how many individuals actually attended meetings or participated regularly in club activities.[38]

In Graz, the more socially prominent members of the local Bürgertum joined liberal state bureaucrats and landowners like Moritz von Kaiserfeld to found a Constitutional Club in May 1848. The Constitutional Club sent petitions and delegations to Vienna and worked to elect its members to the Austrian Parliament in June 1848. Also in June, the more progressive democratic forces in Graz—students, writers, small-scale producers, and the editor of the democratic paper *Leaves of Freedom and Progress*—created a Committee to Watch Over the Elections to Parliament. In August, many of the same men founded a Graz Democratic Club, which demanded radical political reform, still stressing the importance of using legal means to attain it.[39] In addition, Styrian liberal activists founded the German Nationalist Association (*Deutscher Verein*), meant

---

36. NBF, 1848, "Wai! geschrirn jetzt fangen die Jüdinen a schon an," Vienna 1848; "Der Frauenaufruhr im Volksgarten, oder die Waschenanstalt der Wiener Damen," Vienna 1848; *Neue politische Strassenzeitung* 2 (August 31, 1848).

37. On Caroline von Perin (1808–88) and the Women's Association, see Daniela Weiland, ed., *Geschichte der Frauenemanzipation in Deutschland und Österreich* (Düsseldorf, 1983), 208–9; 286–7. Among other actions, Perin's association organized a demonstration of 300 women before the Austrian Parliament on October 17, 1848, after which the press referred to her as "dirty amazon" and "unfeminine lover of a demagogue." Like other political associations, Perin's eventually collapsed in October, riven by the opposing attitudes toward private property and its uses that distinguished moderates from radicals. After the October uprising in Vienna, Perin herself was betrayed to the police and arrested. She was allowed to emigrate to Munich in 1849, but she lost all rights to her children, and her companion, democratic activist and writer Alfred Julius Becher, was shot in prison.

38. NBF, 1848, "Euer Majestaet," Vienna, April 14, 1848; Häusler, *Massenarmut,* 202–5.

39. Krones, *Kaiserfeld,* 51, 54–55; Pfeisinger, "1848 in Graz," 231–48; Pirchegger, *Steiermark,* 392–96.

to protect so-called German interests from Slovene attacks in Styria. This apparently became necessary in May after Slovene activists publicly expressed their preference for an Austria oriented toward Slavic peoples rather than toward a greater German Reich.[40]

In Vienna, when a Czech deputation demanded autonomy for the lands of the Bohemian crown in April of 1848, Ludwig von Löhner founded the Association of Germans from Bohemia, Moravia, and Silesia to protect the "badly threatened interests of Germans" in those three provinces. This new club promised to alert German Bürger to Czech attacks on the former's "natural rights and cultural heritage" by petitioning the government, publishing nationalist pamphlets, corresponding with local German newspapers, electing German-identified deputies to the Austrian Parliament, and using members' personal connections to keep Germans aware of local Czech nationalist activities.[41] Löhner's group was the only German liberal association to establish a network of local clubs extending beyond a single city or province. German liberal associations in Bohemian towns like Eger, Karlsbad, Leitmeritz, Reichenberg, Saaz, and Teplitz organized themselves during April and May 1848. Their founding statements used a common wording taken from Löhner's Vienna association.[42] In June, the association broadened its horizon to include Germans from all provinces in Austria, changing its name appropriately to the Association of Germans in Austria. By August, local branches of this German association had sprung up in twenty-four more towns and districts in Bohemia, five in Moravia, and two in Silesia.[43]

The degree of activity in officially non-political organizations like the civic guard and the academic legions serves as an additional indicator of

40. Pfeisinger, "1848 in Graz," 231.

41. Hans Kudlich, *Rückblicke und Erinnerungen* (Vienna, 1873), 1:228–29; 299; "Die Lage in Boehmen," *Die Grenzboten*, 7 (1848): 179. For an election statement by the association, see NBF, 1848, "Wahlmanifest des Vereins der Deutschen aus Böhmen, Mähren und Schlesien zur Aufrechthaltung ihrer Nationalität." On the German casinos in Bohemia, see [Alfred Klaar] *Franz Schmeykal. Ein Gedenkschrift* (Prague, 1894), 23–36.

42. Sieber, *Löhner*, 67.

43. Kudlich, *Rückblicke und Erinnerungen*, 1:229; NBF, 1848, "Aufforderung zur Theilnahme an dem konstitutionellen Verein in Teplitz," "Statuten des deutschen konstitutionellen Vereins in Teplitz," "Vom konstitutionelle Verein zu Leitmeritz," "Deutsche Brüder," "Programm für die am 28., 29. und 30. d. M. in Teplitz abzuhaltende Versammlung;" *SRG*, August 11, 1848; Constant von Wurzbach, *Biographisches Lexikon des Kaisertums Österreich*, 60 vols. (Vienna, 1856–1923), 15:391. The Association of Germans in Austria had a membership in Vienna of about 200. Participation outside Vienna was probably limited to correspondence with the Vienna branch, distribution of the newspaper, and intermittent petition activity. When the association sponsored a Congress of Bohemian Germans at Teplitz in August 1848, the small number of participants reflected the as yet limited interest in developing a specifically German nationalist politics in Bohemia.

middle-class political involvement. Joining one of these paramilitary bodies was a primary form of middle-class political expression in 1848, since the guards functioned exclusively to protect Bürger material interests. Urban civic guard units were infused with political overtones. In Vienna, the political attitudes of guard companies strongly reflected the social composition of each of the districts they served. Local political conflicts were played out as often in the context of district guard companies as they were in political clubs. And despite a chronic decline in guard membership and popular interest during the long periods of quiet in 1848, the guards involved more people in political discussions on a daily or weekly basis than did the early clubs.[44]

Periodicals, journals, and newspapers represented another important forum for developing common points of view and a common discourse within the loose liberal movement. Abolition of censorship—a major demand in March—and new press laws had paved the way for a veritable explosion in the press. Beside the thirty-nine papers published in Austria before 1848, 170 new publications sprang up during the revolutionary year. These journals represented all shades of political opinion, from Catholic conservative on the right to liberal and democratic on the left. In addition, many of the papers already founded during the *Vormärz* changed their appearances and contents literally overnight to reflect the new turn of events. From business papers to fashion magazines, most of them assumed a more democratic tone, so as not to be accused by their readers of reactionary sympathies.[45]

The competition among new publications was especially fierce in the cities. In Vienna, where the competition was stiffest, twenty-six of the fledgling newspapers in 1848 survived for less than a week, and thirty-four published only one issue before collapsing. Here the most successful new papers were the *Constitution*, a liberal journal with occasionally radical leanings favored by imperial civil servants, and the more moderate *Presse*.[46] In Graz, nine new papers joined the two that had previously served the Styrian public. Their

---

44. Wenzel Dunder, *Denkschrift über die Wiener Oktober-Revolution. Ausführliche Darstellung aller Ereignisse aus ämtlichen Quellen geschöpft, mit zahlreichen Urkunden begleitet* (Vienna,1849), 13–14, 92–93. The number of Viennese Bürger active in the national or civic guard fell immediately after the March events from 30,000 to below 10,000. The May uprising brought the number back up to 60,000, but by October the number had again fallen to around 18,000.

45. Reinhold Enöckl, "Der Einfluss der revolutionären Wiener Journalistik auf die Politik des Jahres 1848" (Ph.D. diss., University of Vienna, 1967); Häusler, *Massenarmut*, 164–72; Rath, *Viennese Revolution*, 90–119. Rath's discussion of the Viennese press includes a useful survey of pamphlets and broadsides with an analysis of their language.

46. Häusler, *Massenarmut*, 167; Adam Wandruszka, *Geschichte einer Zeitung. Das Schicksal der "Presse" und der "Neuen Freien Presse" von 1848 zur zweiten Republik* (Vienna, 1958). The *Constitution* sold 40,000 copies per day at its height of popularity. On its readership in 1848, see Heindl, *Gehorsame Rebellen,* 201–2.

names illustrated the new revolutionary image their owners tried to cultivate for themselves. Instead of *Official Grazer* or *Inner Austrian Journal of Industry*, publishers chose names like *Peoples' Newspaper*, *Leaves of Freedom and Progress*, or *Peoples' Resounding Katzenmusik*, billed as "Austria's cheapest freedom-breathing newspaper." *Katzenmusik* referred to the 1848 custom of harassing those suspected of counterrevolutionary sympathies by singing and making noise outside their houses at night. Many papers in fact recreated this form of harassment in print, a trend that led even some liberals in 1848 to question the wisdom of allowing complete freedom of the press.[47]

The newspapers coordinated revolutionary activities, often by announcing upcoming demonstrations and sometimes by warning the public against unpopular or little-understood government measures. By consistently commenting on government measures and by publicizing political club activities, the newspapers tried to keep political issues at the forefront of public concern. Perhaps most importantly, the papers helped to create a liberal community in discursive terms by casting every local issue in a new political language. Quick to point out, for example, similarities between the Vienna of 1848 and republican Rome or revolutionary Paris, (1789, 1792, or 1830, depending on one's point of view), the newspapers drew on imagery from popular foreign or historical subjects, creating a kind of popular political shorthand for understanding the complicated events of 1848. Finally, the liberal papers believed it was their mission to enlighten the popular classes about the new rights and duties of citizenship that the revolution had bestowed. The *Constitution* called itself a "daily for the people's constitutional life and instruction," defining its primary goal as providing "a guide to the culturally uneducated public regarding its interests."[48]

Both the press and the political clubs contributed actively to another important new aspect of bourgeois public life in Austria: elections to new or reconstituted legislative institutions. During the spring and summer of 1848, the government held a series of elections for deputies to the German Parliament at Frankfurt, to the Austrian Parliament, to some of the reconstituted provincial diets, and to several town councils. Each of these elections, combined with the periodic election of officers in national guard units, contributed to the growing public sphere of politics among the middle-class populace. Electioneering also encouraged the formation of the earliest local party organizations in Austrian cities and towns.

Election committees made their first appearance on the scene in the spring of 1848 largely as informal, ad hoc groups that might exist for a few weeks prior to the election, then disband. They presented a candidate to the voters

47. Krones, *Kaiserfeld*, 47–48; Pfeisinger, "1848 in Graz," 93–95, 244–46.

48. *Constitution*, March 20, 1848.

of a certain district by sponsoring a speech and perhaps printing a pamphlet or poster publicizing the candidate's name or his position on a popular issue. In larger cities the committees might be affiliated with existing political or social clubs, as in Vienna, where the Legal-Political Reading Association organized a committee in April to elect its own candidates to the Frankfurt Parliament. As an early organizer, the Reading Association managed to have twenty-six of its members elected to the Austrian delegation to Frankfurt. By the summer, however, when elections were held to the Austrian Parliament, other political clubs contested the elections, and the Reading Association had less success.[49]

In both Vienna and Graz, political differences between moderate liberals and radical democrats developed quickly, and elections were harder fought by all sides than in most towns. In Graz the moderate Constitutional Club urged voters not to elect workers, since these lacked the necessary worldly experience, farsightedness, and conviction necessary for political life. For the moderates, reputation, integrity, and good Bürger behavior far outweighed a candidate's stand on any particular issue. Thus, the *Gratzer Zeitung* recommended that those elected be men unlikely to abandon the path of "steady and sober progress." The German Association in Graz, together with the more democratically oriented Association to Watch Over the Parliamentary Elections endorsed another group of citizens, mostly on the basis of their more progressive and nationalist convictions.[50]

Several candidates contested the Viennese elections to the Austrian Parliament. Pamphlets and speeches assailed voters daily for weeks, and the unresolved issue of the franchise for wage laborers made the outcome unpredictable.[51] All of these rudimentary efforts at organization and voter mobilization resulted in a voter participation rate that by later standards was still quite low. In Vienna, 18,000 people voted for the Austrian Parliament—a small percentage of eligible voters but a large number compared to many districts where turnout fell below a hundred. Rural or small-town voting rates in 1848 remained far below those for urban districts.[52] In fact, urban committees of moderate liberal notables often chose candidates to run for election in nearby rural districts. Democrats rarely ventured out of the cities. Their own favorite

---

49. Reschauer, *Leseverein*, 25–28. By the summer of 1848 many members of the Legal-Political Reading Association found themselves increasingly in rival democratic and moderate liberal political camps, making it much harder to run a single slate of candidates.

50. Pfeisinger "1848 in Graz," 146–47.

51. SRG (2), July 14, and (3), July 18, 1848; Häusler, *Massenarmut*, 262–63.

52. For a useful survey of 1848 voter turnout both in Vienna and the other provinces, see Karl Obermann, "Die österreichischen Reichstagswahlen 1848. Eine Studie zur Fragen des sozialen Struktur und der Wahlbeteiligung auf der Grundlage der Wahlakten," MÖSA 26 (Vienna, 1973): 342–74.

issues—rent control, price freezes—held little appeal for peasants and farmers. A Graz newspaper bitingly characterized the concerns of the new rural voters in South Styria near Cilli in the following words: "One God, one emperor, one religion, no *Robot*, no tithe, no chickens, no eggs, no cheese [all references to dues in kind], no burdens—otherwise things can remain as they are."[53] The statement reflected the fact that rural voters of all types were extremely concerned with the abolition of feudalism.

The future liberal cabinet minister Carl von Stremayr has left an account of the informality with which electoral organization might spread from city to neighboring countryside. A young law student in 1848, Stremayr discovered that one of his professors, a member of the Graz Constitutional Club, had recommended him in a local newspaper for election to the Frankfurt Parliament. Stremayr then received an invitation to speak on election day at Kindburg, a small town in rural Upper Styria. Terrified, but encouraged by his fellow students, Stremayr traveled to Kindburg, where he found a stage set up in the marketplace and hundreds of farmers gathered around for the spectacle. Stremayr spoke briefly, did not give a detailed program, but emphasized his support for close political ties to Germany, an end to feudalism and absolutism, and his allegiance to the emperor. As far as he could determine, anything more would not have interested his rural audience. In fact, the other, more radical-sounding candidates alienated the peasants, who voted overwhelmingly for Stremayr.[54]

Despite minimal organization and low voter turnout in 1848, Austrians did elect new institutions in which the previously unrepresented Bürgertum now played a major role. In provincial diets that met after March 1848, representatives of both the so-called Bürger estate and the peasantry demanded immediate representation, either by appointment, election, or both. The protocols of one diet recount how this broadening of representation was achieved, using an official language that barely betrays the social conflict that lurked behind the process. Claiming a sudden illness, the mayor of Linz had declined to attend the opening session of the Upper Austrian Diet on March 21. The evidence suggests, however, that the illness had been induced by his unwillingness to give way to the demands he expected the Bürger would make. In the mayor's absence, the Linz city council, "informed of the lively desire of the local citizens . . . to participate . . . and reminded of the reward due them for having maintained peace and order during the recent agitated days," asked the Linz Bürgertum to elect ten responsible citizens from among its own ranks to attend the diet as deputies. On their arrival at the opening session of the diet, an enthusiastic crowd of onlookers acclaimed the new deputies with shouts of "long live

53. *Der Herold*, July 3, 1848; Pirchegger, *Steiermark*, 389.

54. Carl von Stremayr, *Erinnerungen aus dem Leben* (Vienna, 1899), 18–19.

the worthy Bürger of Linz!" Two weeks later the same diet voted to add nine peasant representatives to its ranks, and on April 22 the vigorous protests of other Upper Austrian towns led to the addition of even more representatives.[55] In Styria, the diet decided that from then on, one-third of its deputies would be elected by the urban Bürgertum and one-third by rural communities. In Moravia, the newly reformed diet was to consist of deputies elected by five categories of citizens: provincial officers, large landowners, urban Bürgertum, rural communities, and intelligentsia (*Intelligenz*).[56]

The deputies elected to the new all-Austrian Parliament in Vienna also reflect political conquests by the urban Bürgertum. Their position in this body made some of them visible symbols of a new middle-class involvement in politics. An occupational breakdown of the 384 parliamentary representatives illustrates both the high degree to which men of non-noble status had been elected and the social limitations of this newly devised system. Nobles of both higher and lesser degree constituted only 12 percent of the legislators, while the rural bourgeoisie made up the largest single occupational bloc with 24 percent. More than a third of the deputies came from traditionally urban middle-class occupations or had university training, while a fifth of the parliamentary deputies were also state or private officials, some of whom also identified with middle-class political interests.[57]

Within the Austrian Parliament two different patterns characterized the deputies' political behavior: (1) Most deputies voted in provincial blocs on major issues, eschewing alliances with deputies of similar backgrounds from other provinces. (2) German-speaking liberal deputies from Lower Austria and

---

55. OL, Flugschriftenversammlung B, vol. 5, *Die Verhandlungen der am 23. März auf dem Landtage versammeltgewesenen Stände des Erzherzogthums Österreich ob der Enns,* sessions of April 4 and July 24, 1848. The citizens of Linz elected six merchants, one lawyer, one manufacturer, one city bureaucrat, and one book dealer to serve as their representatives. Twelve urban deputies were later added to represent the smaller provincial towns, and these included two physicians, an innkeeper, an apothecary, a scythe maker, a hat maker, a beer brewer, and three local mayors.

56. *Verhandlungen des Provisorischen Landtages des Herzogthumes Steiermark* (Graz, 1848), June 13, 1–3; Karl Hugelmann, *Die österreichischen Landtage im Jahre 1848* (Vienna, 1928), 50–53, 56–81; Anton Springer, *Geschichte Österreichs seit dem Wiener Frieden 1809* (Leipzig, 1863–65), 2:373. For a discussion of education or membership in the intelligentsia as a particular qualification for suffrage rights, see below 54–55.

57. Dunder, *Denkschrift*, 37–46; Sheehan, *German Liberalism*, 56–57. The following is an occupational breakdown by percentage of the German liberal deputies who listed Bürger occupations: lawyers 12.5 percent, physicians 5.7 percent, industrialists 4.6 percent, professors 3.4 percent, merchants 2.3 percent, journalists 2.3 percent, miscellaneous bourgeois occupations 5.7 percent. An interesting aspect of this apparent conquest of the Austrian Parliament by the German middle classes was the comparatively smaller number of state bureaucrats and civil servants to serve in this body. By contrast, officials accounted for about a third of the deputies in both the Frankfurt Parliament and the Prussian Diet in Berlin.

Bohemia in particular—but not exclusively—began to form interregional interest groups around clusters of issues. These deputies created three loosely allied factions: the Union of German Austrians, the Center Club, and the small Democratic Left. Other German deputies, especially the Tirolean clericals, dissociated themselves completely from the three liberal blocs.[58] Although its name suggested otherwise, the Union of German Austrians opposed close links with the other German states. It was strongly centralist and socially moderate, usually supporting the Austrian cabinet. The Center Club also backed an independent Austria but held more socially progressive positions regarding internal matters. The Democratic Left, on the other hand, favored close cooperation with the Frankfurt Parliament and inclusion of the monarchy within a newly united Germany. It came the closest to representing the Vienna democrats' radical social positions in the parliament. The Democratic Left was a popular favorite with the Viennese crowds, tending, as it often did, to antagonize other nationalists with its strongly anti-Slav rhetoric.[59]

During the early months of the revolution, bourgeois activists had worked to institutionalize their new political power on many fronts. Political clubs and a freer press functioned both to educate and mobilize citizens about their new constitutional rights. The clubs also continued to reproduce in miniature those new forms of appropriate public group behavior, like parliamentary procedure, that were now to inform political institutions as well. Middle-class representation in the monarchy's new legislative bodies, from city councils to provincial diets and the parliament proved that the Bürgertum had acquired some political power. And yet this optimistic appraisal represents only a part of what actually took place in 1848. As Bürger activists struggled to gain power, they encountered unexpected opposition, finding political conflict where they had expected to find harmony. Liberals believed that by seizing power in the name of all society, they could give their particular version of the revolution a powerful moral justification that was lacking in the selfishly parochial counterclaims made by rival social groups. The promise of a just order created in everyone's interest justified the bourgeois acquisition of power. Yet the liberals soon discovered that vociferous sectors of the popular classes, along with the former elites and even some Slavic bourgeois groups, questioned the benefits conferred on them by German liberal rule. In fact, these latter groups were prepared to fight ac-

58. OL, Flugschriftenversammlung A, vol. 22, "Programm des linken Centrums." These early factions were very loose and not subjected to any organizational discipline. Nevertheless, the Left Center, a grouping that later united most deputies from the three earlier liberal groupings, did draw up statutes declaring, "As a rule, party members must vote in parliament the way the party has determined beforehand."

59. Party programs in SRG, July 21 and July 28, 1848. Parliamentary deputies may have frequented political club meetings in Vienna, but the clubs did not develop institutional relationships with any of the loose parties in the parliament.

tively against them. This discovery elicited a bitterly defensive reaction among liberals, but it also produced several more detailed ideological justifications of their vision.

In mapping their ideologies in 1848, liberals also found that they often disagreed among themselves over what specific content to give to their new, generally agreed upon principles. Raw interest politics soon pitted sections of the Bürgertum against one another in 1848, as they tried to apply their new moral order to society. What exactly made a citizen, for example? And who actually belonged to the political nation, from which governing power was now said to derive? Were the rights of citizenship natural in origin, or did they have to be earned? What were the social responsibilities of the local commune to its citizen members, as well as to those who did not qualify for full membership? To address these issues, I turn now to a discussion of the development of liberal discourse about society in 1848–49.

Liberal Ideology: Defining Community and Nation in 1848

The revolutionaries who had unseated the old order in March 1848 deplored that regime's ramshackle bureaucratism and its senseless feudal hierarchy. Yet with what were they to replace it? Formal and informal discussions of this question dominated political activity and organization at every level throughout 1848, with German liberals elaborating ad hoc political programs based largely on their practical experience. Although few of these programs were ever implemented, their development—together with the elaborate justifications devised for them—help us to understand a larger liberal project as its most devoted supporters conceived of it.

Liberals in 1848 saw the March revolution as an opportunity to reconstruct society. The unfortunate tumult of the March days that had given them this opportunity should not be repeated by other groups. The glowing myth of their heroic revolt coexisted uncomfortably in the minds of many liberals with the equally strong memory of violent threats posed by an angry proletariat against private property. This latter fear motivated the more immediately conservative concerns of the revolutionaries, particularly the repeatedly expressed need to secure private property. In an anonymous pamphlet circulated on March 15, one Bürger revolutionary tempered his enthusiasm for the recent constitutional changes with warnings against those who sought to profit from public disorder. "*The great work has been completed.* Unfortunately it has been associated with deeds of which every citizen would be ashamed, were it not known that only robbers are finding pleasure in destruction and burning. . . . Every respectable citizen must now wish to have peace again, so that he can go about his own business. . . . Thieves wish to encourage the people to be disorderly so that they can steal. . . . *Whoever is a partisan of freedom is already peaceful*."[60] Taken together, these conflicting attitudes toward the March events produced an often self-contradictory program, meant to create a new civic order while protecting an endangered one.

Most liberals did not question that the ultimate source of legitimacy for this new order derived from the emperor. During the revolution every political faction tried to appropriate the unifying symbolism of the emperor for its own position, and he remained a powerful symbol throughout 1848 for both the continuity of law and the unity of the empire. The liberals hoped to preserve the best aspects of their society and the powerful continuity symbolized by the crown. At the same time, the liberal movement clearly sought to reform the bankrupt political order beneath the crown. "We declare ourselves opposed to bureaucratism," announced the Society of the Friends of the People, "[and] we declare ourselves opposed to the indolent nobility, which wedged itself between the people and the throne and which only wants to retain its ancient privilege and particularist interests."[61] Liberals warned constantly against the dangers to their vision of community posed by the particularism of a federalist nobility interested only in preserving its local prerogatives.

As we have already seen, liberals found models for the new order primarily in the *Vormärz* traditions surrounding the voluntary association. For many Bürger, associational life offered a compelling vision of society and its governance, one that contrasted individual responsibility to the traditional patriarchy of the old regime. The Bürger's concept of political society rested on the belief that membership within any community conferred specific rights and duties on the citizen. It was the active fulfillment of these obligations that gave the individual citizen the moral right to participate in the governance of the community.

Neither the bourgeois association nor its ideal of community resembled a democratic republic of activists, all social distinctions among them erased. Rather, the liberal association substituted new forms of hierarchy for the feudal or absolutist ones the Bürger had rejected. "To be free is to make reason the constituting principle of one's life," wrote student activist Johann N. Berger in a pamphlet on freedom of the press. In his belief that freedom required the self-imposition of discipline, Berger built on the implicit sense of hierarchy that characterized the liberals' attitude toward the popular classes, those people who had yet to internalize self-discipline. Noting that "people are not free in one blow; they become free, they develop and educate themselves to freedom, and freedom exists precisely in carrying out this process," he argued against giving the masses complete liberty until they had received enough education to

60. Rath, *Viennese Revolution*, 80–81.

61. *Vorträge des Dr. Schutte*, ed. Chaises, vi.

make proper use of it.[62] The chaos of March 1848 confirmed for the liberals that the working classes held a narrowly selfish understanding of politics, desiring only to improve their own material situations without regard to the rest of society. Education would help workers to see the larger common interest of society. According to liberals, that common interest was founded in the preservation of order, of common rules of civility in political practice, and of a respect for private property. Both the democratic and liberal political clubs professed a dedication to the education of the working classes, believing that responsible citizenship would be the end result.

Austrian liberals shared John Locke's belief in reason as a common law available to teach all mankind "who will but consult it, that being all equal and independent, no one ought to harm another in his life, health, liberty or possessions."[63] Yet in calling upon reason as the means to educate the masses to the responsible uses of freedom, liberals implicitly posited a darker side to human existence, a realm of unreason. Throughout 1848 liberals painted a disturbing picture of those who in John Stuart Mill's words "have not attained the maturity of their faculties," such as children, dependents, and "backward states of society in which the race itself may be considered in its nonage." Although Austrian liberals produced no theorists of the stature of Mill, their actions both in 1848 and later in the 1860s suggest that they fully shared his belief that "liberty, as a principle, has no application to any state of things anterior to the time when mankind have become capable of being improved by free and equal discussion." Citizens thus earn political rights by proving their ability to use them properly.[64]

The particular meanings liberals gave to general ideas like freedom or education in 1848, and the centrality they assigned to private property as the external indicator of these qualities, did not always resonate well with the rest of society. For all its universalist claims, the world of the voluntary association was itself highly limited, a world inhabited primarily by Bürger, bureaucrats, gentry, and an occasional enlightened noble. And while the association may have served the Bürgertum as a model for a reformed public sphere, it reflected a limited and narrow experience of the world. Despite their claim to speak for the whole of society and its needs, the liberals' programs rested on their own assumptions about property, one's place within a system of production, one's level of education, and one's gender. The language of a universal Bürgertum had enabled the middle-class revolutionaries to rally a socially diverse fol-

---

62. OL, Flugschriftenversammlung A, vol. 24, Johann N. Berger, "Die Pressefreiheit und das Pressegesetz" (Vienna, 1848), 1.

63. John Locke, *Two Treatises of Government* (New York, 1965), 311.

64. John Stuart Mill, *On Liberty* (New York, 1973), 484–85.

lowing for the purpose of reforming the half feudal, half absolutist state. Yet almost immediately, the liberals had to confront the fact that even the Bürgertum encompassed groups whose short-term interests were at best difficult to reconcile and at worst downright hostile to one another.

The liberals ran into trouble, for example, when they tried to apply the theoretical inviolability of private property with consistency to real world situations. In the economically troubled period of 1846–48, producers demanded contradictory measures to address their economic woes. Small producers who considered themselves the backbone of local Bürger society did not conceptualize the freedom of property ownership in quite the same way as more affluent industrialists did. While they might support the new political freedoms, small producers often viewed strict economic freedom as an infringement of their own rights. As one Upper Austrian Mittelstand group put it in a petition to the Austrian Parliament, "We want to be free, but along with freedom we also want to ensure our [economic] survival." The petitioners claimed that the larger good of the community depended on the secure foundation of a solid Mittelstand. This in turn required the "maintenance of a healthy *Bürgerstand* with its own appropriate rights." For these small producers, economic freedom had to be tempered with concern for the existing order, since only some form of economic regulation could prevent the proletarianization of the Mittelstand.[65]

In Vienna, the most troublesome social and economic issues rarely pitted the property-owning classes against the propertyless and dependent wage laborers as one might expect. Rather, various elements of the urban Bürgertum fought one another, thereby challenging the very idea of a middle-class consensus. Issues like housing, rent postponement, cheap credit, and how far to extend suffrage rights elicited conflicting views among urban Bürger and increased social tensions. What exactly was the freedom brought by the revolution, and how should it relate to the uses and privileges of property?

The demand for rent postponement by artisans and shopkeepers who had been hard hit by financial depression constituted the most divisive of these issues in Vienna. When quarterly rents fell due in April of 1848, landlords called for their prompt payment, thereby asserting what they considered to be legitimate property rights. Mass demonstrations and the radical press harassed landlords, accusing them of everything from a lack of charity toward the suffering artisans to rent gouging. In demanding a rent postponement, the artisans were not challenging the sanctity of private property. Rather, they implied a different standard for property's use, one that from their point of view replaced

65. OL, Flugschriftenversammlung A, vol. 25, "Petition der Gewerbsinhaber aus Oberösterreich an den österreichischen Reichstag" (Ried, 1848). The petition had 3,649 signatures from producers in the towns of Braunnau, Gmunden, Ried, Schärding, and Vöcklabruck but not from Linz. It also urged that restrictions be placed on Jewish emancipation for economic reasons.

the landlords' legal formalism with the realistic needs of the artisanal business community. The artisans used a moral rhetoric that contrasted their own economic productivity with the unproductive economic activity of the landlords (collecting rents). Without a rent postponement, artisans hard hit by the revolution could not maintain the profitability of their businesses. Without their businesses, nothing could be produced.[66]

The question of providing cheap credit for the same artisans also split the Viennese Bürgertum badly in 1848. A proposal to finance interest-free loans for artisans by forcing wealthier property owners to contribute to a credit fund led the latter group to accuse the former, once again, of violating property rights. Eventually, a private credit institution for artisans was set up in June, but its crash in September renewed the simmering conflict between wealthier and poorer capitalist producers. The artisans called on the city government to bail out their bank, demanding a guarantee of its investments. The moderate majority on the city council refused to take this course of action. As with the issue of rent postponement, most councilors accused the artisans of behaving like the unemployed wage laborers who constantly demanded government-funded welfare projects. The artisans should behave, they felt, like responsible property owners and stop treating government protection as if it were a fundamental right.[67]

On the new city councils and in many of the provincial diets, the perception of poorer artisans as potential traitors to the Bürgertum shaped ongoing discussions of what constituted citizenship and who might exercise it. Moderate liberals used these discussions to redefine citizenship and remove their more radical opponents from active participation. In framing suffrage laws for the Austrian Parliament, for the diets, and for the municipalities, moderate liberals in city and national government increasingly set limits on the right to vote. Every individual in the new polity enjoyed the basic civil rights bestowed by citizenship, yet suffrage qualifications restricted the right to vote and run for office to a socially responsible minority. For nineteenth-century liberals, active rights of citizenship belonged to individuals who demonstrated reasonable behavior in certain distinct situations. Only those who passed certain tests of reasonableness earned full personhood and the attendant rights and opportunities that attached to it. Devising such tests was a difficult task and often hard to justify, given the liberals' universalist discourse. Yet the dangers of civil unrest made this evident compromise of principles a pressing necessity.[68]

---

66. Häusler, *Massenarmut*, 205–8, 212; Rath, *Viennese Revolution*,176–78. (See also the example from the First Viennese Democratic Women's Association, p. 40.)

67. Häusler, *Massenarmut*, 348–54; Rath, *Viennese Revolution*, 306–12.

68. *Ämtliche Vehandlungs-Protokolle des Gemeindeausschusses der Stadt Wien vom 25. Mai bis 5. Oktober 1848* (Vienna, 1848). See the city council's discussion on September 2, 1848,

In the case of elections to the Austrian Parliament, for example, the Vienna government was forced to concede the vote to some wage laborers and dependent workers after an uprising in May 1848. Alexander Bach, now a member of the Vienna city council, helped the government avoid full democratization by suggesting that laborers should vote in their place of permanent residence, or *Heimat*. With few exceptions, *Heimat* implied one's town of birth. This clause allowed the liberals to support a more democratic suffrage while effectively disenfranchising the considerable number of workers who had emigrated to Vienna from Bohemia and Moravia in the previous months or years.[69]

The Viennese municipal suffrage law, adopted after the repression of worker disturbances in August of 1848, still reflected the myth of a Bürgertum uniting all property owners, great and small. It gave the right to vote to all male taxpayers. In making this decision, the city council followed the logic that had informed the original Bürger challenge to the old regime in March. Their tax payments entitled property owners with even the smallest stake in the affairs of the city to participate in municipal decisions. Yet following further disturbances in September and a violent uprising in October of 1848, the city council began to revise its definition of active citizenship. By the spring of 1849, the councilors had imposed a minimum annual tax payment of five florins as a qualification for the right to vote, thereby disenfranchising numerous artisans and small property owners.[70]

The Vienna city council further stratified the liberal definition of citizenship by creating a hierarchic curial voting system based on tax and educational qualifications. Citizens who paid up to ten florins in annual taxes voted in the third curia. Medium-sized property holders and the educated intelligentsia elected the second curia, while a small number of the wealthiest artisans, merchants, houseowners, and industrialists elected the first curia. Since each curia elected the same number of deputies, this arrangement gave the wealthier citizens a proportionately greater voice in city government and effectively removed propertyless wage laborers from any voice at all. As for small property owners, although they constituted a numerical majority of all voters, their

---

of whether or not to allow an upcoming democratic demonstration. "The right of association is indeed holy," explained one councilor, "but it cannot be allowed to threaten our property and our families."

69. Obermann, "Reichstagswahlen," 342–74. Local authorities used other means, such as an indirect, two-tier voting system, to prevent laborers from gaining a substantial voice in the *Reichstag* elections. In Vienna, 26,000 people were listed as eligible to vote out of a general population of 411,000. Of these, 18,500, or 71 percent of those eligible and 5 percent of the entire population, actually voted in the *Reichstag* elections.

70. *Ämtliche Vehandlungs-Protokolle der Stadt Wien*, 43–47.

challenge to the moderates' concept of private property throughout 1848 justified the decision to diminish their voice in city politics through the curial system.[71]

The discussions about who might vote in which curia began in August 1848, before the council had actually imposed the minimum tax qualification of five florins. This early discussion already indicated in some detail the kinds of concerns that the liberal Bürgertum of the nineteenth century consistently raised. It shows an awareness of the split between poorer and wealthier producers, as well as an assumption that socialization through higher education would make poorer voters more likely to identify their interests with those of the wealthier classes. It also shows that the liberals never viewed property ownership as an end in itself. Rather, they viewed ownership as one of a few reliable indicators of a person's capability to exercise reason. Defending the placement of teachers in the second curia, for example, when their economic status qualified them to vote in the third (if at all), one deputy explained that it was necessary "to use the intelligentsia to counterbalance the large numbers of tax proletarians," those who paid the very minimum in taxes. Another deputy pointed out that the teachers, in contrast to the poorest taxpayers, "will have both the knowledge and also the necessary [free] time to make excellent city councilors."[72]

Liberal initiatives in those provincial diets that met after March 1848 had the same double-edged quality. They insisted on the universal rule of law, on community control over local revenues, and on ending so-called feudal privilege and social hierarchy. Yet by debating the boundaries of the enfranchised community of active citizens, they created new sets of social hierarchies. In Upper Austria, for example, the first-time bourgeois appointees to the diet mentioned above made their presence felt within hours of taking their seats. To the traditional address of thanks that the executive committee of nobles had planned to present to the emperor, the "worthy Bürger of Linz" added a list

---

71. *Ämtliche Vehandlungs-Protokolle der Stadt Wien,* 43–47, includes the August 1848 franchise provisions. For a useful discussion of the 1849 law, see Boyer, *Political Radicalism,* 15–16.

72. *Ämtliche Vehandlungs-Protokolle der Stadt Wien,* 45. All of the measures instituted here for the first time in 1848 served as models for future discussions of voting rights in the monarchy down to 1918. While liberal politicians in later periods often protested the unfairness of curial or two-tiered systems of voting, they did not abandon them when they gained the opportunity to do so. In fact, many liberals involved in writing the 1867 constitution argued that retaining the curial system would strengthen the legitimacy of the new document by making it appear consistent with Austrian tradition. That system was not exactly traditional but had been invented in 1848 for local elections and revived in 1861 for local and provincial ones. The liberals' community statutes of 1862 would also retain the residence (*Heimat*) requirement for voting in order to exercise social control over the lowest classes.

of their own demands, starting with an explicit catalog of new rights for the citizen and outlining the contours of their ideal polity. Those rights included the abolition of censorship, the right of association, protection from arbitrary arrest, and freedom of education. In a reference to the economic condition of the province, the Bürger demanded improved teacher training and the founding of a special ministry for industry and trade. As far as participation in the political community was concerned, the new deputies demanded suffrage laws based on property and educational qualifications rather than on traditional feudal privilege, thereby expanding their own influence at the expense of both the nobility above and the poorer classes below.[73]

This influence is apparent in the new community statutes debated by the Upper Austrian Diet in April. Voting members of a community were adults who could demonstrate their independence by showing that they owned enough property to be able to feed a family. Dependence, meanwhile, was linked to poverty and criminality in the rhetoric of the deputies and served as the major reasons for which inhabitants might be denied full membership status. In an interesting privileging of gender prejudice over the sanctity of private property, women could not obtain or inherit member status as individuals. They could only achieve it by marrying a member of the community.[74] Bürger deputies to the diet displayed the same preoccupation with issues of property and independence when it came to deciding who might vote in provincial elections. As one liberal deputy put it, "we should only prevent those individuals from voting who live from a daily wage or who enjoy contributions from a charity institution . . . in short, those who are not independent."[75]

Despite this apparently conservative bent directed against the lower classes, the liberals could also sound like radicals when it came to establishing the legitimacy of their political power against that of the traditional elites. In discussions of the future makeup of the diet, for example, liberals denounced the role that privilege had traditionally played in the composition of its predecessors. One deputy wanted a diet slanted more toward the so-called productive elements in society and suggested the following three categories for election: rural (including both peasants and noble landowners), commerce/industry, and education. "Since up until now, only unabashed members of the privileged es-

73. Hugelmann, *Österreichischen Landtage im Jahre 1848*, 50–53, 56–81.

74. See OL, Flugschriftenversammlung B, vol. 5, "Die Verhandlungen der am 23. März auf dem Landtage versammelt gewesenen Stände des Erzherzogthums Österreich ob des Ems," session of April 4, 1848. Membership was denied to anyone prosecuted for theft or begging, for inability to prove financial solvency, for taxes over a year in arrears, and dependence on a charity or welfare institution in the preceding three years. Once a woman was granted membership in the community, she retained it even if her marriage was later annulled.

75. OL, Flugschriftenversammlung B, vol. 5, "Protokoll nr. 1 über die am 24. Juli 1848 von den gesammten Herrn Ständen des Landes ob der Ems mit Zuziehung aller Herren Mitglieder des provisorischen Landes Ausschusses zu Linz gepflogene Verhandlung."

tates have spoken, someone from the other categories must speak his mind. The institution of [privileged] estates should be abolished . . . for a long time it has not had a good reputation. . . . I believe that work itself should be the basis for deciding representation."[76]

In Styria, the reconstituted diet drew up new community statutes that gave complete power over local revenues and administration to urban citizens, in line with antibureaucratic sentiment there. Whereas the state had formerly appointed city officials and mandated city affairs, the language of the new law stipulated universal community control over the administration of community funds through the process of elections. At the same time, like their colleagues in Lower and Upper Austria, the liberals introduced a hierarchy of citizenship into their universalist vision. The deputies distinguished mere inhabitants of the community from its tax-paying members with the phrase "whoever does not share in the burdens of the community should have no voice in the administration of community funds."[77]

Unlike their Lower and Upper Austrian counterparts, some of the Styrian deputies at least recognized the potential contradiction in their principles when it came to the issue of women property owners. As in Upper Austria, a Styrian woman gained rights of community membership (without the right to vote) only when she married one of its members. On June 16, however, one deputy unsuccessfully posed the question: "Why, since we decided that an individual is a member through ownership of either landed property, a house, a business, or the equivalent, [should not] women, who are often in possession of these qualifications, qualify to vote, albeit by proxy? Since it is the ownership of taxable property that makes someone a member of the community, I therefore believe that in writing the paragraph this way we have emancipated women."[78]

Although debated in this context, the issue of women voters was not settled or even addressed coherently in 1848. The phenomenon of an unmarried woman owning enough property to vote was considered a major exception to the norm in the liberal cosmology, no matter how often it might really have occurred. Otherwise, legislators would have been forced to choose between one of two sacred and in this case contradictory principles: the sanctity of property ownership and the belief that women's participation in politics was inappropriate. In 1848, liberals had no pressing reason to grapple with such a theoretical issue. According to Bürger gender assumptions, women simply did not own property, although legally women often owned landed or business property.

---

76. OL, Flugschriftenversammlung B, vol. 5, "Protokoll nr. 1."

77. *Verhandlungen des Landtages Steiermark*, June 16, 1848, 28–30.

78. *Verhandlungen des Landtages Steiermark*, June 17, 1848, 30.

Voting distinctions were applied to other groups as well. Liberal attitudes toward the peasantry betrayed a similar mistrust of that group's ability to transcend its sectarian interests and consider the community as a whole. "Traditional education made people stupid," noted one *Schwarz-Roth-Gold* correspondent who regretted the ignorance of most peasants about their national identity and the liberal political ideals it embodied. "The majority of Austrian peasants doesn't even know that there is a Germany and that it is their fatherland!" Attributing peasant ignorance to a lack of progressive education in rural areas, the journalist continued, "[traditional forms of education] did not want to . . . provide our children with the example of the free men of their national past, out of fear that it would teach them [to think] independently."[79]

Liberals suspected that once it had been emancipated from feudal laws, the peasantry would withdraw from responsible political involvement and become the political pawns of the noble landowners.[80] In discussing the issue of representation to the Moravian Diet, German liberals there betrayed both these fears about the peasantry and their own belief that they themselves had created the revolution for the benefit of the entire nation. Against the protests of the landowners, the liberals recommended that the diet allot one deputy for every 3,000 town residents and one for every 20,000 rural residents, arguing that "if we don't ensure the towns a certain preponderance, the liberal principle will be endangered. The cities fought for the revolution . . . and created freedom in Austria. We know the nature of the peasants; once they are rid of their *Robot*, they will no longer bother with politics, or even worse, they will be swayed by their traditional love of the old-fashioned ways."[81]

The question of who made up the nation whose interests the liberals served was further complicated by the growth of political nationalism. During 1848–49 the liberals faced political challenges to their own local and state power couched in the language of national identity. The appearance of Czech, Italian, Polish, and Slovene nationalism (among others) in the political arena forced liberals to respond to an issue that they had not at first believed to be relevant to politics. This development encouraged the first ongoing discussions among liberals of the meaning of one's national identity in politics. Since many German liberals believed that their Germanness lay primarily in their adherence to an ideal liberal culture, and that this identity was open to people

79. SRG, August 22, 1848.

80. On the failed attempts by urban democrats to win peasants and farmers for their cause, see Wilhelm Wadl, "Die demokratische Bewegung in Kärnten im Jahre 1848," *Österreich in Geschichte und Literatur* 28 (1984): 64–86.

81. Springer, *Österreich*, 383. The liberals added, "We can also see through the so-called liberalism of the noble landowners who demand the election [of an equal number] of deputies from the towns and the countryside, because they can influence their dependent cottagers and the naturally conservative peasants."

who spoke any language, they could not understand a politics based on mere ethnic identity. At the same time, Germans also grappled among themselves with the issue of unification with the other German states and what form, if any, it should take.

Some liberals who embraced the idea of unification with Germany downplayed the political significance of ethnic identity. If German was privileged to be the language of the bureaucracy, the military, and educational institutions, there were objective justifications for this privilege. Was not German the most internationally recognized and culturally advanced language of those in use in the monarchy? Furthermore, the privileges enjoyed by German culture were not necessarily limited to German speakers in the monarchy. German identity was open to anyone wishing to adopt German cultural values. The statutes of the German Constitutional Association in Teplitz stated that "membership in the association is open to any Austrian citizen without regard to religion, nationality, or estate." And in a united Germany, liberals assumed that the cultural rights of ethnic minorities would be respected.[82]

Ludwig von Löhner's Association of Germans in Austria reflected some of these attitudes when it invited "Austrians with German sympathies"—not necessarily Germans—to join. The club did not define German nationality in a racial, ethnic, or even a linguistic sense, and membership was not technically limited to Germans. Members were only required to "wear the German colors" (black, red, and gold) and to pay a monthly contribution of at least twenty kreuzer. For this, the first German nationalist organization in Austria, national identity itself derived from a public expression of liberal political sympathies. The group's publication, *Schwarz-Roth-Gold* claimed that one's Germanness "is based not simply on the soil of birth or language of culture, but rather on . . . nobility of action and the worthiness of conviction." In fact, a reading of the Association's statutes would seem to make greater sense if one were to substitute the word *liberal* wherever the word *German* appears.

In July 1848, one writer for *Schwarz-Roth-Gold* suggested that precisely those qualities that distinguished German culture from other cultures could also regulate the relationship between Germans and non-Germans. "We believe in the holy spirit of humanity . . . which is embodied in the German people, whose breath . . . serves to awaken all peoples . . . so they might become great and do well on earth. We want a German Austria . . . a powerful leader for all our brother nationalities, not through the [coercive] power of the crown of Charlemagne, but rather through the voluntary respect that we earn when we deal in freedom and humanity. . . . Therefore our highest commandment: Thou shalt love humanity above all else!"[83]

82. NBF, 1848–71, "Statuten des deutschen konstitutionellen Vereins in Teplitz."

83. SRG, July 11, 1848.

The journal also gave voice to a certain confusion among German nationalists about whether German and Austrian national identities were in fact synonymous. In explaining its emblematic use of the German colors, for example, *Schwarz-Roth-Gold* suggested the existence of both a specifically German ethnic consciousness and of a higher Austrian nationality uniting Austrians of different cultural origins. Austria's revolutionary course had taken it "out of the [black] night of destructive fragmentation and isolation, through [the red dawn of] joyous consciousness of national unity, to achieve the [gold] light of spiritual unity among all peoples and races that inhabit Central Europe."

Such idealism, which allowed for autonomous development of individual national consciousness as a prelude to forming a larger Austrian nationality, typified the attitude of some German Austrian activists. These people envisioned a new Austrian nationality, which they equated with a loyalty to the new liberal principles of constitutionalism. "Teach your children that they are not [simply] Hungarians, Germans, Slavs, [or] Italians," counseled one observer, "but rather citizens [Bürger] of a constitutional Austrian state." Warning that the demands for individual national rights would sunder the "brotherhood, sworn on that great day," the writer admonished his readers to remember March 13. "On that day we were one people and acted in unison. . . . The old state collapsed! A new state arose [and]—a new people! Therefore let us have only one nationality and no national divisions!"[84]

Others, however, could not accept as legitimate Czech nationalist demands for Bohemian provincial autonomy and Czech linguistic parity with German. These demands, as with the Slovene demonstrations in Styria, seemed to imply a profound suspicion of German motives as well as an irrational unwillingness to adopt the so-called higher culture. In fact, to many liberals, Czech nationalist programs only made sense if understood in political terms, as providing reactionary aristocrats with a front for their own agenda of federalism, feudalism, and states' rights. These contradictions became particularly acute during the siege of Prague by General Windischgrätz in June 1848. Germans in Prague, upset by the recent convocation of a Congress of Slavs in their city, at first welcomed the violent efforts of the reactionary general to end the congress and take over administration of the city. Many liberals and democrats in Vienna shared this enthusiasm, celebrating the siege as a victory for German liberalism. Others were not so certain. When the Association of Germans in Austria met to discuss these events, the Viennese members displayed little happiness about the June days in Prague. Noting that Windischgrätz had installed the "reactionary Count Leo Thun" to administer the province, a man "who had [also] betrayed the demands of Czech democrats," the liberals could not endorse the general's action. Association members in the other towns and cities of

84. *Wiener Zeitschrift für Kunst, Literatur, Theater und Mode* 60–61 (1848): 239.

Bohemia also admitted that while Windischgrätz might have saved Prague for the Germans, he would just as easily march against Germans if ordered.[85]

After the siege of Prague, the Germans in provincial Bohemia sometimes interpreted Czech hostility toward them as a result of Count Thun's political influence.[86] According to one association correspondent from Rumberg, "Luckily, not too many Czechs have been infected with [Thun's] poison as yet. . . . The German will protect his rights but will never try to take away the rights of those who speak a different language." In a similar vein, a song composed by the Eger branch of the association asserted, "And though the German colors / May shimmer on our breast / Still no Czech need worry."[87] The "Freedom Song of Bohemia" downplayed the importance of ethnic differences in the face of political issues, declaring, "and whether the tongue, whether the mouth / Speaks in German or Czech / Only a freely spoken word guarantees / Truth, duty, and justice."[88] Such generosity of spirit toward the recent enemy was perhaps easier to indulge in after the clear defeat of the Czechs and the Slav Congress.

The question of unification with Germany complicated the issue of political nationalism even more, often pitting Austro-German nationalists against one another. What was to be their future relationship to the newly unified Germany that was gradually emerging from the work of the Frankfurt Parliament? At first, in March 1848, many German Bürger and university students had seen in the revolution an opportunity to join a greater united Germany founded on liberal or democratic ideals. Austria's close relationship with the other German states seemed a powerful guarantee of imminent reform. Enthusiastic liberals had incorporated the German colors (black, red, gold) into their costume and hung the new German flag from their houses.

In this context, Francis Palacký's famous rejection of the Frankfurt Parliament's invitation in April and his support for an autonomous, Slavic Austria seemed a shocking denunciation of both German cultural values and political liberalism. The tendency among many German liberals to equate (unfairly) Slavic nationalism with the sponsorship of reactionary Russia only aggravated this view. When Slovenes in Graz displayed their own Slavic red, white, and blue colors publicly or founded a political association there, German liberals reacted with profound bitterness, believing that these events reflected the local popularity of reactionary conservationism.[89] Yet only a few months after this

85. SRG, July 18, 1848.

86. SRG, July 21, 1848. See the account of a conversation between Thun and German liberal Ignaz Kuranda.

87. SRG, July 11, 1848, "Die deutsche Städte Böhmens an die Hauptstadt Prag." For the text of the song, see SRG, July 21, 1848.

88. NBF, Flugblätter 1848–71, undated.

89. Pfeisinger, "1848 in Graz" 103–6.

so-called colors incident, liberals in the Styrian Diet continued to treat the Slovene minority as a potential political ally. In June, German liberals proposed that a Slovene translation of the diet proceedings be published in local German newspapers, to make the legislative session more accessible to the Slovene minority. Noting that "many of the Slovenes who read the Graz newspapers are very intelligent people," one liberal suggested that it would make Slovenes happy "and give them more trust in us" if the translations were appended to the Graz newspapers.[90]

German activists themselves were also uncertain about what exactly they expected to gain from participation in a unified Germany. During the summer of 1848, enthusiasm for Austria's incorporation into a unified Germany seems to have waned considerably. Often this change of heart among German Austrians had to do with the fear that weaker Austrian manufacturers could not compete with their German counterparts in an open market. This concern had surfaced frequently before 1848 in industrialists' discussions of the advantages to be derived from Austria's possible entry into the German Customs Union (*Zollverein*).[91] These economic worries had been driven into relative obscurity for a time by the euphoria of the March days, only to reemerge as the Frankfurt Parliament discussed unification more seriously. One petition to the Austrian Parliament from small producers in Upper Austria expressed the fear that too much freedom would destroy the Austrian Mittelstand completely.[92] Noting that complete freedom of trade as contemplated by the Frankfurt Parliament was responsible in France and Belgium for the introduction of "that terrifying feature of modernity—the proletariat," the petition urged the deputies to temper their enthusiasm for free trade with some restrictions. A similar petition to the parliament from a Prague Handworkers' Association echoed the same fears: "The experience of England and France has taught us that so-called freedom of industry and trade, the unlimited application of machines, the super power of big capital only crushes the Mittelstand and acts as midwife at the birth of the fearsome proletariat."[93] Yet restrictions on industry or trade were not likely to be retained should Austria join the other German states in the *Zollverein*.[94]

Delegates to the First Congress of Bohemian Germans, a modestly attended meeting of associational representatives from Northern Bohemia in

90. *Verhandlungen des Landtages Steiermark,* June 14, 1848, 12–13.

91. SRG, July 11, 1848; *Mittheilungen für Gewerbe und Handel* 1 (Prague, 1835): 26, 125–27, 349–53.

92. SRG, July 11, 1848, has a discussion of economic arguments for and against German unification.

93. NBF, 1848, "Hohe Reichstagsversammlung," September 22, 1848.

94. OL, Flugschriftenversammlung A, vol. 25, "Petition der Gewerbsinhaber aus Oberösterreich" (Ried, 1848).

August 1848, also expressed ambivalence toward the potential results of unification. However much they supported increased political ties with the new Germany, the delegates also blamed their recent economic woes specifically on competition with *Zollverein* goods.[95] The delegates to the First Congress of Bohemian Germans also struggled hard to develop administrative solutions to the nationality conflict in Bohemia. Many of them favored a future division of the entire monarchy into districts (*Kreise*) based on ethnic composition rather than on historical provincial boundaries. Yet this did not solve the problem of the smaller islands of German or Czech speakers who lived interspersed in otherwise more ethnically homogeneous areas (as was the case for the Germans in Prague, Brünn, or Iglau). Most delegates were not prepared to go as far as one Viennese speaker who urged, "We must concern ourselves with saving and protecting the vital part of German Bohemia and abandon the sick and lazy ones to their own devices."[96] They also considered such ideas as dividing Bohemia into Czech and German administrative districts or dividing the Bohemian Diet into separate German and Czech curias. All these solutions would be raised again and debated starting in the late 1880s and continuing until the collapse of the monarchy in 1918.[97]

Many German liberals also began to understand that their insistence on unification with Germany weakened their political position at home, where they had to work closely with other nationalist groups in the Austrian Parliament. If forced to choose between liberal and national political identities, many deputies preferred to work for liberal constitutional institutions that would ensure the survival of their particular vision of community.[98] The failure of the Frankfurt Parliament to negotiate an acceptable form of German unity combined with the resurgence of conservative fortunes both in Prussia and in the Habsburg monarchy led to new combinations and alliances. The failed Viennese uprising of October 1848 reinforced for German liberals the urgency of finding political solutions more acceptable to other groups in order to save what remained of the revolution.[99]

---

95. This conference was sponsored by the Association of Germans in Austria. For an account, see Polišenský, *Revolutionary Year,* 178–84; NBF, Flugblätter 1848–71, Kronländer 1848, and Wien 1848.

96. Sieber, *Löhner*, 142–43.

97. Polišenský, *Revolutionary Year*, 178–83. For statements from the second conference of Bohemian Germans held at Eger in November of 1848, see articles in *Deutsche Zeitung aus Böhmen* (Prague, 1848), November 28 and December 1, 1848.

98. Sieber, *Löhner*, 143–47; see also Lasser's statement to the constitutional committee of the Kremsier *Reichstag* in February 1849 cited below, 64.

99. OL, Flugschriftenversammlung A, vol. 22, "Programm des linken Centrums." The removal of the parliament from revolutionary Vienna to provincial Kremsier in October 1848 meant that radical Viennese deputies lost contact with organized pressure groups, and the democratic left could no longer count on popular uprisings to aid its cause.

Some German nationalists like Löhner decided that to reach a compromise with the other nationalist parties over a constitution was more important than waging a principled, but losing, battle for German unification. This recognition underlay much of the work of the constitutional committee of the Austrian Parliament, which struggled from January to March 1849 to produce a draft constitution for the Austrian half of the empire.[100] The German liberals on the committee worked hard to create a centralized structure for the monarchy. They came to consider the achievement of centrally guaranteed institutions and civil rights within the multinational monarchy to be more desirable than German unification. In February 1849, for example, Baron Joseph Lasser of Upper Austria told his fellow committee members, "I see true freedom in the homogeneity of certain basic institutions that guarantee freedom of the individual, freedom of the municipality, and the cohesiveness of the entire empire. Out of these considerations I renounce my German sympathies."[101]

In January 1849 the committee presented the full Austrian Parliament with a draft preamble to the new Austrian constitution that defined both the powers of the crown and the rights of the citizen. This liberal document, the only one to be discussed and voted on by the whole parliament, boldly proclaimed that "all sovereignty proceeds from the people." This statement alone incurred such displeasure from the crown that it had to be amended to read "from the sovereign and the people." The parliament then approved the rest of the preamble, which abolished titles of nobility, demoted the Catholic Church to equal status with other religions and sects, and introduced civil marriage, equality before the law, freedom of the press, and the right of association. The preamble gave the emperor almost unlimited powers in the sphere of foreign policy. Typical of the liberals, however, a treaty only required parliamentary sanction if it involved any financial obligation by the people.[102]

A special paragraph in the preamble guaranteed each nationality the "inviolable right to preserve and cultivate its nationality in general and its lan-

---

100. *Protokolle des Verfassungsausschuss im österreichischen Reichstage, 1848–1849*, ed. Anton Springer (Leipzig, 1885), 4. Three representatives from each province—thirty in all—sat on the constitutional committee, including German liberals Rudolf Brestel (Vienna), Franz Hein (Silesia), Josef Lasser (Salzburg), Cajetan Mayer (Moravia), and Viennese democrats Adolf Fischhof and Joseph Goldmark. Despite the apparently federalist structure of the committee, which gave each province equal representation, this arrangement actually favored the liberal centralists. There were several smaller ethnically German provinces represented by liberals, while federalists came mostly from two of the largest provinces, Bohemia and Galicia.

101. Karl Müllner, "Freiherr Josef Lasser von Zollheim, eine Biographie" (Ph.D. diss., University of Vienna, 1962), 11.

102. Macartney, *Empire*, 417–18. The *Reichstag* established a political system that gave parliamentary deputies considerable power. Cabinet ministers were responsible both to the emperor and to the parliament, and the government could not dissolve the parliament for a period longer than three months. Legislation that passed the parliament three times remained valid, even without imperial sanction.

guage in particular. The equality of rights in schools, the bureaucracy and public life of every language used locally (*Landesüblich*) is guaranteed by the state."[103] This paragraph stated a formal principle open to diverse interpretations. The deputies agreed that a group had the right to cultivate its particular cultural heritage, yet the question of how far this right extended into the realm of public life remained controversial. Did the equality of languages in local use apply to schools beyond the primary level, for example, or to bureaucratic institutions beyond the village or town level? The Czechs could interpret the paragraph as endorsing bilingual universities or the use of Czech at the highest level of the provincial bureaucracy, while for the German liberals it applied only to local situations. And what was the difference between a legitimate language in local use and a mere dialect? The committee expected to elaborate more specific applications of the principle as it negotiated the future organizational and administrative structure of the monarchy.

All participants understood that it was the question of Austria's ultimate state structure—whether federalist or centralist—that would decide how the nationality clause was eventually to be applied. The federalists, led by Palacký and his son-in-law Francis Rieger of Bohemia, proposed that the committee specify the powers of the central government first and that everything else be left to the provincial governments. Most of the German liberals fought hard to enumerate the powers of the provincial diets first and leave the rest to the central government. They opposed any solution to the nationality question that gave individual provinces substantial autonomy. Germans made up the largest national group in the monarchy as a whole, but they were scattered across many regions. In some provinces like Bohemia and Moravia, they constituted a distinct minority. They therefore saw the central government as their most effective champion. Rudolf Brestel of Lower Austria suggested dividing provinces with sizable ethnic minorities like Bohemia into large districts drawn along national lines and setting up special courts to arbitrate nationalist disputes. In this he returned to a favorite liberal theme of communal self-determination combined with centralism at the state level. Rieger faulted this solution for failing to account for the many small islands of one nationality surrounded by another. He considered district autonomy even less practical than provincial autonomy.[104]

Cajetan Mayer of Moravia/Silesia intervened to give an eloquent justification of the centralist vision that also influenced future German liberal positions

103. Gerald Stourzh, "Die Gleichberechtigung der Nationalitäten und die österreichische Dezember Verfassung von 1867," in *Der österreichische-ungarische Ausgleich von 1867. Vorgeschichte und Wirkungen*, ed. Peter Berger (Vienna, 1967), 193. Stourzh gives an excellent account of the history of this clause, placing it in the context of Pillersdorf's April 1848 constitution and the draft of the Frankfurt Parliament Bill of Rights.

104. Springer, ed., *Protokolle*, 32–34.

on nationalism. Conjuring up the old regime, Mayer reminded his colleagues how Metternich had supposedly held the Austrian peoples together with an iron fist, suppressing all autonomous national and provincial life. "We are proving him right if we keep demonstrating that there is no other way to keep us all together." He asked the committee members to trust one another and to work together for a common goal. "Up until now we could not be Austrians, we loved our individual provinces more, as a way of opposing oppression from above. . . . If the Germans were formerly the lords and Slavs the servants, this was only true because the government was German and it oppressed both nations. The government didn't know Slavic. The organs of our common oppression therefore spoke German." Mayer then added, "the Germans want to be emancipated as much as the Slavs. Whoever transfers the Slavs' hatred of the bureaucracy to a general hatred of the Germans is simply showing the truth in Metternich's principle of divide and conquer."[105] Mayer's ability to disconnect the interests of average German speakers across the monarchy from those of the German-speaking bureaucracy demonstrated his acute understanding of the many-layered nationality problem in Austria. At the same time, Mayer drew a very different conclusion from the Czech nationalists, who located the problem in the very existence of a powerful central government rather than in the specific abuse of power by that government.

The majority of the constitutional committee, politically weighted toward the centralists, voted with Mayer to limit provincial autonomy from above by a strong central parliament and from below by giving some power to semi-autonomous districts and municipalities. To avoid any confusion about the ultimate source of authority, they added a clause authored by Lasser, which stated that in cases where jurisdiction between parliament and the diets remained unclear, the matter should be decided in favor of the central government, not even by the monarch. For German liberals this solution guaranteed the implementation of a consistent code of laws, civil and religious rights for the diverse peoples of the monarchy, while freeing local communities from the rule of a hitherto arbitrary bureaucracy.[106]

The committee also decided after much debate that the central parliament and not the provincial diets would regulate industrial, economic, and tariff policies, as well as school and religious matters. Czech deputies had argued that given the enormous variety in regional conditions and needs, industrial codes must be set by each province. In addition, the federalists warned that future cen-

105. Springer, ed., *Protokolle*, 42–43.

106. Springer, ed., *Protokolle*, 49–53. Fischhof, one of the Viennese democrats who were more wary of the central government's intentions than the liberals—a position that put the former on the side of the Slav federalists with whom they otherwise had little in common—suggested giving decisive power to the imperial parliament (*Reichsgesetzgebung*) instead of to the imperial government (*Reichsregierung*).

tral governments might pay too little attention to the economic development of certain provinces while encouraging growth in others. As an example, they blamed the Vienna government for the decline of the Bohemian linen industry in the 1840s. In response, liberals argued that industrialists had to be confident of consistent conditions for labor all over the monarchy. "Could a manufacturer in Bohemia survive if local laws limited the working day there to six or eight hours while in neighboring Moravia it was set at twelve?" asked Brestel. Furthermore, some provinces might even return to guild regulation of labor as well as to a system that limited the numbers and types of industries that could be started in a given locality, both of which measures the liberals deplored. In fact many small producers in 1848 who feared the disastrous effects of open competition with large-scale or foreign firms had already demanded precisely these kinds of remedies from the diets and parliament.[107]

Liberal committee members also argued that industrial laws were far too important and complex to be left to the discretion of individual provinces, which might hurt general economic development by pursuing separate courses. Echoing this sentiment, Emil Vacano of Upper Austria described the ideal industrialist as "a cosmopolitan when it comes to business practices, [for whom local] limitations would have a disadvantageous influence." In this way centralist bureaucrats and liberal businessmen reinforced one another's theoretical commitment to a policy of state centralism.[108]

The full Austrian Parliament never voted on these recommendations, and the work of this committee was suddenly cut short. Throughout February 1849 committee members voiced fears that the imperial government might attempt to undercut their work by dictating its own constitution. Sure enough, on March 6, Count Francis Stadion assembled the leaders of the parties to read them the text of a rival constitution he himself had drafted at the request of the emperor. The next day the cabinet dissolved the parliament, simultaneously publishing Stadion's constitution. The deputies were dismissed for having wasted their time on "dangerous theoretical discussions." Scarcely one year to the day after the March revolution had toppled the Metternich regime, a new government forbade any observance of that anniversary.[109]

---

107. Springer, ed., *Protokolle*, 73–76.

108. Springer, ed., *Protokolle*, 73–77. In answer to the Czech accusation that the central government bore responsibility for the decline of the Bohemian linen industry in the 1840s, Brestel declared that tariff regulation and popular education were the best ways to raise the level of industry. He added that the depression of the 1840s had been caused by events in the United States and in Spain, as well as by the introduction of mechanization, not by the workings of the Austrian central government.

109. Wolfgang Häusler, "Noch sind nicht alle Märzen vorbei . . . ." Zur politischen Tradition der Wiener Revolution von 1848," in *Politik und Gesellschaft im alten und neuen Österreich*, ed. Isabella Ackerl, Walter Hummelberger, and Hans Mommsen (Vienna, 1981), 1:92-93; Macart-

The government appeared to have destroyed the German liberal movement completely. Political clubs had gradually been outlawed following the October uprising in Vienna, and the few elected institutions that continued to meet—mostly city councils—lost their ability to make political decisions and served instead as local administrative bodies for implementing government policy.[110] The press was once again subjected to a severe censorship. Across the monarchy revolutionaries of all nationalities and political beliefs were arrested or subjected to police harassment. Caroline von Perin, who had founded the Women's Democratic Association, managed to emigrate to Munich after six months' imprisonment, although the state confiscated her personal fortune. Only Justice Minister Anton Schmerling's timely intercession saved Carl Giskra, the student representative to the Frankfurt Parliament, from imprisonment. Even so, the government ended his promising career and those of others like Stremayr, prohibiting these student deputies from practicing law. Several other revolutionaries, including Hans Kudlich and the democrats Joseph Goldmark and Ernst Violand, managed to escape abroad. Other liberals like the lawyer Alexander Bach joined the bureaucracy of the new regime.[111]

Most liberals sought refuge from the confusion and violence of the revolutionary year in a rededication to work and family. Prague Professor Leopold von Hasner spoke for many in later years when he reminisced that the era that began in 1849 was one in which "I belonged almost completely to my teaching and research activities and not at all to the events of the outside world."[112] Yet as the next chapter will show, liberal ideas and much of liberal political discourse survived to structure the new regime's thinking about a host of economic and social issues. The public discussion of these issues that had been raised in 1848 continued during the next decade, albeit within bureaucratic circles and devoid of their more overtly political implications. And in the 1860s, when the government again conceded a form of constitutionalism, liberal political culture and its rhetoric proved only to have been dormant, not dead.

---

ney, *Empire*, 423. Attempts to commemorate the March 1848 fallen were met with arrests and police harassment.

110. Leopold Kammerhofer, "Das politische Vereinswesen und der deutsch-österreichische Liberalismus in Zisleithanien von 1867 bis 1879" (Ph.D. diss., University of Vienna, 1986), 21. In December 1848 the cabinet had sent a memorandum to the provincial governors outlawing democratic or radical political associations.

111. Weiland, *Frauenemanzipation*, 208–9; Macartney, *Empire*, 423. On Schmerling's intercession for Giskra, see Paul Molisch, "Anton von Schmerling und der Liberalismus in Österreich," *Archiv für österreichische Geschichte* 116 (Vienna, 1943): 15–17.

112. Hasner, *Denkwürdigkeiten*, 51.

CHAPTER 3

The Struggle for the State, 1849–67

> The visions that malcontents and utopian dreamers sought to realize through political and social upheaval are now being achieved through legal . . . means, with the help of government economic reforms.
>
> Ernst von Schwarzer (1857)[1]

> Not the points of swords, nor the strict regimen of military discipline, nor the strength of clerical powers and hierarchy, nor the refinements of the bureaucratic regime . . . can gain for itself the kind of authority that dwells [alone] in the people.
>
> Carl Giskra (1861)[2]

The revolutions of 1848–49 left several important legacies to Austrian liberalism. One consequence was that much of Bürger society viewed the state as the appropriate place where reform of society should occur. This meant a revived importance for the Austrian bureaucracy, both as instrument and as originator of social policy. Along these lines, it is tempting to see the period 1849–67 through the lens of a persisting bureaucracy, that is, to see liberalism itself as a variation of bureaucratism. This would be a mistake. While connections among the bureaucracy and the liberals were many and complex, while an uneasy and socially conservative consensus united the two in the 1850s, their commonalities must not be made the starting point for understanding liberalism in the period after 1848.

Another consequence of 1848 was the new meaning attached to concepts such as the people's right to legislate. The Bürgertum had asserted the rights of society to legislate for itself in 1848, but this apparently democratic ideal turned out to mean several different things in practice, as arguments over suffrage laws in 1848 suggested. In the 1850s the rights of the people became

1. Ernst von Schwarzer, *Geld und Gut in Neuösterreich* (Vienna, 1857), 6–8.

2. Carl Giskra, "Wahlrede des Dr. C. Giskra für die Landtags-Candidaten des II. Bezirks in Brünn" (Brünn, 1861), 1.

understood in a more limited, abstract sense. The Bürger exchanged representative for popular democracy, claiming as a group to speak for the needs of the entire nation. Finally, it is worth noting that the informal public culture of associations, however socially conservative in the 1850s, kept alive many of these abstract principles both in their rhetoric and in their structures of governance.

A Fragmenting Consensus: Liberals and Bureaucrats, 1859–61

Soon after its introduction, Stadion's constitution, which retained many liberal features from the Kremsier draft, was itself superseded by a newly emerging absolutist system. The successful reimposition of order in Italy and Hungary, together with Stadion's illness, enabled Emperor Francis Joseph and his new minister president, Count Felix Schwarzenberg, to renounce constitutionalism altogether. On December 31, 1851, Francis Joseph issued the Sylvester Patent, which revoked the Stadion constitution, abolished the local institutions of self-government, and established the Habsburg monarchy as a centralized, unitary, and absolutist state.[3]

This new absolutism differed markedly from its ramshackle *Vormärz* predecessor, particularly in the renewed sense of mission it gave to the bureaucracy. Foreign policy requirements and Austria's lagging economy dictated a new policy of reform from above. No longer simply the passive upholder of the social status quo, the bureaucracy assumed an activist role once again in the formulation and administration of social and economic reforms.[4] Historian Harm-Hinrich Brandt has assessed the Austrian regime of the 1850s as a "new type of military-bureaucratic autocracy," not unlike Napoleon III's regime in France, "in which socially reactionary elements mixed with social reformers whose ideas had gained substance through the experience of the revolution."[5]

3. For an excellent analysis of the neoabsolutist regime, particularly from the point of view of state finances, see Harm-Hinrich Brandt, *Der österreichische Neoabsolutismus. Staatsfinanzen und Politik, 1848–1860* (Göttingen, 1978) 1:246–80. On the fate of communal self-government, Karl Ucakar and Manfried Welan, "Kommunale Selbstverwaltung und konstitutioneller Rechtsstaat," in *Wien in der liberalen Ära,* ed. Czeike, 15–19.

4. Brandt, *Neoabsolutismus,* 2:256–57. Calling the regime a "naked bureaucratic centralism, stripped of all constitutional forms, which observed neither the constitutional principles of the liberal bourgeoisie nor the pretensions of the traditional aristocratic classes," Brandt shows how in theory, "The traditional role of the monarch as gathering point for the various component parts of the monarchy and their representatives changed to an equalizing and united principle of rule that was conveyed through a uniformly and centrally directed bureaucracy."

5. Brandt, *Neoabsolutismus,* 1:255.

There was much in this program to please Austria's liberals. In his 1857 survey of Austria's productive resources, Ernst von Schwarzer praised the technical and economic accomplishments of the new regime, noting that "any form of state [not simply a democratic one] is capable of furthering the happiness of the people united under its rule." In short, "everything genius, science, practical understanding, and statesmanlike insight could think of" had been brought together by the government in a unitary policy for the modernization of the entire monarchy.[6]

Yet despite all this, the 1850s was a decade of bitter exile and political frustration for many former liberal activists. While they may have welcomed the new centralization of the state administration, they regretted the loss of communal autonomy and parliamentary government. Under this new regime, the individual could only influence community affairs by joining the state service. Some former liberals developed the concept of consultative liberalism to give intellectual justification to a system of reform from above. This bureaucratic philosophy claimed to encourage civic participation at the municipal level in order to draft the best citizens into the bureaucracy for the ultimate benefit of the state. Yet to many, the cabinet's early abandonment of the 1849 communal statutes suggested that even this kind of limited participation depended for its effectiveness on the whim of the absolutist system. In fact, the conclusion of a Concordat with the pope in 1855 led many liberal observers to surmise that despite the efforts of so-called reform bureaucrats, the reactionaries in the government held the upper hand.[7]

Liberal opposition did not simply derive from the government's apparently reactionary religious sympathies. Before 1848 they had complained about the ways state economic policy had hampered capitalist development. Now the state fostered development in a manner unresponsive to the immediate wishes and needs of Austria's broad middle class. The new policies of rapid modernization generally favored the interests of the largest industrialists and bankers at the expense of the smaller manufacturers who had made up the backbone of the local Bürgertum. Too often, access to credit remained beyond

6. Schwarzer, *Geld und Gut in Neuösterreich*, 6–8.

7. See the useful discussions of the Concordat in Boyer, *Radicalism*, 19–21; also Boyer, "Religion and Political Development in Central Europe around 1900: A View from Vienna" *Austrian History Yearbook* 25 (1994): 13–57; Karl Vocelka, *Verfassung oder Konkordat? Der publizistische und politische Kampf der österreichischen Liberalen um die Religionsgesetze des Jahres 1868* (Vienna, 1978); Erika Weinzierl-Fischer, *Die österreichischen Konkordate von 1855 und 1933* (Vienna, 1960). Several historians have argued that the Concordat reflected not a political victory of religious reactionaries over the state but rather a rearticulation of josephenist principles regarding the church-state relationship. Boyer also notes that the cultural shock waves produced by the Concordat prevented the absolutist regime from enjoying greater public support for its program of economic modernization.

the latter's grasp. The government's desire to regain its influence over the German states also drew the fire of business and industry. A trade treaty designed to integrate the Austrian economy more fully with the German Customs Union by reducing tariffs up to 50 percent was concluded in 1853 over the protests of many Austrian industrialists. When economic crisis hit in 1857, Austria's textile and iron manufacturers were quick to blame the tariff reductions, warning that "Austria would tumble from the heights of its enlightened economic intentions if it renounced the principle of protecting its industry."[8] Nationalization and a rapid expansion of the railroad system may have also benefited industrial development and trade in the long run, but they proved a heavy burden on state finances and short-term credit. So too did the mobilization of Austria's forces in 1854 during the Crimean War. This event, along with the expansionist economic policies of Finance Minister Bruck, rapidly increased Austria's budget deficit to unmanageable proportions. Liberals derived little comfort from any of these developments.

Some liberals acquiesced in the new system, or even worked for it, because of their disillusionment with popular democracy. Throughout Central Europe the 1850s witnessed a new, often uncomfortable consensus between Bürger and bureaucrats, forged from their mutual antipathy to the recent popular uprisings. This consensus facilitated a general bourgeois accommodation to absolutism in Central Europe in the aftermath of the revolution. Fear of violent revolution drove the once liberal middle classes to come to terms with a new absolutist government that promised them security in exchange for a renunciation of the political rights gained in 1848. Many Bürger saw the reform-minded system of absolutism as a potent ally of middle-class economic power at the local level. These perceptions helped redirect bourgeois efforts away from the realm of politics and back to local economy and local society. Scholars consider the upper state bureaucracy in particular to have mediated this tradeoff between state and civil society. They point out that a number of prominent 1848 liberal leaders like Alexander Bach subsequently gained important positions in the state bureaucracy, giving them enormous influence over government policy. And it has been argued for the Austrian case that in the early 1860s it was this same generation of bureaucrats, those "sympathetic to a moderate absolutist ethos," who helped replace absolutism with a form of limited constitutionalism.[9]

---

8. *Denkschrift der am 6. Dezember 1858 in Wien versammelten Eisenindustriellen* (Vienna, 1859), quoted in Herbert Matis, "Sozioökonomische Aspekte des Liberalismus in Österreich 1848–1918," in *Sozialgeschichte heute. Festschrift für Hans Rosenberg zum 70. Geburtstag*, ed. Hans-Ulrich Wehler (Göttingen, 1974), 248. See also Brandt, *Neoabsolutismus*, 1:415–16; Charmatz, *Deutschösterreichische Politik*, 138. A government inquiry into the economic crisis of 1857 concluded that the new trade policy was not to blame.

9. Boyer, *Radicalism*, 18–19.

This period should not, however, be seen primarily in terms of some general consensus linking Bürger and bureaucracy if such a view causes the historian to lose sight of other, equally important developments. True, there were important transformations within the state bureaucracy in the 1850s. During that time, a process of *embourgeoisement* proceeded apace, both in that group's social makeup and in its cultural outlook.[10] It is also true that after their experience of "mob rule" in 1848, many liberals did see reform from above as the only kind of change that would not disrupt public order or threaten property. However, the theory that highly placed bureaucrats sympathetic to moderate liberalism somehow mediated between state and civil society in the 1860s confuses some important divisions between liberal and bureaucratic interests. From the experience of 1848 liberals may have learned the dangers of mobilizing the propertyless masses and the Mittelstand, but in the long term that experience did not diminish their zeal for self-government. Nor did it weaken their commitment to the voluntary association as the model for responsible citizenship. By the 1860s, most liberal leaders revived their earlier demands for constitutional review of the budget by an elected parliament, the restoration of communal autonomy and the abolition of the hated Concordat, each of which (with the possible exception of the last) was completely antithetical to the belief system of most state administrators.

Historians sensitive to the important ideological contributions state bureaucrats made to the liberal movement at some historical moments have been less sensitive to the differences that divided the two at other times. The socially conservative consensus that joined the interests of Bürger society and state administration for a time in the 1850s did not survive into the next decade. The typical portrayal of liberals and bureaucrats during the reform period 1859–65 defines the ideology of the former far too much in terms of the agenda of the latter. This results in a twisted vision of liberal ideology, one that stresses issues like state centralism, German as the bureaucratic language of state, and a desire to give the state more power over the church.

The categorization of all the individuals who worked to reform Austria in the 1860s as "liberal bureaucrats" or "bureaucratic liberals" obscures the powerful ideological distinctions that divided many of them. Those who shared in a bureaucratic ethos supported the empowerment of the administration to reform society from above. Their rhetorical concession to the need for some consultation from below suggested one way to institutionalize and at the same time effectively limit popular participation. These men spouted sentiments that sounded liberal on occasion, but they abandoned their progressive sympathies when it came to implementing fundamentally liberal reforms after 1861. Still other bureaucrats were liberals, not at all "sympathetic to a moderate absolutist

10. Heindl, *Gehorsame Rebellen*, especially 93–224.

ethos," and strongly opposed to the restrictive implications of consultative liberalism. They believed in constitutional change that would give legislative power to an elected body.[11]

The political reforms that emerged from the failures of the absolutist decade revived the liberal movement in the 1860s and helped produce a liberal constitution in 1867. Two different struggles shaped these reforms: (1) a struggle between liberals and bureaucrats played out within the cabinet and (2) a larger political struggle that joined liberals and bureaucrats together against the politically conservative forces of federalism. If the positions of liberals and bureaucrats seem interchangeable at times, this confusion is partly due to the narrowness of the political stage on which these struggles were enacted. They involved a very limited number of men, largely of socially homogenous backgrounds, who used a similar rhetoric to make their arguments. The ultimate success of the reform process changed the relation between the liberal movement and the Austrian state bureaucracy; it clarified their points of agreement and highlighted their significant differences. It gave the liberals their own, more distinctive voice.

In 1859, financial crisis and military defeat in Italy forced the government to reform the structure of the monarchy. The Viennese banking community refused to fund a swollen state deficit without some assurance of responsible constitutional reform, and the Hungarians continued to demand the reinstatement of the 1848 constitution. Francis Joseph's need to restore state solvency, to avoid outright revolt among his Hungarian subjects, and to regain public support for government policy forced him to allow discussion of measures to limit his absolute powers. For liberals, this meant a chance to revive constitutional life. For conservatives, it meant a chance to resurrect the power of the individual diets. For all concerned it would be a long and unpredictable process, punctuated by the emperor's tendency to vacillate unpredictably between opposing political reform programs.

In the early phases of constitutional transition, from 1859 to1861, Ignaz von Plener and Anton Ritter von Schmerling were to play critical, though very different, roles. It is their views that form the context for the following discussion of the reform process. Both men worked in the cabinet to reform the absolutist system, yet they disagreed over fundamental political goals. Most historians considered that the two adhered to a similar, bureaucratic philosophy regarding reform, but this account will stress their basic differences.

11. For examples of this undifferentiated view, see Mechtild Wolf, *Ignaz von Plener. Vom Schicksal eines Ministers unter Kaiser Franz-Josef* (Munich, 1975); Boyer, *Radicalism*, 19–25. Boyer suggests a provisional categorization by generation as a way to understand political differences within the bureaucracy and the liberal movement.

The government's first reform program, published in August 1859, promised to reinstate the communal statutes of 1848 and floated the idea of a future review of the budget, without specifying who was to do the reviewing.[12] The financial community's less-than-enthusiastic response to these suggestions, however, forced even more concessions from the unwilling monarch. Now Francis Joseph enlarged his advisory council (*Reichsrat*) to give it a more visible role as watchdog over the financial affairs of the state. The large majority of *Reichsrat* appointees were conservative aristocrats who favored reviving an archaic type of federalist system wherein the provincial diets, dominated by a feudal nobility, would become the locus of political power.[13] This modest series of steps was hardly the reform that the banking community or the liberal public had expected. Liberal reaction was skeptical, particularly since the government made no effort in the following weeks to implement the promised changes, and since so few liberal sympathizers had been appointed to the Reinforced *Reichsrat.* As Styrian liberal Moritz von Kaiserfeld wrote pointedly in the *Grazer Tagespost*, "The state is in no position to satisfy the bank, because—let us say openly what everyone is thinking—it has no credit. Only parliamentary control of financial affairs can ensure such credit."[14]

The small group of liberals appointed to the Reinforced *Reichsrat* largely represented the interests and demands of the Viennese banking community, neatly summed up by Anselm Rothschild in 1860 as "no constitution, no money."[15] They had a tireless if unlikely spokesman in Ignaz von Plener, who became finance minister in April 1860. Plener appears to have been the first and only exponent of a liberal constitution within the cabinet during this period. Despite his close association with the absolutist state bureaucracy of the 1850s, Plener consistently upheld a liberal position in the face of his fellow bureaucrats' disapproval in the 1860s. His open intransigence eventually earned him the support of other cabinet members, like former 1848ers Baron Joseph Lasser and Freiherr Adolf Pratobevera, who rejoined the liberal fold through their support for Plener. Yet Plener also managed to maintain the respect of the emperor. His liberal constitutional positions were not born of 1848 revolutionary experience; rather, they derived almost completely from his connections to the

12. Macartney, *Empire*, 498. As a further token of good intention, the government granted equality to the Protestant and Greek churches and promised a revision of the Jews' legal status.

13. Josef Redlich, *Das österreichische Staats- und Reichsproblem* (Leipzig, 1920), 1/1:489, 1/2:226–27; Macartney, *Empire,* 501. A rescript of March 5, 1860, increased membership of the reinforced advisory council *(verstärkte Reichsrat)* from ten to sixty, giving it the right to advise the emperor about the state budget, to examine the closed accounts, and to advise him on the proposals of the state debt committee.

14. GT, October 29 and December 16, 1859.

15. Friedrich Schütz, *Werden und Wirken des Bürgerministeriums* (Leipzig, 1909), 152.

financial world. In this Plener represented a new liberal ideological synthesis, shaped more by pragmatism and the socially conservative consensus of the 1850s than by the idealism of 1848.

Plener was born in 1810 to a German middle-class family with a tradition of service to the state. Both his grandfather and father had distinguished themselves as bureaucrats in the state service. Ignaz himself joined the state administration in 1836 as a provincial bureaucrat for the Ministry of Finance in Vienna, then later in Bohemia, Hungary, and Galicia. In his first years at the Finance Ministry Plener worked beside Bach, Doblhof-Dier, and Pratobevera, all interns for the same department. Yet these professional connections did not draw Plener into the loose *Vormärz* reform movement. Many of his colleagues played significant roles in the German liberal movement of 1848, but Plener, who was stationed in Eger, Bohemia, did not participate at all in revolutionary activities.[16] During the 1850s Plener's reputation as a hard-working and creative bureaucrat brought him to the attention of such disparate figures as Finance Minister Bruck, a centralist, and *Statthalter* (later Interior Minister) Goluchowski, a conservative federalist, both of whom helped to advance Plener's career. Early in 1859 Francis Joseph named Plener to the *Reichsrat*, and in April 1860 he succeeded Bruck as finance minister.[17]

Considering his inactivity in 1848 and his work for the absolutist regime of the 1850s, Plener did not seem a likely spokesman for liberal demands. Yet his ties to the Viennese banking community and his grim realism about the monarchy's financial plight made him a strong advocate of liberal reform. Plener favored a constitutional government responsible to an elected parliament, a demand that went well beyond the consultative liberalism of contemporaries like Schmerling. Repeatedly, as we will see, he suggested liberal measures to an unwilling monarch. As early as 1860, Plener extracted a series of remarkable concessions from the emperor designed to reassure the public that the government took its reform activities seriously; among them Francis Joseph's agreement that no new taxes would be raised nor loans floated without the consent of the Reinforced *Reichsrat*.[18]

---

16. HHSA, Nachlass Plener, family documents, ct. 2; Ernst von Plener, "Ignaz von Plener," *Biographisches Jahrbuch und deutscher Nekrolog* 16 (Berlin, 1914): 262; Wolf, *Plener*. Ignaz von Plener's father had been granted a title by the emperor in 1856.

17. For the circumstances surrounding Plener's appointment as finance minister following Bruck's suicide, see Brandt, *Neoabsolutismus*, 2:893–900.

18. HHSA, Nachlass Plener, "Autobiographisches" and "Politische Aufzeichnungen," ct. 4 and 5. Plener claimed to have authored the original draft of the imperial decree of July 17, 1860, the first step toward constitutionalism. Plener also extracted concessions from the emperor designed to reassure the public that the government took its reforming activities seriously. He convinced Francis Joseph to publish the otherwise secret report of the state debt commission, to publicize the government's long-term plans for balancing the budget, and, most importantly, to concede that no new taxes would be raised nor loans floated without the consent of the *Reichsrat*.

In September 1860, this *Reichsrat* presented the emperor with majority and minority reports on the future of the monarchy. The federalists—aristocrats more socially acceptable to the emperor than the financiers and lawyers who represented liberal ideas—desired a reconstruction of the monarchy that would give the provincial diets key legislative powers.[19] The liberal minority offered a different plan, backing a centralist government structure but adding an elected parliament. Following the desires of the socially more congenial federalists, the emperor issued a series of statutes on October 20, 1860, known as the October Diploma. In this document he promised to enact, amend, or veto legislation only in consultation with the provincial diets and the *Reichsrat*. While the *Reichsrat* would now legislate on matters of concern to the entire monarchy—taxation, weights and measures, commerce and customs, or military conscription—everything else, including education and religious matters, would be left to the individual diets. These, in turn, would be constituted according to pre-1848 forms of representation.[20]

In cabinet discussions Plener immediately attacked the Diploma in exceptionally direct, acerbic, and occasionally condescending tones. In early October he told the emperor and Goluchowski that the financial community would never accept a state reorganization based on pre-1848 forms of representation and election. Plener cited the very text of the October Diploma to justify his demands for an Austrian parliament with the right to legislate in all areas of government, repeatedly questioning the utility of the federalist scheme that divided the legislative power among twenty-one provincial diets. Calling such a plan "an absurdity that no one in Austria except for a few aristocratic groups desires," Plener stubbornly and consistently rejected Goluchowski's conservative reform proposals.[21]

Plener's dire predictions about the public mood proved completely accurate in November 1860 when Goluchowski unveiled the statutes for electing the new provincial diets. These laws gave noble large landowners an overwhelming majority of representatives and ensured that the diets would resemble their *Vormärz* predecessors. Liberal journals, which had expressed a cautious optimism at the news of the October Diploma, now greeted the

19. Liberal reaction to federalist proposals in 1860 often bordered on contempt, as with *Die Presse*'s claim that, "No one in the monarchy could believe for even a moment that the majority of the people, or even of the educated people, stands behind this [federalist] *Reichsrat* majority." PR, September 29 and 30, 1860.

20. Redlich, *Staats- und Reichsproblem*, 1/2:228–29. The October Diploma guaranteed the emperor's subjects full equality before the law, freedom of religion, equal opportunity to fill state offices, and equality in military and tax obligations.

21. Redlich, *Staats- und Reichsproblem*, 1/1:619. Either out of principle or as an attempt to stall publication of the Diploma, Plener offered to resign. Francis Joseph, however, did not wish to see the effectiveness of the new laws undercut by his resignation. Wolf, *Plener*, 19.

statutes with a storm of protest. Despite harsh censorship, the German liberal press managed to convey outrage at this betrayal.[22] City councilors in Graz, Salzburg, and other Austrian towns who had accepted bureaucratic absolutism in the 1850s now promised to boycott elections to the diets and even to resign en masse.[23] As Plener had predicted, the banking community had few illusions about the October Diploma either. Austria's credit at home and abroad remained so low that no new funds could be raised.[24]

When Goluchowski complained that "the rotten influence of the [liberal] press" had poisoned the public mind against the October Diploma and asked the emperor for extraordinary censorship measures, Plener retorted that the press merely reflected the public mood. Lasser now agreed with Plener, pointing out that simply giving the individual diets equal rights would encourage separatism; what Austrians really wanted was their own elected central parliament with increased legislative powers. Negative reaction in Hungary also helped convince Francis Joseph that the October Diploma would have to be modified. His conservative advisors had assured him that the Diploma would at the very least satisfy his recalcitrant Hungarian subjects. When this expectation also proved completely illusory, the emperor turned to the centralists for a solution, dismissing Goluchowski and replacing him with Anton Ritter von Schmerling.[25]

Plener's repeated urgings that nothing short of a genuinely representative and centralist constitution could restore the confidence of the financial community in the state seem to have had their effect. Yet to understand Schmerling's ambivalence toward the liberal movement it is important to distinguish between the two major elements—representation and centralism—within the reform plan that he now developed. As we will see, Schmerling created a political system that gave the German liberals important advantages in national politics. Yet he did so as a loyal bureaucrat. Schmerling championed limited constitutional concessions as a way of mobilizing financial resources for the state, not to make Austria's government a representative one.

---

22. PR, November 10, 1860. Several liberal journals had already complained about the slow pace of reform in the summer and fall of 1860, particularly the delay of a promised statute granting Jews civic equality.

23. Redlich, *Staats- und Reichsproblem*, 1/1:673.

24. Macartney, *Empire*, 509; Redlich, *Staats- und Reichsproblem*, 1/1: 684–85. Plener vetoed all attempts to send troops to Italy, which Piedmont was busy unifying in Austria's absence. The financial situation would not allow such action.

25. Redlich, *Staats- und Reichsproblem*, 1:674–75; 679–83; HHSA, Nachlass Schmerling, "Denkwürdigkeiten," fol. 24. According to Schmerling, Plener was in constant contact with the liberal press in Vienna during this period, and especially with August Zang, owner of *Die Presse*. See *Der Vater der Verfassung. Aus den Denkwürdigkeiten Anton Ritters von Schmerling*, ed. Lothar Höbelt (Vienna, 1993), 52.

Born in 1805, Schmerling, like Plener, belonged to a generation that had come of age well before the revolution of 1848. Schmerling's family had received a title in the eighteenth century for service in the judicial administration. Unlike Plener, however, he had clearly sought out political involvement in the 1840s. In the years leading up to 1848, he had played a visible role in the Lower Austrian Diet reform movement. A member of the Legal-Political Reading Association, Schmerling knew personally many of the men who joined the cabinet or who sat in the Austrian Parliament as German liberals in 1848. Yet in contrast to most of his well-known contemporaries, Schmerling achieved popularity with the liberal public for his deeds before and after the revolution, not during it.[26]

For most of 1848 Schmerling led the Austrian delegation to the German Parliament at Frankfurt, serving as justice minister for the provisional German government there. A moderate, Schmerling played a major role in the suppression of left-wing agitation in September 1848.[27] From June 1849 until January 1851, he served as minister of justice in the Schwarzenberg cabinet. During his tenure he reformed criminal procedure and implemented a policy of trial by jury. These achievements added to his popularity in liberal circles, although in the case of juries, Schmerling simply implemented a promise made in the 1849 constitution that he had personally opposed. Schmerling also seems to have acted with moderation toward Hungarians accused of subversive activity in 1848–49, a fact that ensured him some popularity in Hungarian

26. HHSA, Nachlass Schmerling, "Denkwürdigkeiten." These autobiographic notes were written in the 1880s with the help of the journalist Friedrich Uhl. The notes often use events of the 1850s and 1860s as a means to justify Schmerling's later career, and thus they are based more on selective recollection and parliamentary protocols than on personal notes actually written in earlier periods. The notes are far more interesting for the prejudices and opinions they convey about individuals and events (for example, the scandalous stories about Carl Giskra) than for their reconstructions of events. Recently Lothar Höbelt edited and commented on selections from these reminiscences in *Der Vater der Verfassung*. A disappointing biography is Alfred von Arneth's *Anton, Ritter von Schmerling* (Vienna, 1894). On the culture in which Schmerling was raised, see Redlich, *Staats- und Reichsproblem*, 1/1:691–92; for Schmerling's *Vormärz* and 1848 activities, see Bibl, *Niederösterreichische Stände*; Paul Molisch, "Schmerling," 5–10. Molisch, who referred to Schmerling as "Vater der Verfassung," wrote this piece under fascism, which may partially explain his strangely ahistoric references to anti-Semitism in Schmerling's career. Despite such shortcomings this piece contains valuable insights.

27. Molisch, "Schmerling," 11–17. Schmerling frequently complained that the younger members of the Austrian delegation to Frankfurt, Johann N. Berger, Carl Giskra, and Carl Stremayr, had become too involved in radical democratic activities. He also took a dim view of events in revolutionary Vienna, believing the October uprising to have been unjustified. Nevertheless, Schmerling opposed Schwarzenberg's reactionary policies, fearing that vindictiveness might damage future developments in Austria. For this reason he defended Berger, Giskra, and Stremayr against government accusations of subversive radicalism, arguing that their talents would still be useful to the state.

circles.[28] When the emperor suspended the constitution in 1851, Schmerling resigned from the cabinet in protest against the new absolutist system. This act of conscience endeared him to the German liberal public, which by 1860 considered him to be one of its heroes. The German liberal press cast Schmerling as a liberal savior in 1860, a role he neither wanted nor could play. Schmerling's views coincided with liberal opinion in the importance he placed both on local self-government and on a centralized structure for the monarchy as a whole. He also considered the liberal parliamentary parties his natural allies in the early 1860s, and in later years he led the Liberal or Constitutional Party in the House of Lords. Yet, as we will soon see, Schmerling opposed the liberals on precisely those political issues that lay at the heart of their program.[29]

Schmerling's political beliefs reflected a complex mixture of bureaucratic legalism and liberalism of the kind that had characterized the Lower Austrian Diet's opposition of the 1840s. His particular philosophy does not really fall within the general category of liberalism even broadly defined after 1861 but represents an altogether different, if occasionally allied, phenomenon. Schmerling had viewed the diet's role as an advisory one, believing that reform must always come from above. Unlike some of his contemporaries, he never made the transition to a belief in the direct political rule by civil society over itself. He did not, however, support a completely autocratic form of state absolutism either, since he insisted on the importance of consultative bodies, which could bring many varied responsible views to the attention of the monarch. For such a system to work, the consultative bodies—hence the term consultative liberalism—had to mobilize the best social forces throughout the monarchy to participate in policy-making. This required conceding a measure of local self-government to encourage the individual's sense of civic duty and responsibility.[30]

---

28. HHSA, Nachlass Schmerling, "Denkwürdigkeiten," ct. 1, fol. 3.

29. For contemporaries' views of Schmerling, see Heinrich Pollak, *Dreissig Jahre aus dem Leben eines Journalisten* (Vienna, 1898), 1:54–55, 103; Krones, *Kaiserfeld*, 211–17; Molisch, "Schmerling," 39–43, 51, which surveys liberal historians' evaluations of Schmerling and his personality. Schmerling's beliefs seem to have been tempered or reinforced at crucial moments by an overbearing personality, a trait reported by many contemporary observers. His steadfast adherence to principle seems easily to have turned into arrogance and stubbornness. Contemporaries felt that Schmerling pursued his policies too obstinately, shutting out the kind of reasonable compromise that could have helped him achieve more of his legislative goals. His oft-quoted utterance to the *Reichsrat*, "We can wait," referring not to Hungary but rather to Liberal Party obstruction of a bill to fund the official government press, epitomized this tendency not to seek compromise. Schmerling also interpreted any criticism of his policies as tantamount to personal attacks. And yet on some occasions, he displayed great political skill, as when he gained the emperor's support for his reform program.

30. For an illuminating discussion of consultative liberalism, its conceptualization of local autonomy, and the influence of Rudolf von Gneist's theories of self-government on Schmerling and his circle, see Redlich, *Staats- und Reichsproblem*, 1/1:715–32.

Following his appointment, Schmerling set to work with the help of Lasser and Hans Perthaler to produce a reform document for cabinet discussion. Speaking for liberal interests in the cabinet, Ignaz von Plener staked out several positions well beyond anything Schmerling was planning. The finance minister asserted that nothing short of Stadion's ill-fated 1849 constitution with its bill of rights, powerful central parliament, and ministerial responsibility would satisfy the financial world. Plener, backed by Lasser, also argued that the reform should be called a "constitution" (*Verfassung*) and that the central legislature should be called a "parliament" (*Reichstag*), as it had in 1848–49. Schmerling and Francis Joseph, however, insisted on referring to the reform as individual "statutes" (*Statuten*) and the parliament as an advisory council (*Reichsrat*), thus emphasizing that body's advisory rather than legislative capacities.[31]

On the other side, the conservative federalists and Hungarians in the cabinet vehemently opposed any central parliament. They also protested against the direct election of deputies to a parliament and against Schmerling's proposed suffrage qualifications, which they considered far too liberal. The emperor refused to countenance any enumeration of basic civil rights or the introduction of ministerial responsibility to parliament.[32] The resulting body of laws, therefore, grew out of a curious mix of liberal demands, conservative intransigence, and bureaucratic mistrust of constitutionalism. Known as the February Patent, the reform ordinances technically elaborated and administered the promises set down in the October Diploma.[33]

The February Patent set up a bicameral central legislature in Vienna, the *Reichsrat*.[34] This body had the right to legislate on domestic issues that affected the entire monarchy, and its consent was required for all legislation, not just taxation. This represented Plener's hardest-won victory and Francis Joseph's

---

31. To support his claims, Plener even polled forty-nine of the Austrian chambers of commerce, each of which considered a constitution absolutely necessary to the restoration of the state's credit. Redlich, *Staats- und Reichsproblem*,1/1:706, 715–16, 735–36; HHSA, Nachlass Schmerling, "Denkwürdigkeiten," ct. 1, fol. 21, 58; Wolf, *Plener*, 76. Others who participated at various times in developing the reform document were Joseph von Kalchberg, a department chief in the Justice Ministry, Cajetan Maier, coauthor of the 1849 Kremsier draft, Lasser, and the elder Plener.

32. HHSA, Nachlass Schmerling, "Denkwürdigkeiten," ct. 1, fol. 127.

33. The text of the Patent is conveniently reproduced in Redlich, *Staats- und Reichsproblem*, 1/2:229–34 along with the *Grundgesetz über die Reichsvertretung*, which elaborated the specific applications of the Patent. Francis Joseph would not allow the October Diploma to be voided or replaced, having only four months earlier referred to it as the "permanent and irrevocable" fundamental law of the monarchy. Yet the language of that document had been vague enough to allow Schmerling's radical change in direction and emphasis.

34. Of the 343 deputies, the 205 from the Austrian half of the monarchy constituted a so-called "narrower *Reichsrat*," which met when matters that did not apply to Hungary were debated. As it turned out, the Hungarians never sent deputies to the *Reichsrat*, so that from 1861 until its suspension in 1865, the narrower *Reichsrat* functioned as the whole body.

biggest concession. In every other respect the emperor's powers remained considerable. The emperor retained absolute control over the field of foreign policy. Internally, he appointed cabinet ministers, and they were responsible to him alone, contrary to Plener's suggestions and later liberal demands for ministerial responsibility to the *Reichsrat*. The emperor could convoke or dismiss the *Reichsrat* at will, and he selected its presiding officers. Certain provisions, chief among them the notorious paragraph thirteen, enabled the emperor to bypass *Reichsrat* consent on legislation if, for example, it was not in session. Another clause stipulated that taxation once voted remained in force until superseded by a new tax law. This prevented the *Reichsrat* from withholding approval of tax collection or the military budget to obtain political concessions. Finally, the *Reichsrat* could technically amend the February laws, but only with a two-thirds majority vote in each house. This was considered an unlikely occurrence, since the emperor himself appointed the majority of deputies to the upper chamber, the House of Lords.[35]

The provincial diets were to elect the 343 representatives to the lower house, or Chamber of Deputies, in proportions based roughly on provincial population and tax contributions. Retaining a traditional system of election by estate, each curia in each diet elected its own representatives to the *Reichsrat*. The new curial system, or interest representation *(Interessenvertretung)*, was meant to reflect economic status as well as traditional feudal social divisions. Property owners who paid a minimum of ten florin in annual taxes were generally eligible to vote in the urban or rural curia. The major chambers of commerce and noble large landowners elected their own deputies in separate curias.[36]

Schmerling's voting system clearly favored the interests of the upper middle classes, most of whom happened to be urban, German-speaking, and

---

35. Two houses made up the new *Reichsrat*: a House of Lords (*Herrenhaus*) and a Chamber of Deputies (*Abgeordnetenhaus*). Schmerling had invented the House of Lords as a means to persuade Francis Joseph of the conservative nature of his intentions and to provide a moderating influence on the Chamber of Deputies. Adult male members of the imperial family, princes of the church, and the leading aristocrats of the monarchy were appointed hereditary members of the House of Lords. In addition, the emperor appointed individuals distinguished by state service or by contributions to education, the arts, and sciences as lifetime members.

36. Jutta Martinek, "Materialien zur Wahlrechtsgeschichte der Grossgrundbesitzerkurie in den österreichischen Landtagen seit 1861 (Ph.D. diss., University of Vienna, 1977). Deputies to the *Reichsrat* were elected by the individual curias within the diets and not by the diets as a whole. This precaution made it less likely that diets with antigovernmental or anticonstitutional majorities would send only hostile deputies to Vienna. In Bohemia, for example, tax qualifications gave Germans a solid majority in the urban curia, while Czechs dominated the rural curia. This ensured that whatever group controlled the Prague Diet as a whole, both would be represented in Vienna. Women property owners were not mentioned in the statutes, an omission that led to their enfranchisement in Bohemia and Lower Austria, where deputies to the diets actually raised the issue for discussion.

liberal in their political convictions. Not surprisingly, some contemporaries and later historians accused Schmerling of having rigged the system for nationalist reasons, giving undue weight to the Germans in the monarchy and slighting the other ethnic groups.[37] Certainly, the system was rigged, but not to favor German speakers as such. By far the best represented group was in fact the noble large landowners, a group neither pro-German nor particularly liberal in its sentiments. Schmerling hoped this supranational group would take the lead and form a strong middle party that would provide the government with unquestioned support. The next best represented groups were the members of those chambers of commerce that elected their own deputies to the *Reichsrat,* and then urban voters in cities with their own charters. Finally, it is worth noting that while the relatively high tax requirement that limited the vote to 6 percent of the population certainly privileged urban German and Italian speakers, it did so more for reasons of class than of ethnic identity.[38]

Two days following the publication of the February Patent Francis Joseph demanded an extraordinary oath from his ministers: "that they would use all their energy . . . to defend the throne against the exaction of further concessions, either by pressure from the *Reichsrat* or the diets or through revolutionary attempts by the masses."[39] Despite each cabinet member's dutiful signing of the protocol, the very significance of the February Patent lay precisely in the way it fulfilled Francis Joseph's worst fears. Those liberals who remained dissatisfied with the constitutional reforms embodied in the February Patent soon found that when they applied some pressure, this conservative document opened the door to more responsible and progressive forms of constitutional rule.

Certainly by the standards of 1848–49 the October Diploma and February Patent hardly deserve the name "constitution." Yet by the conservative continental European standard of 1861, the Patent was far more liberal. It gave Austrian citizens an incomparably larger voice in their own government than the French had during the last years of the Second Empire. The Patent may not have been as progressive in its language as the 1830 Belgian Constitution, which served as a model for nineteenth-century European liberals. Yet despite an enviable catalog of civil rights and a statement that authority emanated from the people and not the monarch, the Belgian constitution enfranchised a much smaller percentage of the population than did the February Patent. The Patent did bring Austrian political rights closer in scope to those of Prussia and several other German states. In fact, during this period Austrians gained more constitutional control over local affairs than did most Germans, even though in

37. Charmatz, *Deutschösterreichische Politik,* 21.

38. Eva Somogyi, *Vom Zentralismus zum Dualismus. Der Weg des deutschösterreichischen Liberalen zum Ausgleich von 1867* (Wiesbaden, 1983), 10–14.

39. Redlich, *Staats- und Reichsproblem,* 1/1:808.

national affairs the Austrian suffrage remained more restrictive than suffrage for the *Reichstag* after 1871.[40] Table 1 compares European states with respect to the proportion of their population that was enfranchised, 1867–78.

By allowing the *Reichsrat* to legislate in all areas of internal affairs and by leaving open the possibility of constitutional amendment, the emperor had given constitutionalism a certain legitimacy. He had also given the liberals a powerful tool for the realization of their program. This would soon be apparent from the demands for further reform made by the liberals elected to the city councils, the provincial diets, and the new *Reichsrat* in the spring of 1861.

The Revival of Public Life

Soon after abolishing the Stadion constitution in 1851, the Schwarzenberg government had revived the old concession system for associations, thereby limiting the gains made by autonomous Bürger social organizations in 1848–49. From now on, all voluntary organizations had to obtain official permission to constitute themselves by submitting their proposed statutes and membership lists to the provincial governments for approval. Furthermore, the government directed local police to observe all public forums for any violation of the ban on politics—from lecture halls, theaters, dance halls, and cafes to railway stations and riverboats.[41] Nevertheless, the numbers of voluntary associations and the percentage of those not associated exclusively with religious or charity efforts grew steadily in the 1850s. These institutions continued in the 1850s to serve as a setting for discussion of often forbidden issues and as an instrument to effect social and economic change at the local level, not merely in the largest cities. Within groups as diverse as industrial associations, rifle clubs (*Schützenkorps*), or singing associations, debate over public policy continued to flare up through the 1850s, albeit in informal settings. Local and parliamentary leaders of the 1860s often established lasting public reputations through their earlier associational activism. The future leader of the German Liberal Party in Bohemia, Franz Schmeykal, played a prominent role in the gymnastics, singing, and rifle clubs, exercising an "animating influence on associational life" in his hometown of Böhmisch Leipa in the 1850s.[42]

---

40. J. A. Hagwood, "Liberalism and Constitutional Developments," in *The New Cambridge Modern History*, ed. J. P. T. Bury (Cambridge, 1971), 10:191; Volker Berghahn, *Imperial Germany 1871–1914: Economy, Society, Culture and Politics* (Providence, RI, 1994), 210–12; James J. Sheehan, *German History 1770–1866* (Oxford, 1989), 716–19. Most German states retained a curial voting system similar to the Austrian one at the provincial diet and municipal levels.

41. Hans Peter Hye, "Wiener 'Vereinsmeier' um 1850," in "*Durch Arbeit, Besitz, Wissen und Gerechtigkeit*," ed. Stekl et al., 292.

42. Alfred Hanke, *Die nationale Bewegung in Aussig von 1848–1914* (Prague, 1943), 35; Hye, "Vereinsmeier," 310–11; [Klaar], *Schmeykal*, 29–30.

TABLE 1. Percentage of Population Enfranchised in National Elections, 1867–78

State	Percentage of Population
Austria	5.9%
Belgium	2.3%
France	25.6%
Germany	21.4%
Great Britain	8.7%
Italy	2.2%
Portugal	5.4%
Sweden	5.9%

Source: F. X. Neumann-Spallart and G. Schimmer, Die Reichsrathswahlen vom Jahre 1879 in Österreich (Stuttgart, 1880), 10. The statistics are for the newly created French Third Republic and the new German Empire, both of which instituted forms of universal manhood suffrage. Neumann-Spallart and Schirmer estimated the following numbers of voters in each curia under the Austrian system for 1879: large landowners, 4,678; chambers of commerce, 515; cities and towns, 196,993; rural communes (Urwähler), 1,088,457; total for Austria, 1,290,733.

In 1859, after a decade of restraint, middle-class dissatisfaction with the political system vented itself publicly in the local festivals organized to celebrate the centennial anniversary of Schiller's birth. These festivals were notable for at least two reasons. First, their character suggests the degree to which a desire for liberal reform still outweighed all other concerns (including nationalist or ethnic ones) among the German-speaking urban Bürgertum in both the ethnically mixed and more homogeneous German-speaking provinces. In 1859, Schiller was still celebrated as the poet of freedom and liberty, not as a symbol of German national accomplishment. In Prague, German and Czech activists used the occasion to stress the importance of a free and liberal public life. Of that celebration Fritz Mauthner recalled, "If one had not otherwise known that . . . this celebration grew out of a political mood of longing for freedom, one could have guessed it from the participation of the Czechs [along with the Germans]." Government officials understood all too well the political significance of these celebrations and often tried to have them halted.[43]

The second important point about the Schiller festivities is that they provided an organizational impetus to promote political reform long after the festivities had ended. The Schiller committees frequently served as both meet-

43. Fritz Mauthner, *Prager Jugendjahre* (Frankfurt/M, 1969), 121, quoted at length in Gerhard Kurz, "Von Schiller zum deutschen Schiller. Die Schillerfeiern in Prag von 1859 und 1905," in *Die Chance der Verständigung. Ansichten und Absätze zu übernationaler Zusammen-*

ing place and training ground for German middle-class men who within two years would be organizing local election committees, choosing candidates, and in many cases serving in the newly constituted diets and parliament. In Prague, two law professors who later served as deputies to the Bohemian Diet, the Austrian Parliament, and eventually as cabinet ministers, Eduard Herbst and Leopold von Hasner, participated in the organizing committee for the celebration, while Professor Alois Brinz, another future deputy, delivered the main speech commemorating Schiller.[44] Enthusiasm generated by the Schiller Year led to the birth of several new associations with a high degree of political consciousness, in particular gymnastic societies (*Turnvereine*) and a new wave of student organizations.[45] Finally, the Schiller Year, combined with new transportation possibilities offered by a growing railway network, inaugurated greater interregional connections among associations across Central Europe in what Robert Hoffmann has called an "interregional festival culture" among Austrian Germans.[46]

The emergence of this increasingly politicized public culture at the end of the decade suggests that despite its efforts at economic modernization, the regime had failed to gain the support of crucial sectors of the populace. The absolutist state of the 1850s may well have favored middle-class economic and social interests, and it may have secured property from the kind of wanton violence that characterized 1848. Nevertheless, these policies clearly did not buy it significant credit with most liberals. While some former liberals who had joined the bureaucratic camp still clung to their belief in the efficacy of reform from above, convinced that self-government could only lead to disorder and violence, most of the newly enfranchised class of the middle and upper Bür-

---

arbeit in den böhmischen Ländern 1848-1918, ed. Ferdinand Seibt (Munich, 1987), 41; Rainer Noltenius, *Dichterfeier in Deutschland. Rezeptionsgeschichte als Sozialgeschichte am Beispiel der Schiller—und Freiligrath— Feiern* (Munich, 1984). Kurz contrasts the politically liberal content of the official 1859 celebrations in Prague with the radically German nationalist content of the 1905 Schiller anniversary there.

44. Elizabeth Wymetal, "Eduard Herbst, sein Werdegang und seine Persönlichkeit vornehmlich auf Grund seiner selbstbiographischen Aufzeichnungen" (Ph.D. diss., University of Vienna, 1944), 19–20. Although generally unhelpful, this dissertation does indicate that Herbst established several crucial connections for his political career in 1859 while helping to organize the festivities surrounding the Schiller Year celebration in Prague.

45. For a typical example from Northern Bohemia of the new interest in founding gymnastic societies at the end of the 1850s, see Hanke, *Aussig*, 35–36. More generally on gymnastics and student organizations, see Paul Molisch, *Geschichte der deutschnationalen Bewegung in Österreich* (Jena, 1926), 62 and Molisch, *Die deutschen Hochschulen in Österreich und die politisch-nationale Entwicklung nach dem Jahre 1848* (Munich, 1922), 32.

46. Hanke, *Aussig*, 36; Robert Hoffmann, "Bürgerliche Kommunikationsstrategien zu Beginn der liberalen Ära: Das Beispiel Salzburg" in "*Durch Arbeit, Besitz, Wissen und Gerechtigkeit,*" ed. Stekl et al., 317–36. Hanke also noted the rise in interregional gymnastics and singing festivals in Northern Bohemia in the early 1860s, some of which were attended by associations from other Bohemian towns as well as from Moravia, Silesia, and Prussia.

gertum would vote overwhelmingly in the spring of 1861 for liberal candidates who supported more, not less, self-government. The response of *Die Presse* to the announcement of the February Patent echoed the mistrust with which Austria's liberal Bürgertum greeted even Schmerling's constitution. The editors did not hesitate to point out the shortcomings of the Patent: no formal list of guaranteed freedoms, no ministerial responsibility, no immunity from arrest for deputies, no direct election of *Reichsrat* deputies, unfair suffrage requirements, no limit on paragraph thirteen, not enough deputies representing Vienna, and too many deputies representing the aristocracy.[47]

The municipal and provincial elections held in the spring of 1861, the first since 1848, allowed a cautious revival of public life throughout Austria. Press censorship, while officially relaxed, remained unofficially in effect. Laws regulating political activity and electoral organizing still forbade the creation of political associations and placed strict limitations on election campaign meetings. By forbidding overt politicking, the laws reflected the often disapproving attitudes the absolutist bureaucracy continued to hold toward any popular political activities. The individual's right to vote was one thing; organizing publicly to discuss issues and influence voters was quite another. A special government ordinance of March 9, 1861, allowed only those electoral meetings to take place that met certain conditions: the police would need to grant permission, a police deputy must be present at all times, only certified voters could attend, and the participants could not discuss political issues.[48]

Despite restrictions, electoral committees sprang up and vaguely worded political programs appeared all over urban Austria for the first time since 1848. In Vienna, with its strong tradition of local activism from 1848, liberals in each district organized voters' meetings to hear candidates and nominate deputies. Each group met regularly in a local hotel, often with over 150 men attending. Voter certificates issued by the government had to be shown in order to gain admission, and members had to respect the ban on political discussion, as more than one committee chair apologetically reminded his audience. Neither stipulation was easy to enforce, since voter lists were incomplete and most participants were eager to debate political issues. At a meeting in Vienna's ninth district one voter pointed out that "if Austria's [political] reconstruction is to be successful, we have to become better acquainted with those men and their

47. PR, editorials of January 8 and February 28, 1861.

48. Karl Hugelman, *Studien zum österreichischen Vereins- und Versammlungsrechte* (Graz, 1879), 44. The government certified voters on the basis of existing tax lists, an unwieldy process that caused endless controversy over who had the right to vote. Johann Umlauft, later democratic Vienna city council member and representative in the *Reichsrat*, petitioned the minister of police on behalf of an electoral group from the sixth district to allow nonvoters to attend the electoral meetings. The minister replied that the high rate of participation and the surrounding press publicity ensured that all citizens would hear about them. PR, January 18, 1861.

principles who will be participating [in politics]." Another speaker favored more open discussion, warning that "dislike of publicity is a characteristic of the opposition [conservative] party; we must build self-confidence to develop our new institutions." Speaking to a third district meeting, lawyer Joseph Kopp articulated the most typical liberal themes in a speech that nearly provoked police intervention. Bravely reminding his audience of what had been won and then lost in 1848, Kopp maintained, "We must not be cheated a second time" and reiterated that "the securest base for freedom, autonomy and welfare in our city of Vienna is the existence of a constitutional and unitary Austria."[49]

Participants at these meetings also debated the qualifications that the best candidates should embody. These included a certain degree of education, self-cultivation, and free time. The ideal liberal candidate was someone "with character," "convictions," and "clear judgment." The candidate should understand "the interests of the whole community" and "have time to represent citizens." He should represent an entire community and not simply a particular interest group. Another meeting stressed "love of fatherland," cautioning voters to reject candidates who supported programs associated with political conservatism: intolerance, religious fanaticism, "social peace at any price," or "no convictions at all."[50]

Given the precarious political situation, the Schmerling government left little to chance. Its members worked hard to ensure the election of as many favorable candidates as possible. These favored candidates were often liberals, due to their strong commitment to a centralized state. Historian Hanns Haas has recounted how the chief of political administration in Salzburg, an ally of Interior Minister Lasser's, used local connections to encourage the creation of an election committee for the city and surrounding rural areas. This organization counted among its earliest members physicians, notaries, officials and small businessmen, regional postmasters, prosperous farmers, and a professor. The committee then wrote letters to more rural notables, who "contacted their own friends and acquaintances, [developing] a kind of chain letter that . . . was meant to be read in intimate social circles." Often this kind of campaign required the notables to walk the countryside for long hours to reach potential voters.[51]

In the first elections of 1861, Viennese and Lower Austrian voters elected an overwhelmingly liberal and experienced diet.[52] No social radicals of the

---

49. "Wählerversammlung bei den 'drei Tauben,'" PR, January 4, 1861; "Wahlcomitè-III. Bezirk," PR, February 5, 1861.

50. "Die Geschäftsordnung einer Wahlversammlung," PR, January 11, 1861.

51. Hanns Haas, "Postmeister, Wirt, Kramer, Brauer, Müller und Wundarzt. Trägerschichten und Organisationsformen des Liberalismus. Das Salzburger Beispiel—vom frühen Konstitutionalismus bis zum Kulturkampf," in *Bürgertum in der Habsburgermonarchie*, ed. Bruckmüller et al., 269.

52. Gustav Kolmer, *Parlament und Verfassung in Österreich* (Vienna and Leipzig, 1902), 1:52. Lists of those elected to the Lower Austrian Diet from each curia appear in NÖLA, Landes-

1848 democrat variety gained election. Their place on the far left of the Lower Austrian Diet was taken by a vocal group of mostly lawyers and journalists who made their priority the fight to extend civil and constitutional rights. Several veterans of parliamentary activity in 1848 belonged to this faction, including the lawyers Johann N. Berger, Ignaz Kaiser, and Eugen von Mühlfeld, all members of the Frankfurt Parliament, along with Ignaz Kuranda, a former editor of the *Grenzboten*.[53] Another, Rudolf Brestel, now an official with the *Creditanstalt* bank, had played an influential role on the Austrian Parliament's constitutional committee in 1849. Almost half the deputies selected by the Lower Austrian Diet to go on to serve in the *Reichsrat* had also been elected to a legislative institution back in 1848, and over half of them had experience as state administrators.[54]

In Bohemia, Czech nationalists demanded an autonomous political status for Bohemia, and the linguistic, educational, and social rights to which their position as the largest ethnic group in Bohemia entitled them. On January 6, 1861, the Czech nationalist leaders Palacký and Rieger concluded a political alliance with a group of federalist noble landowners headed by Count Heinrich Clam-Martinitz. Under the terms of the alliance, which dominated Bohemian politics until 1890, the Czechs modified their social demands and gained the crucial political support of the conservative landowners for their nationalist demands. Since neither the Czech nationalists nor the German liberals controlled much more than 40 percent of the seats in the Bohemian Diet, the balance of power rested with the all-important large landowners' curia. The immediate result of this Czech alliance with the landowners was to make compromise with the German liberals at the provincial and national level more difficult to achieve. Shared social and economic concerns among the two bourgeois groups—concerns that might have provided the basis for a rapprochement—were effectively negated.[55]

Despite the apparent gulf separating the two sides, local elections in ethnically mixed areas in 1861 could produce temporary alliances. In Prague, where neither believed themselves politically strong enough to challenge the existing city government, Czech nationalists and German liberals joined forces to form

---

registratur, 1793–1904, fas. 49, ct. 9. In 1861, statistics from actual races were only cited in the Landesregistratur if the results were disputed. This seems to have occurred most frequently (if at all in 1861) in the rural curia, where between 350 and 450 people, or 25–30 percent of those eligible, voted in the first round of balloting.

53. Kuranda was also one of two Jews elected by the Lower Austrian Diet to serve in the Chamber of Deputies.

54. These included two cabinet ministers, Adolf Pratobevera (justice) and Schmerling.

55. Bruce Garver, *The Young Czech Party 1874–1901 and the Emergence of a Multiparty System* (New Haven, 1978), 49–54. The German liberals, meanwhile, concluded an alliance with the constitutionalist large landowners. Control of the Bohemian Diet thereafter depended on which faction won elections in the large landowner curia.

a single election committee. This remarkable alignment occurred precisely at a time when both groups were busy battling each other for election to the diet. Following the Prague election, the German liberals felt obliged to publish an "explanation" in a local newspaper. Citing as a justification Czech promises of full equality for both groups in city government, the newly elected councilors stressed that the alliance would be discontinued for the elections to the diet.[56]

The German liberal program for Bohemia decisively rejected the idea, popular among many state bureaucrats during the 1850s, that economic development could be encouraged only by reform from above, without guaranteeing some input from below. Instead, the program argued that economic development required a degree of political freedom to flourish: "Commerce, manufacture, and industry can never prosper in a country where there is no freedom of speech, freedom of the press, freedom of religion, or right of association." Mixing political idealism with economic pragmatism, the liberal program called for the improvement of education, the creation of more hospitals, improvements in local sanitary conditions, and an expansion of the railway network to improve commerce and to aid the poorer regions of Bohemia. The program ended on a warning note that raised the issue of nationality and its relation to liberalism: "All honorable and capable men of either nationality who live in our province would support what we have said here. But . . . while liberal ideas are important for deciding the elections to the diet, they cannot be decisive. We are also concerned to preserve the rights . . . of Germans in Bohemia. Our election motto is: liberal and German."[57]

The Bohemian Party produced several leaders of the German liberal movement in Austria, including Prague University professors Alois Brinz, Eduard Herbst, and Leopold von Hasner. Famous for his incisive speaking style, irony, and sarcasm—which terrorized opponents—as well as his detailed knowledge of financial matters, Herbst became the acknowledged leader of German liberal parties in the *Reichsrat* for the next twenty-five years. Franz Schmeykal, a lawyer from Böhmisch Leipa, would gradually construct the most sophisticated and effective provincial liberal political organization in the monarchy. Rounding out the list of Bohemian leaders, Prince Carl Auersperg,

56. Gary Cohen, *The Politics of Ethnic Survival: Germans in Prague, 1861–1914* (Princeton, 1981), 45–47; Hasner, *Denkwürdigkeiten*, 61–62; *Tagesbote aus Böhmen*, March 10, 1861. Leopold von Hasner, professor at the University of Prague and future liberal cabinet minister, recalled being asked to run for election to the Bohemian Diet both by local German liberals and by Francis Rieger and Francis Pstross (later the first Czech mayor of Prague) for the Czechs. Hasner later assumed that his reputation as a political moderate, his knowledge of the Czech language, and the fact that the Czechs could not put up a successful candidate against him in the majority German district of Prague—Altstadt—had led to this curious invitation.

57. *Tagesbote aus Böhmen*, March 11, 1861.

a liberal aristocrat known as "first cavalier of the *Reich*," led the constitutionalists in the Bohemian large landowners' curia.[58]

Moritz von Kaiserfeld, a veteran of the 1848 Diet and a frequent commentator for the Graz newspapers, organized a liberal party in Styria. Kaiserfeld drafted several party programs and appeals to the Styrian voting public, reaching beyond local economic issues to demand freedom of conscience and freedom of religion.[59] The signatories included 1848 veterans like Carl von Stremayr, who had sat in the Frankfurt Parliament as a young student and had suffered subsequent government persecution. In 1861, while recovering from a case of typhus, he discovered that he had again been nominated to run for election, this time to the Styrian Diet. Stremayr eventually served in three liberal cabinets as minister of education and religion and briefly headed another. Carl Rechbauer was another 1848 veteran who won election to the new diet and later to the *Reichsrat*. More a political activist than the old-fashioned Kaiserfeld or the administrator Stremayr, Rechbauer joined the left-liberal Progressive Party in the 1870s and served as president of the *Reichsrat* Chamber of Deputies from 1873 to 1879.[60]

More than that of any of his contemporaries, Carl Giskra's career epitomized the evolutionary process shared by the liberals of 1848 who returned, often following years of privation, to lead the movement in the 1860s. Barred from practicing law by the absolutist government because of his involvement in both the academic legion and the Frankfurt Parliament, Giskra had suffered years of poverty and frustration. Eugen von Mühlfeld, among others, had given Giskra odd clerking jobs in his Vienna law practice. Not until 1860, after repeated petitioning, did Giskra finally receive permission to practice law, albeit in Brünn rather than in Vienna. The government demanded that he prove his loyalty in a provincial post before allowing him to practice in Vienna, where, as a former radical, he would be in a position to cause more political trouble.[61]

---

58. Cohen, *Politics*, 66–67, 164–65, 181–83, 191; [Klaar], *Schmeykal*, 30–63; Rudolf, "Karl Auersperg," 29–32; Wymetal, "Herbst."

59. SLA, Familienarchiv Kaiserfeld, Sch. IV, Heft 166. One of these programs, signed by Kaiserfeld and thirty-eight colleagues, appeared in December 1860, making it the first program of a provincial liberal party in the new era.

60. Diethild Harrington-Müller, *Studien zur Geschichte der Fortschrittsklubs im Abgeordnetenhaus des österreichischen Reichsrats, 1873–1910* (Vienna, 1972), 180–81; Stremayr, *Erinnerungen*, 37–38.

61. Dieter Haintz, "Dr. Carl Giskra: Ein Lebensbild 1820–1879" (Ph.D. diss., University of Vienna, 1963) is extremely useful for Giskra's political career. According to Schmerling, only his personal interventions obtained full rehabilitation and permission to practice law in Brünn for Giskra. Schmerling, however, uses this incident in order to portray Giskra's later political opposition to the Schmerling government as a personal betrayal. See *Denkwürdigkeiten*, ed. Höbelt, 112–13; 114–20 for more scandalous tales of Giskra's apparently unspeakable behavior.

In Brünn, Giskra was in constant demand as an attorney. He rapidly made up for the lean years he and his family had suffered by gaining as clients local industrialists, among them Alfred Skene, the textile magnate.[62] Contemporary accounts noted the strong impression that his charismatic speaking style and romantic good looks made on his audiences. The mayor referred to him as "the rising star of Brünn." In 1861 he won election to the Brünn city council, to the Moravian Diet, and to the *Reichsrat*, and in 1866 Giskra was elected mayor of his adopted city. In the following year he achieved his greatest triumph: in an ironic turn of events, the former police suspect was himself appointed minister of the interior and placed in charge of all police activities.

The effects of such extremes on a man like Giskra are important to understanding the mentality shared by many of the liberal deputies to the first *Reichsrat*. In a speech to his voters in Brünn, Giskra observed with some irony that everyone seemed to be calling himself "liberal" in 1861 and that from these claims, "one might assume that the reactionaries had simply disappeared overnight, and that it was difficult to understand just where these millions of liberals had been hiding during the past years." Men like Giskra saw themselves as victorious martyrs whose virtue had outlasted a daunting array of forces mounted against them by a reactionary government. This conviction exaggerated their assessment both of their own capabilities and of their importance to the liberal movement. Giskra's philosophy clearly put him on the side of virtue in an historic struggle between light and dark. His extreme view of politics formed the basis for the powerful rhetoric that endeared him to much of the liberal public, both in Brünn and in Vienna.

In the same speech, Giskra openly recalled the recently concluded "twelve-year period of unjustified tutelage" and claimed that "the teachings of history [must have finally convinced] the monarch that all government power originates in the people."[63] Was Giskra still a populist demagogue? Did his belief in the people as the authentic repository of legitimacy make him a democrat? The preliminary answer to these and similar questions must be negative. Liberals in the 1860s derived their moral authority from an ideology that proclaimed their unique ability to represent the best interest of the *Volk*. If that belief had led many in 1848 to support universal manhood suffrage, at least at the communal level, we will see that the experience of the 1850s made them drop whatever tendencies toward a system of direct democracy they harbored. By the 1860s, liberals had fully reinterpreted democratic discourse to support a theory of representation claiming that only the middle class understood the overall needs of society.

---

62. Haintz, "Giskra," 61–63; Harrington-Müller, "Fortschrittsklub," 182.

63. "Wahlrede des Dr. C. Giskra für die Landtags-Candidaten des II. Bezirks in Brünn," 1.

The deputies elected by the diets to the first *Reichsrat* were socially a far more homogeneous group than their predecessors in the Austrian *Reichstag* of 1848–49 had been. Gone were the peasant landowners who had comprised the largest occupational group in 1848. In their stead, the noble large landowners, with over a third of the deputies, constituted the largest social group. Such were the effects of Schmerling's ten-gulden suffrage minimum and two-tiered voting system in rural areas that the large landowners dominated political life outside the cities. State and private officials elected in the urban and chamber of commerce curias increased their representation above the 1848 level, as did industrialists and merchants, while lawyers remained as the backbone of the German liberal movement. The deputies' backgrounds appear even more socially homogeneous when one considers the overlap in some of their occupations. Of the state and private officials who joined liberal parties, for example, a fifth were also listed as landowners, while a quarter of the liberal landowners were also state officials. Just under a third of the German liberal deputies had belonged to at least one of the elected bodies in 1848 (*Reichstag*, Frankfurt Parliament, provincial diets), and a tenth served concurrently as mayors of their municipalities. The ages of the deputies further reflected the homogeneity of their experience: two-thirds belonged to a generation that had come of age well before 1848.[64]

The Struggle to Govern: Liberals in Parliament, 1861–65

The implementation of the February Patent only encouraged the parliamentary liberals to articulate their political demands with increasing radicalism in the years following 1861. Intended to coopt the bourgeoisie into a moderate bureaucratic consensus, the document immediately aggravated the differences between those who favored representative government and those who clung to bureaucratic reform from above as the best way to transform society. In the years following the violence of 1848, these differences had been masked by a socially conservative consensus holding that Austrian society was not yet mature enough for true constitutionalism. For more than ten years, liberal Bürger had renounced their former political activism, unable to reconcile the contradictions between their ideals of political democracy and the social anarchy that often resulted from their own revolutionary reforms in 1848. Now, a decade later, the choices were different.

---

64. Pieter M. Judson, "German Liberalism in Nineteenth-Century Austria: Clubs, Parties and the Rise of Bourgeois Politics" (Ph.D. diss., Columbia University, 1987), 461–62; Oswald Knauer, *Das österreichische Parlament von 1848–1966* (Vienna,1969); *Reichsratsalmanach* (Vienna, 1864). Of the liberal deputies to the *Reichsrat* in 1862, 65 percent were between the ages of forty-one and fifty-six, 22 percent were younger than forty-one, and 13 percent were older than fifty-six. Twenty-eight liberal deputies had served in some elected capacity in 1848–49.

Toward the end of April 1861, the newly elected deputies to the *Reichsrat* gathered in Vienna for the opening of the first legislative session. The government had hastily erected a temporary wooden structure near the Schottentor to accommodate the Chamber of Deputies. Although their new home did not have room for committee meetings or party headquarters, the deputies continued to meet in this "Schmerling Theater" (as the enemies of the February Patent called it) for the next twenty-five years.[65] Not long afterwards, the German liberal deputies in both houses began to form loose political parties distinguished by general programs. The liberal faction in the House of Lords issued a program that stressed centralism and denounced all concessions to federalism.[66] In June, the Viennese press reported the formation of three liberal parties in the Chamber of Deputies: Unionists, Great Austrians, and Autonomists.[67] All three parties played on memories of 1848, warning against any unconstitutional interventions by the cabinet. Both Unionists and Great Austrians vowed to introduce a law creating ministerial responsibility to the *Reichsrat,* the former declaring that "in case of a conflict between the cabinet and our convictions, we must adhere to the latter."[68] All three desired constitutional guarantees of "equality of all citizens before the law, equal opportunity for public positions and titles, equal rights for all legally recognized religions and nationalities, guaranteed freedom of the press, of teaching and research, of . . . privacy of letters, of petition, the right to assemble, the right to form associations . . . and the right to trial by jury in criminal cases."[69] What distinguished the small Autonomist Party from the other two was its willingness to negotiate a compromise settlement with the Hungarians who refused to attend the *Reichsrat* sessions. The Autonomists supported an extension of civil and political rights, but they also counseled patience and pragmatism in pursuing them, claiming that "we find true guarantees of freedom and justified national development not in the words of the constitution but in the autonomy of the local community."[70]

---

65. The House of Lords met in the more comfortable quarters of the Lower Austrian Diet.

66. PR, May 31, 1861, evening edition. The constitutionalist lords supported equality of all citizens before the law, equality among nationalities, freedom of worship, and freedom of the press (but within limits to discourage its misuse), but they remained silent on ministerial responsibility and deputies' immunity from prosecution, two issues of paramount importance to the liberals in the lower chamber.

67. PR, June 10 and June 13, 1861. The Unionists' name was taken from the inn where its members met to constitute themselves. The party numbered about eighty members and was the only German liberal party to take in non-German-identified deputies, including a group of twelve Ruthenian deputies from Galicia. Its emphasis on party discipline and on maintaining the centralist state structure reflected the leading role played by the Bohemian Germans in its direction.

68. "Programm der Unionisten im Abgeordnetenhaus," in *Reichsrathsalmanach*, 17–18.

69. "Programm der grossösterreichischen Partei," in *Reichsratsalmanach*, 22.

70. "Programm der deutschen Autonomisten," in *Reichsratsalmanach*, 23–24; "Statuten der Unionisten," in *Reichsrathsalmanach*, 18–20; Krones, *Kaiserfeld*, 175–80. Of the three liberal

These early party programs demonstrate that from the start, the parliamentary liberal movement was not about to subordinate itself to the consultative role envisioned for it by the Schmerling government. Furthermore, despite Schmerling's best hopes, the disproportionate representation given to the large landowners did not result in the creation of a large, progovernment party of the center as the cabinet had hoped. Instead, the noble landowners split into mutually hostile pro- and anticonstitutionalist groups. The former aligned themselves with the liberals, while the latter joined with the conservative, federalist, and Slav factions. Furthermore, few landowners who did join liberal parties achieved leadership positions in the 1860s. Unlike their counterparts in Prussia and the other German states who often dominated both local and parliamentary politics, noble landowners in Austria followed the lead of more activist middle-class professionals and businessmen.[71]

On April 29, 1861, deputies to both houses of the *Reichsrat* took the oath of office in an atmosphere of general excitement in Vienna. "A survey of the records from that stirring period in parliamentary history must fill every Austrian with pride," wrote Heinrich Pollak, political reporter for the *Morgenpost* of the 1861–63 parliamentary session. "What an abundance of spirit and perception is contained in the individual speeches!"[72] The German liberals in the *Reichsrat* not only learned how to make speeches in those early years; they also wrote a remarkable amount of legislation. Not content to wait for the government to introduce this or that reform, they plunged ahead with their own program. In particular the liberals attacked constitutional shortcomings, as if they could legislate away the structural limits the emperor had placed on their powers. In this attempt they received the enthusiastic support of the liberal press in Vienna and several of the provincial capitals. At the same time, the memories of 1848 loomed large at the Hofburg, and Schmerling often found it necessary to warn the new liberal parties not to act independently

---

parties, only the Unionists explicitly addressed the question of party discipline. An elected committee of six ran internal party debates, planned agendas, and represented the party. Members were expected to submit their legislative initiatives to the club for discussion before raising them in the Chamber, and Unionist deputies were bound to vote a certain way if two-thirds of the party members voted to make an issue into a "party issue" (*Parteifrage*). Members paid nominal dues to cover certain party expenses. Frequent laments in the press about the lack of party discipline in the 1860s reflect the fact that many of these rules could never be enforced.

71. Of the most prominent liberals in the 1860s, Berger, Brinz, Giskra, Hasner, Herbst, Mühlfeld, Rechbauer, Karl van der Strass, and Karl Wiser were lawyers. Berger, Hasner, and Alexander Schindler were lawyers who, along with Kuranda, also had experience as journalists. Brestel was a bank director and Skene a textile magnate. On the political role of large landowners and local notables in the liberal parties of imperial Germany, see Dan White, *The Splintered Party: National Liberalism in Hessen and the Reich* (Cambridge, MA, 1976); Sheehan, *German Liberalism*, 82, 160–65.

72. Pollak, *Dreissig Jahre*, 1:68.

but to follow the cabinet's lead if they wished to ensure the success of constitutionalism.

The liberals of the 1860s did face a difficult situation, as they challenged their former bureaucratic allies for the sole power to govern. Without a legally organized mass base in society, parliamentary liberals had few means by which to enforce their demands. Legal constraints still forbade political meetings, much less the organization of local political associations. Not surprisingly, the press quickly assumed a paramount role within the movement. Newspapers provided a public forum for the discussion of issues from a liberal point of view, and they helped maintain a connection between elected officials and their constituents. In particular, *Die Presse*, and after 1864 the *Neue Freie Presse* in Vienna, reported domestic and international events relying on liberal opinions as major points of reference and interpretation. Their news columns related party news, published liberal electoral programs and endorsed liberal candidates. Their editorials usually sided with the liberal parties against the government, although they frequently lamented the parties' inability to act even more forcefully and with greater discipline.[73]

Knowing that the function of their press extended well beyond general reporting or editorializing, several liberal politicians became adept at manipulating the press. Deputies mixed freely with reporters in the buffet area of the parliament building, frequently giving journalists advance copies of upcoming speeches. Committee chairs reported personally on their activities to the press, and some cabinet members like Lasser enjoyed giving journalists off-the-record information. Ignaz von Plener remained in "constant communication with August Zang," editor of *Die Presse*, while Carl Giskra and Eduard Herbst both cultivated particularly close relationships with the *Morgenpost's* Heinrich Pollak. Each used these connections regularly to plant rumors, leak secrets, or to justify their actions. Many deputies also used editorial space to publicize their own views or to pressure the government on a specific issue.[74] The same was true of liberal newspapers in the provinces. Moritz von Kaiserfeld wrote

73. On the newspapers, see in general, Wandruszka, *Zeitung*. Other Vienna papers that generally supported liberal positions included Kuranda's *Ost-Deutsche Post* (until 1866). According to Schmerling, who had a disastrous relationship with the press, the press encouraged liberal deputies to behave more radically than they might otherwise by making them answerable to its democratic standards. Molisch, "Schmerling," 45.

74. Of the cabinet members in the Schmerling government, Lasser seems to have been on the most familiar terms with the press. On one occasion he gave several journalists a demonstration of his staff's ability to open and examine their private correspondence without detection. Pollak, *Dreissig Jahre*, 1:71–73. On Plener's relations with Zang, see *Vater der Verfassung*, 52. Zang's own understanding of the power of the press is captured in an anecdote related by Julius Fröbel. In an audience with Schmerling, who had threatened to bring a lawsuit against his paper, Zang is supposed to have replied, "I made you a minister, I will just as easily bring you down." Julius Fröbel, *Ein Lebenslauf* (Stuttgart, 1891), 2:336.

frequently to the editors of the *Grazer Tagespost* suggesting the point of view they should adopt on certain issues. Upper Austrian liberals founded the Linzer *Tages-Post* in 1865 to ensure their views would be aired, while in Laibach, the *Laibacher Tagblatt* was meant to present educated circles with liberal positions. In Prague, the journal *Bohemia* became the official organ of the Bohemian German Liberal Party.[75]

The liberal deputies and their press conceptualized the legislative sessions as struggles of epic significance. As in 1848, they referred to political opponents in a language that rendered all conflict in moral terms. This rhetoric lent a messianic air of inevitability to a future liberal victory and offered a compelling justification for liberal opposition to the system itself. But if they invoked a recognizable moral language to describe their struggles in general, they used different arguments from the ones they had employed to make their case in 1848. The liberal insistence on locating executive power in the *Reichsrat* was no longer justified by theories of popular democracy. Like Plener in the cabinet, the liberals had shifted their arguments away from the idealism of 1848 and had adopted more socially utilitarian forms of reasoning. In doing so, they battled the bureaucracy on its own turf. The liberals challenged the view that the bureaucracy represented the best vehicle to transform Austria into a modern, powerful state. Instead, they placed themselves squarely in that position. More and more, the liberals justified their claim to rule by characterizing themselves and the social groups they spoke for as the vanguard of economic, political, and social progress. Liberals continued, however indirectly, to champion eventual political democratization and equality in Austria, thereby appropriating twin legacies for themselves: the popular idealism of 1848 and the hardnosed bureaucratic pragmatism of the 1850s.

Early in the first *Reichsrat* session, the liberals fired a substantial volley at the bureaucratic heart of the February Patent. In an attempt to legislate the elusive *Rechtsstaat* into existence, Giskra introduced a bill that would make the cabinet directly responsible to the *Reichsrat* for the execution of legislation passed by that body, demanding that every new law passed by the parliament and sanctioned by the emperor be cosigned by a responsible cabinet

75. Krones, *Kaiserfeld*, 203–4. In February of 1864, the *Grazer Telegraf* in fact proclaimed itself "the official organ of the Styrian Autonomist Party," and its editors worked closely with Kaiserfeld on political strategy. GT, February 21, 1864. On the Laibach papers, see Peter Vodopivec, "Liberalismus in der Provinz? Das Beispiel des Triestiner Hinterlandes" in "*Durch Arbeit, Besitz, Wissen und Gerechtigkeit*," ed. Stekl et al., 82–83. On the *Linzer Tages-Post* see Kurt Wimmer, *Liberalismus in Oberösterreich am Beispiel des liberal-politischen Vereins für Oberösterreich in Linz 1869–1909* (Linz, 1979), 194. According to Karl Czörnig's statistics for 1858, before Austria lost its Italian provinces, there were 354 newspapers or journals being published in the monarchy: 182 in German, 108 in Italian, 39 in Hungarian, 31 in Slavic languages, two in Rumanian, and one each in Greek, Russian, and French. Karl von Czörnig, *Österreichs Neugestaltung* (Stuttgart, 1858), 624.

minister.[76] The liberals rightly feared that the state bureaucracy did not yet accept the legitimacy of the constitution and that cabinet ministers did not treat enforcement of the new laws as a priority. In support of the motion, Eugen von Mühlfeld stressed that the participation of the people through their representatives in the legislative process included the right to watch over the execution of the resulting laws. "The wisest laws, passed for the good of the people, are worthless if they are not carried out. If the administration (*Verwaltung*) were not responsible to the legislature, the rights of the people would lose all meaning."[77]

By claiming that the cabinet was in some way responsible to the legislature, rather than to the emperor alone, the concept of ministerial responsibility attacked the basis of the bureaucratic order. Rejecting a consultative role outright, the liberals were clearly behaving as if they already enjoyed full constitutional equality with their sovereign, an assumption that is not unambiguously supported by the texts of the October Diploma and February Patent. The liberals' interpretation of those documents constituted an aggressive encroachment against the emperor's prerogatives, and for this reason Schmerling worried that this conflict would turn the emperor against the entire constitutional experiment. In June Schmerling opened a cabinet discussion by noting that while public opinion, the Chamber of Deputies, and even the House of Lords were all "possessed of a mania for ministerial responsibility," his colleagues should oppose any attempts to transform "His Majesty's government into a government of the parliamentary majority." At the same time, however, Schmerling could not afford to estrange his supposed allies in the *Reichsrat* and on the stock exchange by openly denying their constitutional claims, even though, like the emperor, he adamantly opposed further concessions.[78]

A majority of cabinet members also opposed granting ministerial responsibility, but the demands of the recalcitrant Plener helped prevent the cabinet from burying the issue altogether. As he had so often before, Plener cited economic considerations to argue for ministerial responsibility, threatening to resign from the cabinet if it were rejected, because he could "only carry out his financial operations if ministerial responsibility were assured." Francis Joseph resolved the matter for a time, informing the *Reichsrat* deputies that he considered his ministers "directly responsible to him for fulfilling their functions, upholding the constitution, and for the exact execution of the laws," and for

76. SPHA 1, May 15, 1861; Kolmer, *Parlament*, 1:78. Parliament would have the right to take legal action against any minister who did not fulfill his constitutional duties. Giskra's motion would also have made all laws enacted under the emergency powers section provisional in nature until the next *Reichsrat* had either endorsed or rejected them.

77. SPHA 1, May 15, 1861; Kolmer, *Parlament*, 1:78–79. The Czech nationalists introduced a similar bill at this time.

78. Franz, *Liberalismus*, 268–69.

these specific functions, responsible to the legislative body as well. This vague gesture of good will satisfied the moderates among the parliamentary liberals for the time being, but the more radical among them did not let the issue die. They raised it repeatedly in the next four years, making it the centerpiece of their legislative attempts to force a *Rechtsstaat* into being.[79] Other legislation meant to undermine the power of the bureaucracy included a bill giving deputies immunity from prosecution for statements made in parliament and one that revived communal autonomy by limiting local bureaucratic powers and eventually separating the local judiciary from the state administration.[80]

From the beginning of the constitutional era, the problems of stabilizing the currency, paying off the tremendous state debt, and balancing the budget overshadowed almost every other issue. In the liberals' worldview, large-scale deficit spending and huge bank loans proved the irresponsibility of absolutist government, especially when so much of the money had funded the military. Budget cutting and keeping a tight rein on currency circulation therefore highlighted the new course. Both Finance Minister Plener and the liberals agreed to lower expenditures as the primary strategy to cut the deficit. Further borrowing on the accustomed scale was out of the question, and the liberals shied away from paying off the debts they had inherited by imposing increased taxes, which could only detract from their political popularity. It should therefore come as no surprise that the primary target of liberal budget cutting was the military, that supposed last refuge of aristocratic reaction. Plener's tireless efforts in the cabinet alone reduced military spending from 179 million florins in 1860 to 118 million by 1863.[81]

79. Franz, *Liberalismus*, 269–70; Müllner, "Lasser," 25–26. Both Pratobevera (justice) and Count Wickenburg (commerce) backed Plener. Lasser too supported the principle of ministerial responsibility but mostly as a way of shielding the emperor from potential criticism. Ministers and not the crown, he believed, should be the target for parliamentary attacks. In 1862 the *Reichsrat* financial committee charged with examining the state budget demanded to know why the government had not yet introduced a law on ministerial responsibility, declaring that "if Austria is not ready for such a law, then it is not ready for a constitution." In the same year, Alexander Schindler interpellated the government, complaining that bureaucrats at all levels made no secret of their opposition to the February Patent and reminding the government of its failure to introduce a loyalty oath for either the civil service or the military. Kolmer, *Parlament*, 1:83, 107; SPHA 1, May 1 and November 25, 1862.

80. Kolmer, *Parlament*, 1:113–15. For an appraisal of the new law and the Liberal Party amendments, see Ucakar and Welan, "Selbstverwaltung," 20–24. The liberals insisted that communal autonomy was the necessary basis for the constitutional state, a belief that reflected the power of the traditions of *Bürgerrecht* within the movement.

81. Macartney, *Empire*, 533–34. Giskra headed a parliamentary budget committee popularly known as the *Streichquartett,* a pun that conjured up both a string quartet and the cancellation of requests. This committee pared down the military budget more drastically than did Plener, calling for a further reduction of the standing army, furloughing more men, and postponing new

The issue of tariffs and trade policy split the liberal parties into two distinct factions, one that demanded an immediate liberalization of tariffs and another that supported retaining relatively high barriers. This internal controversy pitted different industrial and regional sectors within the movement against one another. The battle did not grow out of a general conflict between agrarian and industrial interests, as it might have in other states, nor did it result completely from a rigid split between so-called economic liberals and political liberals within the parties, as some historians have claimed. As in 1848, the issue of free trade in Austria involved more than simply the economic concerns of a variety of industries; it depended on the aggressively German orientation of the monarchy's foreign policy.[82]

Schwarzenberg had attempted to bring Austria's policies more in line with those of the German *Zollverein* in the 1850s. The vision of a politically united Germany under Austrian leadership had motivated this gradual reduction in tariffs, as had the neoabsolutist desire to encourage modernization. This policy had raised the ire of several industrialists' organizations which blamed the economic crisis of 1857–58 on the tariff reduction.[83] When in the early 1860s France and England concluded a commercial treaty that came close to introducing free-trade conditions, Prussia (and by extension the *Zollverein*) negotiated a similar treaty with France. The Association of Austrian Industrialists (*Verein der österreichischen Industriellen*) feared that the Austrian government would seek to negotiate a similar treaty in order to maintain its political influence among the German states. In a strongly worded memorandum, the industrialists warned that "Austria cannot be allowed to increase the damage that the Prussian-French treaty will cause our industries by negotiating a similar treaty itself."[84]

As part of a bid to establish Habsburg political hegemony in Germany, the Schmerling cabinet did propose in 1865 a trade treaty with the *Zollverein* that committed Austria to an eventual elimination of tariff differentials. Signed in April 1865, the treaty became the focus of a bitter debate in the Chamber of Deputies. Speaking in its favor, Rudolf Brestel and Moritz von Kaiserfeld admitted the short-term hardships the treaty might cause Austrian industry but

---

weapons purchases, all measures that arguably contributed to Austria's defeat by Prussia in 1866. These austerity measures were continued by the conservative Belcredi cabinet in 1865–66.

82. Matis, "Sozioökonomische Aspekte," 244–49.

83. Charmatz, *Deutsch Österreichische Politik*, 138. Before 1849 Austria had no history of trade treaties with other European countries. The autarkic policies of Joseph II and his successors had raised prohibitive trade barriers against raw materials and finished products from the outside world. In 1853 trade treaties with Prussia and the other German states had freed most raw materials from duties, while industrial tariffs fell by 25 to 50 percent.

84. Charmatz, *Deutsch Österreichische Politik*, 137–38. An official investigation of the 1857 crisis found the industrialists' criticism of trade policy to be largely unjustified. Brandt, *Neoabsolutismus*, 1:415–16.

emphasized its long-term beneficial effects, including the political credit to be reaped from tying Austria's fortunes more closely to those of the *Zollverein.* For these men and their allies, free trade, like the destruction of the guilds, was an integral part of a moral vision of historical progress. Johann Demel pointed to a logical contradiction between the industrialists' enthusiasm for the newly introduced industrial code, which had freed the labor supply, and their opposition to free trade. To him the two measures were inextricably linked. Eugene Kinsky echoed this opinion, asking, "If we now consider the Austrian people mature enough [for a constitution], why should they not be mature enough to buy or sell freely?"[85]

Alfred Skene, the Moravian textile magnate, led the liberals opposed to the trade treaty in the *Reichsrat,* while the Association of Austrian Industrialists waged a bitter campaign in the press.[86] Opponents doubted Austria's short-term ability to compete successfully against European industry without some moderate tariff protection. "It may be that those who are full of free-thinking ideals see a happy system far in the future," said one, "but I cannot vote for a system that will destroy us in the immediate future and that is based on the ruins of the present generation."[87] Despite a sizable liberal opposition, the treaty was ratified. Following this defeat, the Association of Austrian Industrialists wasted little time preparing for future confrontation. In a new program, the association regretted that free trade had been introduced before internal conditions favored unlimited competition. Noting that they had always supported the eventual introduction of free trade once freedom of capital, of land disposition, and of a mobile labor supply had taken root in Austria, the industrialists vowed to continue their opposition.[88]

The terms of this debate reflect the problematic position of general liberal theory when applied to specific economic situations, an issue that had caused serious divisions in 1848 and would do so again with the onset of depression in 1873. In towns and villages across Austria liberals supported free trade as part of their general program until specific free-trade policies began to affect their own businesses adversely. As Peter Vodopivec has noted for the German middle class in Krain, its newspapers referred often and approvingly to the theories of Adam Smith, Richard Cobden, and John Stuart Mill. Liberal leaders

85. Kolmer, *Parlament,* 1:198.

86. Charmatz, *Deutsch Österreichische Politik,* 138–39.

87. SPHA 3, May 19, 1865; Kolmer, *Parlament,* 1:197.

88. Charmatz, *Deutsch Österreichische Politik,* 138. In their new program the industrialists stepped up demands for transportation improvements, river regulation, and large-scale railway planning, along with lower interest rates. They also demanded that the government establish a central organ for commercial interests and that the cabinet create an expert commission to advise on future tariff policy. In effect, this early defeat made the industrialists better prepared to pressure both *Reichsrat* and cabinet in future debates over commercial policy.

consistently praised economic freedom as a fundamental prerequisite to any kind of social progress. Yet the question remained whether, in Vodopivec's words, "local enthusiasm for liberal economic principles merely reflected a political commitment to the general ideological orientation of liberalism in Austria."[89] The most ardent supporters of free-trade legislation may well have been bureaucratic reformers, those who had attempted to create an economic modernization of Austria in the 1850s. Their policies had raised popular resentment in business and industrial circles because they paid little heed to the particular needs and desires of those most deeply involved in Austrian industry.[90]

The liberals were not the only force in the *Reichsrat* to challenge Schmerling's system. From 1861 to 1865 conservative groups intent on undermining the effectiveness of the February Patent clamored for their own federalist reform, which would give greater power to the provincial diets. In June 1863, the governing board of the Czech National Party narrowly approved a motion to boycott the *Reichsrat* altogether. From 1863 until 1879 the Czech nationalists used this form of passive resistance to agitate for more extensive provincial autonomy and for a federal state structure. The Poles too desired special concessions for Galicia and refused to recognize the right of any central parliament to legislate for Galicia on internal matters. Periodically, they threatened to boycott the *Reichsrat* to make a parliamentary quorum impossible. Clerical deputies from the Tirol and Upper Austria meanwhile opposed any attempt by the central *Reichsrat* to legislate religious or social policy, and the Slovene deputies clamored for linguistic concessions.[91]

The loose federalist alliance among these groups consistently questioned the competence of the *Reichsrat* to decide almost any issue. The federalists also focused their efforts on the definition and enforcement of national equality with regard to language use in the administration. Casting the battle between centralization and federalism as a question of ethnic survival, Palacký told the House of Lords: "Federalists believe they can best protect their nationality only when individual provinces are assured their autonomy." Rieger too warned the *Reichsrat* deputies that the Czechs "don't want simply to vegetate, and we don't want our language confined simply to farmers and nursemaids." He demanded the kind of national equality that would function "realistically in every aspect of public life." The desire for linguistic equality was even more pressing

89. Peter Vodopivec, "Die Sozialen und wirtschaftlichen Ansichten des deutschen Bürgertums in Krain vom Ende der sechziger bis zum Beginn der achtziger Jahre des 19. Jahrhunderts" in *Geschichte der Deutschen im Bereich des heutigen Slowenien. 1848–1941,* ed. Helmut Rumpler and Arnold Suppan (Vienna, 1988), 98–101; Haas, "Trägerschichten des Liberalismus."

90. Matis, "Sozioökonomische Aspekte," 242–54.

91. Kolmer, *Parlament*, 1:142, 173. Both the cabinet and the liberal parties were more likely to negotiate with the Poles, allowing Galicia substantial internal autonomy, because unlike Bohemia, Galicia had no German liberal constituency.

for the Slovenes, whose institutional power and local influence were far less established than that of the Czechs.[92]

German liberals often misinterpreted such nationalist demands, seeing in them conservative or federalist-inspired attacks on the young and vulnerable institutions of the *Rechtsstaat*. In cases like this they backed the Schmerling government to the hilt, denying that the use of German in state institutions constituted a form of national privilege and explaining its use in purely functional terms. If Slovenes and Czechs used an empirical argument—how many people spoke a given language—to argue for institutional bilingualism, German speakers maintained that cultural superiority, not population statistics, should determine language policy. Was not German the only common language among educated people in Central Europe? Could the Czechs or Slovenes boast of similar academic achievements? "After all," suggested Alois Brinz with typical sarcasm, "we can never achieve . . . brotherhood among Austria's nationalities if we can't even understand what each other is saying." It was not the numbers of German speakers in the monarchy but rather their historic role in creating a common public culture in Central Europe that justified their language's hegemonic position.[93]

By 1865 liberal opposition and federalist intransigence had completely eroded the cabinet's legitimacy. Schmerling had made no headway on the problem of Hungary, and he seemed to flaunt his increasing disregard for the role of the legislative bodies in the governing process, relying on paragraph thirteen to pass key legislation. The liberal leadership responded with harsh words and organized opposition to almost every measure the government brought before the *Reichsrat*. Interpellations frequently attacked what they now called the government's "phony constitutionalism" (*Scheinconstitutionalismus*). And liberals persisted in their demands for a law on ministerial responsibility.[94] Early in

92. SPHA 1, June 19 and 23, 1861; Kolmer, *Parlament*, 1:88–89. The example of the Slovenes also differs from that of the Czechs since there were some Slovene politicians from Carniola in the 1860s who opposed a politics of ethnicity and supported a progressive alliance with the liberal parties. Vodopivec, "Die Sozialen und wirtschaftlichen Ansichten des deutschen Bürgertums in Krain," 86–88.

93. Kolmer, *Parlament*, 1:89; *Das Deutschtum in Krain. Ein Wort zur Aufklärung* (Graz, 1862); Pieter M. Judson, "'Not Another Square Foot!' German Liberalism and the Rhetoric of National Ownership in Nineteenth-Century Austria," *Austrian History Yearbook* 26 (1995), 89–90. Responding to a Czech interpellation in 1862, Interior Minister Lasser stated that an official's ability to do his job was the primary consideration in bureaucratic appointments. No matter what his ethnic background, any candidate fluent in German would be considered qualified. Francis Joseph endorsed this position, and he also insisted upon the retention of German as the language of command in the army. SPHA 1, May 17, 1862; Kolmer, *Parlament*, 1:89; Deak, *Beyond Nationalism*, 178–89.

94. SPHA 3, November 14 and 28, 1864. This strategy involved some political risk. Even though the tide was running against Schmerling in the lower House, the liberals could not be certain of attaining the necessary two-thirds majority vote.

1865 they decided to legislate a constitutional amendment to change paragraph thirteen.

In April the constitutional committee of the Chamber passed the desired amendment with a ringing endorsement of liberal constitutionalism. "The February Patent," it asserted, "does not allow the government to publish laws . . . without the constitutionally required consent of the legislature, even when the *Reichsrat* is not in session. . . . Until now, however, the government's interpretation and use of paragraph thirteen has not agreed with the views of this committee. . . . Therefore . . . the committee [has proposed] a law that will eliminate any future doubts about the meaning or use of paragraph thirteen."[95] In an eleventh hour appeal to the *Reichsrat* Schmerling reiterated his government's commitment to constitutional rule. Nevertheless, the lower house voted by a margin of 102 to 48 to adopt the amendment.[96] The results reflected the enormity of the split between bureaucracy and legislature. As the *Neue Freie Presse* noted with some satisfaction, the parliamentary situation had changed considerably since 1861. Some of the moderates who supported the amendment were voting against the government for the very first time.[97]

The paragraph thirteen vote exposed Schmerling's lack of influence in the *Reichsrat,* but it was hardly the only reason for his fall in the summer of 1865. Schmerling had by now lost Francis Joseph's confidence, due primarily to the complete failure of his Hungary policy. The situation had developed no further than where it had stood in 1861. Hungary had never recognized any links with the other parts of the monarchy beyond the common dynasty. Since 1861 Schmerling had rejected Hungarian demands for the recognition of the April 1848 constitutional laws. At the time, most liberals in the *Reichsrat* applauded his uncompromisingly centralist position. In the cabinet, however, some liberal voices had already supported compromise and negotiation with the Hungarians. Both Plener and Pratobevera favored accepting the Hungarian position as a basis for further discussion. Plener especially saw no reason why the government might not allow the Hungarians to create their own cabinet for matters not common to the entire monarchy. This minority opinion, however, did not prevail. Instead, Schmerling proclaimed a provisional martial law and dissolved the Hungarian Diet along with all other representative institutions.[98]

---

95. PA, Verfassungsausschuss, ct. 2/A, folder 6, "Bericht des Ausschusses über den von dem Abgeordneten Dr. Berger bezüglich des Par. 13 des Grundgesetzes über die Reichsvertretung von 26. Februar 1861 gestellten Antrag auf authentische Erläuterung der gedachten Verfassungsbestimmung."

96. Kolmer, *Parlament*, 1:180–81. Seventy-seven liberals, twenty-two Slavs, and three clerical conservatives voted against the government, while thirty-eight progovernment liberals, three Slavs, and seven clerical conservatives voted against the amendment.

97. NFP, June 17, 1865.

98. Redlich, *Staats- und Reichsproblem*, 2:83–94.

This unproductive policy drew criticism from the Autonomist Party a year later, when nothing in the situation had changed. As long as the Hungarians did not participate in constitutional life, the Autonomists feared that the Austrian constitution would achieve neither legitimacy nor permanence. In 1862 Kaiserfeld openly attacked Schmerling's non-policy of waiting. "Those proud words [of Schmerling's] 'we can wait' have proved to be a delusion, both here and in Hungary. If only we could wait! Yet we know that we don't dare wait because we are only injuring ourselves and that only our . . . enemies will benefit from this deplorable quarrel." By 1865 Kaiserfeld publicly supported the adoption of Hungary's Laws of April 1848 as the basis for negotiation. He now believed that the liberals would have to accept a division of the monarchy in order to guarantee the survival of constitutional rule in Austria.[99]

Francis Joseph also recognized the futility of the waiting policy toward Hungary, but for a very different reason. By 1865, the possibility of war with either Prussia or Italy loomed on the horizon. In either case, ongoing passive resistance in Hungary could become more than a domestic nuisance. In December 1864 the emperor undertook his own private negotiations. Typically for Francis Joseph in the 1860s, this personal maneuver was carried out without the knowledge or approval of the cabinet. When these negotiations came to light, Schmerling's position as state minister became untenable. Having lost the confidence of both emperor and *Reichsrat*, Schmerling resigned on June 27, 1865.[100]

Both contemporaries and later historians sympathetic to the liberals' cause have tended to judge them harshly for their abandonment of Schmerling. The liberals of this period are often accused of clinging blindly to principle, unwilling to compromise and politically immature, willing to make grandiose gestures but unwilling to act constructively on their principles. Yet it is worth remembering the fundamental opposition of interests that divided the semi-absolutist bureaucrat Schmerling from the parliamentary liberals, who, as this account should make clear, were intent on guaranteeing themselves a voice in government at whatever cost.[101]

Crisis and Opportunity, 1865–67

The next two years brought further political confusion, and Austria's constitutional system hung in the balance between two opposed visions: liberal cen-

---

99. Krones, *Kaiserfeld*, 187–88, 223–26. In February 1865 Kaiserfeld met with Count Menyhért Lonyay, a prominent ally of Deak, in Pest. This first meeting produced only a better awareness of each other's positions. It was followed by increased contacts, which were crucial for winning a majority of German liberals to the Autonomist position regarding Hungary in 1867.

100. Kolmer, *Parlament*, 1:201–3.

101. Franz, *Liberalismus*, 294; Walter Rogge, *Österreich von Villagos bis zur Gegenwart*

tralism and conservative federalism. In retrospect the possibility of a reversion to a federalist model seems unrealistic given the modern needs of the state, but it appeared a very real possibility to contemporaries. When the emperor appointed the conservative Count Richard Belcredi to succeed Schmerling, most liberal observers doubted the new cabinet would openly attempt to undo the February Patent, given the liberals' strength in the *Reichsrat*. Nevertheless, on September 20 an imperial manifesto suspended the *Reichsrat* indefinitely. The suspension did not apply to the provincial diets, however. They received the friendly assurance that the government would convoke them "for a hearing and consideration of their views." The suspension of the *Reichsrat* gave Francis Joseph more leeway to negotiate with Hungary, and it also allowed Belcredi to pursue his own aims more completely. These rapidly became apparent as the new cabinet chief outlined his desire to replace Schmerling's centralist system with a federalist alternative more congenial to conservative groups in the diets.[102]

This new development galvanized the liberal parties, bringing them together in a new unity of purpose. Referring to the suspension as a *Staatsstreich* or coup, moderates, leftists, and Autonomists banded together to fight the government in the individual diets.[103] German liberals from the different provinces coordinated a strategy and drew up an address protesting the suspension of the *Reichsrat*.[104] When the government opened the diets with a reading of the September Manifesto, a barrage of indignant protest struck the imperial officials in every diet with a bloc of German liberal deputies.[105] Yet even as liberals protested and conservatives rushed to present their demands to a sympathetic government, events in Hungary and Europe soon forced the emperor to retreat from his flirtation with federalism.

(Vienna and Leipzig, 1873), 2:301. Franz concluded that "indecision in practice was the fate of the liberals, who were otherwise so unmovable in their theory."

102. Kolmer, *Parlament*, 1:205–7; Redlich, *Staats- und Reichsproblem*, 2:432–36, 786–87. Among Belcredi's first actions were a promise of a coronation in Prague and linguistic concessions to Czechs and Slovenes. Macartney, *Empire*, 540.

103. Kaiserfeld editorial in GT, October 27, 1865.

104. On the coordination of liberal efforts, see Brinz's letter to Carneri in *Briefe zur deutschen Politik in Österreich von 1848 bis 1918*, ed. Paul Molisch (Vienna, 1934), 21–22; Krones, *Kaiserfeld*, 230–31.

105. Franz, *Liberalismus*, 293; Kolmer, *Parlament*, 1:210–15; Rogge, *Österreich*, 2:301. The Styrian Autonomists led the way, and the Graz Diet was the first to adopt the common resolution condemning the September Manifesto. The diets in Carinthia, Lower Austria, Salzburg, Silesia, Upper Austria, and Vorarlberg followed suit. In Lower Austria, much against the will of the government representative, the liberals actually proceeded with elections for the suspended *Reichsrat*. In Carniola and Moravia, the balance among German liberals, Slavs, and conservatives was so close that neither side could pass a motion either in favor of or against the *Reichsrat* suspension. In Bohemia, where the Czech and aristocratic federalist parties held a numerical edge over the German liberals, the federalists prevailed. In addition to these cases, the diets in the

In June 1866 war broke out pitting the monarchy against Prussia and Italy. Although the Austrians managed some significant victories to defeat Italy (including a naval one), they were speedily routed by the Prussians at Königgrätz in Bohemia. Besides the questionable capacities of some of the military commanders, the Austrian army was poorly equipped with old-fashioned armaments. Plener's and Belcredi's budget cuts had taken their toll. Austria's economic situation certainly could not bear the burden of yet another war, although one argument for fighting the war was the hope of a heavy indemnity after a speedy victory to restore the monarchy's finances.[106] For the liberals, there could be only one explanation for the war's sorry outcome. The emperor's suspension of the constitution had seriously weakened the morale of the nation. The German liberals blamed the Königgrätz disaster on this political event. The Graz city council voted an address to the emperor that linked Austria's defeat to the government's halfheartedness in implementing the promised constitution. In Vienna, the liberal city council presented Francis Joseph with a similar address, which assigned responsibility for the recent "defeat in the field" to "the unfortunate policies . . . that His Majesty's advisors have pursued for a number of years now."[107] In a meeting with the emperor, Mayor Andreas Zelinka of Vienna repeated the city council's conviction "that it is the present domestic political situation that is causing the people so much worry."[108]

With the benefit of hindsight, historians have marked the summer of 1866 as that crucial moment when Austro-German political links to the rest of the Germans in Central Europe were severed. Indeed, Austria itself was expelled from the German Confederation. The explicit goal of political hegemony in Germany, which had provided the impetus for so many domestic and foreign policies since 1848, vanished overnight. Yet as long as a German liberal government ruled in Austria, as long as German cabinet ministers oversaw and regulated a German-speaking bureaucracy and middle-class Germans maintained their privileged place in Austrian society, German-speaking Austrians did not view themselves as a minority under siege. The defeat of 1866 did not

---

Bukowina, Dalmatia, Galicia, Görz, Istria, Trieste, and the ever-reactionary Tirol voted resolutions of thanks for the suspension of the *Reichsrat*.

106. Macartney, *Empire*, 541–44.

107. NFP, July 14, 1866, reproduced the text of the Graz resolution. It was followed by the Graz and Vienna addresses. The Klagenfurt city council debated and narrowly defeated a similar resolution. NFP, July 17 and 20, 1866. For the text of the Vienna address, see *Protokolle der öffentlichen Sitzungen des Gemeinderathes der k.k. Reichshaupt- und Residenzstadt Wien*, 2:1782–83, 1779–80, 1815–16 (498th session, July 17), 1866. On the mood in Vienna, Pollak, *Dreissig Jahre*, 1:173.

108. Kolmer, *Parlament*, 1:230–31. On hearing the emperor's negative reaction to the address, the Vienna city council had declared itself ready to resign en masse and to hold new elections.

provoke in the monarchy widespread outbursts of German nationalism directed against other national groups. If anything, the defeat provided German liberals with more rhetorical ammunition for their battle to establish a liberal constitutional order. Austrian Germans preferred to see their country's defeat in terms of the ongoing constitutional crisis. Certainly, many of them regretted the circumstances that had pitted them against their fellow Germans in Prussia. Some believed, however mistakenly, that Austria could eventually take its revenge on Prussia in alliance with the South German states. These hopes were not completely dashed until the final unification of Germany took place in 1871.

The most important change in German liberal attitudes in 1866 had less to do with the German states to the north and west and more to do with Austria's Magyar neighbor to the east. Dualism appeared increasingly attractive now to Austrian Germans, and even some strict centralists began to appreciate its allure. Many believed that a dualist solution would strengthen the political position of German liberalism in Austria; without Hungary, Austria would be a more fully German state in character. Kaiserfeld openly linked a dualist settlement to the maintenance of German liberal hegemony in the Austrian half of the monarchy. Stating that "there is no great power in the world today that does not have its leading nationality," he called for centralist institutions favoring Germans in Austria and Magyars in Hungary. Yet Kaiserfeld's concern was directed more toward the survival of political liberalism than toward Germanness per se, since to him the two were inextricably bound together.[109]

The most influential political leaders now engaged in a waiting game, calculating the most politically advantageous moment to announce their conversion to dualism. Supporting dualism too soon would cost the liberals valuable negotiating leverage for constitutional revision. And the eventual price of their support for dualism would be high: the restoration of the *Reichsrat* and a more progressive constitution.[110] By the fall of 1866 the political situation of the monarchy had reached yet another of its periodic stalemates. The Hungarians

109. GT, March 6, 1866; Krones, Kaiserfeld, 28–50. In a letter to the Hungarian deputy Agostin Trefort, Kaiserfeld elaborated further the advantages a dualist system offered both Magyars and Germans: "If a [single] general *Reichsrat* could have been established for the entire empire, it would have remained a battleground for national hegemony; there could have been no purely political majority in such an institution . . . . In fact, the otherwise geographically and politically disparate Slavs would have used such a *Reichsrat* as a means to unite and establish their own hegemony over the empire."

110. Molisch, *Briefe*, 32–33. Many nominal centralists supported a dualist settlement in principle yet wanted the *Reichsrat* to play an active role in the negotiations. In the fall of 1866, representatives of the Autonomists and centralists met repeatedly to try to develop a consensus position on the subject of dualism. Serious divisions persisted, with textile magnate Alfred Skene the most outspoken of the strict centralists. At one meeting in Vienna Ignaz Kuranda, himself formerly a strict centralist, pleaded with his colleagues to endorse a moderate form of dualism and seek an understanding with the Autonomists.

remained eager to negotiate but would not compromise any part of their program. Francis Joseph might have been grateful that they had not added to their demands after Austria's military defeat. Yet he remained committed to Belcredi's federalism, which in theory promised equal degrees of autonomy to every province, not simply a dualist compromise with Hungary. Francis Joseph could not accommodate both the Hungarians and the Austrian federalists within the same compromise plan. Dualism could not succeed as long as federalism remained on the agenda.

Into the complex political impasse the emperor introduced a new factor. On October 30 Francis Joseph made the Saxon Friedrich Ferdinand von Beust foreign minister. With this appointment the emperor aimed to regain some footing for Austria among the South German states, perhaps even someday to challenge Prussia's hegemony. Yet this was not to be Beust's primary achievement. Beust forced all sides out of the political stalemate. His ambition, his determined personality, and above all his position as an outsider helped him to achieve results that no Austrian or Hungarian politician could equal. Beust was no genius, and his political abilities were no greater than those of his contemporaries, despite the exalted self-evaluation he has left us in his political memoirs. Neither his intelligence nor his political instincts exceeded those of Andrassy, Belcredi, Deak, or even Schmerling. In fact, once his status as outsider had worn off somewhat, Beust's personality contributed to some egregious political blunders. In 1866, however, this aggressive newcomer made a virtue of his ignorance and managed to revive the flagging momentum of the Hungarian compromise *(Ausgleich)* negotiations.[111]

Belcredi now took the next step in his own federalist plans. Having promised to submit any settlement with Hungary to the diets for their approval, he issued a patent on January 2, 1867, announcing elections. These he hoped would return more conservative majorities to those bodies previously dominated by the German liberals. The diets would then elect deputies to a so-called extraordinary *Reichsrat*, to vote on the compromise with Hungary.[112] German liberal reaction to Belcredi's January announcement was unanimously

111. Franz Ferdinand von Beust, *Aus drei Vierteljahrhunderten* (Stuttgart, 1887), 2:84–85; Pollak, *Dreissig Jahre*, 1:183; Redlich, *Staats- und Reichsproblem*, 2:512–24. The appointment was unusual for a number of reasons. Beust had no experience with Austrian affairs and was, as Belcredi reminded him, "a foreigner, a German, and a Protestant."

112. Kolmer, *Parlament*, 1:244–45. To ensure a federalist majority in the extraordinary *Reichsrat*, Belcredi announced a change in electoral procedure: the diets would be free to elect their *Reichsrat* deputies by a vote of the entire body instead of by curia. The latter system had always ensured some representation for substantial ethnic minority groups to the *Reichsrat*, and in particular the German liberals who despite their minority status still managed to dominate the urban and chamber of commerce curias in provinces like Bohemia, Moravia, and Carniola. The new election procedure could have prevented the election of any German liberals from Bohemia to the extraordinary *Reichsrat*.

hostile. The liberal press derided the idea of an extraordinary *Reichsrat*, warning this new body would not solve any constitutional problems and demanding a restoration of the February Patent. The *Konstitutionelle Vorstadt-Zeitung* called on the public not to make itself "accomplices of the September [Patent] politicians" but to follow its legally elected leaders. Liberals across Austria agreed to boycott any extraordinary *Reichsrat*.[113]

After fourteen months of rule by paragraph thirteen, liberal anger reached new peaks, as is evident from the apocalyptic language employed by Ignaz von Plener in a letter to his son Ernst. Certainly no fiery personality, Plener called the prevention of the extraordinary *Reichsrat* "a question of life and death for Germans and friends of the constitution alike." He warned, "If Belcredi tries to call the extraordinary *Reichsrat* without the participation of the Germans, then the people of Vienna will drive the illegal body out of the city, a sight I certainly would enjoy. You know that I am usually calm about such matters, but the ruthlessness of the present ministry, which is driving the emperor and the monarchy to ruin, demands heaven's punishment, which will be forthcoming!"[114]

While Belcredi appeared undaunted by the fierce opposition to his latest plan ("If Schmerling could govern for five years without the Czechs, I ought to be able to govern for at least that long without the Germans"), Beust worried that liberal anger might subvert his delicate negotiations with Hungary. This concern gradually brought Beust closer to the Liberal parties. As a result of personal meetings with Giskra, Kaiserfeld, and Plener in January, Beust now concluded that only a *Reichsrat* with a German Liberal majority could ensure success for the Hungarian *Ausgleich*. A federalist majority would demand similar arrangements for each province and jeopardize the compromise work of the last months.[115] Consequently on February 7, both Beust and Belcredi presented their cases to the emperor. Belcredi argued for federalism while Beust advocated restoring the February Patent. When the dust had settled after the stormy four-hour session, the victor's laurels went to Beust in the form of the added responsibilities of Austrian minister president. Against his personal inclination, Francis Joseph decided to dismiss Belcredi, drop federalism, and once again to rely on the German liberal parties in the *Reichsrat*.[116]

---

113. KVZ, January 4, 1867; NFP, January 3, 1867; Molisch, *Briefe*, 36. In a letter to Pratobevera, Herbst reported there was "not the slightest disagreement that the German deputies would refuse to participate in any election to a *Reichsrat* that was not carried out strictly according to the [February Patent]," nor would anyone accept such a mandate if elected.

114. HHSA, Nachlass Plener, letter to Ernst von Plener of January 10 and January 17, 1867; also excerpted in Molisch, *Briefe*, 36. Also Krones, *Kaiserfeld*, 265.

115. Beust, *Aus drei Vierteljahrhunderten*, 2:86–87; Pollak, *Dreissig Jahre*, 1:108; HHSA, Nachlass Plener, letter to Ernst von Plener of January 5, 1867.

116. Redlich, *Staats- und Reichsproblem*, 2:559–67, gives a detailed account of the confrontation.

While this battle was fought in government circles, new elections to the diets took place. For the first time since 1861, the deputies faced their voters. The press and politicians worked hard to convey the degree to which the recent political crisis personally affected the voter, asking the public to participate in the resistance by electing liberal candidates. Candidates' speeches painted the situation in more partisan, more explicit, and even more uncompromising terms than in 1861, while the press reported approvingly on the new enthusiasm that the crisis had produced for the party. In a speech to his Brünn constituents, Carl Giskra called the extraordinary *Reichsrat* the "illegal and unconstitutional work of a new absolutist regime." The German liberal election committee in Prague assured voters that "the Germans in Bohemia will not participate in the illegal elections [for the extraordinary *Reichsrat*] and will not accept election to that body." In Vienna, a Lower Austrian Election Committee constituted itself and sponsored the first speeches of the campaign, held in the stock exchange. By January 28, the *Neue Freie Presse* was able to publish a list of all the German liberal candidates endorsed by the liberal parties across the monarchy, an organizational first for the liberals.[117]

At the local level several party leaders worked to institutionalize their political power through the officially nonpolitical associations. In the summer of 1862, for example, a group of German notables in Prague had met to found a German Casino, electing Franz Schmeykal, a lawyer from Böhmisch Leipa, as its first president. According to Schmeykal's biographer, the Casino served a dual purpose from the start, as a center for both German social life and liberal political debate. Soon it became the most influential organizational center of the German Liberal Party in Bohemia. The German Casino was exceptional for the substantial wealth and social influence of its members.[118] The memberships of comparable associations for Bürger social life reflected the more limited social makeup of the local middle classes. In a city like Salzburg, members of the urban patriciate socialized with Mittelstand artisans in organizations such as the Educational Association, intended to promote the general improvement of local education and cultural life. According to Robert Hoffmann, these associations, in tandem with the local newspapers, soon influenced public opinion in favor of liberal positions, even creating a bourgeois "mass movement." And according to Hanns Haas, the very constitutional conflicts of the 1860s themselves encouraged the growth of a politically conscious public in the Salzburg region.[119]

---

117. Kolmer, *Parlament*, 1:246–47; Molisch, *Briefe*, 36; NFP, January 6 and 28, 1867.

118. [Klaar], *Schmeykal*, 34–35; Cohen, *Politics*, 66–68. The founders and directors were lawyers, wealthy merchants, manufacturers, professors, and officials, each of whom contributed one hundred florins. By November of 1862 the association counted 632 members, and by 1870 it had grown to 1,098.

119. Hoffmann, "Bürgerliche Kommunikationsstrategien zu Beginn der liberalen Ära: Das Beispiel Salzburg," in "*Durch Arbeit, Besitz, Wissen und Gerechtigkeit*," ed. Stekl et al., 317–36;

In Vienna, the democratic *Konstitutionelle Vorstadt-Zeitung* did its part to raise the political consciousness of its readership for the elections. The newspaper offered a first prize trip to the Paris World Fair and a second prize of four gold ducats (third prize was a complete edition of Schiller) for the best essays on the question: "Which form of government in Europe best embodies the spirit of our century, and by what government measures can social and economic ills be abolished most rapidly and assuredly?" Such means encouraged the reading and voting public to consider at length the significance of casting its ballots for constitutionalism, the avowed agent of both moral and economic progress.[120]

The press endorsement of candidates did not solve growing problems of party discipline. In Vienna, with its strong tradition of political activity dating back to 1848, factionalism flourished in many districts. The *Konstitutionelle Vorstadt-Zeitung* deplored this fact and demanded that so-called spoilers retire in favor of the strongest candidate wherever possible. The newspaper also advised the Lower Austrian liberals to follow the example of the more disciplined German Liberals in Bohemia, emphasizing that the party could only triumph if voters respected the decisions of the Lower Austrian Central Election Committee.[121]

Such calls for party unity were not uncommon in 1867, although no effective political organizations yet existed that could enforce them. The highly touted Lower Austrian Central Election Committee was in reality a loose group of diet incumbents and "Viennese Bürger and industrialists." Although the committee considered endorsing candidates for each district, many members did not want to give the impression they were handing out "good conduct grades" (*Wohlverhaltungszeugnisse*) to deputies who had voted a particular way. They simply allowed all incumbents (and anyone else) to join their committee without seeking to enforce any particular candidate on local constituencies.[122]

These early organizational efforts betrayed a sense of ambivalence toward the function of a party organization. The legal restriction on political organizations was responsible to a degree for the distant attitude of some incumbents toward their voters. A private group like the Central Election Committee ul-

Hanns Haas, "Salzburger Vereinskultur im Hochliberalismus (1860–1870)," in *Vom Stadtrecht zur Bürgerbeteiligung. Ausstellungskatalog 700 Jahre Stadtrecht*, ed. Rainer Wilflinger and Peter Michael Lipburger (Salzburg, 1987), 174–98; Haas, "Trägerschichten des Liberalismus," 259.

120. KVZ, January 13, 1867.

121. KVZ, January 29, 1867; Maren Seliger, "Liberale Fraktionen im Wiener Gemeinderat 1861 bis 1895," in *Wien in der liberalen Ära*, ed. Felix Czeike, 62–90. Based on their approaches to specific social and economic issues, Seliger locates three distinct liberal groupings on the Vienna city council.

122. KVZ, January 5, 1867; NFP, January 3, 1867.

timately remained no more than a private group. It could build no official organizational ties to local constituent groups and consequently developed little sense of constituent opinions and concerns. Furthermore, liberals in some German-speaking provinces ignored local constituencies. Local incumbents rarely faced organized opposition. Individual clerics or conservative newspapers might criticize the liberals, but this only provided the latter with local targets who were not yet politically threatening. All of this would change rapidly after 1867. The growing efforts by the Catholic Church to mobilize rural voters for conservative ends and new associational laws would give the liberals new reason to compete for voters. Yet their early experience as both party and popular movement in one made the parliamentary leaders of the 1860s loath to adapt to the changing situation. It would not be easy for many of them to expand their horizons and modify their style when politics came to include activities beyond the limited scope of *Reichsrat* or diet speech-making.

The 1867 election results indicated the liberals had retained their popularity among enough voters in the German-speaking regions and generally in the urban and chamber of commerce curias to maintain their strength. Beust himself had campaigned strongly for a Liberal Party majority for the *Reichsrat*. At Herbst's request, he had signaled the Bohemian large landowners that the emperor desired a Liberal majority for the diet. The German Liberals now resumed negotiations among themselves to develop a common position on Hungary and a strategy for reforming the February Patent. The few strict centralists among them rejected the government's already concluded settlement with Hungary as an unacceptable basis for discussion. Intransigents like Skene opposed any dualist settlement at all and sought to maintain the monarchy as a unitary state. Most centralists, among them Plener and Lasser, opposed the specific financial arrangements of the compromise, considering them too onerous for Austria and too advantageous for Hungary. The majority of German liberals, however, belonged to an opportunist faction now led by Herbst and Kaiserfeld. They accepted the principles of Beust's settlement with Hungary but did not wish to agree to the settlement too easily for fear of losing their political leverage.[123]

In a gesture of good will toward the liberals, Beust now convinced Francis Joseph—not without some difficulty—to appoint Giskra president of the Chamber of Deputies. The *Neue Freie Presse* hailed this appointment as a "guarantee of Beust's intentions to work closely with the Liberal Party in the *Reichsrat*." In a scene redolent with irony as well as triumph, the tanner's son Carl Giskra, 1848 firebrand and former police suspect, welcomed the deputies

123. Beust, *Aus drei Vierteljahrhunderten*, 2:111; Kolmer, *Parlament*, 1:251; Molisch, *Briefe*, 38; FA, ct. 51, fasz. 11; NFP, February 14, 1867, *Abendblatt*. In all, the liberals elected 118 deputies of the186 who attended the *Reichsrat* in 1867 (fourteen Czechs abstained). The conservatives and federalists elected sixty-eight deputies.

back from their long absence. True to his customary rhetoric of passion, pathos, and exaggeration, the new president painted a somber picture of the recent interregnum in Austrian constitutional life. During this short but significant period without a *Reichsrat*, Austria had managed "to lose a beautiful province [Venice]," suffer the attacks of an enemy who had "reached the gates of the capital," give up its "unity of a thousand years with its motherland, the [German] Empire," sustain a financial crisis damaging to the economy and welfare of the people, and worst of all, "weakened that feeling of belonging to a great community that holds all Austrians together."[124]

In case this message was not absolutely clear, the liberals drafted a scathing reply to the speech from the throne that had opened the session. In a stern rebuke to the emperor, they reiterated their belief that material progress could only flow from constitutional reform: "The most important matters of state were decided without the people's representatives exercising their necessary participation and control, thereby severely damaging the credit of the *Reich*, which in turn had grave material consequences for everyone." The deputies served notice that constitutional revision could no longer be postponed. Ministerial responsibility, revision of Paragraph Thirteen, a catalog of civil rights, and a revision of the Concordat were no longer subject to negotiation. They represented the absolute minimum price for liberal assent to the *Ausgleich* and cooperation with the government. In the spring of 1867, the liberal parties seemed poised to attain their most cherished political demands: the creation of a truly constitutional state with adequate guarantees of civil rights for its citizens.[125]

The conflicts that pitted the liberals against the Schmerling and Belcredi cabinets had produced a more intense sense of party identity among the liberals by 1867. The liberals' legislation in the 1860s, even when it failed to become law, gradually altered the traditional ways in which economic, legal, political, and social issues were conceptualized and addressed in Austria. Their version of the *Rechtsstaat* became the standard against which political reform was to be measured. Their concept of communal autonomy replaced a bureaucratic one in shaping legal and political relations in towns across Austria. Their arguments either for or against free trade determined how economic issues would be argued for the next twenty years. A new, self-confident liberal ideology, derived both from the idealism of 1848 and from the bureaucratic pragmatism of the 1850s, increasingly dominated both press and parliamentary institutions. This discourse made clear moral divisions in the world, leaving no question about where each player stood. It demanded fulfillment of the liberals' program as a

---

124. NFP, May 15, 1867; Beust, *Aus drei Vierteljahrhunderten*, 2:112; SPHA 4, May 20, 1867; Kolmer, *Parlament*, 1:256.

125. Kolmer, *Parlament*, 1:260–62.

moral imperative. The liberals' popularity with the public grew out of their success at portraying these early constitutional battles in moral terms, battles in which the Bürger public participated vicariously through press reports and informal associational discussions. Yet there were potential limits on the ability of this discourse to inform future debates. If the liberals' popularity derived from the specific demands they made of the state, what would happen if those demands were met? Once a constitution had been secured, could the liberals transfer the moral power of their rhetoric of the 1860s to the new challenges of economy and society in the 1870s?

CHAPTER 4

Building a Liberal State

> From this day forward we live under a constitution. The ruins of the bureaucratic police state lie at our feet.
>
> *Konstitutionelle Vorstadt-Zeitung* (1867)[1]

> Just because you were born human beings does not mean that you have any right to a vote. You will earn this right [only] when we see that you have a real interest in it, an interest indicated by your payment of direct taxes.
>
> Carl Giskra (1868)[2]

Since 1860, the liberals had advanced their general program resolutely against opposition from the monarch, the bureaucracy, the Catholic Church, and much of the nobility. Finally in December 1867, after years of struggle, the emperor ratified a liberal constitution and appointed Austria's first parliamentary cabinet, the so-called Bürger Ministry (*Bürgerministerium*). Their bitter experiences under both Schmerling and Belcredi regimes led liberals in the press to offer a cautious assessment of the chances that the new constitution would survive. Nevertheless, many believed they stood on the threshold of a new golden age that promised unlimited individual freedoms, social progress, and economic expansion. The long-overdue institution of a *Rechtsstaat*, the implementation of the new industrial code of 1859, and substantial reforms in education and religion would quickly revolutionize Austrian society.

This chapter examines the new constitution and government as a way to explore three related questions about liberal ideology and bourgeois influence in Austria. First, given the opportunity to reform Austria's internal system of government, what kind of political order did the liberals actually create? Second, what specific meaning did the liberals of 1867 give to their general principles, such as progress, freedom, and order, as they went about constructing

1. KVZ, December 12, 1867.

2. Carl Giskra, 1868, quoted in Wilhelm Angerstein, *Österreichs parlamentarische Grössen* (Leipzig, 1872), 20.

and then governing the *Rechtsstaat*? Finally, what do the liberals' accomplishments reveal about the extent of Bürger political influence in a state traditionally dominated by other social groups like the regional nobility and imperial bureaucracy? Historians have written surprisingly little on the 1867 laws, preferring, in the words of Gerald Stourzh, "to concentrate their efforts on the countless reform projects for the transformation of the monarchy." Available historical discussion of the laws conveys neither the liberals' own understanding of what they hoped to accomplish with the constitution nor an evaluation of their relative success in establishing the bourgeoisie as a significant contender for political power in the monarchy.[3]

Writing Their Constitution

In the spring of 1867, several factors increased the liberals' relative bargaining power with the state, enabling them to impose a constitutional revision. Most notable among these were the emperor's desire for a speedy conclusion of the *Ausgleich* with Hungary and his replacement of the federalist Belcredi with the more sympathetic Beust. Nevertheless, liberal unwillingness to endorse the *Ausgleich* too soon left an impression of vacillation and disunity within the parties. Some stalwarts like Lasser and Plener also complained that they were being kept out of the main negotiations because of their centralist sympathies. In particular, Plener chided Herbst for being "outwardly friendly to the *Ausgleich* while declaring it an impossibility in private conversation." Leopold von Hasner also voiced centralist reservations about the *Ausgleich*, with the result that he was suddenly appointed to the House of Lords to remove him from the debate in the Chamber.[4]

Kaiserfeld too expressed pessimism concerning the party political situation in letters to his wife in Styria. Assailing the liberals' apparent lack of party discipline, Kaiserfeld had nothing but admiration and respect for Julius Andrassy and the other Hungarian politicians he met during this period. "If only we had similar people among us!" he wrote to his wife in May. "With us things are going badly. Irritability, poor judgment, and boundless vanity are the essence of our character." Yet Kaiserfeld did not perceive the significantly different circumstances that separated the Hungarians from their neophyte Aus-

3. Gerald Stourzh, "Die österreichische Dezemberverfassung von 1867," *Österreich in Geschichte und Literatur* 12 (January 1968): 2. Two excellent evaluations of one element of this period, Francis Joseph's own relationship to the Bürger Ministry, are Fritz Fellner's articles, "Kaiser Franz Josephs Haltung in der Krise des Bürgerministeriums. Nach Aufzeichnungen und Briefen Ignaz von Pleners," MÖSA 6 (1953): 327–37 and "Kaiser Franz Joseph und das Parlament, Materialien zur Geschichte der Innenpolitik Österreichs in den Jahren 1867-1873," MÖSA 9 (1956): 287–347.

4. Molisch, *Briefe*, 39–40; Hasner, *Denkwürdigkeiten*, 86–88.

trian counterparts. The Hungarians had the advantage of unitary administrative traditions and of a far more unified political nation.[5]

The liberal press also interpreted as a sign of political weakness the liberals' unwillingness to commit themselves one way or another on the question of the *Ausgleich*. Throughout 1867, the press lamented an apparent lack of discipline among the liberal parties, fearing that this would undermine the chances for success of the constitutional revisions. "Instead of all those who share basic beliefs joining firmly with one another and striving to achieve the triumph of their ideas in an organized partnership, everyone fluctuates . . . and instead of [creating] disciplined parties, the deputies move in disorderly masses."[6] From the point of view of constitutional reform, however, the consequences of this apparent lack of discipline were not as dire as either Kaiserfeld or the press painted them. During the 1867 session, only the *Ausgleich* created any real internal disagreement. Since this issue had already been settled by the emperor, the liberals could afford a few symbolic quarrels over it. The parties had far less difficulty achieving a broad consensus regarding their most important challenge, the revision of Austria's constitutional laws.

On June 17, Beust presented the *Reichsrat* with the drafts of four constitutional laws. Two of these made the necessary constitutional alterations required by the *Ausgleich*, while the others revised the hated paragraph thirteen and established the concept of ministerial responsibility to the *Reichsrat*. The liberals welcomed these concessions but had more ambitious plans. Taking matters into their own hands, within a week they had created a special constitutional committee to evaluate the government's drafts and to draw up their own set of constitutional proposals. This action gave them greater control over the reform agenda and made them less dependent on proposals from the government.[7]

The new commission swiftly revised the government's proposals for the new emergency paragraph and the law on ministerial responsibility with an eye toward strengthening the constitutional position of the *Reichsrat* vis-à-vis the emperor. Both houses quickly passed this key legislation, and the emperor sanctioned it before the end of July. "Only a few years ago we would have celebrated a ministerial responsibility law like the one passed today in the Chamber

5. Krones, *Kaiserfeld*, 271.

6. NFP, May 7, 1867.

7. Kolmer, *Parlament*, 1:276–84; Stourzh, "österreichische Dezemberverfassung," 1–16 and "Die Gleichberechtigung der Nationalitäten und die österreichische Dezemberverfassung von 1867," *Der österreichische-ungarische Ausgleich von 1867*, ed. Berger, 186–218. The committee of thirty-six numbered twenty-nine German liberals, including Brestel, Herbst, Kaiserfeld, Plener, and Rechbauer, five Poles, and the Slovene leader Louis Toman. The only Ruthene to sit in the *Reichsrat* was included on the commission by the liberals to demonstrate their liberality toward the other nationalities and to embarrass the Poles. Many of these deputies had served in the Kremsier *Reichstag* nineteen years before, and two of them, Brestel and the Pole Florian Ziemialkowski, had even sat on that body's constitutional committee.

as a triumph of constitutionalism," noted the *Neue Freie Presse*. "And today such a law was quietly passed, as if it were some [minor change] and not an institutional guarantee of the highest constitutional privilege, [which] is shared by hardly any other European state."[8]

The constitutional commission then elected a subcommittee of seven, which assumed the greater task of drafting further constitutional revisions. As in 1849 at Kremsier, Rudolf Brestel played a leading role on the subcommittee. In July he formulated a working paper to guide the efforts of the full commission, which proposed five laws to implement the *Ausgleich* and to revise the Austrian constitution. These laws enumerated the rights of Austrian citizenship, guaranteed the separation of judicial authority from the administration, elaborated administrative and executive powers, and instituted a supreme court to rule on potential constitutional conflicts. The liberals hoped that, taken together, these measures would finally bring the elusive *Rechtsstaat* into being and diminish any future possibility of arbitrary rule by the executive and the bureaucracy.[9]

The broad scope of these laws immediately raised the question for several deputies of whether the *Reichsrat* was in fact drafting a brand new constitution or simply reforming existing laws. Brestel's working paper left little doubt that the liberals viewed their task strictly as a revision of existing constitutional laws, the October Diploma and February Patent. Sensitive to accusations in the Czech press and from the federalist opposition that they had arrogated to themselves the powers of a constituent assembly, the liberals did not want to expose their new document to charges of illegitimacy. It was bad enough that the Czechs did not participate and that the federalists and clerical conservatives opposed almost every one of the new reforms.[10]

The critical task of drawing up a preliminary bill of citizens' rights went to subcommittee member Eduard Sturm, a lawyer from Brünn. In formulating his draft for Austria, Sturm examined bills of rights from the Frankfurt Parliament of 1848, the Kremsier constitutional committee of 1849, and from the Belgian, Dutch, and Prussian constitutions. The resulting proposal created an Austrian citizenship for the first time. Citizens were considered equal before the law, and they were allowed the right to settle anywhere in Austria. They were guaranteed immunity of person, property, and mail and an equal opportunity to

8. NFP, July 11, 1867; Stourzh, "Österreichische Dezemberverfassung," 5.

9. PA, Verfassungsausschuss, ct. 1, 2/a; Stourzh, "Österreichische Dezemberverfassung," 5. Brestel, Froschauer (subcommittee chair), Kaiserfeld, Klier, Kuranda, Sturm, and Ziemialkowski made up the subcommittee. Later, Kremer and von Waser joined its ranks after Kaiserfeld and Ziemialkowski were elected to the committee that negotiated the financial settlement with Hungary.

10. PA, Verfassungsausschuss, ct. 1, 2/a.

compete for state offices. This bill of rights allowed freedom of belief and public worship and granted to every citizen the same civil rights no matter what the individual's religious beliefs. The law also guaranteed the rights of recognized religions to administer their own internal affairs but warned that, "like every association," they were subject to the higher authority of the state. In a pointed reference to the institutionalized privileges enjoyed by the Catholic Church, Rechbauer amended this clause to state further that no citizen who did not wish to could be compelled to take part in a public religious function.[11]

The constitutional laws also abolished press censorship, instituted trial by jury, and guaranteed freedom of speech, of education, and of instruction. Other reform efforts failed but not without vigorous debate. Herbst, Mühlfeld, and Kuranda, for example, argued strenuously, if unsuccessfully, against the death penalty. Another reform effort that failed was a repeal of existing laws criminalizing homosexual acts, proposed by Minister of Justice Ritter von Komers in June 1867.[12] In most cases, the new constitutional pledges that passed had to be supplemented by legislative initiative. The most controversial of these initiatives followed in 1868 when, over the powerful objections of the clerical opposition, the liberals passed three laws designed to free Austrian society from the fetters of the Concordat. The first of these laws regulated the relation between church and state, the second introduced civil marriage, and the third greatly diminished church influence over the schools. With these laws the *Reichsrat* laid the basis for later reforms designed to lessen the influence of the Catholic Church on society and place responsibility for education more firmly in the hands of secular authorities.[13]

In July the *Reichsrat* passed a law granting the long-desired freedoms of association and assembly to Austrian citizens. In apparent contrast to their open

---

11. HHSA, Nachlass Plener, ct. 44; PA, Verfassungsausschuss, ct. 1, 2/a, protocol of committee meeting, September 21, 1867; Stourzh, "Österreichische Dezemberverfassung," 10. This was the only place in the constitution that referred to "Austria." Formally the new constitution applied simply to those kingdoms and lands represented in the *Reichsrat*. Out of concern for the committee's legitimacy, Eduard Sturm advised that the commission follow the example of Stadion's ill-fated 1849 constitution as closely as possible. The emperor could hardly object to civil rights and structural reforms that his own octroyed (yet never implemented) constitution had guaranteed in 1849. The legally recognized religions were Catholic, Calvinist, Greek, Jewish, and Lutheran.

12. KVZ, July 17, 1867; Hubert Kennedy, *Ulrichs: The Life and Times of Karl Heinrich Ulrichs, Pioneer of the Modern Gay Movement* (Boston, 1988), 148, 162–63. After lengthy debate the committee voted to retain the death penalty. When Herbst took over the justice ministry in 1868, he rejected Komers's reform proposal and decided to maintain the existing law against homosexual acts.

13. Kolmer, *Parlament*, 1:304–6, 324–27; Vocelka, *Verfassung oder Konkordat?*, 68–90 .

concept of religious and educational freedom, however, the liberals placed heavy restrictions on the rights of association and assembly. In line with traditional associational procedure, political associations would have to apply to the state for approval of their statutes, and a police officer had to attend all their open meetings. Women, minors, and foreigners were barred from membership in political clubs, and these groups were not allowed to found branches in more than one locality.[14]

The liberal press criticized the law's inconsistencies and restrictiveness, interpreting these as signs that the Beust government (which had presented the original draft) still did not trust Austrian citizens. The *Neue Freie Presse* ridiculed the clause that restricted membership in political clubs, conjecturing that "foreigners must have been responsible for Austria's past problems like the revolutions of 1848" and pointing out to its readers that under the new law not even Beust (a foreigner) could join a political association. The *Konstitutionelle Vorstadt-Zeitung* criticized the way the text stated "associations are allowed to be formed," instead of proclaiming this as a fundamental right of the people. The paper further accused the government of using the constitution to reimpose a policy more appropriate to the absolutism of earlier years. "If two hundred Bürger or workers wish to create an association, a single fearful, intolerant, or reactionary bureaucrat will be able to deny it in the name of the public good!" Nevertheless the paper called on its readers to "Form Associations!" hoping that the progressive citizens of Vienna (including workers "who also have rights") would rush to found democratic political clubs.[15]

Why in 1867 did the liberals limit the right of association for which they had fought so hard since 1848? Believing themselves to be the new governing class, liberals gave themselves leeway to control potentially dangerous situations: lingering memories of the violence of 1848 combined with the growth of new workers' organizations led the liberals to restrict the freedom of association. Whenever possible, as we will see, liberals used their government powers to limit the workers' abilities to constitute themselves as a class. They harassed working-class organizations by limiting the right of association, and they consistently denied workers' demands for political representation. In redesigning the boundaries of citizenship in 1867, the liberals clearly worked to increase the rights of those who were already enfranchised and not to draw the unenfranchised into public life.

In fact, most of the new constitutional laws required the resolution of some contradiction inherent to liberal ideology. In most cases the liberals had to balance the broad freedoms embodied in their universalist principles against

---

14. Hugelmann, *Österreichischen Vereins-und Versammlungsrechte*, 64–66.

15. NFP, July 7, 1867; KVZ, November 23, 1867. In the next weeks, the latter paper devoted substantial space to describing the founding of various new political associations.

the need to protect property and the social order. As in 1848, two very different struggles determined the particular resolution in each case. The first of these struggles challenged the dominance of an identifiable enemy, the so-called feudal classes who benefited from all the benighted, particularist, irrational restrictions and petty hierarchies of the old order. This battle had unleashed a veritable explosion of emancipatory rhetoric in 1848, in which both the liberal press and *Reichsrat* deputies continued to indulge themselves more than twenty years later. In this war, the liberals spoke for a universal political nation trying desperately to free itself from the fetters of ignorance and economic backwardness imposed by the Catholic Church and noble privilege.

The second struggle in this two-front war pitted the liberals against the emerging interest politics of the organized working classes. In the mid-nineteenth century this struggle was understood in much different terms from the open war on so-called feudal reaction discussed above. Starting in 1848 the liberals had to fight to control the defections of lower-class groups from their self-proclaimed sponsorship of the universal nation. The emerging opposition of workers' groups in the 1860s confused and embarrassed the liberals. They often attributed this opposition to the dark influence of conservative or Catholic reformers who had seduced workers with simplistic promises of material gain, made at the expense of the good of the whole community.[16] The liberals adopted a rhetoric at times condescending, at other times disciplinarian, to persuade the workers to adhere to the interests of the nation as a whole as the liberals saw them. This rhetoric demanded of the workers that they submit to liberal tutelage until such time as they had gained economic independence and the ability to make mature political judgments themselves. Most liberals believed that the long-term interests of all producers, including the workers, converged in the liberals' program of political freedom combined with an unrestricted internal labor market.

The anticlerical passions of many liberals and their obsession with establishing a secular school system show us how they understood the connections between their struggle against the old regime and their concern for finding a solution to the threats from below. The popularization of empirical science, particularly Charles Darwin's theories of evolution, bolstered the liberals' claim that society itself could be studied and manipulated. The free schools could mold responsible citizens by teaching them to internalize the rational behavior so necessary to the reproduction of capitalist relations. Only the schools could liberate students from the false values of ignorance, superstition, and exaggerated piety inculcated by the church hierarchy. Only the schools could

16. Wilhelm Wadl, *Liberalismus und soziale Frage in Österreich. Deutsch liberale Reaktionen und Einflüsse auf die frühe österreichische Arbeiterbewegung 1867–1879* (Vienna,1987), 56–57. Wadl characterizes the fear of a Catholic worker alliance as "die liberale Urangst."

take students from all social or ethnic backgrounds and make them citizens who shared a common Austrian identity.[17]

This concern for social engineering may appear to contradict the liberal emphasis on individual achievement. Nevertheless, the reader should recall that free will itself was almost always qualified in liberal theory by a presumption of its user's education or property ownership. The presence of either or both of these conditions indicated that the individual in question was a reasoning being, one who could be trusted to use freedom properly. A radical such as John Stuart Mill still believed that, "Liberty, as a principle, has no application to any state of things anterior to the time when mankind have become capable of being improved by free and equal discussion." Liberty, he thought, could not be applied to those who have not attained "the maturity of their faculties," such as children, dependents, and "backward states of society in which the race itself may be considered in its nonage." Liberals might argue about how to determine the line between those who were reasonable and those who weren't, but they did not question the necessity of that boundary itself.[18]

The concern to create a single, progressive Austrian identity as a means to bring Austria's disparate social, ethnic, and national groups into harmony, surfaced once again in discussions surrounding the law on the linguistic rights of the citizen. Sturm and the subcommittee presented the constitutional commission with a draft that followed the general principles of linguistic equality established in the Kremsier draft of 1849: "All national groups within the state are equal, and each one has the inviolable right to preserve and to cultivate its nationality and language." Yet the men of 1867 added some detailed qualifications upon which one influential group insisted.

The Bohemian liberals demanded an explicit constitutional guarantee that no German speaker would ever be forced to learn the Czech language in school. Recalling Belcredi's failed attempt to impose a Czech language requirement on administrators in linguistically mixed areas of Bohemia, the Bohemian liberals vowed to oppose any linguistic settlement that did not take their special interests into consideration. They added a clause stating that, "in those provinces inhabited by several nationalities, public educational institutions should be set up so that without being forced to learn a second language, those nationalities that are in the minority have adequate opportunity for an education in their own language."[19] The addition of this sentence to article 19 may have pleased the Bohemian Germans in the short run, but it subverted their efforts twenty years

17. Wadl, *Liberalismus*, 161–62. Darwin was popular in people's libraries (see below, ch. 5).

18. Mill, *On Liberty*, 484–85.

19. Stourzh, *Die Gleichberechtigung der Nationalitäten in der Verfassung und Verwaltung Österreichs 1848–1918* (Vienna, 1985), 200–201. Calling Belcredi's statute a *Sprachenzwang* or forced language law, was of course only the German liberal interpretation of a law that many Czech nationalists saw as a question of fairness.

later to institutionalize German as Austria's official state language, and it freed other national groups from the necessity of learning German.

The Slovene leader Louis Toman offered a further amendment to the law on language stating that "the equality of every normal provincial (*landesüblich*) language in schools, official posts, and public life is guaranteed by the state." The liberals reluctantly accepted this amendment, hoping to conciliate the Slavs and to ensure sufficient support for the Bohemian Germans' amendment. The liberals also approved Toman's suggestion in order to head off a more worrisome Polish amendment giving the provincial diets sole responsibility for implementing linguistic equality. This Polish suggestion would have allowed the various majority nationalities in the individual diets to define and implement legal equality among ethnic groups. In fact, it was left to the new court system to decide what constituted an eligible language or ethnic group to begin with and how to apply the laws guaranteeing linguistic and ethnic equality to those eligible groups.[20]

As it turned out, various political groups interpreted the constitutional pledge of the law on linguistic equality quite differently. Most liberals believed that by recognizing the linguistic rights of non-German speakers at the local level, this law ended all conflict around nationality issues in Austria. The liberals took a conflict involving differences over language use and implemented an apparently pluralist solution, one that seemed to ensure at least a legal equality of all languages in use at a local level. However, for all its guarantees of equality, this solution still imposed a significant degree of homogeneity on a linguistically heterogeneous population. As we have seen, the liberals justified the exclusive use of German in the bureaucracy and military with functional arguments. For the sake of bureaucratic efficiency, non-German speakers whose ambitions reached beyond local horizons could only gain social advancement by learning a second language. Many liberals also argued that since the German language had attained a higher degree of civilization, measured in global terms, than any other language in use in the monarchy, it should therefore remain the official language of the state.

This discussion should again alert the reader to contradictions in the constitutional provisions that seem to result from different liberal ideological imperatives. The new Austrian citizenship guaranteed the individual a high degree of personal freedom from interference by the state or the privileged

20. Stourzh, *Gleichberechtigung*, 204–5; Dietmar Baier, *Sprache und Recht im alten Österreich. Artikel 19 des Staatsgrundgesetzes vom 21. Dezember 1867, seine Stellung im System des Grundrechte und seine Ausgestaltung durch die oberstgerichtliche Rechtsprechung* (Munich, 1983). Deeming it inappropriate "to promise something that might be accomplished wherever feasible but that should not be unconditionally guaranteed in advance," Hasner altered Toman's amendment when it reached the House of Lords by changing the word "guaranteed" to "recognized."

classes. At the same time, the very idea of inventing a common Austrian citizenship betrays the liberals' intentions to forge a single identity that could transcend local forms of difference. It is true that civil and linguistic rights gave to individuals a considerable local freedom of action. However, restrictions on associations, the continued privileging of the German language, the school reforms, and the attempt to exercise a form of tutelage over the working classes all worked to impose on the individual a specific version of an Austrian identity. That identity was not a random one but rather a particular Bürger ideal. Liberal theory may have celebrated the strengths that diversity among citizens contributed to society as a whole, but liberal practice worked to erase diversity in its conceptualization of citizenship.[21]

The constitutional commission considered several other amendments to the February Patent designed to strengthen the foundations of the *Rechtsstaat*. One amendment created both a high court of administrative justice and a supreme court. The administrative court was formally established in 1876 to hear cases involving bureaucratic infringements of individual rights. The supreme court addressed cases involving general constitutional principle. The existence of both courts ensured the separation of judicial from administrative power, long desired by liberal critics of the bureaucracy. According to the laws that established this separation, bureaucrats, cabinet ministers, and even the emperor himself were now obliged to swear an oath to protect the basic constitutional laws of "the kingdoms and lands represented in the *Reichsrat*."[22]

The recent *Reichsrat* suspension of 1865–67 caused the committee to add a clause specifying that "the emperor convenes the *Reichsrat* annually in January." This measure ensured parliament's ability to oversee critical annual decisions, not simply to be informed of them later on by the cabinet. Brestel also favored bringing the *Reichsrat* closer in size to the 446-member Hungarian Parliament. Other deputies raised the possibility of having *Reichsrat* deputies elected directly by the voters instead of by the diets. Carl Rechbauer even suggested scrapping the *Herrenhaus* completely and replacing it with a Federal House (*Länderhaus*), which would represent the individual provincial governments.[23] None of these last three suggestions gained a serious hearing.

21. There is a striking similarity between the concerns of Austrian liberals to create a unitary citizenry and the fears expressed by many contemporary academics and politicians in the United States, that too much regard for cultural differences among groups will result in a dangerous weakening of the bonds that hold the nation together. See the essays of bell hooks in *Black Looks: Race and Representation* (Boston, 1992).

22. Baier, *Sprache und Recht*, 45–54, 129–30; Stourzh, "Österreichische Dezemberverfassung," 12–13.

23. Fellner, "Kaiser Franz Josef und das Parlament," 297; PA, Verfassungsausschuss, ct. 1, 2/a; Stourzh, "Österreichische Dezemberverfassung," 8. The clause was amended by the *Herrenhaus* to read: "The emperor convenes the *Reichsrat* annually, when possible in January."

According to the earlier constitutions, the diets regulated the election of the *Reichsrat* deputies, in proportion to provincial population and tax contribution statistics. The liberals could not increase the size of the central *Reichsrat*, nor could they introduce direct elections to it, without infringing on the rights of those diets. This explains why liberals preferred not to state explicitly what they believed implicitly, namely, that in cases of disagreement between the two, the diets would always be subordinate to the *Reichsrat*.

Throughout the summer and fall of 1867, an Austrian deputation met with its Hungarian counterpart to hammer out the final details of the *Ausgleich* legislation. The financial agreement with Hungary turned first and foremost on the issue of how much each half of the new dual monarchy would contribute to fund the common institutions. To the annoyance of the Austrians, the Hungarians repudiated any responsibility for the state debt incurred during the last twenty years of what they considered to have been illegal absolutist rule. Other aspects of the *Ausgleich* like industrial tariff policy caused considerable disagreement as well. The liberal press frequently harped on the sacrifice everyone seemed to require of Austria, given the low quota negotiated by the Hungarians. The press found some consolation, however, in the fact that Austrian taxes would now contribute to maintaining purely Austrian institutions instead of financing the whole monarchy as they had during the years of Hungarian passive resistance. Austria would also be at liberty to reform its tax system without Hungarian interference.[24]

The liberals who dominated the Austrian delegation came away from this first round of negotiations with Hungary believing themselves to be the financial losers. Having compromised more than they would have liked for the sake of achieving their domestic reform program, the liberals vowed to gain a better position for Austria when the *Ausgleich* agreement came up for renewal in ten years. Given the differences between the two political systems and between the two political nations, such a reversal would be difficult to achieve. The very liberality of Austria's new constitution toward its diverse national and social groups made it unlikely that the Austrian side could present a united front in the near future. By contrast the more illiberal political system in Hungary ensured that nation's leaders a greater degree of political unity.

During these six months of constitutional revision, fears that the constitutional reforms would somehow be sabotaged at the last minute dominated liberal attitudes toward the emperor and Beust. These suspicions were so great that during the final debate over the Hungarian *Ausgleich* law, Rechbauer proposed that the *Reichsrat* tie the *Ausgleich* directly to the other constitutional revisions. According to this measure, the emperor's desired *Ausgleich* could only take effect simultaneously with the other constitutional reforms. On

24. KVZ, July 12, 1867; NFP, December 13, 1867.

December 21, therefore, the emperor sanctioned the entire bundle of legislation, and Austria entered a new constitutional era.[25]

The Viennese liberal and democratic press reacted enthusiastically to the *Reichsrat*'s accomplishments taken as a whole, despite its earlier criticism of Liberal Party compromise or hesitation on specific reforms. The *Neue Freie Presse* noted with satisfaction on December 21 that "in a few hours the emperor will have sanctioned a constitution, filled to an extent we would never have dreamed (we have to admit) with constitutional freedoms!" Adding that the Concordat's days were clearly numbered, the paper even admitted on the sensitive subject of the *Ausgleich* that, "Whatever was to be achieved inside a dualistic system for the liberal part[ies], has been achieved." Warning that it would now require an exceptional degree of work, patience, and courage on all sides to make the new system work, the paper recalled the many constitutional disappointments of the last seven years. "We cannot fool ourselves about the reason why the masses are not inspired to jubilation over this completed work. Austria has greeted new [constitutional] eras too often [in the last years]."[26]

"From this day forward we live in a constitutional state," rejoiced the more democratically inclined *Konstitutionelle Vorstadt-Zeitung*, "the ruins of the bureaucratic police state lie at our feet." Pointing out the fundamental difference between the old system and the new, the paper concluded that "we no longer obey any [absolutist] authorities, only the law." The *Vorstadt-Zeitung* admitted that it too had often complained of the halfheartedness of the reforms and warned of even more difficult battles that lay ahead: revoking the Concordat, broadening the franchise, introducing direct elections to the *Reichsrat*. Nevertheless, the new list of civil rights meant that every "citizen can raise his head proudly as a free man." These laws would ensure the rise of "a fresh, new movement that would lead civil society to the realization of truly democratic principles."[27]

Later that same week after much difficult negotiation (mainly with Francis Joseph and Herbst) Beust was able to announce to the public the successful formation of Austria's first parliamentary cabinet, popularly known as the Bürger Ministry. This cabinet was a parliamentary government in two senses. First, its members were all deputies in the *Reichsrat*. Second, the majority of the new ministers represented the liberal political majority in the *Reichsrat*. Liberal Prince Carl Auersperg of Bohemia headed the new cabinet, while Beust was

25. Stourzh, "Österreichische Dezemberverfassung," 1–2. What is often referred to as the constitution of 1867 for convenience sake was really a bundle of six fundamental state laws and the law that guaranteed they would all be issued simultaneously. These technically amended the existing October Diploma and February Patent.

26. NFP, December 12, 1867.

27. KVZ, December 12, 1867.

promoted to the position of foreign minister for the monarchy as a whole, with the special title of *Reichskanzler*. The other liberal deputies whose social status gave the cabinet its nickname were Johann N. Berger (minister without portfolio), Rudolf Brestel (finance), Carl Giskra (interior), Leopold von Hasner (religion and education), Eduard Herbst (justice), and Ignaz von Plener (commerce). Two other ministers who were neither Bürger nor liberal rounded out the cabinet: Count Eduard Taaffe (Austrian defense minister and vice chair of the cabinet) and the Pole, Count Adam Potocki (agriculture).[28]

Enthusiastic well-wishers published articles and poetry celebrating the cabinet ministers as modest Bürger whose ascent into governing circles reflected the new political power of the Bürgertum. "The times are calling you! These are days of creation / Create! Produce! Your time burns bright!"[29] The press fostered a short-lived cult around the Bürger ministers, explaining their historic significance to the public through all manner of symbolic imagery and written text. Their portraits adorned newspapers: dressed in black suits, three of them wearing professorial eyeglasses, serious with a touch of defiance, they gazed firmly ahead to the future. That image suggested an internal fortitude that had helped them to overcome the obstacles of the past nineteen years, their awareness of the grave tasks that lay ahead, and their determination to conquer the highest reaches of the state for the people they represented.

The liberal newspapers also resorted to imagery culled from accounts of the ancient Roman Republic to create a contrast between the sincerity of the unpretentious yet articulate Bürger, called to serve their fatherland, and the feudal pretension of the men who had traditionally surrounded the monarch. The *Konstitutionelle Vorstadt-Zeitung* hailed Giskra in particular, calling him "at every time the very embodiment of German Austrian liberalism." The paper did not doubt the tanner's son's pride in his modest Bürger origins. Dealing "with excellencies and highnesses all the time" would not change his simple manner or his honest outlook. "He has," proclaimed the *Vorstadt-Zeitung,* "the confidence of all the people." German liberal press and liberal public alike considered these men, who had themselves authored the new constitution, to be the surest security for its successful implementation and the continuation of progressive reform.[30]

---

28. Beust, *Aus drei-vierteljahrhunderten*, 2:162–67; Molisch, *Briefe*, 45–46; Pollak, *Dreissig Jahre*, 1:219–24; Redlich, *Staats- und Reichsproblem*, 2:655–61; Rudolf, "Karl Auersperg," 76–112. Beust tried to present Auersperg as a political conservative to a skeptical Francis Joseph. As a devoted party man, however, Auersperg would not assume the cabinet presidency before Herbst and Giskra had agreed to serve in the cabinet. Not surprisingly, Beust also had some difficulty persuading Francis Joseph to accept Giskra as minister of the interior.

29. Krones, *Kaiserfeld*, 303.

30. KVZ, December 21, 1867.

The Bürger Govern, 1867–70

The Bürger ministry governed for two years before it collapsed, beset by controversy and frustration. Its efforts in most areas have not been judged a resounding success. Historians have explained the government's short and rocky life span by enumerating the personal antipathies and rivalries that dominated relations among the individual ministers. Carl Auersperg's optimistic "all for one and one for all" motto for the cabinet was gradually replaced by the cynical Berger's punning observation, "how can we support one another when we can't even bear one another?" The fact that the ministers spent as much time sparring among themselves as they did working together is born out by a survey of cabinet protocols and contemporary memoirs. Herbst and Giskra apparently regarded each other with jealous suspicion: after Auersperg and later Taaffe resigned from the cabinet, each took pains to prevent the other from being named minister president. And so great was Berger's disregard for the popular Herbst and Giskra that he eventually aligned himself with Taaffe and Potocki. According to the others, Berger spent his time writing sarcastic observations about his pompous colleagues on scraps of paper during cabinet meetings. Plener viewed the three of them as woefully inexperienced and occasionally disrespectful of the emperor, claiming that alone of the cabinet liberals, he commanded the Emperor's trust. All four—Plener, Berger, Giskra, and Herbst—seem to have had little regard for Hasner's capacities.[31]

Nevertheless, it would be a mistake to blame the cabinet's ultimate failure on the personal foibles of its members. Nor should we attribute much significance to the other common argument made by historians, that the new ministers were simply too used to being in constant opposition to the government and therefore unable to act responsibly once they had gained power themselves. The problem was much bigger than any of these explanations suggests. The act of legislating a constitution at a moment when the emperor was politically vulnerable did not by itself change the social balance of power within the monarchy. The liberals would have to struggle against competing social forces to institutionalize the *Rechtsstaat* in all areas of public life. In this fight they could not rely on the monarch. Francis Joseph was no more committed to this particular constitutional experiment than he had been to any other one. He may have signed the new laws into being, but he continued to rule as he had before, often seeking advice outside the cabinet, negotiating policies behind his ministers' backs, and undercutting their ability to act effectively. Beust too continued

31. Fritz Fellner, "Kaiser Franz Josephs Haltung," 327–37; Haintz, "Giskra," 69–198; Heinrich Pollak, *Dreissig Jahre*, 2:129–36; Samuel Sandler, "Das Bürgerministerium, 1868–1870" (Ph.D. diss., University of Vienna, 1930), 36, 69–70; 106, Rogge, *Österreich von Villagos*, 3:84; Rudolf, "Karl Auersperg."

in his earlier role as all-around advisor to the emperor, meddling in internal affairs, which he had so recently (and so successfully) dominated. This approach accorded well with the traditional way in which Francis Joseph had conducted state affairs.[32]

Liberal cabinet members often learned, to their surprise and annoyance, that they lacked the emperor's support or, worse, that his outside advisors were interfering in domestic issues where their official competence did not extend. In particular, Francis Joseph often communicated privately with Foreign Minister Beust and Defense Minister Taaffe on domestic policy matters, and both of them negotiated with the regime's opponents behind the backs of their liberal colleagues in the cabinet. As a result, individual liberal ministers and on occasion a majority in the cabinet threatened to resign over the emperor's apparent lack of support for his own government.

Significant social groups also fought the Bürger Ministry and the constitution. These included the Catholic clergy, much of the absolutist bureaucracy, and the federalist nobility who sought a more decentralized system of government. In addition, bourgeois nationalist groups like the Czechs allied themselves for a time with the federalist nobility, demanding a reorientation of power away from the *Reichsrat* to the diets. These latter groups rejected the December constitution and saw in federalism their best chance for achieving further linguistic reforms. Politically less influential yet vocal groups, such as urban workers and small urban property owners, also opposed various aspects of the new liberal order.

The victory of the liberal *Rechtsstaat* remained conditional as long as these politically influential sectors of Austrian society, starting at the very top, contested the new system. Their opposition immediately threatened the liberals' attempts rationally to legislate a constitutional system into existence. At the same time, the liberals could count on the fact that the interests of oppositional groups did not coincide with one another completely. For example, imperial bureaucrats might oppose liberal reform legislation, but, like the Schmerling regime of the early 1860s, they concurred with the liberals on the basic importance of maintaining a strongly centralized state system. This prevented them from allying with the more extreme members of the federalist nobility.

The liberals also understood that these powerful forces threatened the very survival of their constitution. They now plunged ahead zealously in the areas of educational and religious reform, hoping to strengthen their popular support by creating an educated and politically progressive citizenry. A future society,

32. Fellner, "Kaiser Franz Joseph und das Parlament" and "Kaiser Franz Josephs Haltung"; Hasner, *Denkwürdigkeiten*, 99–100. There is some evidence that Beust recommended Karl Auersperg to the emperor believing that he (Beust) could more easily retain a free hand in Austria's internal affairs. Rudolf, "Karl Auersperg," 79.

so enlightened, would diminish the demagogic powers of the church and conservative nobility in the battle for the people. The liberals had less success, however, negotiating the problems facing them in the present. Viewing their own legislative accomplishments in moral terms, as gains for enlightenment, progress, and civilization, made liberals ill-equipped to handle the angry and obstructionist responses of conservatives. The liberals' self-righteous rhetoric, so important to their survival during the long years of opposition, prevented them from negotiating creatively with their opponents to ensure the implementation of their legal and political reforms. In the case of problems like the Czech opposition in Bohemia or the social question in the cities, liberal rhetoric actually substituted for creative legislation.

The short reign of the Bürger Ministry constituted the most radical attempt of any post-1848 government to remake Austrian society in a new image. For this very reason the first liberal cabinet inevitably disappointed its supporters and exhausted its members, failing to transform Austria overnight. This was not for lack of trying: Herbst and Giskra in particular used their ministerial positions to impose liberal assumptions, beliefs, and behaviors on the bureaucracy. The later, less ideologically pronounced liberal cabinets would have far more success in transforming Austria's administration, largely because they identified broad areas of consensus and adapted their goals to traditional patterns of doing business.

Not surprisingly, the Bürger Ministry's sweeping religious reforms and the liberals' new school policies passed in 1868–69 encountered strong opposition at all levels of society. The first of these laws created the option of civil marriage and transferred local record keeping, and by implication jurisdiction over all marriages, from the churches to the state authorities. Many *Reichsrat* liberals who had pressed for a law requiring civil marriage in all cases treated this law as a compromise, one that clerics, however, viewed as a direct attack on the fundamental rights of the church in Austria. The second of these laws elaborated the principles that would structure the future relation between the schools and the church. This law removed from the church the right to oversee the school system, giving it instead to the central state.[33]

This same point alienated the federalists in the *Reichsrat* who wanted complete jurisdiction over the schools for the provincial diets. Since the school law merely elaborated a series of fundamental principles, however, its implementation would require a further series of laws and a later political battle to set up the new system. The third confessional law listed the principles that would

33. Vocelka, *Verfassung oder Konkordat?* 56–90, 168–70. These laws were actually adopted as a milder and more realistic alternative to outright renunciation of the Concordat. Not until the ecumenical council of 1870 adopted the dogma of papal infallibility, which Beust interpreted as a one-sided alteration of the agreement with Austria, did the emperor allow the government to repudiate the Concordat.

regulate interfaith marriages and the relations among legal confessions. The *Reichsvolksschulgesetz*, promulgated a year later, outlined the mode of financing for the new school system, the curricular requirements, and a new system of teacher training. The law also stipulated that both boys and girls attend school for at least eight years. The new law provided that students might attend confessional schools as long as these schools followed certain basic guidelines, including the eight-year requirement and a minimum of hours devoted to secular subjects.[34]

In May 1868, before passage of these laws had been assured, the cabinet almost resigned over reports that the emperor opposed the laws regulating religion and education. Only six months earlier, Francis Joseph had assured Carl Auersperg that he supported legislation to reform education and to regulate religion. Without the emperor's assurance on this issue Auersperg would not have agreed to serve as minister president, and none of the liberal deputies would have joined the cabinet. Now, under strong pressure from clerical and conservative circles to repudiate the confessional laws, Francis Joseph appeared to lend public sympathy to the legislation's opponents. Although the emperor did sign the new laws, he warned the cabinet that he would not tolerate any further religious legislation of the kind being mooted by *Reichsrat* liberals, such as mandatory civil marriage.[35]

Taaffe reported with disapproval to the emperor in Budapest that noisy public demonstrations had broken out in Vienna celebrating the passage of the May Laws. Soon the vigorous opposition raised by clerical, federalist, and conservative opponents dwarfed the Vienna celebrations. The creation of a centrally mandated secular curriculum and the loss of direct church control over religious instruction angered clerics, particularly in the Tirol and Upper Austria. The pope entered the controversy, denouncing the confessional laws as an illegal breach of the Concordat. Conservatives and federalists in agricultural regions angrily opposed the strict requirement of eight-year schooling for all boys and girls. They wanted the diets to decide on the minimum amount of schooling, taking into account the requirements of local agriculture. In many parts of the monarchy such as Galicia, Dalmatia, and especially the Tirol, bureaucratic and clerical opposition prevented the implementation of the school laws.

---

34. Vocelka, *Verfassung oder Concordat?* 99–100. The liberal press raised the question of Jews and interfaith marriages, pointing out that since Jews still faced discrimination, placing all recognized faiths on an equal legal footing meant that discrimination against Jews would now have to be based more on racial prejudice.

35. FA, ct. 51, fas. 11, politischer Nachlass, untitled manuscript by Karl Auersperg, 1868, 7–10; Fellner, "Kaiser Franz Joseph und das Parlament," 312–14; Rudolf, "Karl Auersperg," 143–50; Sandler, "Bürgerministerium," 44; Beust, *Aus drei-Vierteljahrhunderten*, 2:193. Not surprisingly, Beust later claimed credit for the passage of the May Laws, despite his refusal to back Auersperg's position during earlier meetings with the emperor.

The new ministers fought back, adopting a firm stand against both their bureaucratic subordinates and the church. In a speech to the civil servants of the interior ministry on January 4, 1868, Carl Giskra had already insisted that the spirit of the constitution must pervade the actions of the bureaucracy. He advised those individuals who could not in good conscience offer unconditional loyalty to the new system to resign their posts. A month later, Justice Minister Eduard Herbst presented the *Reichsrat* with a law enabling the government to discipline judicial civil servants who undermined the new system. Several *Reichsrat* liberals went further, calling for a purification of the civil service and demanding that all bureaucrats swear an oath to the constitution. In September 1868 Giskra circulated a memorandum instructing civil servants to handle any clerical opposition to the confessional laws with the "utmost severity" and warning civil servants themselves against any display of disloyalty to the new constitution.

These efforts by the cabinet failed to quell resistance to many of the new laws. In July 1869, in a highly visible gesture, the emperor commuted a prison sentence meted out to Bishop Francis Joseph Rudigier of Linz for inciting opposition to the government and disturbing the peace. The bishop had published pamphlets that urged noncompliance with the new laws and had used the pulpit openly to condemn the government. The government had decided to prosecute him as an example, although he was certainly not the only cleric to engage in such acts. The police confiscated the pamphlets, and at the trial that followed, a jury declared Rudigier guilty of disturbing the public peace. He was then sentenced to a two-week prison term. The entire procedure was "unavoidable," declared Ignaz von Plener to his son Ernst. "The cabinet had to draw the line somewhere," to demonstrate that even "church officials are subordinate to the state."[36] Yet even as the cabinet tried to draw that line, the emperor seemed to display his sympathy for the law-breaking cleric by commuting the sentence. Like many other liberals, Ignaz von Plener concluded from this frustrating episode just "how little His Majesty agrees with the new laws . . . and how little he actually sympathizes with his present government."[37]

In fact, the vehemence with which both liberal deputies and press attacked the church reflects more the heightened symbolic significance of this

36. OL, Flugschriftenversammlung B, "Der Pressprozess des Bischoffs Franz Josef Rudigier in Linz von seinem Ursprunge bis zum Schlusse durch das Schwurgericht" (Linz, 1869); Kolmer, *Parlament*, 1:315–16, 327–28; 367–73; Molisch, *Briefe*, 52; Vocelka, *Verfassung oder Konkordat?* 162–66; Wimmer, *Liberalismus*, 26–27, 57–64. Several bishops endorsed Rudigier's confrontational approach, while Vienna's Cardinal Rauscher advocated taking legal steps to oppose the new laws.

37. Molisch, *Briefe*, 52–53. The emperor's pardon of Rudigier was raised hastily during a brief absence of Giskra, Herbst, and Plener from Vienna and according to the latter was never fully discussed in their presence.

conflict for liberalism than its practical consequences. Particularly at the local level, the church certainly led the fight against many liberal reform efforts. The liberals rightfully worried about the actual implementation of their legislation. Yet as several historians have shown, the Concordat was by itself not the obscurantist unenlightened medieval document the liberals depicted but rather an example of centralist Josephenist state policy of the kind often praised by the liberals. Certainly the Concordat did not give the church the singular power over society that the liberal popular press claimed for it. Nevertheless, despite its actual content, the Concordat came to embody all the principles against which liberalism claimed to fight. In the particular context of the 1860s, the Concordat offered a crucial target for liberal anger and frustration with the bureaucratic absolutism of the recent past, where other potential targets like the emperor could not be touched. And if the liberal obsession with the church finally declined in the late 1870s, a strong local tradition of anticlericalism survived, particularly in the western and Alpine regions of the monarchy.

Throughout 1868, the ongoing boycott of the Bohemian Diet by Czech nationalist deputies and an increasing number of Czech nationalist public demonstrations challenged the government to deal effectively with political nationalism. The liberals had given little thought to this issue. Most of them expressed the optimistic belief that the constitution itself addressed the complaints raised by nationalists, since it ensured the rights of national groups to use their languages at the local and provincial levels. In any case, the liberals suspected their Czech opponents of whipping up nationalist emotions to justify their real political interest, namely the replacement of the centralized political system with a loose federalism dominated by the provincial diets.

Liberals fought Czech demands for greater Bohemian autonomy not simply because they opposed the use of the Czech language (which they did in any case) but because the implementation of these demands would seriously weaken the centralist system of government. Of course the implementation of the kind of federalist reform demanded by the Czechs would have the additional consequence of greatly diminishing the importance of German as the state language. Yet by playing down the nationalist dimension of the conflict in Bohemia, the liberals seriously underestimated the ability of Czech nationalism to mobilize broad sections of the Czech-speaking middle classes for their federalist political goals. Within the cabinet Giskra and Berger often inclined toward negotiation with the Czechs, believing that a mutually acceptable compromise was possible. Prince Carl Auersperg too, although a strict centralist, believed that negotiation might at least bring an end to the Czech boycott of the *Reichsrat*. Hasner, Herbst, and Plener, all deputies from Bohemia, adopted a much harder line toward Czech demands. The question remained, however: What kind of compromise and what kind of negotiation should the government engage in? The liberals wanted at least to explore the possibility of discussions, particularly with the emerging Young Czech faction within the nationalist party.[38]

Beust and Taaffe, however, began their own negotiations with the Czechs, suggesting subtly that a federalist compromise might indeed be possible. They thus removed any possible impetus for the Czech nationalists to negotiate with the liberal cabinet. In fact, they encouraged the Czechs in the belief that they might gain more if they waited, especially since the present liberal government might be of short duration. The emperor too sent confusing signals on this issue. He deplored Czech nationalist street demonstrations and unrest, and he strongly backed the problematic decision of the liberals in the cabinet to impose martial law in Bohemia. Yet Francis Joseph did nothing to prevent Taaffe and Beust from negotiating behind the backs of the rest of the cabinet, an act that could only raise Czech hopes that a future government might be more sympathetic to their federalist demands.

In June 1868, an angry Prince Carl Auersperg asked the emperor to relieve him of his post as minister president, citing Beust's interference as the reason for the request. "The unexpected . . . entrance of [Beust] into political negotiations with leaders of the Czech party has severely compromised my position, and the fact that the governor of Bohemia was earlier and better informed about . . . this meeting and its goals than your most loyal and obedient minister president remains for me an undeserved and grievous sign of disregard."Pointing out that Beust's negotiations would only encourage the Czech nationalist factions to hold out for better terms from a friendlier government, Auersperg deplored the way in which he and the rest of the cabinet had been kept ignorant of negotiations that held such serious domestic consequences.[39]

In September 1868, Carl Auersperg threatened resignation again on learning that Beust had continued his secret negotiations with the Czechs, with the apparent approval of both the emperor and Taaffe. This time, Beust's actions directly undermined a separate government initiative. Auersperg had accompanied the emperor on a trip to Prague in the hope of opening negotiations

---

38. FA, ct. 51, fas. 11, politischer Nachlass, untitled manuscript by Karl Auersperg, 1868, 20–21; Garver, *Young Czech Party*, 60–75; Pollak, *Dreissig Jahre*, 15–18; Rudolf, "Karl Auersperg," 178–79. Somewhat optimistically, the cabinet hoped by this action to split the Czech National Party and perhaps reach a compromise solution. The younger generation of Czech politicians, themselves liberals, shared the German liberal commitment to educational reform and they also expressed some discomfort about the political alliance that tied them and their Old Czech colleagues to the conservative nobility in Bohemia. They opposed the party's boycott of the diet and later of the *Reichsrat*.

39. FA, ct. 51, fas. 11, politischer Nachlass, copy of letter of resignation of June 24, 1868, untitled manuscript by Karl Auersperg, 1868, 19–23; Molisch, *Briefe*, 48–49; Pollak, *Dreissig Jahre*, 2:18; Rudolf, "Karl Auersperg," 178–87.

between his government and representatives of the Young Czech faction. He hoped to detach this group from the boycott of the *Reichsrat* imposed by intransigents among the Old Czechs. Beust, however, had proceeded secretly to Prague in advance of Auersperg, and in discussions with Palacký, leader of the Old Czechs, he had revealed the government's intentions.

Auersperg found Francis Joseph strangely unsympathetic to his complaint that Beust had overstepped his bounds. Although this version of events is drawn largely from Auersperg's own account, there is little reason to doubt its accuracy, given Beust's admitted predilection for involvement in Austrian internal affairs. There is even less reason to doubt that the emperor would have sided with Beust, given his own understanding of his prerogatives. After Carl Auersperg left the cabinet, the remaining liberals insisted they would only accept Taaffe as minister president if there were an end to "all one-sided actions by the [new] minister president in domestic political affairs." From now on, any domestic initiative could only follow full cabinet discussion.[40]

During the same period, the government faced demands and demonstrations of a different kind from growing working-class organizations in Vienna. Mass demonstrations for universal manhood suffrage and the legalization of unions elicited the suspicions of the more conservative ministers and bureaucrats, as did most meetings and discussions in workers' clubs. In particular, Taaffe, backed by the emperor, demanded that the cabinet take harsh measures against the young workers' movement. As with the decision to impose martial law in Bohemia, the cabinet reluctantly approved highly illiberal measures to combat this apparent threat to public order. The government forbade public demonstrations and dissolved several workers' organizations. Both the liberal press and several liberal deputies, among them some cabinet ministers, expressed misgivings about limiting the workers' constitutional rights of assembly and association. One paper reminded its readers that government persecution of social democracy might turn "tomorrow against democracy and the next day it will be liberalism's turn. The issue of freedom is the same for all parties who oppose reaction."[41]

Interior Minister Carl Giskra came under much public criticism for his leading role in the government's campaign against the workers. In May 1868 Giskra had addressed a delegation of workers with sarcasm bordering on contempt. "Do not think that we will introduce mob rule here in Austria. . . . Just because you were born human beings does not mean that you have any right to

40. FA, ct. 51, fas. 11, politischer Nachlass, copy of letter of resignation of September 16, 1868, untitled manuscript by Carl Auersperg, 1868, 19–23; Molisch, *Briefe*, 48–49; *Dreissig Jahre*, 2:18–28; Rudolf, "Karl Auersperg," 178–87. Molisch, *Briefe*, 50–51, 66. Plener later wrote that Beust's "biggest mistake was his involvement with the Czech demands for a compromise. I blame him the most for that."

41. NWT, October 15, 1868; Wadl, *Liberalismus*, 80–82.

a vote. You will earn this right [only] when we see that you have a real interest in it, an interest indicated by your payment of income taxes." Several observers noted with irony that the 1848 radical and later police suspect Carl Giskra had taken such a harshly reactionary position toward the workers. The new minister of the interior, however, was well aware that the emperor had raised questions about his own reliability when Beust had first suggested his name for a cabinet post. Giskra seems to have used his meeting with the workers as an opportunity to prove both his reliability and his willingness to act forcefully against any revolutionary threat.[42]

Most liberals agreed that the workers should only gain the right to vote when they had proven that they would use it wisely. As in the suffrage discussions of 1849, they frequently cited the twin elements of education and independent property ownership as reliable measures of an individual's political maturity. At the same time liberals in the legislative bodies and in the press voiced disapproval of the government's aggressive tone and oppressive measures. They feared that a working class alienated from the rest of society would easily be seduced by Ferdinand Lassalle's radical theories of state socialism. These liberals advocated active engagement with the workers, encouraging the young workers' movement to organize self-help institutions similar to those popularized by Schulze-Delitzsch in Germany as a means of gaining education, economic independence, and political maturity.

Several prominent liberals supported self-help associations organized by and for the benefit of workers in Vienna, Linz, and other industrial centers. Many lectured in working-class educational associations and supported working-class libraries. Some, like Max Menger in 1866, advised workers how to set up economic associations like consumer cooperatives and credit institutions. For such institutions to succeed, however, the workers had to be educated in the bourgeois virtues of thrift, domestic economy, and sobriety. This would facilitate their eventual rise into the lower reaches of the Mittelstand. As one early proponent of self-help associations noted in 1857, "A nation [like ours] that has hardly emerged from the primitive conditions of a natural economy cannot be transformed overnight into a nation of sober housekeepers. This nation must be educated to thrift, it must learn the value of its own work and the true value of money . . . it must learn how to delay gratification for a safer future."[43]

This attitude reinforces the points made in the discussion of the constitutional laws of 1867 regarding the need to balance individual rights and

---

42. Angerstein, *Parlamentarische Grössen*, 17–20; *Für das Volk*, May 20 and June 5, 1868; Haintz, "Giskra," 147–54.

43. Bernhard Friedmann, *Die Wohnungsnot in Wien* (Vienna: 1857), 6; Max Menger, *Die auf Selbsthilfe gestützten Genossenschaften im Handwerker- und Arbeiterstande* (Vienna, 1866); Wadl, *Liberalismus*, 110–18; 153–99.

safeguard private property. The liberals could not empower a substantial group of people who did not subscribe to their own values and ways of life. In theory, liberals endorsed the right of the individual to self-determination, a key element in the formation of a truly pluralist society. Yet government actions limiting worker involvement in politics betrayed the liberals' need to make the workers over in their own bourgeois image before granting them rights to full participation in community politics.

Even as they moved to outlaw working-class political organizations, liberals in the cabinet, the parliament, and in the press opposed the government's traditional ban on trade unions. In December 1869, the day after a mass demonstration of thousands of workers in Vienna had presented the cabinet with the same demand, Justice Minister Herbst introduced a law in the *Reichsrat* to repeal the ban. This legislation was easily approved in 1870, and even the *Neue Freie Presse* maintained that "no one supported [the ban on unions] any longer." At the same time, however, the government continued its active persecution of workers' associations. Only two weeks before it approved the repeal of the ban on unions, for example, the government arrested the leaders who had organized earlier demonstrations and tried them on charges of treason the following summer. Four of the leaders received prison sentences of five to six years, while the rest received lighter sentences.[44]

The cabinet faced yet another kind of problem from both colleagues and opponents in the *Reichsrat*. The liberal parties in parliament often pushed the cabinet to take even more extreme measures. Despite passage of the new confessional laws, for example, many *Reichsrat* liberals continued to call for a formal repudiation of the Concordat by the government and the imposition of obligatory civil marriage. These demands only angered Francis Joseph and lowered his esteem for the liberal cabinet ministers, who it seemed could not or would not control their more radical allies in the *Reichsrat*.[45] The liberal ministers could do little to quell radicalism in the *Reichsrat*, partly because they relied completely on the liberal deputies in parliament to pass even noncontroversial legislation and partly because the liberals in parliament seemed only good at making opposition. "You know," wrote Kaiserfeld to Stremayr, "our undisciplined party differs more and more with the government, even though this government sprang from the heart of the party! . . . At least we all agree that mistrust is our highest party commandment. At the very instant when one of us enters a government position, he loses his colleagues' trust and any influence over them."[46]

44. Wadl, *Liberalismus*, 82–83, 223–28. Some liberal deputies did support continuing the ban. Alfred Skene, textile magnate from Brünn, argued strongly from personal experience of worker violence against lifting the ban.

45. Fellner, "Kaiser Franz Joseph und das Parlament," 314–18.

46. Krones, *Kaiserfeld*, 305–6.

The problem of *Reichsrat* support for the government became more critical as conservatives, federalists, clerics, and nationalists attempted various forms of obstruction as a means to prevent more reform legislation from becoming law. In 1869 they threatened to boycott the *Reichsrat* and leave it without a quorum. This would undoubtedly bring down the cabinet and perhaps even the December constitution. With the exception of Berger, the liberals in the cabinet agreed that only electoral reform could save the system. If local constituencies were to elect *Reichsrat* deputies directly, it might free parliament from the federalist influence of the diets. Ignaz Plener complained of the Slav boycott to his son Ernst, noting that "direct elections are becoming a necessity to prevent the complete collapse of the *Reichsrat* . . . the whole institution will not be worth much if it is not relieved of its dependence on the diets."[47]

Like many later reformers of the Austrian electoral system, the liberals believed that the direct election of deputies would encourage the formation of broadly based parties organized around common ideologies. Election by the diets returned too many deputies who focused their energies on localist or nationalist concerns. Francis Joseph encouraged each faction in the cabinet to draw up a memorandum stating the arguments for or against a system of direct election. When it became obvious that a majority in the cabinet supported reform, he agreed that Giskra should explore a new system of direct election, even though it brought the resignations of Taaffe, Potocki, and Berger. Yet within a few months the emperor made clear his opposition to any reform that required the dissolution of the diets. The exhausted Bürger Ministry collapsed, defeated by a combination of political isolation and the machinations of the emperor and his associates.[48]

Vowing never again to rely on support from the liberal parties, Francis Joseph replaced the Bürger Ministry with successive governments of federalist sympathizers under Counts Adam Potocki and Carl Hohenwart in 1870–71. These cabinets, it was hoped, would negotiate a new constitutional settlement designed to bring the Czech nationalists, conservatives, clericals, and federalists back into the political system.[49] Several liberal observers feared that the

47. Molisch, *Briefe*, 60.

48. Fellner, "Kaiser Franz Josephs Haltung," 331–37; "Kaiser Franz Joseph und das Parlament," 322–25; Kolmer, *Parlament*, 2:6–17; Molisch, *Briefe*, 60–61; Sandler, "Bürgerministerium," 96–113. Plener suggested that "the real reason for Giskra's resignation is his conviction that he is not capable of bringing order to the chaos of nationalist and political confusion, and that this particular situation offers the chance to go out in the blaze of glory surrounding the nonrealization of a liberal idea: direct elections."

49. On the Potocki and Hohenwart cabinets, Garver, *Young Czechs*, 56–57; Kolmer, *Parlament*, 2:52–58, 67–88, 110–202; Jan Kren, "Die böhmischen Länder in der Krise 1870/71," *Bohemia. Zeitschrift für die Geschichte und Kultur der Böhmischen Länder* 28 (1987): 312–30; Macartney, *Empire*, 581–85.

1867 constitution would not survive these federalist experiments. They need not have worried. It was precisely the dualist arrangement with Hungary that ensured the survival of the 1867 constitution against federalist and conservative attack. The Czech nationalists demanded an *Ausgleich* for Bohemia. Any such arrangement altering the dualist structure of the monarchy and diminishing the influence of the two existing states required Hungarian agreement, and this the federalists could never obtain.

In two short years Austrian liberals had legislated a responsible, activist concept of Austrian citizenship, complete with civic rights explicitly enumerated in the new constitutional laws. In addition, the liberals' school reform gave powerful institutional support to this new concept of citizenship. The mass education of Austrian boys and girls from all backgrounds would prepare them to assume the adult responsibilities of citizenship. Austrian schools would create the cadres of a mass liberal society that did not yet exist, by training students in empirical, rationalist, positivist thinking. Teaching individuals to free themselves from the grasp of religious, localist, and nationalist interests would diminish the dangerous influence of those forms of difference and introduce citizens to liberal, universalist principles of tolerance. Eventually the schools might even imbue children with a specifically Austrian identity, one completely free from the trammels of nationalism and localism. Such an identity would transcend all those local forms of difference that the liberals viewed with suspicion.

Conceptions of difference among various groups in the monarchy had to be decreased, if not erased, for the constitution to take root. Linguistic, religious, ethnic, class differences might season social life, might be displayed in parades and in museums, but they would only be salutary in a society of people who shared the same fundamental loyalties to progress and civilization. This explains the restrictive laws on association, Giskra's harsh treatment of the workers' deputation and demonstrations in 1868, and the imposition of illiberal measures to pacify Bohemia. That the liberals could argue in good faith against carrying their own program to its logical end, namely a completely democratic franchise, demonstrates not so much their hypocrisy as the tension between progressive reform of society and the protection of material interests, both of which elements had characterized Austrian liberalism since 1848.

It would also be mistaken, I think, to conclude that the liberals' recourse to illiberal measures suggested that the position of bourgeois groups in Austria was exceptionally weak by European standards of the 1860s. It should hardly come as a surprise that a liberal bourgeoisie might deploy those very policing institutions it had deplored under absolutism only a decade earlier. Which nineteenth-century bourgeois society in Europe did not find occasion to resort to illiberal measures, even if those measures contradicted the liberal belief in individual freedom and pluralism? Surely the Austrian liberals were no less worthy of the name than the French, German, or British liberals of the same period.[50]

This brings us to the second important lesson of 1867 and the Bürger Ministry. The liberal bourgeoisie managed to implement its desired state form only to a limited degree. Politics represented a contested, changing compromise among competing classes and groups for institutional power, just as it did in every European state that developed constitutional life in the nineteenth century. From the point of view of 1867, the new liberal institutions may appear to have been too much at odds with the traditional ones to succeed. Despite numerous attempts in the previous century, the monarchy had never completely succeeded in imposing consistent centralized institutions of rule. The liberals' attempt to do so did not, at first, fare much better. The broad middle classes had indeed gained access to the highest levels of power in Austria, but they were not alone at the top. Other groups and institutions, including the monarch, the army, the bureaucracy, the regional aristocracy, and later the working classes, all managed to assert or preserve different modes of behavior and rule to some extent until the fall of the empire in 1918.

The liberals learned only a part of this lesson following the collapse of the Bürger Ministry. They understood that political success could not be legislated from above but must somehow be derived organically, from within society itself. Starting in 1868, therefore, they sought a means to effect political transformation from below. They turned once again to the voluntary association, that critical institution that had served them since the *Vormärz* as the model for the ideal liberal society.

---

50. Sanford Elwit, *The Making of the Third French Republic: Class and Politics in France, 1868-1884* (Baton Rouge, 1975), 19–52. Elwit's discussion of liberalism in the early years of the French Third Republic stresses the transformation in the content of traditional liberal and radical ideology that took place in the decade after 1848 and that resembled closely the path taken by the Austrian liberals during the same period.

CHAPTER 5

Building a Liberal Movement: The Political Clubs, 1867–73

"Let us now create associations!"

Konstitutionelles Vorstadt-Zeitung (1867)[1]

The constitution of 1867 removed the last legal barriers to the formation of political organizations. Almost overnight, liberal political associations sprang up in every region of Austria. They joined an existing network of cultural, educational, and philanthropic organizations that had increasingly structured the public life of the urban Bürgertum since the early nineteenth century. Bürger activists had long considered the voluntary association to be an important institution for the enlightenment and reform of society. The centrality that they assigned particularly to reform gave even the most avowedly unpolitical of associations real political potential.[2] Existing associations that conceived their task as helping to spread progressive ideas undermined the very legitimacy of religion and tradition. There could be little doubt, for example, about the political content of the ideas propagated by a group like the German Association for the Spread of Generally Useful Knowledge based in Prague. To the reforming members of this organization, spreading "generally useful knowledge" meant exposing the *Volk* to a liberal, scientific, progressive, and anticlerical critique of traditional society.[3]

1. KVZ, November 23, 1867.

2. There is now an enormous literature on the nature and significance of middle-class voluntary associations in Central Europe. A brief list of important works for this particular study follows: Blackbourn, "Discrete Charm of the German Bourgeoisie," in *Populists and Patricians*, ed. Blackbourn, 67–83; Blackbourn and Eley, *Peculiarities of German History*; Cohen, *Politics*; William Hubbard, *Auf dem Weg zur Grossstadt. Eine Sozialgeschichte der Stadt Graz 1850–1914* (Munich, 1984), 113–25, 152–78; Koshar, *Social Life*; Thomas Nipperdey, "Verein als soziale Struktur in Deutschland im späten 18. und frühen 19. Jahrhundert. Eine Fallstudie zur Modernisierung I," in *Gesellschaft, Kultur, Theorie*, ed. Nipperdey, 174–205; Peter Urbanitsch, "Bürgertum und Politik in der Habsburgermonarchie. Eine Einführung," in *Bürgertum in der Habsburgermonarchie*, ed. Bruckmüller et al., 165–76.

3. *Deutscher Volkskalender für 1876* (Prague, 1875), 128.

Voluntary associations organized around cultural activities engaged in quasi-political activities both explicitly in their discussion circles and lecture series and implicitly through the repetitive use of symbols and rituals that stressed the organizations' autonomy from the state. Public festivals organized by these groups could, on occasion, take on implicitly political overtones. They provided a public forum for the expression of social values often at odds with those propagated by the government or church. Singing, athletic, and historical associations all helped to establish and reinforce the legitimacy of middle-class society's alternative vision of the world in public. Growing communications and railway networks at mid century contributed to the interpenetration of these shared values and political identities in several geographic regions. Robert Hoffmann has shown, for example, how the new railway that connected Salzburg to Vienna and South Germany dramatically increased the degree of local participation in interregional singing and athletic festivals in the early 1860s. This rise in participation and travel in turn helped to popularize a German liberal identity that reached well beyond local or provincial roots.[4]

Given the implicit political character of the cultural, educational, and philanthropic associations, what was the role of the exclusively political club to be? The legalization of political associations certainly presented middle-class activists with new organizational opportunities for their specifically political ambitions. Yet, particularly outside Vienna, liberal activists did not generally engage in a rhetoric of interest group politics. They did not see the political club as a vehicle to accomplish partisan goals. Rather, local liberals tried at first to apply the moral and humanitarian discourse of nonpolitical associational life to the previously forbidden arena of politics. According to this rhetoric, liberal political clubs, like other kinds of associations, existed for the betterment of the entire community, not simply to advance the interests of one group, faction, or party. This is what the Constitutional Association of Laibach meant when it claimed that "only a liberal city council can guarantee an impartial, objective exercise of city powers," and praised its municipal representatives as "an objective, impartial city council [proudly working to] further the cause of progress."[5]

This rhetorical denial of interest group politics even within specifically political associations helps to explain the public response to the long-

4. Robert Hoffmann, "Bürgerliche Kommunikationsstrategien zu Beginn der liberalen Ära: Das Beispiel Salzburg," in *"Durch Arbeit, Besitz, Wissen und Gerechtigkeit,"* ed. Stekl et al., 317–36; Dieter Düding, *Organisierter gesellschaftlicher Nationalismus in Deutschland (1808–1847). Bedeutung und Funktion der Turner- und Sängervereine für die deutsche Nationalbewegung* (Munich, 1984); Klaus Tenfelde, "Adventus. Zur historischen Ikonologie des Festzugs," *Historische Zeitschrift* 235 (1982): 45–84.

5. *Bericht des constitutionellen Vereines in Laibach über das siebente Vereinsjahr 1874* (Laibach, 1874), 21; *Bericht des constitutionellen Vereines in Laibach über das elfte Vereinsjahr 1878* (Laibach, 1879), 4.

awaited opportunity to form political clubs. Associational statistics for the years 1867–72 show that the number of political associations grew rapidly but that it remained relatively small when compared to the number of purely social or charitable clubs. One year following their legalization, for example, Austrians had founded 64 political clubs, compared with over 5,000 of the nonpolitical variety. By 1872, that number had grown to 555, or 5 percent of all associations in Cisleithania, compared to over 10,000 nonpolitical associations. And of these political associations, only a minority were liberal in their orientation.[6]

Commenting on this statistical phenomenon from the vantage point of the 1880s, Karl Hugelmann attributed what he called the slowness and unevenness of liberal political development to the general apathy and immaturity of Austria's bourgeois classes. Superficially at least, the figures could indeed support Hugelmann's conclusion that civic quietism and bourgeois timidity had retarded the development of a self-confident involvement in politics. For several later scholars, Hugelmann's conclusions about an immature bourgeoisie provided additional anecdotal proof of their own theories regarding the monarchy's supposedly slow rate of industrial development.[7]

Given the continued proliferation of bourgeois associational life in Austrian society, and given its implicitly moral and political overtones, should one expect German Austrians to have joined the more narrowly and explicitly political organizations in greater numbers? Did not their existing associations already fulfill many implicitly political functions, such as the elaboration of bourgeois values and the institutionalization of local social hierarchies? The same sense of moral purpose that had spurred the social clubs on to reform during a time of political repression may well have lessened the apparent need for purely political clubs after 1867. Instead of becoming the most important local instrument for carrying out the long-term interests of the local Bürgertum, the average political club served more as an agitational vehicle, popular in election years and during political crises but otherwise appealing to only a limited number of activists.

---

6. Karl Hugelmann, "Beiträge zur Geschichte und Statistik der politischen Vereine in Österreich," in *Österreichische Zeitschrift für Verwaltung* 13 (Vienna, 1880): 123–24. New clubs were unevenly distributed throughout Austria, with Styria and Lower Austria having the highest concentration and Istria and Dalmatia the lowest. For informational studies of political associations in the Austrian monarchy as a whole, see Judson, "German Liberalism in Nineteenth-century Austria," 293–346, 383–437; Kammerhofer, "Politische Vereinswesen."

7. Hugelmann, "Beiträge," 124–25; Ritter, "Austro-German Liberalism," 238. In the atmosphere of recrimination and confusion that followed the liberals' fall from parliamentary power in 1879, observers tended to read back organizational passivity and political immaturity to explain the sudden weakness of liberalism in 1879. Harry Ritter has noted that "the terms and metaphors which control present-day discourse about nineteenth-century liberalism are, to a great extent, taken over directly from the figurative language of pathology invented in some cases . . . by insecure or disillusioned turn-of-the-century liberals themselves."

The growth pattern among liberal political clubs during the four years following their legalization confirms this idea. The initial urge to found political clubs reflected a strong determination by local liberals to protect the political gains they had only recently won from the forces of reaction. The stormy and short-lived career of the Bürger Ministry (1868–70) combined with the conservative, pro-Czech experiments of its successors, the Potocki and Hohenwart cabinets (1870–71), made the survival of the new system seem doubtful at best. And as early as 1868, clerical conservatives began to organize their own network of political associations dedicated to the destruction of the liberalized school system and confessional legislation. Citizens in the provincial capitals and major towns hurried to found political clubs, both as a response to threats against the constitution and as an additional means of consolidating their institutional power base.

Yet this period of initial danger to liberalism lasted only a short time. The next eight years saw far fewer political attacks on the young constitutional system. With a liberal cabinet under Adolf Auersperg firmly in control (1871–79), German liberal hegemony seemed assured at both the state and local levels. During this period membership in liberal political clubs leveled off and then actually declined, indicating among other factors a confidence in the apparent permanence of constitutionalism.

Membership Recruitment and Organizational Structures

Most of the new liberal political clubs recruited their members from existing local associations, which in turn lent their organizational forms to the new groups. Social composition of a political club depended largely on the special characteristics of the local Bürgertum. In more rural localities, the initiative to found a liberal political club was taken by small shop owners, innkeepers, or postmasters. In such provincial towns, groups of about twenty male citizens, usually including municipal council members, met privately to gauge the feasibility of founding a local political club. The meeting drew up tentative statutes and a program that was sent to the provincial government for approval. The group then published announcements for a public meeting, inviting like-minded men to participate in the founding of the new association.[8]

8. See AVA, Ministerium des Innern, Politische Vereine, ct. 785–87; NÖLA, Statthalterei Vereinskataster, Kategorie XIX, "politische Vereine 1868–1879"; OL, Vereinskataster, A. Rubrik 1–10, "politische Vereine"; SLA, Vereinskataster, "politische Vereine"; for membership lists where available. Also Haas, "Trägerschichten und Organisationsformen des Liberalismus." For occupational breakdowns of founding memberships in small-town liberal clubs, see Erhard Unterberger, "Der Liberalismus in St. Pölten (1870–1918)" (Ph.D. diss., University of Vienna, 1966); Josef Tuma, *Jahresbericht des liberalen Vereines in Wels über das 1. Vereinsjahr vom 11. 2. 1868 bis 12. 2. 1869* (Wels, 1869); Wimmer, *Liberalismus*, 26–27, 156–71.

In cities like Vienna or Graz with a stronger tradition of organized political activism, the internal controversies that had divided liberals and democrats in 1848–49 revived overnight. In fact in Vienna some districts boasted three or four rival liberal or democratic clubs. Their existence reflected widely divergent economic or social concerns within a larger, more heterogeneous middle class. Thus in Vienna wealthier citizens joined liberal or so-called Bürger associations, while artisans, teachers, and some lower-level professionals revived the democratic club tradition. Nevertheless, differences in program or social recruitment between liberal and democratic clubs in the 1860s and 1870s were not so great as to suggest that the two represented fundamentally different political phenomena. The democrats shared the organizational structures and basic political views of their liberal colleagues, as a closer inspection of statutes and programs will indicate.[9]

Club statutes generally invited citizens of any class or background to join the universal struggle to achieve a liberal society in Austria. In practice, however, the clubs welcomed only a small proportion of society into their organizations. As noted earlier, the law that regulated political associations automatically excluded women, minors, and foreigners from participation. Any male citizen of the community over the age of twenty-one could join at the founding meeting, provided he supported the associational program and had no criminal record. At subsequent meetings, however, the statutes helped ensure that the membership would remain solidly middle class. After the founding meeting, a new applicant had to be sponsored by current members. The club then exercised its right to accept or reject the potential inductee by a secret vote. Even the democratic clubs, ideologically more inclusive, retained the custom of voting to approve new members. In general, patterns of middle-class sociability functioned to ensure that only a certain type of person, usually a friend, colleague, neighbor, or relative of a member, applied for admission in the first place.[10]

Club statutes often contained other qualifications designed to limit membership further. In Klosterneuburg, for example, the more exclusive Liberal Citizens' Association implicitly limited its membership to property owners by stipulating in 1868 that new members be tax-paying citizens. In 1875 the association amended this statute to admit only those taxpayers whose status gave them the right to vote in provincial elections. Clearly, the political associations did not simply seek to mobilize as many people as possible for their cause. While they viewed their programs as universal in application, they only sought out members who resembled themselves.[11]

---

9. Kammerhofer, "Politische Vereinswesen," 96–97; Seliger, "Liberale Fraktionen im Wiener Gemeinderat," 62–90.

10. Hugelmann, *Österreichischen Vereins-und Versammlungsrechte*, 57–66.

11. Hugelmann, "Beiträge," 169. Wiener Stadt und Landesarchiv, politische Vereine, 1750/41.

The imposition of dues required to finance club operations also set an informal limit on the type of person who joined a club. Most clubs charged members a florin to join and set yearly dues at between 50 kreuzer and 1.20 florins. Some, however, charged substantially more. In Vienna, two-thirds of liberal political associations set their annual dues at 2.4 florins or higher, while in Prague the powerful Casino charged dues of 12 florins. Democratic clubs, on the other hand, charged less. They clearly intended their lower dues to attract a larger membership and to reflect their more populist ideology.[12]

Associational statutes usually provided for an executive committee consisting of a president, one or two vice presidents, a secretary to keep the minutes, and a treasurer. This group ran the club on a daily basis, representing it to the public, preparing the agenda for and organizing the general meetings. According to the statutes, a committee member's term of office might range in length from a few months in the democratic associations to a year in the others. The statutes provided individual members with an avenue of recourse against arbitrary rule by the executive committee. Any member could have an item placed on the agenda for discussion if he obtained the signatures of anywhere from seven to twenty-one other members. And just as the liberal constitution of 1867 had separated the judiciary from the administrative bureaucracy, each side in the case of an internal conflict could appoint an equal number of independent arbitrators (*Schiedsrichter*) who in turn selected a neutral judge to decide the matter. Both sides had to abide by the decision or forfeit their membership in the association, just as those who violated the laws of the *Rechtsstaat* might be punished by their exclusion from civil society.[13]

Liberal associations rarely functioned in practice exactly as they did on paper. Despite provisions for a healthy rotation of office, for example, club records show the same men to have generally won reelection to the executive, often for periods of up to twenty years. In Prague, the treasurer and secretary of the German Casino in 1892 had both sat on the executive board in 1870, while the same man, Franz Schmeykal, served as president for over twenty years. Nor was it at all exceptional that in 1880, for example, over 60 percent of the men elected to the executive committee of the Constitutional Association in Laibach in 1868 still served on that board.[14]

---

12. AVA, Ministerium des Innern, ct. 785–87, particularly numbers 21–23, 47, 86–90, 93 and 95; Cohen, *Politics*, 66–73; Anton Kiemann, *Die ersten vierzig Jahre des Vereines Deutsches Kasino in Prag, 1862–1902* (Prague, 1902), 11. The Casino raised its dues in 1875 to twenty florins.

13. AVA, Ministerium des Innern, ct. 785–87.

14. William Hubbard, "A Social History of Graz, Austria, 1861–1914" (Ph.D. diss., Columbia University, 1973), 221–39; Herbert Lukas, "Der Welser Stadtsekretär August Göllerich (1819–1883). Ein oberösterreichische Liberaler" (Ph.D. diss., University of Salzburg, 1981); Unterberger, "Liberalismus in St. Pölten," 5–12, Wimmer, *Liberalismus*, 166–71; *Bericht des constitutionellen Vereines in Laibach* from 1871 and 1881. Other examples of longevity include

From the start these same executives exercised enormous power within the clubs, and they were rarely challenged by dissenting motions. In fact, few if any issues arose during the 1860s and 1870s to test the clubs' ability to settle internal disputes. Accordingly, the practice of executive rule created difficulties after 1880 when internal tensions did begin to surface, and at precisely the moment when the clubs tried to broaden their appeal to gain a more socially diverse membership. Fights, when they erupted, were bitter and often resulted in permanent splits within the associations. In the 1880s, factions tended to withdraw to found rival clubs rather than submit to arbitration.

Programs

Every liberal association claimed that rooting the 1867 constitution firmly in Austrian society would lead to further material progress and spiritual enlightenment. Clubs defined their primary function in terms of protecting the new constitution, with the Vienna democrats demanding further reform. In 1869, the liberals of Linz, Upper Austria, declared their primary goals to be "the protection and further extension of constitutional freedoms" and "the encouragement of spiritual and material progress." A year later, the liberals of St. Pölten in Lower Austria stated their determination to uphold constitutional rights and to work for material and spiritual progress. In Mährisch-Ostrau, Moravia, the Austrian Constitutional Association pledged to "encourage the spiritual and material interests of Moravia in a liberal direction and to bring all citizens of Mährisch-Ostrau an understanding of their new constitution." In Styria, the Peoples' Association of Weiz called for a general acceptance of the new constitution, promising to work for its further extension "in a democratic sense." Elsewhere in the Alpine provinces, the Liberal Peoples' Association of Villach, Carinthia, vowed to "uphold the constitution and further develop the rights of the people through all legal means."[15]

As in 1848, many associations saw their biggest task as the education of their fellow citizens about the benefits of liberal constitutionalism. In Bohemia, the German Political Education Society *Böhmerwald* in Seewiesen called for the "general education of its members, for the enforcement and further extension of the constitutional laws of 1867, and the specific education of all members of society on the rights and duties of the citizen." In nearby Sichelsdorf, a

---

Johann Ofner in St. Pölten, Karl Wiser and August Göllerich in Linz, Franz Gross in Wels, and Joseph Kopp and Max Menger in the German Association in Vienna. On Schmeykal and others in the Prague Casino, see Cohen, *Politics*, table 9, 299–302.

15. AVA, Ministerium des Innern, ct. 785–87, 14, 44, 52, 84; Unterberger, "Liberalismus in St. Pölten," 7–8; Wimmer, *Liberalismus*, 172; Kammerhofer, "Das politische Vereinswesen," 96–102. Kammerhofer traces the links among clubs based on similarities in the wording of their programs.

German liberal club named Progress promised to encourage both the general enlightenment of the people as well as their "specific education concerning their civic rights and duties." And in the Northern Bohemian district of Teplitz-Schönau, the German Political Association tied the further progress of constitutionalism to its intended education of the people concerning those same civic rights and duties. In its 1868 program, one of the earliest of many Viennese liberal clubs, the Association for Constitutional Progress in the Fourth District, pledged "to increase people's knowledge of modern constitutionalism in Austria, while working for the immediate and thorough enforcement of the new laws and the extension of civil liberties using all legal means."[16]

The "German national interest" was a less clearly defined issue that nevertheless generated some concern among local liberal groups in the 1870s. Although party leaders in the *Reichsrat* tended to view the German national issue as a constitutional question that had been settled in 1867, local clubs often saw the issue differently. Politically active German-speaking liberals who lived in ethnically mixed regions of Bohemia, Moravia, Silesia, Styria, and Carniola faced local Czech, Pole, or Slovene political challenges to their hegemony couched in nationalist rhetoric. Some Bohemian associations called for the "protection of German national interests in Bohemia," the "awakening," "development and strengthening of German national consciousness," and "defense of German nationality." One club went so far as to define its German ethnic identity in terms of language, specifying that "the language of the association is and will remain the German language." Others promised vigilance on the national front to guard German national interests. Yet no club program before 1880 defined these interests specifically, nor did any venture beyond this vaguely articulated commitment to "vigilance."[17]

Local concern with the political, social, and above all with the perceived economic challenge from other national groups preoccupied German-speaking activists all over Austria, not simply those who lived in areas of conflict. A handful of early clubs in Lower Austria and Vienna even targeted nationalism as their primary concern, calling themselves "German nationalist associations" instead of liberal or constitutionalist societies as the others did. In Vienna, Joseph Kopp and a group of progressive liberals that included Max Menger and Heinrich Jacques founded a German Association in 1869. In the 1870s this club functioned occasionally as an extraparliamentary arm of the

16. AVA, Ministerium des Innern, ct. 785–87, 2, 47, 59, 62.

17. AVA, Ministerium des Innern, ct. 785–87, 2, 44, 59, 66. For a contrasting approach to nationalism in an ethnically mixed province with a much smaller German minority, see the actions of the Laibach Constitutional Club recounted by Peter Vodopivec in "Ansichten des deutschen Bürgertums in Krain," 90–92. Here the German liberals criticized the nationalism of the Slovenes, claiming that what really separated the two groups was not their ethnicity (since some well-known Slovenes joined the Liberal Party) but rather their differing political ideologies.

Progressive Party, which increasingly employed a more sharply nationalist rhetoric than the other liberal parties. The club sponsored a series of German Austrian Party conferences in the early 1870s, inviting liberal deputies from all parts of Austria to develop a common program and strategy. The German Association was meant to coordinate the activities of a potential network of similar nationalist associations across Austria that did not materialize before 1880. The program of the German Association promised "to promote the interests of Austrian Germans in general and in particular to protect their national interests."[18]

The German Association desired a close economic and political alliance with the new German Empire and suggested granting political autonomy to Galicia in order to ensure Germans a more pronounced majority in the rest of Cisleithania. In this sense the association advocated more practical steps for ensuring the survival of German hegemony than had its predecessors in 1848. Yet the members still clung to a cultural and political understanding of their own national identity and avoided defining themselves as a closed group, bounded by common racial or even ethnic characteristics.[19] The German Association saw German national survival as inextricably linked to the survival of liberal cultural values like the extension of constitutional rights and expansion of the franchise. Those German speakers who did not identify with cultural or political liberalism were no more part of the ethnic community promoted by the nationalist association than were the rival Slavs. While the specific attributes of Germanness may not have been contested or even much discussed in 1870, it is important for later developments to see the relative openness with which German liberals continued to define their national community.

The programs of the Viennese democratic clubs made more specific demands on the new constitutional system, in contrast to liberal generalizations about broadening the constitution. A typical Viennese democratic program desired the direct election of all parliamentary deputies and the abolition of the curial system of voting. It also demanded a broader franchise, which would, among others, give schoolteachers an automatic right to vote. The democrats criticized the restrictions on the 1867 press and associational laws, demanded "a more equal division of the tax burden," and usually made some mention of

18. AVA, Ministerium des Innern, ct. 785–87, 96; NÖLA, NÖ Statthalterei, 104, 1868–1879, fas. 4; Walter Gruber, "Der Politiker Josef Kopp. Ein Beitrag zur Geschichte der Verfassungspartei" (Ph.D. diss., University of Vienna, 1949). Kopp had been a member of both the Vienna city council and the Lower Austrian Diet since 1867. He was not a democrat, although many of the more moderate liberals painted him as such. His interest in workers' cooperatives and in overhauling the curial system of election made him an occasional ally of the democrats (as in 1871, when he ran unsuccessfully for mayor against the establishment's Cajetan Felder), but they did not share his strong emphasis on German nationalism. Kopp and his colleagues stood for an ideologically more progressive form of liberalism and a more activist rhetoric.

19. AVA, Ministerium des Innern, ct. 785–87, 96.

a "social problem" or a "workers' question." They ventured beyond the liberal position of equality among religions to demand obligatory civil marriage and the removal of religious instruction from the schools.[20]

Democrats used more colorful language than liberals and voiced a theoretical belief in social equality far more aggressively than the liberals. Their programs hearkened back to what they remembered of the heroic traditions of artisanal radicalism in 1848, traditions to which most liberals reacted with understandable ambivalence. In 1868 and again in 1873, democratic associations and newspapers in Vienna celebrated the twentieth and twenty-fifth anniversaries of 1848, thereby openly appropriating the revolutionary events for their own traditions. The democrats' interests in fostering the young working-class movement also occasionally set them apart from mainstream liberals. Yet despite some disagreement with liberals over franchise reform or associational restrictions, the two competing visions of society continued to share most elements and differed only in degree.[21]

The democrats, themselves prosperous artisans, journalists, or manufacturers, never dreamed of attacking the sacred foundation of bourgeois society and the *Rechtsstaat*, private property. Yet, as in 1848, differing definitions of property and its uses often led to political disagreement. Democrats desired legislation to improve their competitive position against larger firms or foreign imports and to increase their own political influence through electoral reform. They hoped the state would direct its attention to the social question because, as owners of small workshops, they dealt directly with workers' problems and demands themselves. They did not want to see the workers turned against the existing system by a hostile state. Yet the democrats' fervent denunciations of the Eisenach program of the German socialists also demonstrated their loyalty to a bourgeois vision of society, albeit one more oriented toward the needs of small property ownership.[22]

During the 1860s and early 1870s, both democrat and liberal groups sponsored associations aimed at integrating the working class into the Bürger community. These associations either encouraged working-class membership in essentially bourgeois (usually democratic) organizations, or they fostered educational programs and economic self-help institutions among the workers. As early as 1866, the Association for Economic Progress in Vienna arranged lectures on social and economic topics for working-class audiences. Founded by bourgeois industrialists, economists, and professionals interested in promoting

20. Hugelmann, "Beiträge," 173–74.

21. Häusler, "Noch sind alle Märzen vorbei . . . ." in *Politik und Gesellschaft*, ed. Ackerl et al.

22. KVZ, December 12, 1867. For an excellent survey of the problematic relationship between the liberal or democratic clubs and early working-class organizations in the 1860s and 1870s, see Wadl, *Liberalismus*, 102–19.

free trade, the association also worked hard to popularize the self-help ideas of the German economist Franz Hermann Schultze-Delitzsch against the statist views of Ferdinand Lassalle's socialist followers. In 1866, for example, Max Menger held a series of well-attended lectures in the Printers' Educational Association on the merits and mechanics of consumer cooperatives.[23]

During the mid 1870s, a few liberal political farmers' associations also appeared in rural regions of Austria. Their statutes paint an interesting picture of a liberal philosophy of education, self-help, and cooperation as they applied to rural Austria. The primary purpose of a Styrian farmers' association was "for us farmers to raise our level of welfare, of self-respect, and of mental independence." To achieve that mental independence, the farmers sponsored lectures and discussions on agricultural matters, maintained a small library, and supported local schools. The club addressed practical issues like increasing soil productivity and obtaining favorable farm legislation. To encourage others to join, the club offered full memberships to "those who work with their hands," at the low weekly cost of only one kreuzer. More affluent and educated members of the community could become supporting members either by contributing their expertise in educational lectures or by a weekly fee of five kreuzer. The rather stern statutes admonished farmers to "follow the club rules, arrive punctually at meetings, pay their dues on time," to "behave in a brotherly fashion toward each other," and never to indulge in any of the rougher and ruder forms of sociability to which they might be accustomed.[24]

Politically independent or liberal farmers' associations represented a rare phenomenon during this period, since the Catholic Church generally controlled the political habits of rural voters in Austria. Liberals too tended to view farmers as the ignorant pawns of the local Catholic priest. Their reform programs frequently contradicted the interests of local agriculture, particularly once the new railroads and freer trade system with Hungary began to bring cheaper foreign grain to local markets. Independent farmers' clubs did not really emerge before the 1890s, and when they did, they tended to shun both liberal and Catholic conservative camps in order to pursue an interest group politics based on their particular economic and social demands. Only in Carinthia and Styria did local liberals manage to develop programs that gained the support of local farmers and landowners, and in these provinces anticlerical farmers remained immune to the blandishments of the Catholic parties.[25]

---

23. KVZ, December 12, 1867; Menger, *Genossenschaften*; Wadl, *Liberalismus*, 163–79. The Laibach Constitutional Association sponsored similar lecture series. Vodopivec, "Ansichten des deutschen Bürgertums in Krain," 112–18.

24. AVA, Ministerium des Innern, ct. 785–87; Bruckmüller, *Landwirtschaftliche Organisationen*.

25. Bruckmüller, *Landwirtschaftliche Organisationen*, 213–14; Wadl, *Liberalismus*, 208–10.

Activism: Issues, Meetings, and Petitions

During their initial growth period from 1868 to 1873, liberal and democratic associations targeted three main issues for their energies: the political power of the Catholic Church, the restrictive and weighted curial electoral system, and the Hohenwart cabinet's federalist schemes. The relative importance of each issue varied regionally, and in urban areas like Vienna social issues also assumed some importance. Liberal hostility to the Catholic Church, for example, was strongest in the Alpine provinces of the West: Carinthia, Styria, Tirol, and Upper Austria. According to liberals in those provinces, the local clergy used every available means to subvert the constitution and avoid implementing school and church reforms. Electoral reform was a major issue among liberals everywhere who wanted to see the *Reichsrat* freed from the federalist influence of the diets. In addition, Viennese liberals had even more immediate reason for demanding electoral reform: the city's special constitutional status placed the tax minimum for the franchise there at twenty florins instead of the usual ten. Viennese democrats and Styrian progressives also demanded a modification of the curial voting system to end the preponderance of the large landowners' curia. Opposition to the Hohenwart regime came from all regions of Austria but was led by Bohemian Germans, who had the most to lose in case of a federalist compromise with the Czechs.[26]

Taken together, these issues motivated the local German-speaking Bürgertum all over Austria to found more clubs and to participate in political club life at a growing rate until the mid 1870s. In Vienna, democrats alone founded eight political clubs in 1868. By 1873 they could boast eighteen clubs, while their liberal colleagues had organized ten. In the rest of Lower Austria the liberals had organized another twenty-three clubs by 1873. In Styria liberals founded thirteen political clubs between 1868 and 1871, including two in Graz. By 1873, Bohemian German liberals could claim at least twenty-five political clubs.[27]

Memberships also seem to have grown continuously, at least through 1873. As table 2 illustrates, the membership of the Upper Austrian Liberal Association in the city of Linz, for example, grew from more than 500 in 1869 to more than 2,500 in 1873. The Friends of the Constitution in St. Pölten, Lower Austria, started with 500 members in 1870 and counted more than 1,000 by 1873.

Liberal clubs in several small towns in Upper Austria quickly grew in the early years. The Liberal Association of Wels went from 190 members in 1869

26. Kiemann, *Casino*; Unterberger, "Liberalismus in St. Pölten," 34–50; Wimmer, *Liberalismus*, 57–63.

27. *Niederösterreichischer Amtskalender für das Jahr 1875* (Vienna, 1875), 499–501; NÖLA, Vereinskataster, Kategorie XIX, Politische Vereine; SLA, Vereinskataster.

TABLE 2. Membership Growth in Two Liberal Political Associations

Club	1869	1870	1871	1872	1873
Upper Austrian Liberal Association in Linz	526	1,857	2,117		2,606
Friends of the Constitution in St. Pölten	500	653	785	1,000	

Source: Data from Unterberger, "Liberalismus in St. Pölten," 8–12; Wimmer, *Liberalismus,* 28, 34–38.

to 210 a year later. Liberal associations in Mauerkirchen and Steyr grew from 114 and 363 members, respectively, to 300 and 369 in the same period. In Graz, the Styrian People's Education Society boasted more than 500 members in the early 1870s. Within six months of its founding in 1868, the Constitutional Club in Laibach, Carniola, also claimed more than five hundred members. The Liberal-Political Association of Sternberg, Moravia, counted almost 400 members at its annual meeting in 1873, while the German-Political Association in Neutitschein, Bohemia, had a total of 480 members. When the democrats' clubs in Vienna combined to form a united electoral organization in 1873, the umbrella association alone counted more than 1,200 members.[28]

The number of general meetings and general levels of attendance also increased rapidly during this same period. In 1870 the Linz association held seventeen meetings; in 1871 this increased to twenty-six and to thirty-six in 1872. The outdoor *Wanderversammlung*, a sort of picnic gathering with lectures or commemorative ceremonies, became a particularly popular club activity. Participation at these socially oriented events ranged from 130 at an early *Wanderversammlung* (which was plagued by rain) to 800 "middle-class persons and their families including a good number of Jews" at an evening celebration with fireworks, held to commemorate both Emperor Joseph II and the martyrs of 1848. In April 1873, over a thousand liberals gathered to celebrate the one hundredth meeting of their association in Linz. More typical perhaps was the experience of the Constitutional Association in Laibach. In its first year, 1869, the club held monthly meetings, each one attended by an average of sixty-nine people. Only two years later, however, the number of yearly meetings had already fallen to about six, with average attendance remaining steady at around seventy per meeting.[29]

Clubs in urban centers made frequent use of organized outings to the countryside. These were usually all-day affairs with meals and speeches and

28. *Bericht des constitutionellen Vereines in Laibach* (Laibach, 1871), 15; DZ, March 21 and April 1, 1873; Hubbard, "Graz," 222; Lukas, "Göllerich," 89–92; *Mittheilungen der Wiener demokratischen Gesellschaft*, July 1, 1873; *Politischer Volkskalender für das Jahr 1871* (Linz, 1870), 65–69; *Politischer Volks-Kalender für das Jahr 1872* (Linz, 1871), 80–81; Wimmer, *Liberalismus*, 28–38.

29. *Bericht des Constitutionellen Vereines in Laibach für das zweite und dritte Vereinsjahr* (Laibach, 1872), 15, 19; Wimmer, *Liberalismus*, 31–37.

might include a rail trip or a steamer cruise on the Danube. When the Viennese Democratic Society and two choral groups sponsored an excursion to Znaim, Moravia, to honor the local *Reichsrat* deputy there in 1873, over a thousand people paid 2.5 florins each to participate. Political clubs also sponsored festivals of commemoration like that organized by the Linz liberals. In 1873, the local German Bürger Association in Znaim, together with the Political Association of Liberals there, devised a celebration to commemorate the twenty-fifth anniversary of both the March revolution and Emperor Francis Joseph's accession to the throne. This incongruous pairing revealed much about the political mythology developed by German liberals in Austria: the justified activism of 1848 combined with the respect for order and continuity symbolized by the emperor.[30]

An increasing rate of participation in many political club activities is also reflected in organizational innovations, such as the one devised by the Upper Austrian Liberals in 1871 to accommodate their growing membership. At that time the general meetings had become so crowded that the executive began appointing committees to prepare presentations so that discussions at the meetings might be more productive. Each committee investigated a topic, whether economic, legal-political, confessional, or school related, which it then presented to the membership for discussion.[31]

The statutes of most clubs outlined a number of specific means by which members might accomplish their program's goals, from petitions and resolutions to lectures and educational projects. Most of these activities were initiated in the weekly, monthly, or semiannual meetings of the full membership and not simply by the executive committee. The Friends of the Constitution in St. Pölten, for example, rarely held a meeting in the early 1870s that did not result in the adoption of some resolution, address, or petition. The local associations bombarded the provincial and Vienna governments with petitions covering a broad range of subjects. They wanted the government to know just how much they opposed the newly espoused doctrine of papal infallibility or the Hohenwart cabinet's attempts to compromise with the Czechs. And they had all kinds of practical suggestions to share with the *Reichsrat* on such problems as how to achieve a just reform of Austria's complex electoral system. In their addresses they often thanked a specific deputy or cabinet minister for a particular act, an especially effective speech, or an edict that had somehow furthered the German liberal cause. Such heroes of the moment often received honorary club memberships, sometimes from towns they had never seen.[32]

30. *Bericht über die zehnjährige Thätigkeit des znaimer deutschen Bürgervereines anlässlich dessen am 11. Juli Stattfindenden Gründungsfeier* (Znaim, 1880), 6; *Mittheilungen der Wiener demokratischen Gesellschaft*, May 15 and June 1, 1873.

31. Wimmer, *Liberalismus*, 34.

32. Unterberger, "Liberalismus in St. Pölten," 54.

Learning, Lectures, and Libraries

Educational projects played a special role in the activities of the liberal associations. All liberal political clubs held lecture or discussion series, and some even published pamphlets for wider distribution. Topics ranged from current events (particularly anticlerical issues in the early 1870s) to local history to popular science. Charles Darwin and his theories seem to have been an especially popular topic of discussion, one lecturer calling them "an infallible weapon in the battle for freedom and progress."[33]

Education was the traditionally favored middle-class means of improving the lot of those less fortunate by teaching them the tools for helping themselves. Now many political clubs began to raise money either themselves or through the institution of a local school penny Association (*Schulpfennigverein*) for public schools and for privately endowed trade schools.[34] Political clubs also subsidized teachers' salaries or offered scholarships to promising students. Some clubs founded or supported a local library (*Volksbibliothek*), often a reading room in the town hall, and some also published a periodical or newspaper, if no liberal organ existed in the community. The Liberal Association in Linz, for example, published both an annual almanac (*Volkskalender*) and a series of informational pamphlets during the 1870s.[35]

In one Carinthian almanac article, Liberal Party *Reichsrat* Deputy Adolf Promber exhorted his readers to "create libraries!" Urging farmers in particular to continue their education after leaving the *Volksschul*, Promber suggested that the long winter months provided ample opportunity for reading. And since farmers were not likely to buy books, the simplest solution was the *Volksbibliothek*. In fact, most liberals foresaw libraries and reading rooms functioning as an adult equivalent to the recently adopted liberal school laws. "The securest basis of any constitutional state, and the most important task for liberalism," wrote the editor of the *St. Pölten Wochenblatt*, "is to achieve a healthy, practical education for the people."[36] Between 1876 and 1883, the Friends of the Constitution in St. Pölten established small libraries of about a hundred volumes each in seven of the neighboring rural communities. In 1882 they created a larger library of 260 volumes in St. Pölten itself, which, with the support of the liberal-dominated town council, grew rapidly in size to 1,500 volumes. Although at first people showed little interest in the new institution, it soon

33. *Bericht über die Thätigkeit des politischen Vereines der Liberalen in Znaim im siebenten Jahre seines Bestehens 1874* (Znaim, 1875), 5–6.

34. *Bericht des constitutionellen Vereines in Laibach (1874)*, 16.

35. *Politischer Volkskalender 1871*; *Politischer Volkskalender 1872*.

36. *Politischer Volkskalender für 1878* (Klagenfurt and Villach, 1877), 1–5; Unterberger, "Liberalismus in St. Pölten," 32. Promber represented Moravia in the *Reichsrat* as a member of the Progressive Party.

gained popularity. Whereas in its first year the librarians had recorded 1,506 book loans, two years later that number had increased over 300 percent to 5,460 book loans.[37]

Peoples' libraries in towns with a large German-speaking population in ethnically mixed provinces like Bohemia or Moravia rapidly took on a heightened significance in the growing nationalist conflicts of the 1880s. As both visible symbols and instruments of German culture there, they often received strong support from town governments. In Iglau, a small Moravian city with a German-speaking population of 83 percent according to the 1880 census, the town council placed two rooms at the disposal of the library, and the local German savings bank contributed to it the annual sum of 300 florins. Writing for the *Deutscher Volks-Kalender für die Iglauer Sprachinsel*, one nationalist liberal described the enthusiasm of the local populace for the library in universal terms, noting that its appeal crossed both class and gender lines: "Young and old race to the library to return their books. . . . Here and there working women disengage themselves from the tightly packed mass of people exiting the cigar factory at the end of a workday, hurrying to the library in order to be at the front of the long line. Already half an hour before the official opening time the small rooms are filled." Men and women of all classes apparently forgot their social differences in their hunger for enlightenment.[38]

---

37. *St. Pöltner Wochenblatt,* January 21, 1886. Occupational Profile of 3,772 Book Borrowers in 1885:

Commerce and Manufacture	1,830	(48.5%)
House Owners and Official	501	(13.2%)
Military Personnel	102	(2.7%)
Female	1,330	(35.3%)
Male	2,442	(64.7%)

Total of Books borrowed: 3,160

The statistics reflect the composition of the local Bürgertum. No farmers seem to have made use of the library in St. Pölten, yet this was precisely the reason why the liberals there set up small branch collections in outlying villages. For statistics and descriptions of other *Volksbibliotheken*, see *Bericht des Vereines der Liberalen in Znaim*, 12–13, *Bericht des znaimer deutschen Bürgervereines*, 5.

38. "Die deutsche Volksbibliothek in Iglau," in *Deutscher Volkskalender für die Iglauer Sprachinsel* (Iglau, 1886), 132–35. The article gave the following statistics regarding library use in 1885–86: 3,565 individuals used the library. Of these, 95 percent lived in the town itself, while the rest came from neighboring villages. As in St. Pölten, women accounted for about a third of the borrowers, despite the author's colorful account that suggests women were the large majority of borrowers. Professions of male borrowers are as follows (figures based on 570 men/quarter).

House or Landowner	29	(5%)
Officials, Lawyers, Professors, Teachers, Officers	58	(10%)
Business and (small or large) Industry	239	(42%)
Commercial Apprentices	73	(13%)
Crafts Apprentices	69	(12%)

The issue of what types of books to include in the peoples' libraries aroused a great deal of interest and discussion. Promber devoted most of his article on *Volksbibliotheken* to dispensing advice on this matter. On the one hand, he believed, one ought to offer books on as many topics as possible so as to retain the interest of the rural readers. On the other hand, "the farmer is no bookworm; if too much is offered him, he might recoil from it, thinking that he was being forced to become a stay-at-home scholar." The books should also be popular in tone and not overly intellectual; "otherwise the farmer might put it aside with anger and vexation." Promber recommended popularly written books about agriculture, science, and geography, next to more amusing books that portrayed the rural life most familiar to the farmer. Austrian history was crucial for the example of famous men and useful to awaken a sense of patriotism. "Next to a history of Austria, a biography of our unforgettable Emperor Joseph II should never be lacking."[39]

The books in the St. Pölten collection came under the headings of "classics, histories and historical novels, science, and periodicals." Care was taken not to include anticlerical works that might offend the religious sensibilities of the rural populace. In Vienna, the Democratic Society scorned the inclusion of "cheap, popular novels," emphasizing instead the importance of "popular works on scientific subjects." In 1873, the third annual conference of the Moravian German Liberal Party decided that the quality of the books furnished to libraries outweighed the quantity. The conference recommended the inclusion of "popular works, including world history, biography, and the natural sciences."[40]

Election Campaigns

The liberal political clubs assumed their most explicitly political function during election campaigns for city councils, provincial diets, and, starting in 1873, for the *Reichsrat*. Every liberal club program considered the "nomination and support of Liberal Party candidates for election" a major contribution to the realization of its goals. Accordingly, liberal clubs took over the direction of political campaigns from the ad hoc temporary committees that had organized them prior to 1867. This change did not involve an appreciable shift in power, since the men who had originally run local political campaigns in the 1860s generally belonged to the same core of activists who had gone on to found the political clubs.

Domestics	27	(4%)
Railroad Employees	16	(3%)
Soldiers	22	(4%)
Workers and Day Laborers	23	(4%)

39. *Politischer Volks-Kalender für 1878* (Klagenfurt and Villach, 1877), 2–4.

40. DZ, June 16, 1873.

Like associational life itself, the election process helped reinforce and solidify the existing patterns of bourgeois predominance at the local level. Particularly in early years, the leading Bürger who had gained social status through associational achievement decided from among themselves whom to elect. At the same time, however, the peculiarities of the curial electoral system prevented a rigid form of local notable politics from developing as it had in parts of Germany or France. In Austria, the professional and commercial classes voted separately from the landowning nobility and in some cities, from the wealthiest industrialists. While the Bürger activists who dominated associational life may have been affluent, they did not generally include the wealthiest men of the community nor the members of the local nobility among their ranks. Whether they qualified to vote in it or not, nobles usually identified their interests with the politically less activist large landowner curia. If they joined in local associational life, they seem not to have usually involved themselves actively in the mechanics of political organizing. Similarly, while the wealthiest merchants and industrialists may have participated more actively in associational life, they often elected their own representatives through the chambers of commerce and industry. This left more room for men whose civic activism itself qualified them for public office.

The institutionalization of electoral organization within the context of the club helped produce a growing politicization of the Bürgertum. Purely in terms of participation in Austrian elections to the *Reichsrat* and diets, the Bürger voting rate in the urban curia increased by 11 percent in Cisleithania between 1867 and 1873, as table 3 shows. Moravia and Upper Austria saw increases of more than 20 percent, while Carinthia experienced an 18 percent rise. And although liberals at all levels continued to claim that they represented the universal interest of the entire *Volk*, some of them clearly had begun to build and mobilize local political machines.

The same men who ran the local associations also often led the liberal parties in the diets and *Reichsrat*. They made up a growing number of activists for whom politics was becoming a time-consuming vocation. What distinguished them from other deputies was precisely the organizational connection they cultivated between their local association and the provincial and national liberal parties. Even after many of these men gained higher office, they continued to concentrate their energies on their local political bases. This allowed them to maintain a firm grasp on growing local political organizations while playing a role in provincial and national politics.

Franz Schmeykal ran the well-organized Bohemian German Liberal Party through his many club positions, including chairmanship of the Prague Casino, for example. Although he never sat in the *Reichsrat*, he used his party position and his seat in the Bohemian Diet to influence decisions of national importance. Karl von Wiser, who presided over the influential Upper Austrian Liberal As-

TABLE 3. Average Participation Rates of Eligible Voters in Urban Curia Districts, in Percentage

Province	1867	1873
Bohemia	47%	58%
Carinthia	36%	54%
Lower Austria (incl. Vienna)	43%	48%
Moravia	59%	79%
Silesia	47%	57%
Styria	47%	52%
Upper Austria	51%	79%
Cisleithania	49%	60%

Source: Data from Neumann-Spallert and Schirmer, *Die Reichsraths-Wahlen,* 33. Statistics for rural districts, where voters chose electors who then chose the deputies, indicate far lower rates of participation ranging from 15% to 35% in both years.

sociation in Linz, sat only briefly in the *Reichsrat* before serving a long term as mayor of Linz. Other local leaders, such as Johann Ofner of St. Pölten in Lower Austria or Franz Gross of Wels in Upper Austria, managed to combine long and successful careers as *Reichsrat* deputies with their duties as town mayors and leaders of local political associations. The Viennese democrats who sat on the city council or in the *Reichsrat* after 1873, such as Franz Kronawetter, Johann Steudel, and Johann Umlauft, also maintained close political ties with local district political clubs. Despite a rhetoric that emphasized their commitment to politics as a civic duty rather than a partisan profession, circumstances and personal inclination combined to make a full-time job out of a former interest for these men. The rapidly changing shape of electoral organization in the 1870s underlined the inevitability of this transformation. Campaign activity grew in scale, requiring far more time, energy, and funds at both the local and provincial levels than it had in the 1860s.[41]

Local elections also became increasingly important, partly because opposition parties soon began to contest them more vigorously. In particular, after 1870, the clerical and conservative parties, which had suffered major setbacks over school and religious laws, began to use their own resources more effectively. Their successful mobilization of a popular opposition meant that liberal parties had to assess their chances more carefully in each constituency and develop more effective campaign tactics if they were to maintain control of

41. Boyer, *Political Radicalism*, 189–91; [Klaar] *Schmeykal*, 32–62; Unterberger, "Liberalismus in St. Pölten," 5–12; Wimmer, *Liberalismus*, 166–71.

the diets and *Reichsrat*. The outcome of each race could no longer be taken for granted. Echoing this new provincial and national concern with local politics, the progressive *Deutsche Zeitung* in Vienna published a "statistical lesson" for its readers in December 1871. A simple table juxtaposing the number and growth rates of liberal associations against Catholic conservative ones conveyed a sobering picture. Whereas both parties could claim an equal number of local political clubs at the end of 1870, by 1871 the conservative clubs outnumbered the liberal ones by a three-to-two margin.[42]

Events themselves often pointed to the danger of complacency at the local level. In 1870, for example, the Liberal Party of Upper Austria discovered to its chagrin on election day that the well-organized conservative opposition had outpolled it in each of the rural constituencies and even in one of the urban ones for the diet. Leaders of the Liberal Association in Linz had campaigned by publishing the party's traditional election proclamation and doing little else. They now saw a need to develop more effective strategies to ensure victory for their candidates. Thereafter, the Upper Austrian liberals adopted some techniques from the opposition at election time, including the popular *Wanderversammlung*, to mobilize their voters. They also added new strategies of their own, such as printing and distributing campaign brochures to reach liberal voters in the countryside.[43]

Liberal electoral organizing in the 1870s aimed primarily to raise voter participation among urban Bürger, not to win voters away from the Catholic, conservative, or Slav opposition. Liberals did not attempt to mobilize new urban social groups for their purposes either. This tendency distinguished the liberal club activities of the 1860s and 1870s from the more conscious efforts at mass mobilization developed later in the 1880s. Progressive liberals like Max Menger or the editors of some of Vienna's more democratic newspapers occasionally called for an extension of the suffrage or for the creation of a workers' curia, in order to coopt new voters and to add new blood to liberalism. Yet in the 1860s and 1870s most liberals concentrated on getting out their own vote, increasing the low rate of voter participation among the urban middle classes.

The dual need for more effective local campaign techniques and a more extensive provincial organization also increased the importance of the men who led the local political clubs. Liberal candidates for provincial or national office relied more and more heavily on local organizations to mobilize support for them at election time. The practice in the 1860s of having a provisional committee nominate candidates for outlying rural districts that they had rarely even visited now gave the local clubs a key role in elections. Besides the candidates who also held local offices, most deputies' reputations rested purely

42. DZ, December 21, 1871, *Abendblatt*.

43. Wimmer, *Liberalismus*, 30.

on their activities in Vienna and not on any connection to their district. It became the often onerous task of the local association to introduce these candidates to the voters and to engender a certain enthusiasm for them.

The increasing importance of local organizations to elections also stimulated the development of provincial electoral organizations to coordinate and direct events. Parliamentary incumbents felt this need particularly after the electoral reform of 1873, when local constituencies gained the right to elect their *Reichsrat* deputies directly. As a result of this reform, parliamentary leaders faced a potential loss of influence to local constituencies, and the creation of provincial organizations institutionalizing their role could help return some of the power to them. As early as 1871, in an attempt to set up a unified organization and a division of competence that might satisfy all involved, provincial party conferences brought deputies together with local club representatives in Bohemia, Moravia, and Lower and Upper Austria. The parliamentary deputies, traditionally isolated from their constituents, attempted nevertheless to impose party discipline on them even at the conferences. The locals meanwhile began to demand a greater voice in choosing candidates for their own districts. Despite professions of unity and mutual respect, the possibility of friction between local activists and the party leaders remained potentially damaging to the future effectiveness of the liberal parties.

The period 1867–73 saw a proliferation of liberal political clubs in cities and towns throughout Austria. Although the memberships of these clubs reflected the full range of social diversity within the German middle classes, the background of the men who led the liberal parties was far more limited. In both the provincial diets and the *Reichsrat*, power continued to be wielded by a relatively homogeneous group of lawyers, university professors, industrialists, and to a lesser extent by large landowners and state officials. The school teachers, artisans, shopkeepers, and smaller-scale merchants who continued to constitute the backbone of the local liberal movements had relatively little influence within the upper echelons of the movement.

This social division caused few problems in the early, "heroic" years of liberalism immediately after political associations had been legalized and when the interests of all liberals in establishing the constitutional state had seemed to coincide. As long as they fought together to establish the constitution, build the new school system, or remove the influence of the church, all these groups had common interests. After 1873, however, these early issues appeared to be resolved. Now economic issues came to the fore, and social differentiation within the movement became more decisive to its development. Gradually associations became spaces in which a variety of economic and social issues might be debated more pointedly, frequently becoming battlegrounds for a growing factionalism. Increasing differentiation within the middle classes and the increasingly outmoded hierarchic structure of the liberal parties also combined to create serious division between local activists and party leaders. While the liberal parties held power in Vienna and in the provincial capitals, these varied potentials for conflict remained implicit. When they lost their *Reichsrat* majority in 1879, however, party activists came to understand more clearly both the dangerous potential for internal conflict as well as the enormous political potential of the clubs for mobilizing new constituents.

CHAPTER 6

Whither Liberalism? Party and Movement, 1873–79

> One really cannot rule with this Liberal Party; some are jackasses, others rogues . . . one becomes exhausted always trying to make amends for their base acts.
>
> Adolf Auersperg (1876)[1]

The decade of the 1870s in Austria was known by contemporaries and historians alike, at first with optimism and later with disdain, as the "liberal era." In the early years of the decade liberalism still connoted unbounded progress for Austria's diverse propertied classes. By the end of the decade, however, tarnished by accusations of official corruption in the wake of severe economic depression, the liberal movement struggled against a growing reputation for unprincipled opportunism and political disunity. For the first time since before 1848, Austrian liberals seemed oddly adrift, lacking a compelling vision for the future.

The monarchy in 1871 was once again poised on the threshold of a liberal future. The short-lived conservative Hohenwart regime had failed in its attempt to satisfy federalist demands of groups like the Czech nationalists in Bohemia. The emperor turned anew to the centralist liberals, charging Prince Adolf Auersperg, younger brother of Carl Auersperg who had led the Bürger Ministry, with the formation of a cabinet. This Auersperg cabinet was to govern the Austrian half of the monarchy for the rest of the decade.[2] To press and liberal public

1. FA, ct. 51, Adolph Auersperg to Johanna, May 28, 1876.

2. On Adolf Auersperg see Irmgard Klebl, "Fürst Adolf Auersperg (1821-1885); seine politische Karriere und seine Persönlichkeit" (Ph.D. diss., University of Vienna, 1971). The following liberal deputies served in the Auersperg cabinet: Anton Banhans (commerce until 1875), Johann Chlumecky (agriculture, commerce after 1875), Sisinio de Pretis (finance), Julius Glaser (justice), Joseph Lasser (interior through July 1878), Hieronymus Mannsfeld (agriculture after 1875), Carl Stremayr (religion and education), Unger (minister without portfolio-cabinet spokesperson). The Auersperg government served from November 1871 until February of 1879, when Auersperg (who had taken over the Interior Ministry as well since Lasser's departure) and Unger departed. Stre-

alike, the new government revived promises of limitless progress on all fronts. These were the final frenzied years of Austria's *Gründerzeit* (1867–73), an optimistic time of perceived economic boom and widespread speculation. Liberal newspapers and journals urged the economic and social transformation of Austrian society, touting the promise of freer trade, an expanding economy, and a better educated society.[3]

Plans for an international World's Fair to be held in the summer of 1873 in Vienna's Prater embodied the expansive optimism of the age. In an artificially created landscape, where architectural achievement appeared to defy nature itself, crowded pavilions and technical displays would catalog both the remarkable productivity and cultural diversity of the liberal monarchy. According to the *Neue Freie Presse*, the exhibition would represent "the cultural and economic achievements of the present" in order to "encourage their continued development in the future." Nature and history, however, conspired to undermine this glorious celebration of the liberal society and its unlimited potential. Bad weather plagued the fair in its opening month, while a cholera epidemic kept down the number of visitors and reduced anticipated profits.[4]

Far worse, however, than the ravages of nature or disease was the spectacular crash (*Krach*) on May 9, 1873, of the Vienna stock market. In a flash, several building ventures, in particular railroad projects, were revealed to have been little more than empty bubbles. Speculators who had amassed fortunes through questionable transactions during the heady days of the *Gründerzeit* now lost them overnight. Some committed suicide in order to avoid angry investors. Among those who lost everything were several small-scale investors, retired people, and widows. All of them had parted eagerly with their life savings in the hope of sharing in the fantastic profit-taking of the early 1870s, and many now faced complete ruin.[5]

---

mayr headed a caretaker cabinet with Taaffe as minister of interior until August when Taaffe was named minister president. For the next months, three liberals (Horst, Korb, Stremayr) reluctantly continued to serve under Taaffe until the emperor approved their repeated requests to resign their posts in June 1880.

3. Helga Maier, "Börsenkrach und Weltausstellung in Wien. Ein Beitrag zur Geschichte der bürgerlichen-liberalen Gesellschaft um das Jahr 1873" (Ph.D. diss., University of Graz, 1973), 118–25. Economic speculation was fueled by a variety of important factors, including exceptional harvests in Hungary, the belief that much of the French war indemnity to the new German Reich after the Franco-Prussian War would be invested in Austrian concerns, and the inflated expectations of the revenues that the World's Fair of 1873 would bring to Vienna.

4. Maier, "Börsenkrach und Weltausstellung," 213, 248; NFP, June 5, 1873. Several newspapers speculated that the dome over the main rotunda at the exhibition, built of glass and steel and apparently a technological marvel, would either sink the building or collapse altogether. It is also worth noting that the choice of the site had required that the bourgeois organizers demolish the popular old *Würstelprater*.

5. The crash was not completely unexpected. NFP, January 1, 1873; Plener, *Erinnerungen*, 2:1; Müllner, "Lasser," 88–89; Rogge, *Österreich seit der Katastrophe Hohenwart-Beust* (Leipzig and Vienna, 1879), 1:147–51.

The drastic fall in prices and subsequent decline in production that followed the crash touched businesses of every size and type, affecting workers, peasants, artisans, professionals, and officials in provincial towns and cities across the monarchy. Overall production in Austria would not reach 1873 levels again until 1881. The economic depression and psychological disillusionment that followed the crash held long-term political consequences. The *Krach* severely damaged popular confidence in the efficacy of liberal principles. This was as much the case for the wealthier urban and provincial bourgeoisie as it was for artisans and small business owners. The *Krach* challenged the largely unquestioned popular belief that a free-market capitalist system would bring growth and prosperity to all of society. Several interest groups now demanded government intervention to guarantee their economic survival. When the Auersperg government proved incapable of ameliorating the immediate effects of the *Krach*, Catholic and Conservative Party politicians blamed liberalism itself for the plight of those hardest hit.[6]

The depression created a populist outcry against the liberal parties as some of the more scandalous details surrounding the *Krach* gradually came to light. In return for financial remuneration, several Liberal Party deputies, it seems, had lent their names to the boards of directors of *Gründer* companies. Some, like Carl Giskra, had joined four or five such boards. After the *Krach*, this practice led to accusations of official corruption and shady financial practices in the highest liberal circles. Increasingly, the *Reichsrat* liberals were portrayed as an elite minority of opportunists feeding off the suffering of the *Volk*, men no longer able to comprehend, much less to represent, the interests of the entire community.[7]

Jungen and *Alten*

These kinds of accusations were not entirely new. They reinforced the earlier complaints some party activists had raised about the unresponsiveness of parliamentary leaders to local concerns. After 1867 some of the new local liberal clubs had started to demand a larger role for themselves in determining party

6. Herbert Matis and Karl Bachinger, "Österreichs industrielle Entwicklung," in *Die Habsburgermonarchie 1848-1918*, vol. 1, *Die Wirtschaftliche Entwicklung* (Vienna, 1973), 132; Eduard März, *Österreichs Industrie- und Bankpolitik in der Zeit Kaiser Franz Josephs I. am Beispiel der k.k. priviligierten österreichischen Credit-Anstalt für Handel und Gewerbe*, (Vienna, 1968), 185.

7. Wilhelm Angerstein, *Volkswirtschaftliche Zustände in Österreich* (Leipzig, 1871), 40; Maier, "Börsenkrach und Weltausstellung," 111; Wadl, *Liberalismus*, 205–7. The Lower Austrian delegation to the *Reichsrat* had the highest percentage of members belonging to boards of directors. Twelve deputies out of eighteen held thirty-eight such positions. Giskra, now representing Vienna's first district, was one of the most egregious examples, with four company positions, assumed only days following his resignation as interior minister. One critic estimated that each of these positions brought Giskra an annual sum of 10,000 florins. Other liberal deputies held even

programs and nominating candidates for election. The stifling authority of party leaders had usually managed to quash the desires of local activists for a greater voice in politics. This kind of internal disagreement flared up noticeably during the brief rule of the conservative-leaning Potocki and Hohenwart cabinets (1870–71). In the election campaign of 1870, a small group of liberal activists calling itself *Jungen* (the Young) made an energetic appearance on the political scene. Consisting at first of a handful of deputies who considered themselves the left wing of the Liberal Party, this group soon attracted the interest and support of a variety of club activists and university students who wanted to transform those parties.[8]

The *Jungen* were outsiders who wanted to become insiders. They were local activists, lawyers, journalists, and schoolteachers with substantial local associational experience, who sought election to the city councils, provincial diets, and the *Reichsrat.*[9] What characterized them most clearly was not their youth but rather their particular relationship to the organized liberal movement. While the *Neue Freie Presse* might contemptuously refer to the *Jungen* as unknowns, they represented important local interests that could not easily be ignored. The *Jungen* wanted to strengthen the rights of local district organizations within the larger party organizations, demanding for the former the right to choose candidates for the diets and the *Reichsrat.*[10]

The *Jungen* also stressed the need to protect Austro-German national interests against what they perceived to be a rising tide of Slav political gains in Austria. Many of them had joined the German Association organized in Vienna by Joseph Kopp in 1869. This new consciousness about German identity developed during the Hohenwart regime (1870–71), when Czech demands for political arrangements like those of the Hungarian *Ausgleich* increasingly dominated Austrian politics. The liberals had traditionally opposed any such compromises, seeing them in purely political, not nationalist terms. In the 1860s party leaders had denounced such schemes as a threat to central, constitutional rule. Now the *Jungen* raised a different concern in the battle against federalism: the endangered German nationality. Rejecting liberalism's cher-

---

more such "advisory positions," including Moravian deputy Eduard Sturm with eight, and Franz, Ritter von Hopfen, former president of the Chamber of Deputies, with six.

8. Eva Somogyi, "Die Reichsauffassung der deutschösterreichischen Liberalen in den siebziger Jahren des 19. Jahrhunderts," in *Gesellschaft, Politik und Verwaltung in der Habsburgermonarchie 1830–1918*, ed. Ferenc Latz and Ralph Melville (Budapest, 1987), 157–87, especially 160–62.

9. Plener, *Erinnerungen*, 2:1, 363. The two earliest *Jungen* activists in the *Reichsrat*, Carl Pickert and Alfred Knoll, were, respectively, a former *Mittelschul* teacher and a lawyer.

10. Except for the university students who supported them, the *Jungen* were not all that much younger than the other liberals. Only about four years separated the average ages of the *Jungen* in the Progressive Party from the *Alten* in the Left Party. Judson, "German Liberalism," 463; Molisch, *Briefe*, 71.

ished belief that a supranationalist Austrian patriotism provided the best guarantee for the rights of German nationality in the monarchy, the *Jungen* began a gradual transformation of the way in which the German-speaking Bürgertum understood its national identity.

While liberals had viewed Germanness as a quality available to all who embraced their progressive political vision, *Jungen* activists like the Bohemian Carl Pickert began to disengage Germanness from its universalist Austrian associations. "We [Germans] were always the saviors of the state, the supporters of the state . . . having always represented the Austrian [state] standpoint while placing our own national interests in the background. . . . We are constantly . . . at a disadvantage against opponents whose nationalism underlies their point of view. . . . We never speak about [our own] national self-interest but always fight for the interest of the [whole] state." This rhetorical transformation obliged those who identified themselves as Germans to rethink their relation both to the state and to other nationalist groups in the monarchy.[11]

The *Jungen* of the early 1870s did not, however, replace liberal ideology with a purely defensive nationalist rhetoric. Nor, in fact, did they privilege the latter entirely over the former. They sought rather to combine their liberal beliefs with a nationalist rhetoric capable of countering the more effective political claims made by the aggressive Czech nationalist movement in Bohemia. Czech activists denounced the privileged position enjoyed by the German language. They attributed its status not to its greater cultural value but to a brutal system of cultural domination. The *Jungen* justified their linguistic privilege by portraying German culture as a powerful vehicle for political progress. An 1871 editorial in the *Deutsche Zeitung*, for example, called on Germans to stand up for their national rights, precisely because "for us, the nationalist position coincides with the free-thinking, enlightened one, since to be German means to be free and to behave ethically." Thus to a great extent the *Jungen* continued to define German identity in terms of belief in progressive cultural values, exactly as did most Liberal Party leaders. Their rhetoric did not convey an essentialist understanding of national identity, and for this reason the *Jungen* did not portray Germans as a full-fledged separate interest group. The German way, they claimed, was still best for both the monarchy and all its peoples.[12]

At first, liberal leaders welcomed the efforts of the *Jungen*, seeing their organizational and ideological innovations as a way to revitalize the liberal parties. Some leaders even borrowed from the nationalist rhetoric of the *Jungen*. When the German Association in Vienna sponsored the first German Austrian Party Conference in May 1870, several Liberal Party leaders (most notably Giskra and Kaiserfeld) attended. The *Neue Freie Presse*, which generally sup-

11. Kolmer, *Parlament*, 2:122.

12. DZ, December 20, 1871.

ported the party leadership in internal political matters, spoke approvingly of the *Jungen* efforts to revitalize the party in a time of crisis.[13]

The program of this first German Austrian Party Conference combined a new concern for national identity with more traditional liberal themes. It claimed a solidarity among all German speakers in the monarchy, stressing that threats against Germans in one province would now be understood as threats against all. At the same time, the program conveyed a desire to return the reforming impetus to an apparently stagnant liberalism. Point five demanded both the direct election of *Reichsrat* deputies and the abolition of the curial voting system. Point six insisted on a complete repudiation of the Concordat and the introduction of compulsory civil marriage, and point seven suggested ways to cut the military budget and equalize the tax burden.[14]

The implicit criticism of the Liberal Party in this program and the desire of the *Jungen* for more democratic party structures alienated several leaders. From their perspective further reforms were out of the question when politics constituted a daily battle to save the precious 1867 constitution. When the German Association organized a second German Austrian Party Conference in 1871, no Liberal Party leaders attended, and the liberal press expressed contempt where it had formerly voiced approval. Commenting on this second conference the *Neue Freie Presse* noted: "we know all too well that this meeting did not include those party members in whose name the conference attempted to speak. . . . What in the world is the point of such an eclectic assemblage, if those people who deserve to be its leaders and who have taken on this [party] role, stay away?"[15]

The *Alten* (the Old), as the leaders were now being called, no longer viewed the *Jungen* as useful to the party and raised objections to their explicitly nationalist bent. "I and most of the other deputies were invited," wrote Ignaz Plener to his son Ernst of the 1871 conference, and "we managed to prevent Giskra, Herbst, and the German Bohemian deputies from attending. The main point on the agenda is celebration of the German victory [against France], [closer] connection to Germany, protection of German nationality in Austria (which is really not in the least threatened, despite the Hohenwart cabinet), etc., and more nonsense of this sort. Naturally [this program created] enormous ill feeling toward us [at court] and plenty of material for slander of the Liberal Party [by its enemies in court circles]."[16]

---

13. NFP, May 24, 1870; Julius Gierschik, *Dr. Karl Pickert. Ein Beitrag zur Geschichte der deutschnationalen Bewegung in Böhmen* (Leitmeritz, 1913), 12. Ignaz Kuranda claimed in 1870 that because the *Jungen* had led the battle against Hohenwart, they had earned the thanks of the entire party.

14. "Programm des ersten deutsch-österreichischen Parteitages in Wien am 22. Mai 1870," in Harrington-Müller, *Fortschrittsklub*, 157–59.

15. NFP, March 1, 1871.

16. Molisch, *Briefe*, 71.

This second conference and its program expressed the *Jungen* position more forcefully than the first one had. Point one did indeed praise the recent Prussian victory over the French and demanded a reorientation of internal policy toward German interests in Austria. "[Maintaining a close] relationship to Germany seems to be the only means to revive Austria's power . . . whose basis, considering culture, history, and politics, is definitely German." While this interpretation of events gained support among the *Jungen* and their student supporters, many of whom waxed enthusiastic over the new united Germany, few of the older liberals agreed. Several could not forget their Great German hopes of 1848 or the bitterness of defeat by the Prussians in 1866.[17]

While the question of how best to articulate Austro-German national interests may have dominated the newspapers, the organizational differences between *Jungen* and *Alten* aggravated their differences. The 1871 program had also recommended a number of organizational reforms to the liberals in order to strengthen party unity and effectiveness from below. These became the focus of a new series of attacks on the apparent complacency of the *Alten* after the fall of the Hohenwart regime. When the liberal Auersperg government took office in 1871, *Jungen* accusations of complacency and corruption overshadowed the issue of German nationalism, a point often overlooked by historians of the period. In the election campaign of 1873, the *Jungen* promised voters not merely a stronger defense of Germanness but more importantly a thoroughgoing reform of the electoral process. A liberal electoral reform sanctioned in April 1873 ensured that *Reichsrat* deputies would now be elected directly from individual constituencies rather than indirectly by the provincial diets.[18] The *Jungen* used this reform to agitate for more local influence in choosing Liberal Party candidates. While not opposing all incumbents, they warned that incumbency frequently led to the kind of backroom deals that had sapped parliamentarians of their reforming energy.[19]

The *Deutsche Zeitung* demanded that election committees in each district have the right to choose their own *Reichsrat* candidates. This was a response primarily to the power of the Liberal Party organization in Bohemia, the only province where liberal efforts were so well organized. "The voters' right to

17. August Göllerich, *Der deutsche Parteitag vom 26. Februar 1871 und seine Beschlüsse* (Vienna, 1871). HHSA, Nachlass Plener, ct. 6; Molisch, *Briefe*, 67–68. The *Jungen* enthusiasm for the new Germany did not, of course, envision a German absorption of Austria as some of the more radical student groups hoped. The difference in generational views is particularly clear from the disagreement between Ignaz Plener and his son Ernst. The elder Plener saw the Prussian victory as a catastrophe and accused his son of being blinded by his admiration for Bismarck.

18. The term *direct* refers to the fact that deputies would be elected by local constituencies and no longer by the diets. Particularly in the case of the rural districts, which retained a two-tiered system of voting for electors who then chose the deputies, the process was anything but direct.

19. DZ, April 9, 1873. Pointing out that every election since 1861 seemed to have presented voters with an emergency situation, the *Deutsche Zeitung*, which supported the *Jungen*, noted that voters had been under continuous pressure for twenty years to reelect incumbents.

self-determination must be protected. In no case should a central or provincial committee have the power to forbid the voters to elect the man who holds their trust and to force on them a different candidate for backroom reasons, as has repeatedly been the case in Bohemia." The *Jungen* proposed that instead of dictating candidates to local committees, the provincial leadership should encourage those committees to take the initiative in finding suitable candidates at the local level. Their battle cry, "Elect new men!" reinforced this populist critique of liberal incumbents. Again and again in 1873, the *Jungen* accused the liberals of having tolerated corruption and opportunism in their ranks for too long, an accusation that gained increasing legitimacy in the wake of the stock market crash. Financial opportunism and government sinecures had, in the eyes of the *Jungen*, drained the party of its former activist vigor.[20]

Not surprisingly, the election campaign of 1873 frequently degenerated into bitter name calling between the *Jungen* and *Alten*, particularly in Bohemia and in the Viennese press. Accusing the *Jungen* of dividing the progressive forces that they claimed to support, the *Neue Freie Presse* asserted that without the *Alten*, no party organization could hope to gain real political influence. The *Deutsche Zeitung* shot back that the *Jungen* and their organization had tremendous support across the monarchy.[21] Both papers used similar rhetoric to claim each party as the legitimate heir to the Austrian liberal tradition. The bitter controversy peaked at the Bohemian German Liberal Party Conference held at Teplitz in May 1873. Speaking for the *Jungen*, Alfred Knoll and Karl Pickert presented a platform amendment demanding more power for local electoral committees and making the issue of German nationalism more central to the party's mission. In his scathing reply, Eduard Herbst derisively accused the *Jungen* of placing the divisive principle of nationalism ahead of freedom itself. The delegates easily defeated the *Jungen* motion. What is most revealing about this episode is the rhetoric employed by Herbst and other party leaders. They were anxious to protect their influence within the party by portraying the controversy as a simple choice between those who represented universal principles of freedom and those who espoused a narrow-minded ideology of nationalism. "After twelve years of defending civil and religious freedom," Herbst and his colleagues added, "if our nation has been called to be the first in the empire, she will become and remain [the first] through hard work and not because she simply announces it for herself."[22]

20. DZ, April 9, 1873; Kolmer, *Parlament*, 2:279. The *Jungen* envisioned the creation of an Imperial Election Committee (*Reichs-Wahl-Comité*) to coordinate local liberal election efforts for all of Cisleithania.

21. DZ, May 8, May 13, 1873; NFP, April 30, *Abendblatt*, May 1, *Abendblatt*, 1873.

22. DZ, May 15, May 18, 1873; NFP, May 18, May 19, *Abendblatt*, 1873; Gierschik, *Pickert*, 13; Molisch, *Briefe*, 83–84; Plener, *Erinnerungen*, 2:1. Over a thousand delegates voted against the *Jungen* proposal, while about forty supported it.

By painting the *Jungen* simply as selfish nationalists, the *Alten* tried to draw public attention away from the issues of local self-determination and political corruption. When they did address these latter subjects, the *Alten* rhetoric cast the argument in similar terms. Did the voters prefer a trusted individual or one blindly loyal to some narrow ideology? The *Neue Freie Presse* maintained that the old Liberal Party's very effectiveness was rooted in the regional friendships and informal contacts among the independent-minded *Bürger Vertrauensmänner* who organized local election efforts. Not a professionally structured organization with artificially imposed programs but rather the traditional collegial network of dedicated citizens would best represent the voter's desires.[23]

Despite the apparent gulf separating *Jungen* from *Alten* in situations like the Teplitz conference, their differences appear minute when viewed in the general context of Austrian politics, even on the vexing question of how much to stress German nationalism. The Teplitz program in fact closed with the claim that the "solidarity and unanimity of Germans in all parts of Austria is the source of the power and meaning [of all civic freedoms]," a statement that barely differs from the opening paragraph of the *Jungen* program. Herbst himself was not above putting his own name to nationalist election appeals later that same year. And while Herbst may have defeated Pickert and Knoll at Teplitz, the issue of party responsiveness to local concerns would continue to divide the liberals well into the 1890s.[24]

From Upper Austria, Styria, Carniola, and Moravia, meanwhile, provincial party leaders called in vain for unity. The party split had not touched local organizations in these provinces, particularly in the first two, where traditional Autonomist rhetoric closely resembled that of the *Jungen*. Here party veterans like Carl Rechbauer, who sympathized with the *Jungen* but remained on good terms with the *Alten* leaders, urged a truce. Party leaders feared that the stock market crash and accusations of corruption would diminish their chances at the polls.[25] Public outrage at those deemed responsible for the *Krach* had run so high that Carl Giskra, who represented Vienna's first district, was forced to return to his native Brünn to run for a seat there. *Jungen* leaders hoped that disaffected Bürger voters would turn to them as an alternative to the discredited leaders, but in Vienna the *Krach* seems to have helped the Vienna Democrats

---

23. DZ, May 31, 1873.

24. *Deutsche Volkszeitung Reichenberg*, September 24, 1873; HHSA, Nachlass Plener, ct. 27. One appeal addressed "to the German people in Bohemia" in September 1873 advised voters to: "Send them a German answer by unanimously electing men on whose loyal conviction for freedom and German tribal behavior (*deutsches Stammesart*) they could count."

25. Leopold Kammerhofer, "Organisationsformen und Führungsschichten," in his *Studien zum Deutschliberalismus in Zisleithanien, 1873–1879* (Vienna, 1992) 23–44, especially 29; Krones, *Kaiserfeld*, 352–53; NFP, May 21, 1873.

most (they elected five deputies to the *Reichsrat* for the first time). In fact, the liberal parties actually emerged from these elections statistically stronger than their numbers in the outgoing *Reichsrat*. This was due not so much to their popularity as to the workings of the curial voting system. Both the Auersperg government's pressure on the voters in the large landowners' curia and a questionable plan designed to buy up as many estates as possible for constitutional landowners in Bohemia helped create a modest landslide for the liberals. Their success, combined with the support of fourteen Galician Ruthenians and the continued boycott by the Czechs, gave the liberals their strongest position yet in the *Reichsrat*.[26]

The election outcome in October 1873, summarized in table 4, reflected several important long-term trends in Austrian electoral geography. The *Alten* demonstrated resilience in the large landowner and chamber of commerce curias and especially in regions where centralism remained an important concern among voters. In the so-called *Sprachinseln*, or "language islands," of German speakers, in provinces as diverse as Moravia and the Bukowina, voters elected centrist deputies who joined either the Left (*Alten*) or the Center Party of liberal large landowners in the new parliament. Painfully aware of their minority status at the provincial level, these voters believed that only a strongly centralist state could guarantee their minority interests. The *Alten* also dominated the election in Bohemia, but here it was their strong organization that carried them to victory rather than their popularity among the voters. The Bohemian German minority lived in contiguous areas and did not share the kind of support for a traditional centralism found in the *Sprachinseln*.

The appeal of the *Jungen* was strongest in the urban curia, particularly in majority German-speaking provinces (Upper Austria, and especially Styria and Carinthia), where traditional concerns about local autonomy canceled any nationalist desire to strengthen the centralized state.

Ideology and Issues in the 1870s

At the start of the new parliamentary session, the *Jungen* and their allies joined to create a Progressive Club in the *Reichsrat*. This new club proclaimed its task "in the Chamber as providing an [impetus for] movement, a forward-pushing

26. Angerstein, *Die Korruption*, 55–57; FA, ct. 51, letters to Adolf Auersperg from his wife Johanna and his brother Karl; Klebl, "Adolf Auersperg," 88–89; Kolmer, *Parlament*, 2: 225–26; Berthold Sutter, "Die politische und rechtliche Stellung der Deutschen in Österreich 1848 bis 1918," in *Die Habsburgermonarchie 1848–1918*, volume 3, *Die Völker des Reiches*, ed. Adam Wandruszka and Peter Urbanitsch (Vienna, 1980), 207; Ucakar, "Demokratie und Wahlrecht in Österreich," 240. In April 1872 Carl Auersperg bought one such estate in his sister-in-law Johanna's name. Some historians consider the 1873 election results to have been disappointing to the liberals (Ucakar) or even view them as a defeat (Sutter). Neither claim is supportable.

TABLE 4. Party Distribution of 353 *Reichsrat* Seats, 1873

Total for Liberal Parties	199	Total for Opposition Parties	125	Total for Allies of Liberals	29
Left (incl. *Alten*)	88	Right (Hohenwart)	43	Vienna Democrats	5
Progressive Party (incl. *Jungen*)	57	Poles	49	Ruthenes	14
Center (Constitutional Landowners)	54	Czechs (Boycott)	33	Independents	10

Source: Data from Sigmund Hahn, *Reichsrathsalmanach für das Jahr 1873* (Vienna, 1873); Knauer, *Das österreichische Parlament* von 1848–1966 (Vienna, 1969); Kolmer, Parlament, 2:281.

element." The Progressives promised to work closely with the traditional liberals on issues of mutual concern while still retaining their independence. In a display of solidarity, the Left joined with the Center (constitutional large landowners) and the Progressives to elect Styrian Progressive Carl Rechbauer president of the Chamber for the new term. By the end of this six-year term, the lines separating the three liberal parties had become confused, suggesting that differences among them were not as clearly defined as the three separate programs indicated. Much political confusion in the *Reichsrat* involved the changeable relations between the Left and the Progressives. In a number of stunning political coups later in the decade, groups of deputies would abandon the Left for the Progressives over the questions of renewing the ten-year financial arrangements with Hungary and the occupation of Bosnia-Hercegowina. By the end of the decade, the ranks of the Progressive Club had in fact swelled to include most of the *Alten* leaders from 1873.[27]

With the bitter election campaign behind them, the Progressives in the *Reichsrat* proposed few changes in the political process or the legislative agenda, a point that implies that *Jungen* attacks had indeed been more about internal party power relations than about ideology. Certainly the *Jungen* did not initiate a new politics organized around the concept of the endangered German nation. Even in their organizational behavior—where one might expect a new model of doing business to have emerged—the Progressives behaved like the *Alten* they had criticized. They too limited their contact with constituents to annual speeches made to local political associations. Nor did the Progressives ever have to choose consciously between their nationalist rhetoric and their liberal convictions in the 1870s.

Liberal and Progressive legislative efforts of the 1870s lacked the urgency and the direction that had characterized them in the 1860s. Liberal rhetoric

27. *Bericht des constitutionellen Vereines in Laibach über das siebente Vereinsjahr 1874* (Laibach, 1874), 9. Quote from a speech made by a liberal *Reichsrat* deputy to the Constitutional Association of Laibach.

and energy had focused on the twin goals of establishing the constitutional *Rechtsstaat* and removing the Catholic Church from its institutional preeminence in Austrian life. These goals had in fact helped to define a clear political identity for all those from various regions across Austria who called themselves liberals. What would constitute liberal ideology in an age with a guaranteed constitution and a government that had repudiated the hated Concordat? Several liberals, including many in the Auersperg cabinet, worked on the remaining tasks required to implement the constitutional order more fully. These administrative tasks, however crucial to the new order, could hardly galvanize the public now that the political battle to establish a constitution had been won. Attempts by others to legislate more radical measures, such as a law requiring civil marriage or further electoral reform, gained some support in parliamentary circles but could not by themselves constitute the raison d'etre of a movement. Leaders discouraged discussion of electoral reform, calling it too soon after the recent reform that had freed the *Reichsrat* from the diets. Also, the very size of the liberal *Reichsrat* majority gave the parties a sense of complacency that reduced the political motivation to address constituents' concerns.

Neither the Auersperg government nor the Left and Progressive parties took action to address the issue that most animated the public: the great depression. Only a week after the *Krach*, the cabinet suspended the Bank Act and set up a fund to help some of the larger banks and firms pay off their major investors. More importantly, the liberals passed legislation in the following years to regulate the stock market and change the system of railroad concessions. Yet the government was reluctant to commit state aid to rectify economic and social ills. Many influential liberals concurred with the position of Interior Minister Lasser (himself a critic of the ill-fated joint stock company concession system), who opposed government aid to troubled companies. Lasser argued that weak and lazy firms should be allowed to die out in order to relieve the market of their oppressive weight.[28]

This *laissez mourir* attitude drew criticism from artisanal producers, small property owners, and their political representatives on the right who demanded stronger state action to mitigate the effects of economic depression. In 1873–1874 such demands also raised fears that the young workers' movement might be driven into the arms of waiting conservative demagogues. A steep rise in permanent unemployment in the first year of depression caused the liberal press to warn, for example, "The ravens of reaction are never far when the field is covered with corpses . . . hawking well-known cures from their . . . [feudal] medicine chest."[29] If most *Reichsrat* liberals had responded with in-

28. Kolmer, *Parlament*, 2:276; Müllner, "Lasser," 88.
29. NFP, February 7, 1874; Wadl, *Liberalismus*, 67.

difference to workers' demands during the expansionist *Gründerzeit*, they now brought their attention to bear on them in the early phases of the depression. In 1874 the workers' association Peoples' Will sent a memorandum to the *Reichsrat* suggesting (among other demands) the creation of *Arbeiterkammer*, or chambers of labor. As drafted by Heinrich Oberwinder, spokesman for the moderate wing of the organized labor movement, the document envisioned institutions that would represent working-class interests in the same way that the existing chambers of commerce represented business interests. Recognizing that the *Reichsrat* would not adopt universal manhood suffrage in the short term, the workers argued that giving every chamber of commerce district its *Arbeiterkammer* would bring workers' concerns into public discussion, give serious consideration to workers' own reform ideas, and eventually enfranchise workers within the existing system of curial voting.

The suggestion of *Arbeiterkammer* was not new in liberal circles, nor was the idea of enfranchising some workers through such chambers. In discussions surrounding the election reform of 1873 Max Menger had suggested a similar way to enfranchise workers. Menger wanted to add workers' sections to the existing chambers of commerce and to give these sections the right to elect one deputy each to the *Reichsrat*. Despite its limited character, Menger claimed this reform would win a significant portion of the working class to "the side of the present state and society and transform a purely revolutionary element into a new force for cooperation in the further development of the state."[30]

Although the 1873 electoral reform, crafted during the last heady days of the *Gründerzeit*, ignored Menger's suggestions, the *Krach* changed the situation considerably. Liberal apprehension at conservatives' attempts to win worker support for their own reform schemes made the liberals more attentive to the demands of the more moderate working-class activists. When Oberwinder's club, the Peoples' Will, presented its petition to the *Reichsrat*, it was Menger's colleague Joseph Kopp, leader of the Progressive Party, who formally introduced it. A special committee was immediately charged to deal with the issues raised in the petition. In December, Ernst von Plener reported the committee's recommendations to the *Reichsrat*.[31]

---

30. Max Menger, *Die Wahlreform in Österreich* (Vienna, 1873), 50, 88. Menger proposed that independent industrial workers over the age of twenty-one who could prove that they owned their place of residence, or that they had worked more than a year for the same employer, or that they had the sum of a hundred gulden on deposit in a savings bank or invested in a self-help organization, would have the right to elect local workers sections. See also Wadl's discussion in *Liberalismus*, 229–30.

31. Ludwig Brügel, *Soziale Gesetzgebung in Österreich 1848–1918* (Vienna, 1919), 109; Plener, *Erinnerungen*, 2:28. The committee recommended not only the creation of *Arbeiterkammer* but also that work hours be limited for women and children, internal sanitary conditions in factories be regulated, and that a system of inspectors be created to oversee the implementation of these reforms.

The ensuing discussion (and the fact that it was postponed until December) suggested that, their fears of a worker-conservative combination having abated significantly, many liberals had returned to their former indifference on this issue. In fact, the parliamentary debate completely ignored the strategic potential of using concessions to strengthen the position of the moderates within the labor movement. The liberals continued to believe that most workers were too immature to join the political community as independent equals. The proof of this immaturity lay in the workers' annoying insistence on defining their interests purely in class terms instead of adopting the liberals' formally universalist vision of community. Arguments based on class challenged the liberals' comforting belief that education would eventually teach everyone in society to adopt bourgeois values. If the workers understood their interests in class terms, then a harmonious solution to the social question was impossible.

The majority on the parliamentary committee did support the creation of *Arbeiterkammer*, but it firmly rejected as premature the idea of allowing those bodies to elect deputies to the *Reichsrat*. Most liberals envisioned *Arbeiterkammer* less as interest groups than as state-sponsored institutions meant to promote working-class self-help and to diminish the likelihood of conflicts between capital and labor. Several committee members argued that the workers' tendency to interpret the world in terms of class conflict was a strong reason not to put the *Arbeiterkammer* on an equal footing with the existing chambers of commerce. According to these deputies the chambers of commerce represented diverse economic and commercial interests rather than the unified class interest of the entrepreneur. The *Arbeiterkammer*, it was claimed, would be organized primarily around the workers' formal class identity as wage earners. "For the first time, the state would formally recognize [the existence of] a class conflict separating capital from labor, giving legal expression to . . . the concept of a separate working class."[32] To avoid the polarization of politics around class issues, some liberals therefore suggested that the *Arbeiterkammer* be organized as distinct sections within the chambers of commerce.

A few *Reichsrat* deputies raised the question of suffrage during the discussion of the petition. Ferdinand Kronawetter, leader of the Viennese Democrats, used the opportunity to demand universal manhood suffrage and to attack the entire curial system of voting. He claimed the *Arbeiterkammer* would only perpetuate an already unfair system of institutionalized privilege. Plener responded, describing the right to vote in Austria as a political function "that the state can give to those who offer a guarantee that they will exercise it properly," and not a natural right.[33] Plener and other moderate liberals also sought to prevent a discussion of direct suffrage for political reasons that had little to do with

32. Ucakar, "Demokratie und Wahlrecht," 245.

33. Plener, *Erinnerungen*, 2:154–55; SPHA, December 17, 1874.

the workers' demands. Such a debate might have revealed a potentially bitter intraparty conflict involving the status of the liberal deputies elected from the large landowner curia. The latter insisted on preserving their privileged position, while increasing numbers of Progressives were privately calling for the complete abolition of curial voting.[34]

Although the Chamber did endorse the committee's findings in favor of *Arbeiterkammer* with limited rights, the government took them as advisory and never implemented them. This *Reichsrat* inaction further damaged the liberals' relation to the labor movement and undermined the influence of those working-class leaders who had argued for a labor-liberal alliance. Citing the betrayal of workers' interests by the parliament as proof of the bankruptcy of the moderate position, radicals within the labor movement urged more confrontational strategies. This reversal had little practical effect in the short run since the effects of unemployment and internal dissension actually weakened the labor movement significantly in the 1870s. In the long term, however, the consequences of liberal inaction were far more serious.[35]

In Vienna, artisanal industry and small business gradually abandoned both the liberal and later the democrat political parties to support conservative social reformist projects during the 1870s. Although this abandonment threatened the liberals' long-term political position, it elicited no positive action from them. Despite the collapse of several productive and consumer cooperatives with the onset of the depression, liberals maintained their belief in the ultimate efficacy of self-help organizations.[36] And while both the Bürger Ministry and Auersperg cabinet conducted surveys of the status of small manufacture, liberal governments remained fundamentally opposed to the basic demands of artisanal industry for a revision of the industrial code. Liberals had generally understood the rapid economic growth that characterized the *Gründerzeit* as a direct result of the freedoms brought by that code. After the *Krach*, they opposed the demands of small manufacturers for a reimposition of restrictive occupational codes, seeing those groups' decline as an unfortunate byproduct of economic progress. These old-fashioned elements of the economy would have to modernize or fall away. The state could not afford to subsidize what many liberals believed to be backward forms of economic activity.

34. Wadl, *Liberalismus*, 233.

35. Wadl, *Liberalismus*, 152. Unlike the situation in Germany, the 1870s actually saw a decline in the organized workers' movement in Austria. In Germany, Bismarck applied a far stronger police harassment as well as social remedies to try to undercut the Social Democratic Party. In Austria, the lack of a united, visible socialist movement made the government far less harsh on the one hand and less impelled to social reform on the other.

36. Wadl, *Liberalismus*, 180–82. Self-help institutions among the artisanal and small manufacturing classes did enjoy a higher survival rate after 1873 than those founded by and for workers. Nevertheless, the efforts of these cooperative associations could not prevent a noticeable decline in economic status among lower-middle-class groups.

When liberals did admit the need for state action on the economy, they discounted in advance the extent to which such measures could cure the crisis. Instead, they assigned to individuals the responsibility for improving the economy through hard work, as an Upper Austrian Liberal Party Conference in 1874 made clear. "We know that [confidence], deeply damaged by the greatest swindle, cannot be [reestablished] by legislation alone and that trust cannot simply be forced on people in this way. We expect that the healing of damage to the economy and the prevention of its repetition must come through the hard work and moral nature of the people."[37]

By 1874 some liberals already expressed the strangely confident opinion that people were beginning to understand that economic recovery would have to be gradual and long term in nature. No interference by the state could alter that fact. "The population quite correctly no longer expects the *Reichsrat* to interfere directly with the economy and only asks that the natural healing process be encouraged by the passage of tax reform, the regulation of stock companies, and [the adoption of] a rational railway policy." More telling than their optimistic statements praising a natural healing process was the gradual abandonment by liberals of their rhetorical confidence in an unregulated system of free-market capitalism. In parliamentary debates of the issue in 1878, a majority of *Reichsrat* liberals demanded the adoption of more restrictive tariffs. This development itself was not so surprising. For most Austrian liberals, free-market capitalism had always meant freedom from internal restrictions on labor and business conditions rather than international free trade. Since the 1860s, several *Reichsrat* liberals, most notably Moravian industrialist Alfred Skene, as well as the Association of Austrian Industrialists, had argued vociferously for the adoption of stringently protective tariffs.

Particularly in less industrialized provinces where liberalism drew its backing from local artisans, small business people, as well as professionals and minor civil servants, liberal enthusiasm for free trade in the 1860s had been more of an intellectual exercise than a pressing concern. Local activists had supported free trade in the same way they supported much of the rest of the liberal canon (civil rights, constitutional rule, secular education), mostly for reasons of principle and not out of any direct experience with the benefits or hazards of free trade. After 1873, however, several local liberal leaders began to distinguish more carefully their progressive political principles from their more theoretical interest in free trade, gradually abandoning the latter altogether. Peter Vodopivec has recently examined this growing dichotomy between liberals' public endorsement of free trade principles and their practical demands for specific protectionist measures, using evidence from local chambers of com-

37. Wimmer, *Liberalismus*, 81–82.

merce in Carniola.[38] This contradiction became even more apparent after 1873, as local clubs discussed ways to represent the needs of small business and industry. Such discussions, however, led neither to significant legislative initiatives nor, as yet, to the formation of a grassroots protest movement.

The general abandonment of free-trade rhetoric by teachers, lawyers, journalists, and civil servants reflected an important transformation in liberal political style. During the 1870s, liberals no longer clothed the special interest politics they had always pursued in their traditional universalist rhetoric of general and individual freedom. Instead, open pursuit of economic interest politics began to replace the earlier moral struggles for a free public life as the very justification for liberal activity.[39] It is not surprising, therefore, that the fortunes of local liberal political clubs, founded to promote an ideology of constitutional freedom, waned altogether in the years following the *Krach*. Club leaders complained repeatedly of any signs of local apathy, warning that "everywhere the downfall of the Liberal Party is being plotted and modern ideas suppressed. . . . We have no reason to give up or retreat," asserted the leadership of the Political Association of Liberals in Znaim "since we represent and defend a good and just cause."[40] Yet even if local populations did not exactly equate liberalism with the depression, and even if they continued to believe in freedom and progress, they saw less and less reason to join liberal political clubs. The original uncertainty about the future of the constitution that had been responsible for mobilizing thousands to join the clubs had worn off. And so had the earlier confidence that liberal constitutional rule alone would create a better world.

Memberships in liberal political clubs declined everywhere in Austria, as did attendance rates and the frequency with which clubs held meetings. The membership of the Liberal Political Association for Upper Austria in Linz, for example, peaked at 2,600 in 1873. Thereafter the membership declined, at first slowly to 1,900 in 1878 and then more drastically to just over 1,000 in 1884. This highly successful organization, which had sponsored twenty-six annual

38. Peter Vodopivec, "Liberalismus in der Provinz? Das Beispiel des Triestiner Hinterlandes" in "*Durch Arbeit, Besitz, Wissen und Gerechtigkeit,*" ed. Stekl et al., 86–88; "Die sozialen und wirtschaftlichen Ansichten," in *Geschichte der Deutschen im Bereich des heutigen Slowenien 1848–1941*, ed. Helmut Rumpler and Arnold Suppan (Munich, 1988), 100–104.

39. Lothar Höbelt, "Kornblume und Kaiseradler. Die deutschfreiheitliche Parteien Altösterreichs 1882–1918" (Habilitationsschrift, University of Vienna, 1990), 5. Höbelt noted that liberal political discourse in the 1870s shifted "away from the high plateau of philosophical conviction to the lower depths of interest politics. The pursuit of economic interests (which had always taken place) was not new; rather, the self-evident legitimacy with which such efforts were now fought served as an indicator for the shift in paradigm that was occurring."

40. *Bericht über die Thätigkeit des politischen Vereines der Liberalen in Znaim* (Znaim, 1875), 14.

meetings in 1872 and thirty-six in 1873, held eighteen in 1874 and only twelve in 1875. By 1878 the number of annual meetings had fallen to three. The membership of the Constitutional Association of Laibach fell from 489 in 1869–70 to just over 200 a decade later, the number of annual meetings falling from eleven to three in the same period. In St. Pölten, the Friends of the Constitution lost almost half its membership of a thousand between 1873 and 1879. As club memberships and meetings declined all over Cisleithania, club structures ossified further, and local activism waned.[41]

In the wake of the *Krach*, the liberal government did make some attempt to regain public support. In June 1873 it decided to prosecute Victor Ritter von Ofenheim, former chief director of the scandal-ridden Lemberg-Czernowitz Railroad.[42] A majority in the cabinet believed that the government would regain some popularity if it prosecuted a public figure who had profited from the speculation surrounding the *Krach*.[43] Yet the decision proved ill-advised. Most of the trial testimony only reinforced the public perception that Ofenheim, although clearly guilty, was a scapegoat for the illegal actions of several corrupt officials, many of whom were close to the government. Ofenheim himself reinforced this image by treating the proceedings as a personal attack by Commerce Minister Banhans, even accusing Banhans of himself having taken bribes. The high (or low) point of this sordid drama came when former Interior Minister Carl Giskra was called to testify. The now tarnished hero of 1848 and 1867 strikingly confirmed popular suspicions of Liberal Party corruption when he explained that he had accepted a 100,000-florin sinecure because "in Austria it is customary to accept gratuities."[44]

Ironically, the jury acquitted Ofenheim in 1875, despite what reads like a preponderance of evidence pointing to his guilt. The unlucky Banhans, in whose name the cabinet had formally brought the charges, was now forced to

41. *Bericht des constitutionellen Vereines in Laibach* (Laibach, 1870), 15; *Bericht des constitutionellen Vereines in Laibach* (Laibach, 1879–80), 20; Unterberger, "Liberalismus in St. Pölten," 11; Wimmer, *Liberalismus*, 38–42.

42. Pollak, *Dreissig Jahre*, 2:287–96. Ofenheim had resigned in October of 1872, after a government investigation revealed the bad state of the railroad. He was later accused of having embezzled funds for the railroad and having profited from selling contracts to his friends. For an exhaustive account of the trial, see Pollak, *Dreissig Jahre*, 3:41–76.

43. Pollak, *Dreissig Jahre*, 3:41–44. Lasser and Unger opposed prosecution of Ofenheim, claiming that the government takeover of the railroad and Ofenheim's resignation from his directorship had accomplished the government's aims. The rest of the cabinet voted to press charges, making Commerce Minister Banhans the actual plaintiff.

44. Pollak, *Dreissig Jahre*, 3:78–87. According to Pollak, who covered the trial and was on friendly terms with Giskra, the latter had wanted to challenge the state prosecutor to a duel to the death on learning that he would be called to testify. Later, he decided to testify in order to clear his name and to show that "he had not become the aged, [corrupt] Giskra but rather had remained the same old Giskra." After the trial, Giskra was banned from appearing at court. A year later, follow-

resign his post as minister of commerce.[45] The trial, which had been intended to showcase the government's determination to prosecute the criminals who had profited at investors' expense, had instead drawn public attention to the financial corruption that permeated Liberal Party circles.

In the next years, the relationship between the Auersperg cabinet and the liberal parties in the *Reichsrat* deteriorated markedly. Conflicts between the cabinet and its parliamentary supporters diminished the emperor's opinion of the liberal parties and brought sharp criticism of the government from the liberal press. Cabinet ministers often reiterated that they enjoyed the trust of the emperor and expressed a desire for even closer relations with the Liberal Party. Yet the major issues now facing the government afforded little opportunity to reconcile the three major players: emperor, parliamentary party, and cabinet.

The approaching renewal of the economic *Ausgleich* with Hungary gave parliamentary liberals an opportunity to air their revised views on free trade and to take some public action on the economy. Economic issues like tariff policy became highly politicized for the first time. If in the 1860s such issues had excited few in public life besides the interested industrialists, now Austrian manufacturers, large- and small-scale alike, clamored for higher tariffs. In the context of a severe depression, political activists treated tariffs and the *Ausgleich* as matters central to the very survival of Austrians in all sectors of the economy.[46] To make matters worse, economic developments since 1867 had further aggravated the structural differences separating the Austrian and Hungarian economies, making it even more difficult to arrive at a coherent tariff policy satisfactory to both sides. In general, the Hungarian government demanded a free-trade policy, hoping to keep foreign markets open to Hungarian grain and to import cheaper industrial products from abroad. Austrian industry, however, demanded higher tariffs to protect itself against foreign imports.

Auersperg himself recognized the politically sensitive nature of the *Ausgleich* negotiations early on. Starting in 1876 he sought to build a parliamentary consensus around the coming compromise between Austria and Hungary, meeting with party leaders, attending party caucuses, and providing party

---

ing the intervention of several of his colleagues, the emperor granted Giskra an audience and lifted the ban.

45. Chlumecky took over as minister of commerce from Banhans, and Mannsfeld replaced Chlumecky as minister of agriculture.

46. Susanne Herrnleben, "Liberalismus und Wirtschaft," in *Studien zum Deutschliberalismus in Zisleithanien 1873–1879*, ed. Leopold Kammerhofer (Vienna, 1992), 175–95, especially 189–91.

47. Éva Somogyi, "Die Reichsauffassung der deutschösterreichischen Liberalen in den siebziger Jahren des 19. Jahrhunderts," in *Gesellschaft, Politik und Verwaltung in der Habsburgermonarchie 1830–1918*, ed. Ferenc Glatz and Ralph Melville (Budapest, 1987), 167. Francis Joseph opposed this policy of working with the parties in parliament, pointing out that the consti-

members with a relatively high degree of information on the progress of negotiations.[47] This promising initiative soon dissolved, since Francis Joseph preferred to limit information about the negotiations to the Austrian and Hungarian cabinets. When the Austrian government did announce a provisional agreement with Hungary in May 1876, some members of the Progressive Party expressed dismay that the government had not held out for better terms for Austria. Georg von Schönerer even proposed that Austria drop all common institutions with Hungary, a suggestion that a majority of the Progressives rejected as too radical.[48]

In November 1876 Moravian textile magnate Alfred Skene, a strong centralist and member of the Left Club, caused a political sensation when he too demanded either a more favorable agreement with Hungary or an end to all common institutions. When only ten members of the Left Club supported his position, Skene and his followers, along with a handful of sympathizers from the Center Party, jumped ship to join the Progressives. In an ironic turn of events, Skene, who had always supported strict centralism and had fought against the 1867 *Ausgleich*, now joined with the least centralist of the liberals, those who preferred a rhetoric of German nationalism to Great Austrian patriotism. Their common opposition to the *Ausgleich* agreement united these disparate groups against the government and against their more moderate colleagues. It is worth noting that a majority of local liberal clubs issued petitions and resolutions strongly supporting Skene's protests against the terms of the *Ausgleich* renewal.[49]

Challenge and Defeat

Confusion among the three liberal parties only increased in the following years over a far different issue: the threat of a Balkan war and Austria-Hungary's subsequent occupation of the Turkish provinces of Bosnia and Hercegowina. The occupation drew sustained criticism of the cabinet and Foreign Minister Andrassy from liberals in all three parties and in the press. In 1878, the issue of whether to approve the Treaty of Berlin, which ratified Austria-Hungary's occupation of the Balkan provinces, completely exploded the Left. A majority

---

tution empowered the Austrian and Hungarian governments to negotiate the agreement alone. Auersperg could inform the *Reichsrat* liberals that the government would adequately protect Austria's interests.

48. NFP, June 26, 1876; Eduard Pichl, *Georg Schönerer*, 6 volumes (Oldenburg i. O., 1938), 1:98; Somogyi, "Reichsauffassung," 167–68. Georg von Schönerer raised the point at a Progressive Club conference held in Wiener Neustadt in June 1876. This type of solution to the *Ausgleich* question was known as "personal union," since it envisioned an end to all common institutions between Austria and Hungary except for the person of the monarch.

49. Plener, *Erinnerungen*, 2:77–81; Somogyi, "Reichsauffassung," 169–72; Rogge, *Österreich seit der Katastrophe Hohenwart-Beust*, 2:336.

of party members led by Herbst denounced the tremendous expense incurred by the occupation of what they considered to be two economically worthless provinces. Pointing out that the acquisition of Bosnia-Hercegowina would only increase the Slav population of the monarchy at the expense of German influence, Herbst reminded the government repeatedly that it could not undertake such a commitment in the Balkans when it had not yet settled its own internal cultural affairs.[50] The Herbst faction too abandoned the Left for the Progressive Party, leaving Ernst von Plener and a small minority whose patriotism led them to support the cabinet and the treaty.[51]

Ironically, Auersperg himself had argued forcefully in the cabinet against undertaking any action that could not be covered financially, and yet this was precisely the outcome of Andrassy's foreign policy. Despite its misgivings, the cabinet worked loyally to implement the emperor's decision in favor of occupying the Turkish provinces and as a result gained the undying opposition of most of its own liberal supporters in the *Reichsrat*. Forced to rely on the conservative and Polish opposition to gain passage of the *Ausgleich*, and sensing a coming disaster over the Berlin Treaty, the long-suffering Auersperg tendered his dual resignation as minister president and minister of the interior in October 1878.[52]

The emperor now attempted to form a new liberal cabinet that better reflected the views of a *Reichsrat* majority and that would undertake to manage the upcoming 1879 elections. In private conferences held with liberal party leaders (Chlumecky, Herbst, Kaiserfeld, Plener, Rechbauer) Francis Joseph discussed the suitability of various potential replacements for Auersperg. On Herbst's recommendation, he chose Baron Sisinio De Pretis, finance minister under Auersperg and a man generally respected by his liberal parliamentary colleagues. In a letter to Herbst, Pretis argued that he could only accept the emperor's mandate with the full backing of the liberal parties and of Herbst in particular. In a friendly response, Herbst promised his own support to Pretis. Nevertheless, lamenting that "the Constitutional Party is no longer what it once was," Herbst warned against the potential difficulty in gaining a clear verdict on any issue from the parties, particularly given recent disagreements over foreign affairs.[53]

---

50. It is worth noting that although the Treaty of Berlin only provided for an Austrian occupation of limited duration, most liberals assumed that occupation would inevitably lead to annexation. In fact annexation did follow thirty years later in 1908.

51. Plener, *Erinnerungen*, 2:92–143. Plener gives a disapproving account of the splits in the left. Although Plener himself voted for ratification of the treaty, even he criticized the government severely over the deficit spending required to carry out the occupation of the new provinces.

52. Klebl, "Adolf Auersperg," 200–208, 214. Auersperg had held both positions since Lasser's resignation earlier in 1878 for health reasons.

53. Molisch, *Briefe*, 71–72, 208. Herbst also suggested that Pretis call a meeting of deputies, particularly the more independent-minded among the liberals, and that he detail his intentions candidly.

These difficulties became apparent when the minister president designate Pretis outlined his ideas to a gathering of liberal deputies on October 23. Confirming his opposition to an eventual annexation of Bosnia-Hercegowina, Pretis proposed to end the occupation of the two provinces as soon as internal conditions there had stabilized. He then requested advance budgetary authorization to carry out this modest goal in the Turkish provinces. Almost immediately, Herbst blasted Pretis's pro-forma support for the Treaty of Berlin, announcing that if Pretis supported Andrassy's foreign policy, he could not give the new cabinet his support. Other deputies now followed Herbst's line, praising Pretis's person but denouncing his support for Andrassy.[54] As a result of Herbst's startling action and the parties' lukewarm response to his program, Pretis abandoned his attempt to form a new cabinet.[55]

Herbst's attack on Pretis seems particularly bizarre in view of its largely symbolic nature. The issues he raised were already settled: Austrian troops already occupied Bosnia and Hercegowina. Viewed in the context of Herbst's earlier political career, however, his actions make more sense. They recall the tactics the liberals had employed in the constitutional battles of the 1860s over issues like ministerial responsibility, battles that had pitted *Reichsrat* against emperor to determine the precise constitutional powers of each. This time the liberals were challenging Francis Joseph's exclusive right to make foreign policy. Still, 1878 was not a simple repetition of an earlier pattern of conflict between monarch and legislature. In 1867 the emperor had acceded to liberal constitutional demands because he needed them to pass the Hungarian *Ausgleich*. By 1878, circumstances had changed significantly. For the first time in twenty years, conservatives and federalists in the *Reichsrat* signaled their acceptance of the constitutional system they had traditionally opposed.

The last straw for Francis Joseph came in January 1879 when 112 liberals defiantly voted against ratification of the Berlin Treaty. Looking back at this event forty years later, Ernst von Plener called the vote an "irresponsible mistake," from which the liberal parties never fully recovered, so greatly did it damage their prestige with the emperor.[56] By contrast, the conservatives looked

54. Plener, *Erinnerungen*, 2:129; Eduard Suess, *Erinnerungen* (Leipzig, 1916), 289.

55. "Erklärung des alten Fortschrittsklubs zum Programm von Finanzminister De Pretis vom 23. Oktober 1878," in NFP, October 24, 1878; "Erklärung des linken Zentrums zum vier-Punkte-Programm von Minister De Pretis," in NFP, October 26, 1878; "Resolution des neuen Fortschrittsklubs zum vier-Punkte-Programm von Minister DePretis," in NFP, October 26, 1878. Soon after meeting with him, the Progressive and Center Clubs published official responses to De Pretis's program. The Progressive Club repeated its specific opposition to the part of the program relating to the Bosnian occupation but stated that "in all other matters the club expresses its confidence in De Pretis." The centrist response (which the thirty-eight remaining members of the Left Club also endorsed) was more positive but stressed that the government must work to restore a balanced budget for Austria as soon as order was restored in Bosnia.

56. Plener, *Erinnerungen*, 2:143.

increasingly responsible, constitutionalist, and *Kaisertreu*.[57] Stung by Herbst's inappropriate behavior and the party's challenge to his foreign policy, the emperor now abandoned the liberals altogether.[58] If their behavior had damaged the liberal parties in the eyes of the emperor, it now threatened to destroy their parliamentary majority in the upcoming *Reichsrat* elections. The task of overseeing the elections and encouraging favorable results for the government in the large landowner curia traditionally fell to the minister of the interior. With Lasser's and Auersperg's departure from the cabinet the liberals had lost effective and partisan allies in this key position. In February 1879 Francis Joseph appointed Count Eduard Taaffe as interior minister. The rest of the cabinet stayed on as caretakers, and Stremayr assumed the additional post of minister president. Taaffe had served briefly in the Bürger Ministry, and he was loyal to the emperor rather than to any party. It would be Taaffe who now presided over the *Reichsrat* elections, scheduled for the summer of 1879.[59]

The liberals assumed wrongly that they would be called to put together a new cabinet following the elections. Francis Joseph, however, had something else in mind. Already in February he had given Taaffe the task of putting together a new cabinet whose loyalty would be "above the parties." Taaffe had been unable to do so, given the strength of the liberals in the outgoing *Reichsrat*.[60] As interior minister and with the emperor's approval, he now worked hard to elect a more cooperative, less ideological parliamentary majority, one that would support a new direction in government. The disastrous outcome of these elections for the liberal parties demonstrated both the shortsightedness of Herbst's intransigence as well as the illusory nature of the large liberal majority

57. Lothar Höbelt, *Kornblume und Kaiseradler. Die deutschfreiheitlichen Parteien Altösterreichs* (Vienna, 1993), 22; Somogyi, "Reichsauffassung," 179–87. The conservative opposition had also endeared itself to the emperor by supporting the negotiated *Ausgleich* with Hungary. Ten years earlier federalist conservatives had fought against the *Ausgleich*. Now that they apparently accepted the constitution, they appeared to offer a far more reliable parliamentary basis for a government than the liberals.

58. Molisch, *Briefe*, 209–10; Plener, *Erinnerungen*, 2:128–31.

59. Plener, *Erinnerungen*, 2:144–47. Taaffe's political intentions were not completely apparent from the start, and there is some evidence to suggest that his first idea was to put together a government of bureaucrats and moderate liberals, at least until after the elections. Ernst von Plener reports that Taaffe invited him to join such a cabinet but that the latter could not meet his conditions, particularly those regarding financial policy (cutting the military budget) and making the new cabinet more representative of the majority parties in the *Reichsrat*. Plener, whose attitude toward Taaffe must be taken into account here, concluded that the latter's behavior during the 1879 elections proved that his ultimate intention was to discredit the liberals.

60. William A. Jenks, *Austria under the Iron Ring, 1879–1893* (Charlottesville, VA, 1965), 29, 32–33. Taaffe had failed to find a workable coalition. He could not yet go all out to the right (it would guarantee the liberals an election victory, particularly with the constitutional large landowners), and he could not persuade even moderate liberals like Plener to join an apolitical compromise cabinet.

in the outgoing *Reichsrat*. Even more than in 1873, internal conflict divided the liberal parties in 1879. The division centered partly on the actions of the liberal deputies who had opposed the occupation of Bosnia and voted against the Treaty of Berlin. The "Committee of One Hundred Twelve," as they now referred to themselves, tried to make a candidate's position on the treaty into a political litmus test of liberal credentials.[61] The question for most liberals was therefore not whether the election would produce a liberal majority but rather which liberals would win—the progressive 112 or the more opportunist minority.

Divisions within the liberal parties went well beyond disagreement over foreign policy, however. In the 1870s progressives in the Alpine provinces adopted increasingly populist nationalist programs, calling in particular for a radical electoral reform that would dispense with the curial system of voting. Liberals in the large landowners' curia feared both this increasingly anticentralist German nationalism and attempts to abolish curial privileges.[62] In addition, the reputation for corrupt opportunism that the liberal parties had acquired in the mid 1870s led several liberal candidates to disavow their party altogether and to run for election as independents. Personal animosities and rivalries added to the chaos that pervaded the liberal camp. What, if anything, held the liberal movement together?

This picture suggests that the liberals had implicit confidence in their continued political, national, and social hegemony. They fought one another over specific points that concerned one group or region because, by itself, their larger vision no longer amounted to a compelling political program. Yet they never imagined themselves as the losers against a revitalized conservative coalition. For the same reason, the liberals also saw no need to pursue new electoral strategies, to mobilize new social groups for their cause, or even to involve local associations more vigorously in the campaign. Their movement was becoming fragmented, but there was no threatening enemy on the horizon to

61. R. D. Anderson, *France 1870–1914: Politics and Society* (London, 1977), 10, 69–70, 164–66; Plener, *Erinnerungen*, 2:152–53. Their adoption of the name Committee of One Hundred Twelve for the election campaign consciously mimicked the French Republican Committee of Three Hundred Sixty-three, those deputies who opposed the anti-Republican deBroglie cabinet in 1877 and who had turned the election of that year into a referendum on their principled resignation. The adoption of this title further annoyed the emperor, who was still smarting from liberal opposition to the Treaty of Berlin. As far as Francis Joseph was concerned, the liberals had no reason to oppose the treaty, since the conduct of foreign policy was his sole prerogative under the constitution. The liberals, especially Herbst, had claimed that in this case, since the treaty required substantial financial obligations that affected the domestic budget, the liberals had a right to review it and to reject it.

62. Krones, *Kaiserfeld*, 410–13; NFP, June 1, 1879; Plener, *Erinnerungen*, 2:154–55. In the spring of 1879, for example, both the Styrian and the Lower Austrian Progressive parties called for the abandonment of curial voting in their programs.

TABLE 5. Average Voter Participation Rates in Urban Curia Districts, in Percentage

Province	1867	1873	1879
Lower Austria	43%	48%	59%
Upper Austria	51%	79%	62%
Salzburg	60%	52%	53%
Styria	47%	52%	48%
Carinthia	36%	54%	43%
Bohemia	47%	58%	52%
Moravia	59%	79%	64%
Silesia	47%	57%	47%
Total Cisleithania	49%	60%	57%

Source: Data from K.K. Statistischen Central Commission, *Österreichische Statistik,* 9, (Vienna, 1885), 5; Neumann-Spallart and Schimmer, *Die Reichsratswahlen vom Jahre 1879,* 33. In some regions in 1879 there were fewer voters, but not necessarily a lower rate of participation, due to the effects of the *Krach* on the number of men who paid enough taxes to qualify to vote.

take advantage of their internal conflicts. The 1879 party conference in Bohemia, for example, paid lip service to the localist concerns that had divided the party in 1873, even as the Prague leaders continued to exercise a tight grip on the party organization.[63]

The liberals' blindness to their potential vulnerability was complemented by the waning public interest in local liberal club activities already noted. Clubs exerted less influence on politics in 1879 than they had in 1873. Not surprisingly, the election results showed a marked decline in voter participation among eligible voters in the urban curia across the monarchy (see table 5). Altogether, the liberals and their political allies lost over fifty seats in the 1879 elections, costing them their *Reichsrat* majority. Some of the liberal losses could be seen as a corrective to their lopsided victory in 1873. And in those curia elected more directly by the people, the liberals actually sustained the smallest losses. In the urban curia, for example, the liberal parties lost just five seats, while in the rural curia they lost nine.[64]

Three developments that had very little to do with their popularity among the Austrian voting public, however, lost the liberal parties their *Reichsrat* majority. First, Taaffe convinced the Czech National Party to end its seventeen-year boycott of the *Reichsrat*, thereby adding over fifty deputies to the anti-liberal forces. Secondly, the fourteen Ruthenian nationalist deputies from

63. DZ, April 10, April 13, 1879; Plener, *Erinnerungen*, 2:148–49. The paper reported that in some Northern Bohemian towns, the decisions of the Prague party conference had not been greeted with enthusiasm, since the provincial party still largely controlled the choice of candidates.

64. Höbelt, *Kornblume*, 20–21. Within those directly elected curia the electorate tended to confirm Herbst's position, generally backing the rebellious One Hundred Twelve against the candidates of the ministerial Bosnian Left, which had supported the treaty.

Galicia who had often voted with the liberal majority in the 1870s were defeated by the Poles. Finally, and most importantly, Taaffe engineered a series of political compromises in the large landowners' curia that reduced the liberal phalanx in the *Reichsrat* by close to thirty deputies and accounted for two-thirds of liberal party losses.

During the election campaign, the new minister of the interior had worked hard to take advantage of liberal disunity and to elect as many men who were independent of party affiliation as possible. This strategy met with only limited success in the urban and rural curias, but it had an enormous effect on the makeup of the large landowner curia. Herbst's divisiveness had already damaged liberal chances among the large landowners, particularly in his own Bohemia. Many of these landowners considered the tactics of the Committee of One Hundred Twelve tantamount to a betrayal of the state interest. The degree to which noble landowners feared the new directions in the liberal movement is reflected in the astonishing fact that Taaffe actually persuaded the usually partisan Carl Auersperg to strike a political bargain with his conservative opponents in Bohemia. The agreement guaranteed each side some representation in the *Reichsrat*.[65] The liberal landowners in Bohemia agreed to elect ten federalist landowners (of twenty-three) partly because the growing political radicalism of the progressives in their own party alarmed them and partly because they believed Taaffe's assurances that he sought to build a nonpartisan centrist coalition government "above the parties."[66]

It was this 1879 swing in the large landowner curia away from the liberal parties to a more independent stance that decided the new political makeup of the *Reichsrat* and made a conservative coalition government possible. Ironically, it was not their implication in financial scandals, nor the *Krach*, nor even their voters' apathy that lost liberals their accustomed parliamentary majority in 1879 but the simple technicality that they had fought this campaign without control of the ministry of the interior. Nevertheless, the liberals certainly recognized a defeat when they saw one. When seventy-seven liberals from the party's various factions met at Linz in late August to plan their strategy for the coming parliamentary session, their program mentioned neither the recent

65. Jenks, *Iron Ring*, 34; Kolmer, *Parlament*, 3:3–6; Plener, *Erinnerungen*, 2:155–56. Auersperg clearly expected that the conservative landowners, as part of their side of the bargain, would end their *Reichsrat* boycott and that they would not align themselves officially with the Czech parties. In this expectation he was bitterly disappointed and later explained this outcome as a betrayal by the conservatives.

66. Jenks, *Iron Ring*, 34–35; Plener, *Erinnerungen*, 2:154–55. Both the emperor and Taaffe still hoped to create a government based on a parliamentary group of unaffiliated centrist deputies. It was hoped that a new coalition of large landowners who had formerly divided along liberal/conservative lines would now provide the basis for such a government. While this specific strategy failed to produce a centrist majority, it did have the consequence of electing far more antiliberal landowners.

controversy over the Bosnian occupation nor German nationalism. In fact, the liberals now seemed to revert to the strategy they had developed a decade earlier against the Hohenwart regime. They reiterated the need to protect the liberal centralist institutions from attack, stressing that any concessions to other nationalities should not contradict the given constitutional framework.[67] "To be in the minority was not a question of politics for us," wrote Leopold von Hasner of this period, "but a question of the very existence of the constitutional state."[68] As they prepared to reengage in the battles of an earlier decade, the liberals largely ignored the changes that had taken place in conservative and Slav strategy. The Taaffe era would not prove a repeat of the Belcredi or Hohenwart years. And while Herbst angrily prophesied that Taaffe could not last more than a few months without turning to the liberals for support, these events technically marked the end of German liberal political supremacy in the *Reichsrat*.[69]

---

67. "Resolutions-Antrag der Linzer Konferenz Verfassungstreuer Abgeordneter am 31. August 1879," NFP, September 1, 1879; Plener, *Erinnerungen*, 2:168–69. The newspaper reported the number of participants at seventy-four, while Plener recorded it as seventy-seven.

68. Hasner, *Denkwürdigkeiten*, 117.

69. Jenks, *Iron Ring*, 28–70. Early votes in the newly elected *Reichsrat* in 1879 were close, and neither Taaffe nor the liberals seemed consistently able to muster an absolute majority. Unaffiliated large landowners made up the balance, however, and on most issues they gave Taaffe the votes he needed to pursue the new course. The liberals assumed that they could topple the new government by forcing new elections. Yet this was precisely what Taaffe meant to avoid. During his first year in office he maintained a conciliatory tone toward the liberals while pursuing policies designed to undermine completely their political influence and legislative accomplishments.

CHAPTER 7

From Liberalism to Nationalism: Inventing a German Community, 1880–85

> We will never accomplish our mission until all social strata of the people take an active part, until those who inhabit the German palaces as much as those who inhabit German peasant huts make a claim to their Germanness.
>
> German School Association (1882)[1]

The 1880s witnessed several shifts of seismic importance in the landscape of Austrian politics. Successive electoral reform meant that politics became defined increasingly by mass participation, which replaced the limited traditions of notable politics. A particularist discourse of German nationalism gradually replaced liberal rhetoric as the motivating force behind the movement, undercutting the traditional Austro-German identification with the state. At the same time, voluntary associations began to translate liberal values into German nationalist terms, transforming liberal rhetorical traditions, ritual, and symbolism into a new culture of community organization.

These transformations had complex, often contradictory effects on the liberal movement. The traditional view, that liberalism collapsed in the 1880s and 1890s because it could not compete with newer mass-based parties organized around nationalist or class interests, simplifies an enormously complex process in which liberals were not always the losers. Certainly Austria's liberals faced the same challenges of democratization as their *Reich* German counterparts. Neither their ideological nor their organizational traditions prepared them for an age of mobilization by interest group, of increased numbers of voters, of higher rates of participation, of more brutal political styles. Throughout Central Europe liberals faced the question of just who their constituency would be in an era of mass politics. After decades of claiming to represent the community's

1. German School Association, MDS 5 (1882): 1.

common interest, by the 1880s it often seemed the liberals in fact only represented themselves.

As it brought more people into active political participation, the new mass politics tended at first to weaken the parties whose ideological appeal had traditionally transcended regional or interest group concerns. During the 1880s parties organized around more specific interests began to challenge not only the liberals but other general coalitions like Hohenwart's conservatives and later even the Czech nationalist parties.[2] This fragmentation of politics along the fault lines of local interest, however, represented only one part of an even larger political transformation. For, if some activists forged successful movements based on narrower interests, the liberals worked to rebuild their coalitions around a new transregional issue: German nationalism. When their opponents challenged the liberals in the 1880s, the latter showed some resilience, developing astonishingly effective responses to hostile new mass political movements at the local level.

The liberal turn to nationalism did not result from strategic choices made by party leaders in Vienna. They often seemed helpless in the face of the political defeats dealt them by Taaffe in the early 1880s. Instead, the transformation of liberal politics derived far more from local initiatives taken within the network of political and social voluntary associations. These demanded new approaches to politics because they understood far better than the leaders the ways in which the locus of power was changing. If liberal leaders adopted nationalist rhetoric reluctantly, local activists saw their own culture endangered in a thousand ways and their access to resources they had always taken for granted increasingly challenged by Slav nationalism.

In the years following the *Krach*, the liberal movement had suffered from local apathy and disillusionment. Now on the defensive, activists built on changed conditions to generate a new vision that revitalized the movement. This activism not only prolonged the life of liberalism; it lent it new energy. Some liberals who had sought in vain for ideological self-definition in the 1870s found what they were looking for in the 1880s. Aided by the survival of the curial voting system in provincial and town politics, and by the emerging role of German nationalism in Austrian politics, bourgeois liberals managed to retain a powerful role for their parties well into the emerging age of mass politics.

The cost of these successful new strategies to the interregional liberal parties at the *Reichsrat* level, however, was severe. During the 1880s successive reincarnations of the old liberal parties (the United Left, the German Austrian Party, and the United German Left) still commanded the votes of between 30

2. Istvan Deak, "Comments," *Austrian History Yearbook* 3 (1967): 303–5.

and 40 percent of the *Reichsrat* deputies, making them by far the largest parties. Yet their size and unity were illusory. By 1897, they had passed from the parliamentary scene. This decline in no way signified the death of political liberalism, as most historians have implied, but rather a reorientation of liberal efforts. A comparison of local associational efforts during this period with those of the big *Reichsrat* parties illustrates the growing irrelevance of the latter and the more successful creativity of the former.

German Liberals in the Opposition

The liberal parties in the *Reichsrat* found themselves constantly on the defensive during the early years of Taaffe's rule. At first, some liberals treated this "Iron Ring" government as a kind of Hohenwart or Belcredi interlude revisited, a transient moment of danger requiring renewed assertions of political unity. They fully expected to regain power within a matter of months. Others, like the liberal large landowners, still smarting from left-wing attacks on their privileged position, actually expressed approval for Taaffe's stated goal to create a governmental party of national conciliation.[3]

Very quickly, however, contemporaries realized that they had erred in their assessments. Unlike Hohenwart or Belcredi, Taaffe gained enough support from antiliberal forces in parliament to establish the Iron Ring government on a long-term basis. His open reliance on the parties of the right, and on the Czechs in particular, canceled any hopes moderates may have had for a broad, apolitical coalition of the center, "above the parties." Bourgeois liberals watched as their unquestioned hegemony in Austria disappeared.

By the spring of 1881, the new government's drift to the right had driven antagonistic factions within the German liberal movement back together to form a new party, the United Left. The United Left formally reunited the right of the liberal movement, those who had supported the Bosnian occupation, with the remnants of the One Hundred Twelve and the old Progressive Party who had opposed it.[4] For the last time, all the German liberal factions united in

3. David Luft, "Die Mittelpartei des mährischen Grossgrundbesitzes 1879 bis 1918. Zur Problematik des Ausgleiches in Mähren," in *Die Chance der Verständigung*, ed. Seibt, 187–244; Plener, *Erinnerungen*, 2:166–68, 213–15. German liberals understood Taaffe's long-term goal as their complete exclusion from government. Any hopes for a cabinet above the parties rested with large landowners and resulted from their own electoral compromise negotiations in 1879. Plener, along with other moderate liberals like Chlumecky, worked hard to avoid any secession by the landowners, fearing the increased influence such a split would give to the more radical German nationalists within the movement. By 1881, however, the dangers of such a secession receded as Taaffe's policies were increasingly perceived as favoring political conservatives.

4. Charmatz, *Deutschösterreichische Politik*, 240–43; Höbelt, *Kornblume*, 21; Plener, *Erinnerungen*, 2:215–18. Plener and Chlumecky led the moderates, while Kopp, Herbst, and

one large parliamentary party. Ernst von Plener welcomed this unification, referring to it as "a great success and a beautiful day." Reflecting on its potential, he recalled regretfully, "If only this large and powerful party had understood how to maintain unity . . . it might have had a more glorious history . . . and Austrian domestic politics would have taken a different direction." Plener, who fought consistently to keep the "short-sighted nationalists" in his party from gaining too much influence, never understood that unity based solely on a denial of difference could guarantee neither greatness nor even coherence.[5]

During the four years of its existence (1881–1885), the United Left worked defensively to protect the legacies of the liberal era, but it failed to create any significant legislative or political initiatives of its own. The constant preoccupation with unity paralyzed the party, leaving its conservative opponents to take the initiative on popular issues like suffrage reform or social policy. This helps to explain the contemporary *bon mot* that claimed, only somewhat unfairly, that the party was neither united nor truly of the left. In fact, by the time of the next *Reichsrat* elections in 1885, party leaders could no longer hold the organization together. The left wing consistently demanded both a stronger articulation of nationalist issues and more progressive stands on social issues from the party than the moderates were prepared to countenance.[6]

The Iron Ring government itself was not particularly united either. Internal disagreement frequently threatened the harmony of this broad coalition. The common antipathy of its members to the United Left only just outweighed their differences with one another. In fact, internal disagreement within the government actually ensured that its attacks on the liberals' legacies never really succeeded as much as apocalyptic United Left election rhetoric liked to claim. Taaffe, too, expended considerable energy to maintain some ideological independence from his coalition partners. At various times the minister president even encouraged the liberals to believe that he might reconstruct his majority, substituting them for the Czechs. This strategy aimed both to keep his own coalition in line and to encourage the moderate German liberals to blunt the antigovernmental rhetoric of their radical nationalist colleagues.

In its first years, the Taaffe government brought legislation to the *Reichsrat* designed to please each of the coalition partners as far as possible and to weaken the German liberals' political position. The Stremayr language ordinances (1880) were viewed by liberals as an outright attack on their funda-

Sturm led the former progressives. The United Left, together with its independent allies, could muster about 160 votes, in addition to three Ruthenes and ten Italians who often voted with it. In a parliament of 354 deputies this still left the party barely, yet decisively, in a minority position.

5. Plener, *Erinnerungen*, 2:218.

6. Höbelt, *Kornblume*, 27.

mental interests in the ethnically mixed provinces.[7] By making Czech an official administrative language (*Landessprache*) alongside German in Bohemia and Moravia rather than simply a language "in use" (*landesüblich*), the ordinances appeared to give Czech speakers an advantage over German speakers in the provincial civil service. Educated German speakers complained that it was only a matter of time before most provincial administrative positions would require a knowledge of both official languages. Only a few German speakers took the trouble to learn Czech, as opposed to the many Czech speakers who learned German.

The United Left responded to the Stremayr ordinances with resolutions sponsored by Eduard Herbst and Count Gundackar Wurmbrand, who declared the German language to be the state administrative language of the Austrian half of the empire. The need for such legislation had never been imagined during the years of liberal party rule, so self-evident were its provisions. Yet now, a variety of groups (including a few conservative deputies) joined forces to support this resolution, albeit for very different reasons. Conservative supporters saw the measure as critical to the survival of imperial institutions like the army and the bureaucracy, while the United Left supported it for nationalist reasons. The government, however, argued successfully that no language could replace German in the inner circles of the bureaucracy, and therefore no law was necessary. The Wurmbrand Resolution failed by one of the closest margins of any vote during the Iron Ring years.[8]

The symbolic failure of the Wurmbrand Resolution combined with the effects of the Stremayr (and subsequent) language ordinances only accelerated a decisive change in attitude already current among German speakers in Bohemia. These groups began to envision the possible administrative division of Bohemia into autonomous Czech and German districts as a way to protect so-called purely German areas from a growing Czech influence in Bohemian public affairs. Their new position repudiated the traditional belief in the central state as guarantor of the Bohemian Germans' survival.[9] This transformation went beyond a perception that the state could no longer be relied on to preserve the Germans' nationalist rights. Many Bohemian Germans also began

7. Jenks, *Iron Ring*, 59–61; Pollak, *Dreissig Jahre*, 3:273; Stremayr, *Erinnerungen*, 60. The Stremayr ordinances put Czech on an equal footing with German in internal Bohemian matters. Stremayr's own role in developing the ordinances is not completely clear, particularly since he had served in past liberal governments. According to an interview by journalist Heinrich Pollak, Stremayr claimed to have actually watered down Taaffe's original language proposals.

8. Jenks, *Iron Ring*, 90–91, 95–102; Plener, *Erinnerungen*, 2:257–64.

9. Plener, *Erinnerungen*, 2:270–73. Plener notes that the idea had already been floated at the Karlsbad conference of the German Bohemian Party in 1880. In the 1884 diet session Herbst made a motion to divide Bohemia into autonomous administrative districts based on local language of use.

to see their own national community as the primary instrument for the spread of culture and social progress. This change in attitude, which we will encounter as part of a larger cultural transformation taking place within voluntary associations, also caused a significant realignment within the parliamentary liberal parties during the 1880s. The Bohemian Germans began to elect deputies whose positions increasingly resembled the more regionalist, radically nationalist positions long espoused by the Styrian Autonomists. In so doing the Bohemian Germans gradually abandoned the centralism that several of their allies, such as the Moravian liberals of the *Sprachinseln* or the Lower Austrian liberals, continued to favor.

The Iron Ring also worked assiduously to break the German liberal majorities in the provincial diets and to diminish liberal numbers in the *Reichsrat*.[10] Using his influence in the various large landowners' curia and forcing government employees to vote for certain candidates or to abstain, Taaffe also managed by 1885 to replace liberal majorities in the Bohemian and Upper Austrian Diets with Slavic or clerical ones. In Moravia, where conservatives in the privileged curias lacked the votes to challenge liberal dominance directly, Taaffe tried to detach the more moderate large landowners from their allegiance to the liberal movement, encouraging them to create a nonaligned *Mittelpartei* of landowners.[11] In 1882, Taaffe's coalition voted to lower the tax qualification for *Reichsrat* elections from ten gulden to five, hoping that newly enfranchised small businessmen, farmers, and artisans would vote against liberalism and that the reform would enfranchise more Slavs than Germans in the ethnically mixed provinces.[12]

Caught between Taaffe's reform proposal and the Vienna democrats' populist demands for universal manhood suffrage, the United Left hastily offered its own suffrage reform, which would lower the tax qualification further to two gulden instead of five. To offset potential losses to the Czechs in Bohemia, the liberals also demanded the creation of from three to six new districts in the suburbs of Vienna to reflect the rapid population growth there. The

---

10. Kolmer, *Parlament*, 3:111–15; Plener, *Erinnerungen*, 2:202–3. In 1879, Taaffe increased his tiny majority in the *Reichsrat* by encouraging the Conservative Party to challenge a recent liberal election victory in Upper Austria on the basis of highly questionable evidence. This initial success for the government deprived the liberals of Franz Gross, one of the most capable leaders of the Progressive Party. The liberals argued the case before the Imperial Supreme Court (*Reichsgericht*), which eventually ruled in their favor. Since, however, the court had no executive power to enforce its decision, the Iron Ring government simply ignored it. In the *Reichsrat* election of 1885, Gross regained a seat.

11. Luft, "Mittelpartei," 194–95; Eduard Vodnarik, *Landesvertretung der Markgrafschaft Mähren vom Inslebentretung der Verfassung vom 26. Februar 1861 bis zum Jahre 1884* (Brünn, 1884).

12. Jenks, *Iron Ring*, 107–13. The government changed the voting structure of the large landowners' curia in Bohemia as well to favor conservative landowners in future elections.

Iron Ring majority rejected these proposals, noting that the liberals could easily have created the new suburban districts themselves back in 1873 when they had instituted direct constituency voting for the *Reichsrat*.[13]

Conservatives also wrote legislation both to dilute the requirements of the liberal school system and to reorganize and strengthen artisan industry. The clerical attempts to revive the role of the church in school curricula, to diminish compulsory education from eight years to six, and to remove young girls from the schools altogether represented the most serious attack on the liberal legacy.[14] Blaming the liberals for aiding heavy industry with generous state funds during the 1870s while ignoring the plight of the handworkers, the conservatives also determined to revive artisanal production by restoring to the vocational guild organizations a measure of power over the labor market. In addition, the government proposed more progressive legislation to institute a rudimentary system of inspection in larger factories (but not artisanal workshops) and some kind of social insurance, both measures that the liberals had discussed and rejected in the 1870s.[15]

Rethinking the Liberal Community

Within a short time, some bourgeois German leaders responded to the traumatic political developments by offering new visions of community. The most successful of these aimed to address two different concerns simultaneously: the challenge of mass politics brought by electoral reform and the new importance of nationalism. In a speech to the Prague German Association in 1883, Professor Philipp Knoll warned his liberal audience that without a broad popular base, the German-speaking bourgeoisie would soon lose its accustomed social hegemony. "If the property-owning class lacks a broad popular base from which it can continually renew itself, composed of those who fight to rise through the ranks and therefore give their actions a greater energy and single-mindedness, then it will degenerate."[16] Knoll hoped to integrate new social groups into the bourgeois liberal movement using nationalist ideology instead of liberal ideals as the glue to unify diverse groups.

Referring to the situation in Prague, Knoll suggested that middle-class liberals start mobilizing German-speaking artisans and workers on the basis of shared national identity and make them junior partners in bourgeois society.

---

13. Jenks, *Iron Ring*, 109–11.

14. Garver, *Young Czechs*, 114; Jenks, *Iron Ring*, 122–40.

15. Kurt Ebert, *Die Anfänge der modernen Sozialpolitik in Österreich. Die Taaffesche Sozialgesetzgebung für die Arbeiter im Rahmen der Gewerbeordnungsform 1879–1885* (Vienna, 1975), 17–32, 58–72, 195–231; Jenks, *Iron Ring*, 181–95, 197–220.

16. Philipp Knoll, "Das Deutschtum in Prag und seine augenblickliche Lage," in his *Beiträge zur heimischen Zeitgeschichte* (Prague, 1900), 191.

This could occur either in large voluntary associations that brought people of diverse social backgrounds together under the direct supervision of a liberal leadership or indirectly by placing liberal advisors on the boards of specifically artisan or workers' associations. By reminding artisans and workers of their German identity and giving them a sense of community membership, liberals might prevent them from voting for, or even becoming, Czechs. In recommending such a course Knoll recognized the reality denied by nationalist ideology itself, that social context and not language use often determined the national allegiance of the individual.[17]

The liberals incurred some risk in mobilizing new social forces as their assimilation might overwhelm and destroy the essentially bourgeois character of the movement. Several activists who worked to transform the liberal movement into a nationalist one saw their ability to manipulate the definition of authentic Germanness as the way to control this heterogeneous alliance. If an expanded political community was to be defined by Germanness, then its leaders could retain their preeminence only so long as the traditional bourgeois determinants of status, property ownership, and education were redefined as specifically German qualities.

The activists who chose to make nationalist rhetoric the basis for a new community politics did so precisely because nationalism offered a compelling vision of social harmony that effectively denied class or regional differences. Bourgeois nationalism assumed that in this time of crisis all Germans throughout Cisleithania shared common interests that transcended regional, economic, and social differences. Activists relied on nationalist appeals to diminish perceptions of social differences among German speakers. In particular, they tried to counter popular images of a callous urban bourgeoisie left over from the time of the *Krach* by stressing the apparent commonalities that united all German speakers. "The German national movement . . . knows no division of the community interest into individual interests . . . the movement detests political organizations that try to invent and sharpen differences between city and countryside. We Austro-Germans desire the welfare of our united people; every member of the race, whether in priest's or bureaucrat's dress, whether in Bürger or farmer's clothing, is welcome in our national union."[18]

This growing importance of nationalist ideology to the bourgeois political community reminds us of similar important developments in Germany, France, and Italy. In the same period, nationalism became an important ideology in those states as well for binding diverse communities together, for teaching bourgeois values, and for suggesting a common outlook for culturally different

17. Cohen, *Politics*, 72–75, 88–91, 100–111.

18. Hans Stingl, *Die Nationalvereine der deutschen Bürger und Bauern* (Krems, 1881), 2–3. Stingl was a nationalist activist from Krems, Lower Austria, who later helped to found the General German Language Association.

populations, now united in a "nation." Yet when Austro-Germans invoked the nation in the 1880s, they did so in new ways that did not necessarily reinforce the power of the central state. In the early 1870s the *Jungen* had raised the question of whether German national interest took precedence over the state interest. With their own government in power, liberals had downplayed such concerns, claiming that their Germanness coincided with the state interest. A decade later, however, the unexpected longevity of a hostile government undermined the traditional German liberal identification with the supranationalist Austrian state. If liberals portrayed nationalist unity as the highest social value in order to quiet class differences within the community of Germans, then that same standard had to be applied to relations between the community and the state as well.

German speakers had to see themselves as an interest group whose primary duty was to help its own. In 1886, Philipp Knoll warned a liberal audience in Bohemia on precisely this score: that "help against the continuous losses of Germans in Austria will not come from above but only from the midst of the German people itself."[19] So while the German liberals expended a considerable effort to remove Taaffe from power and regain control of the state, they also began to redefine themselves as an interest group rather than as a *Staatsvolk* interested only in the universal community good. As one nationalist pamphlet put it in 1887, "We have to learn to place our national well-being inside the monarchy ruthlessly ahead of everything else . . . we must endeavor to make this idea and its implications clear to every last one of us . . . and we must fight ruthlessly to realize our program until we have reached our goal. Without making our national well-being into our highest priority, without a national egoism, we will always be at a disadvantage in comparison to the other nationalities."[20]

It was a hard lesson that required a war on two fronts. Ignorant peasants and workers had to be taught their national identity, and liberal party politicians had to abandon their traditional identification with the state. On the latter front this ideological war intensified the internal struggle within the United Left between the moderates who continued to identify their interests with those of the state and the radicals who pursued an openly nationalist politics. Plener, a proponent of the moderate view, defended the pro-state position, writing that "the old [liberal] party had always viewed itself as the pro-state party [and seen this] . . . as its strong point. By proving that the state interest, state unity, and protection of Germanness all coincided . . . the state party rose above the non-German nationalist parties, who could not see beyond their limited horizons."[21]

19. "Parteibildung und nationale Aufgaben der Deutschen Österreichs," in Knoll, *Beiträge*, 402.

20. *Die Deutschen im Nationalitätenstaat Österreich* (Meran, 1887), 6.

21. Plener, *Erinnerungen*, 2:213. So great was Plener's desire to topple the Taaffe regime, however, that he too adopted a sharply nationalist rhetoric in the late 1880s.

Others argued that if the Germans refused to organize themselves as an interest group as had the Czechs or the Poles, they could look forward to further political impotence and greater defeats.

The tensions that pitted loyalty to the nation against loyalty to the state surfaced early on at a major party conference held in November 1880 in Vienna, before the various German liberal factions formally joined to create the United Left. A circle of former university student activists attending the conference, including Victor Adler, Heinrich Friedjung, Victor von Krauss, and Engelbert Pernerstorfer, attempted to prod the liberal movement toward a more decidedly nationalist, interest group orientation. Franz Schmeykal first offered a draft program meant to promote party unity. According to Plener, it "criticized the government's policies, emphasized the nationalist interests and demands of the Germans, but also stressed the importance of the Austrian state and the maintenance of free institutions against attacks from the right." Friedjung, however, went further and proposed the creation of a German Peoples' Party [*Deutscher Volkspartei*], whose program demanded a pledge from all members to vote according to a nationalist standard on all issues and included plans to broaden the suffrage. While the majority of deputies were not yet willing to go to this extreme, most recognized the tactical need to incorporate a stronger nationalist rhetoric in their program.[22]

When this attempt to transform the liberal parties failed, the Friedjung group turned its attentions away from party politics to developing a program for what it claimed would be a completely new type of politics based on a progressive combination of nationalism and social reform. In the next two years the group founded a variety of organizations and publications, each geared toward forging that new politics. The culmination of these efforts, the Linz Program, appeared in the August and September issues of Pernerstorfer's *Deutsche Worte* in 1882. In this document, the radicals claimed to move beyond the limits of progressive liberal politics to a new communitarian vision, one that rejected the individualistic outlook of traditional liberalism.[23]

More than a new type of politics, however, the Linz Program demonstrated a kind of creative pragmatism, the kind that the United Left, in its efforts to hold the movement's diverse groups together, could not generate. This is evident more in the document's general intent than in any of its specific points. The program's insistence on granting Galician autonomy to ensure the Germans numerical preponderance in Austria and its insistence on guarantee-

22. William J. McGrath, *Dionysian Art and Populist Politics in Austria* (New Haven and London, 1974), 169–70; Plener, *Erinnerungen*, 2:199–200. For the text of Schmeykal's resolution, see PR, November 16, 1880.

23. DW, October 1, 1883; McGrath, *Dionysian Art*, 193–94. Engelbert Pernerstorfer wrote on the need to destroy associational life precisely because it fostered the kind of liberal individualism that was antithetical to the new politics. "We must give up the idea of being able to achieve an active national and political life through political societies."

ing German as the official state language, for example, could certainly have been supported by many in the United Left. Even the Linz Program's demands for the nationalization of railroads, the institution of national insurance, social security, and accident insurance, and the protection of both peasantry and factory labor did not venture much beyond the ideas of the populist Vienna democrats, ideas also endorsed by some liberals in the United Left.[24]

What is exceptional about the Linz Program is its balanced attempt to combine both nationalist and social appeals. Despite their efforts to the contrary, most contemporary movements chose one path or the other. Artisanal radicals tended to focus more on social and economic issues, while bourgeois groups tended to invoke nationalism as a way to cover social divisions. The Linz Program failed to ignite a new movement in Austrian politics, partly due to its authors' marginal position in existing political organizations and to their almost immediate disagreement over the place of Jews in the national community. Georg von Schönerer later insisted that the Linz Program include his racist, anti-Semitic definition of the German community, something that many of his colleagues could not support.[25]

Other, more politically fruitful developments, however, occurred at the local level, where associational culture provided a critical context for political transformation within the German liberal community in the 1880s. As liberals like Philipp Knoll in Bohemia searched for more effective means to solidify their rapidly diminishing control over an expanding political society, they focused their attentions more frequently on the club movement and the possibilities it offered for mobilizing new supporters. In this they were aided by the fears generated by the first decennial census to classify Austrians on the basis of their "language of use" (*Umgangssprache*) and the developing rhetoric of a German *Nationalbesitzstand.*

The census results shocked the bourgeois German-speaking political community, particularly since they followed so closely on the 1879 liberal fall from power in the *Reichsrat*. The census raised fears of a severe German

24. For the origins of the Linz program, see the excellent account in McGrath, *Dionysian Art*, 165–81. See also Paul Molisch, *Geschichte der deutschnationalen Bewegung in Österreich* (Jena, 1926), 118–21; Andrew Whiteside, *The Socialism of Fools: Georg Ritter von Schönerer and Austrian Pan-Germanism* (Berkeley and Los Angeles, 1975), 91–93.

25. McGrath, *Dionysian Art,* 177–83, 196–207; Whiteside, *Socialism of Fools*, 69–140. A Progressive Party member in the 1870s, Schönerer was also known as a champion of agrarian reform in the *Reichsrat*. Well acquainted with the most technical aspects of farm production and finance, he had gained political support particularly among Lower Austrian farmers and later artisans, who felt increasingly alienated from the old liberal parties. By 1879, Schönerer's position on nationalism had become radicalized through his close relations with anti-Semitic student groups at the University of Vienna. He had voiced an uncompromising support for social reform and drastic military budget cuts throughout the 1870s, but these progressive elements gradually faded before his growing preoccupation with a highly anti-Semitic form of German nationalism in the 1880s.

demographic decline in ethnically mixed regions. Previous censuses had only guessed at the ethnic composition of Austria's crownlands. Due to the predominance of German usage in commerce and government, as well as to a restrictive franchise that gave high taxpayers a larger voice in running things, Germans had typically overestimated their numbers in ethnically mixed cities and regions.[26] The 1880 results suggested to Germans that they had suffered an egregious demographic decline and that a hostile government had influenced the process in favor of the Czechs in Bohemia. The use of this document to determine the language of instruction for local schools made this and all subsequent censuses objects of considerable political controversy.[27]

Using the census to represent the size and power of the German nation in Austria transformed the ways in which activists spoke about the national community. The census reduced the complex reality of individuals using more than one language depending on social context (family, business, social life) to the apparently simple fact of national identity. Nationalist activists portrayed the census as an elaborate form of national accounting, with statistical gains or losses determining the relative access of a nationality to state resources. This contributed in turn to the popularization of the term "national property" (*Nationalbesitzstand*) of the German people.[28] *Nationalbesitzstand* referred both to the national ownership of specific geographic places and to the wealth, power, and cultural capital produced by Germans in those places. Its use reflected a rhetorical attempt by activists to show very different groups of German speakers across the monarchy that they shared a culture and a common national property. German speakers were encouraged to develop a feeling of national ownership by imagining their commonalities with one another in physical and geographic terms, as well as in cultural or linguistic ones. Instead of focusing on individuals or groups who had adopted the Czech language or on compara-

26. Cohen, *Politics*, 20. Cohen gives a useful critique of the reliability of some earlier census estimates.

27. Emil Brix, *Die Umgangssprachen in Altösterreich zwischen Agitation und Assilimation. Die Sprachenstatistik in den zisleithanischen Volkszählungen 1880 bis 1910* (Vienna, 1982); Brix, "Die Erhebungen der Umgangssprache im zisleithanischen Österreich (1880-1910). Nationale und sozio-ökonomische Ursachen der Sprachenkonflikte" *MIÖG* 87 (1979): 363–439. Political activists on all sides complained about the way in which the census was taken. Czechs suspected that the notion of *Umgangsprache* would favor German interests since many Czech speakers used the German language in their business or professional dealings. Many on both sides demanded that people be asked to report their nationality instead of their language of use, but the government wanted to avoid legitimizing national identities, and this concept was probably a foreign one to most citizens of the monarchy in 1880 and 1890. The occasion of the decennial censuses increasingly resembled political campaigns, with nationalists exhorting inhabitants to categorize themselves according to national loyalty and watchdog groups springing up to make certain that no undue pressure was put on individuals to declare themselves as speakers of the wrong *Umgangsprache*.

28. Judson, "Not Another Square Foot," 83–88, 91–95; Plener, *Erinnerungen*, 2:65.

tive birthrates to explain their supposed demographic losses to the Czechs, activists spoke about populations in terms of land.[29] Such imagery implied that nationalist conflict was really about private property and its potential loss. As one nationalist activist wrote in 1881, "The periodic attacks against everything German in the ethnically mixed lands are highly dangerous not only to our national welfare but also to our economic well-being."[30]

The first census results, together with the antiliberal policies of the Iron Ring, also helped the local political clubs to renew their sense of purpose. Liberal clubs began to display a new vigor, sparked by the fight for national survival. One sign of this renewal was the decision by clubs in all parts of Austria to adopt German nationalist names. Girding themselves for the impending battle against the dual forces of Slavic nationalism and clerical conservatism, the liberals of St. Pölten in Lower Austria, for example, changed their club's name from the Friends of the Constitution to the German National Association. Instead of simply working to extend the constitutional freedoms of 1867, their new program promised "to protect and encourage the national and economic interests of German Bürger and farmers in a progressive sense." The St. Pölten liberals replaced their vaguely articulated concern for German nationality with a specific promise to "support only tried and true German nationalist candidates for all offices." They also offered material support to their persecuted brethren in ethnically mixed regions by taking out corporate memberships in some of the newly founded German defense organizations discussed below.[31]

Elsewhere in Austria, liberal political associations took similar steps to combat the emerging threats both to their German nationality and to the liberal accomplishments of the last two decades. In doing so, they highlighted the concept of a German national identity and its fundamental importance to both the individual and community. The Liberal Association of Linz became the German Association, whose new program called for the clear defense of German nationality against any attack. The liberals of Krems, Lower Austria, who had founded a Constitutional Progressive Association in 1868, changed their club's name in 1881 to the German National Association. The Liberal Political Progressive Association of Stöckerau, Bohemia, became the German People's Association, while the Constitutional Society of Germans in Bohemia, the political arm of the Prague Casino, became the German Club in Prague. By 1885, eleven of the twenty-four liberal political associations in Moravia, where the nationality conflict was admittedly less antagonis-

29. *Deutsche Volkskalender für das Jahr 1889. Herausgegeben vom Bund der Deutschen Nordmährens* (Olmütz, 1888), 55. "Not another square foot!" was a slogan adopted by the Union of Germans in North Moravia (*Bund der Deutschen Nordmährens*).

30. Stingl, *Die Nationalvereine*, 1.

31. Unterberger, "Liberalismus in St. Pölten," 18–20.

tic than in Bohemia, had nevertheless included the adjective German prominently in their clubs' names.[32]

The liberal associations also revived their petitional activity during the 1880s. The clerical conservative school legislation of 1883 and 1888, for example, called forth the wrath of German liberal clubs all over Austria. One typical letter to the *Reichsrat* from the Upper Austrian German Association lashed out against Education Minister Lienbacher's proposed bill, calling it "a regression into Austria's darkest hours, when she had suffered under the oppression of the Concordat." Even worse, this was happening at a time when economic and social problems threatened to overwhelm political life completely. "Any solution to the social question requires the existence of good schools for the people. And now the government is applying an axe to the roots of this educational system."[33]

If the school issue was one of the most popular subjects for liberal petition activity in the 1880s, it was by no means the only one. The unsuccessful attempt to establish German as the official *Staatssprache* in Austria, for example, drew countless petitions and local resolutions in favor of the measure. In general, the political clubs followed the lead of the parliamentary parties, protesting any anti-German liberal measures by the government and commending the grand but increasingly ineffective gestures of the United Left leadership in defense of the German liberal nation.

This attempt at reorientation often sparked renewed interest in club activities, but it did not completely rejuvenate the clubs, particularly in the more homogeneously German-speaking regions. Neither the St. Pölten nor the Linz political associations succeeded in actually increasing its membership; at best the rate of decline was slowed.[34] Foremost among the reasons for continued decline was an increasingly strong disillusionment with the effectiveness of legislative institutions and parties and the competition of new political groups organized around specific local social and economic concerns. Liberal leaders themselves sensed the dramatic change brought by their frustrating inability to

32. Cohen, *Politics*, 150, 164–66; Judson, "German Liberalism," 375–76; Wimmer, *Liberalismus*, 43–44; "Politische Vereine," in *Die Vereine in Mähren, nach dem ämtlichen Zusammenstellung geordnet* (Brünn, 1885). Krems in particular became a center of German nationalist activism in the 1880s. Hans Stingl, a local Krems activist, joined the *deutscher Schulverein* and founded the General German Language Association in 1885. Stingl also published numerous tracts on nationalist topics, including a dictionary of terms designed to prevent local officials from using words of a non-Germanic origin.

33. Wimmer, *Liberalismus*, 185–87. The proposed reform of the school system also occasioned a strongly worded petition from an organization of women teachers in Vienna with liberal sympathies. *Mittheilungen des Vereines der Lehrerinnen und Erzieherinnen in Österreich* 11 (1888): 1–3.

34. Unterberger, "Liberalismus in St. Pölten," 12; Wimmer, *Liberalismus*, 42–43. During the five-year period 1873–78, the membership of the St. Pölten club had fallen from a record high

influence legislative politics in the *Reichsrat* and the diets. Ernst von Plener wrote of this period, "It was impossible to deny the winds of dissatisfaction that ran through the movement: the party thrust into a minority position, the failure of our parliamentary attacks, the quiet progress of government concessions in administrative and school matters to the right."[35]

Others noted that while liberal political clubs might redouble their efforts at election time, they could never elect a liberal parliamentary majority under such hostile political circumstances. Even if the liberals had managed to elect more urban and rural deputies, Taaffe could always maintain his majority by manipulating the voting in the large landowners' curia. Not surprisingly, the various factions in the United Left drew different conclusions regarding strategy from this recognition. On the right of the party, men like Chlumecky continued to assert that only by gaining the favor of the emperor through statesmanlike moderation could Taaffe be defeated and the liberals returned to power. Plener might have positioned himself with this group, but his overriding desire to defeat Taaffe pushed him further to the left. The progressive and nationalist factions of the movement, meanwhile, argued for the adoption of a more pugnacious strategy based on German self-help.

Nationalist Associations and a New Political Culture

The self-help strategy produced a new type of organization beginning in the 1880s, one that addressed the most pressing national political issues in ways that gave its members an immediate sense of accomplishment. Like the new organizations based on local social or economic interests, the new type of nationalist association took direct action, bypassing the increasingly frustrating route of legislation for strategies involving local and regional self-help efforts. And while avoiding formal political issues in order to maintain a favorable nonpolitical status with the police, nationalist associations actually helped to bring thousands of previously uninvolved men and women into the political arena, often under liberal auspices.

The most successful of these, the German School Association (*Deutscher Schulverein*), mobilized thousands of new activists in the 1880s for the German nationalist cause. Founded in 1880 by the same activists involved in creating the Linz Program, the School Association grew out of discussions in the German Association about the condition of German speakers living in ethnically mixed border regions of the monarchy. In his research on the status of German speakers in the South Tirol, Engelbert Pernerstorfer came across the writings of a German priest who had worked to preserve German culture

---

of 1,000 to 678, while that of the Linz club had declined from 2,600 to 1,000. During the 1880s, after changing their names and altering their statutes, both clubs retained stable memberships.

35. Plener, *Erinnerungen*, 2:196.

through education. From this priest's experiences, the German club concluded that hundreds of children could be taught German at the relatively small expense of hiring a few teachers. A voluntary association would raise the money to fund German schools in all those regions where the small size of the German-speaking population did not warrant a state-supported school in that language.[36]

At a meeting in May 1880 a committee formally established the new German School Association. On June 26 a call for all German speakers to support the new organization appeared on the front page of the *Deutsche Zeitung*. Over a hundred prominent men from the fields of politics and culture, including Johannes Brahms and Ernst Mach, signed the appeal. And although the idea had originated with the young radicals who opposed the apparent quiescence and moderation of the liberals in the *Reichsrat*, many prominent elected officials added their names to the public appeal. On July 2, the almost 4,000 members of the fast-growing association met to adopt the statutes and to elect a central committee. The meeting chose Moritz Weitlof, an energetic organizer—and after 1885 a liberal nationalist *Reichsrat* deputy—to be its first chairman. Members also chose radicals Engelbert Pernerstorfer and Victor von Krauss to serve as secretary and vice chairman, while Victor Adler joined the executive committee along with another future nationalist *Reichsrat* deputy, Otto Steinwender. Georg von Schönerer was elected to the organization's board of overseers.[37]

From the start, individuals representing a broad spectrum of positions within the larger liberal movement joined the organization, from parliamentary moderates to radical nationalists. If the impetus for the organization had come from the younger radicals, the group soon came to resemble other groups in the informal liberal associational network in its inclusion of party notables. By 1882, the executive board included United Left *Reichsrat* deputies Ernst Bareuther, Gustav Gross, Carl Hoffer, Max Menger, Adolf Promber, Robert von Waltherskirchen, and Adolf Weisenburg, as well as a former school director for Vienna. In its early years, at least, the School Association seemed capable of accommodating diverse views, since it portrayed the cause of saving the German language in the border regions as above politics. The organization even called upon German-speaking clerical conservatives to join its efforts.

36. McGrath, *Dionysian Art*, 168; August Ritter von Wotowa, *Der deutsche Schulverein 1880–1905* (Vienna, 1905), 7–9. In December 1879, Max Menger raised the question of how extensively the use of the German language had actually declined in those areas. The association elected Victor Adler, Heinrich Friedjung, and Engelbert Pernerstorfer to a committee charged with further exploration of the question.

37. DZ, June 16, 1880; McGrath, *Dionysian Art*, 169; Wotowa, *Schulverein*, 10–12. Weitlof was a prominent member of the Lower Austrian Diet and Vienna city council, elected to the *Reichsrat* in 1885.

With some exceptions, however, conservatives refused this invitation, viewing the association as a tool of the liberal parties.[38]

The association circumscribed the formal constitutional restrictions against forming branches of the same club in different communities. A central committee in Vienna published manuals advising local activists on how to found their own branches. These kits contained sample statutes and instructions on forming a group, how to keep proper records of the membership, club income, and local expenditure, and they included sample posters announcing meetings. Yet while these local organizations constituted themselves officially as independent entities, the central committee kept a tight rein on their actions and retained ultimate control over the disbursement of funds to schools.[39]

The immediate popularity of the School Association, documented in table 6, was truly phenomenal. By the end of 1881 almost 39,000 people had already paid what von Krauss referred to as the "duty-gulden [*Pflicht Gulden*] of every German" to join one of the 271 local branches. Five years later, more than 100,000 people belonged to 980 local chapters across Austria, making the School Association one of the largest bourgeois voluntary associations in the German-speaking world.[40] The provincial distribution of the membership reflects the particular importance of the association to German speakers in ethnically mixed areas of Bohemia and Moravia, although Lower Austria and Vienna also provided a substantial number of members.

Within six months the School Association had raised over 58,000 florins. More than 50,000 of this sum was invested as an endowment by the central committee. Another 5,000 florins paid for teachers' salaries, school books and books for school libraries (which often doubled as local *Volksbibliotheken*), and school supplies in ethnically contested regions of Bohemia, Moravia, Silesia, Styria, Carniola, and Galicia.[41] The rapid growth in membership soon gave the association the financial means to publish a periodical journal, the *Mittheilungen des deutschen Schulvereins*. The *Mittheilungen* gave members a further

38. MDS 4 (1882): 15.

39. MDS 1 (1881): 3; Wotowa, *Schulverein*, 19–20. Local branches elected representatives to attend the annual School Association conventions and elect the central commitee. They also had the opportunity to bring policy questions to the larger membership for a vote. While the local branches elected their own officers and supervised their own fund-raising activities, the central committee received the collected funds, decided how the income of the entire organization would be spent, and remained the final arbiter of all disputes. Very soon the rapid increase in membership and the increased field of activity required the central committee in Vienna to hire salaried accountants and secretaries.

40. Geoff Eley, *Reshaping the German Right* (New Haven, 1980), 366. In 1885, none of the nationalist pressure groups in the German *Reich* came close to the School Association in membership.

41. Wotowa, *Schulverein*, 12.

TABLE 6. Membership in the German School Association, 1886

Province	Population	German-Speaking	Branches	Members
Bohemia	5,527,263	37.17%	441	44,608
Lower Austria	2,169,032	96.86%	154	22,641
Moravia	2,140,820	29.38%	129	13,751
Styria	1,186,393	67.00%	92	9,620
Silesia	550,662	48.91%	42	5,207
Upper Austria	752,064	98.48%	56	4,869
Carinthia	344,064	70.22%	35	2,257
Tirol/Vorarlberg	897,124	59.44%	12	1,576
Carniola	477,607	6.15%	6	1,330
Dalmatia	120,515	4.27%	3	584
Bukowina	568,453	19.14%	33	332
Cisleithania	21,794,231	36.75%	980	107,835

Source: Data from Wotowa *Schulverein,* 72; Wandruszka and Urbanitsch, ed., *Die Habsburgermonarchie 1848–1918,* vol. 3, *Die Völker des Reiches,* table 1, 38. Provincial statistics and percentages of German speakers are taken from the 1880 census figures for those who reported German as their Umgangssprache or language of daily use.

sense of individual accomplishment by linking the daily, local activities of the School Association with the ongoing struggle for national survival at the state level. Combining enthusiastic reports of local club fund-raising activities with general statistics on the progress of German-speaking schools in Austria or the dangers of ethnic decline, the *Mittheilungen* attempted to transform all German national triumphs or worries into the personal concern of each member.

Each issue of the *Mittheilungen* carried transcripts of the annual conventions, speeches by the executive officers, and reports of constant fact-finding missions made to remote areas of Bohemia and Moravia by the apparently tireless Vice Chairman von Krauss. They also contained descriptions of new schools, local festivals honoring the association, and constant pleas for more support. Every issue carried a dire warning by Chairman Weitlof simultaneously commending the membership for its efforts ("we are finally beginning to achieve something in the fight to help our brothers in distress maintain their most holy possession, their nationality") and also stressing how much more work remained to be done.[42]

The periodical printed its share of entertaining and educational articles, such as the one that appeared in the December 1885 issue warning its readers against the proliferation of non-German words in daily conversation. "Consider your own home, German housewife! After you married, wasn't it one of your first projects to arrange a *salon* in your house? Wasn't it an effort to choose the

42. MDS 1 (1881): 1.

decor, and choose the *sofa*, the *canapée,* and the *ottoman*? A General German Language Association is being formed to fight this spreading plague of foreign words, and our motto is: 'Never use a foreign word for anything that can be expressed in good German!'"[43]

The School Association also published inexpensive almanacs with articles that encouraged all Germans to take up the battle for ethnic survival. In subtle ways the articles defined the norms of Germanness for those outsider social groups now being mobilized for the cause. Writers presented a clear picture of what kinds of practices, behaviors, and traditions were authentically German and which were not. All of these publications, directed at German speakers in small towns and rural areas, aimed not only to generate enthusiasm for the nationalist cause but also to define for thousands of individuals their national identity. As in 1848 and again in the 1870s, the specific content of German cultural identity was closely associated with bourgeois views of the world and forms of behavior.[44]

Articles in these almanacs also show the extent to which politics permeated the fabric of this officially nonpolitical association. Some compared the struggle of Austria's Germans in the nineteenth century to the wars of the ancient Teutonic tribes against the Romans, a double metaphor, since many nationalists criticized the contemporary Catholic Church for encouraging Slavic nationalism. Still others, as we shall see, called upon Austrian women to aid their men in this time of ultimate struggle. One almanac for 1884 even raised tariff issues and the question of guild regulation. The article in question praised the nascent efforts of the United Left in the *Reichsrat* to legislate tariff and welfare relief for artisans and farmers without returning Austria to the days of strict guild regulation of employment. The author noted that while in Germany the Progressive Party was tied to a policy of free-trade "Manchesterism," the Austrian liberals resembled Bismarck in their calls for some regulation of social and economic conditions.[45]

In describing the public response to its appeals, the *Mittheilungen* suggested that it drew its membership from all social groups and that nationalist unity had indeed superseded class differences in this association. In fact, however, the School Association's membership came largely from the middle and lower-middle strata of the Austrian Bürgertum. The occupational breakdown

43. MDS 17 (1885): 3.

44. Pieter M. Judson, "Inventing Germanness: Class, Ethnicity and Colonial Fantasy at the Margins of the Habsburg Monarchy," in *Nations, Colonies and Metropoles* ed. Daniel A. Segal and Richard Handler, *Social Analysis* 33 (1993): 47–67; "Deutschnationale Politik und Geschlecht in Österreich 1880–1900," in *Frauen in Österreich. Beiträge zu ihrer Situation im 19. und 20. Jahrhundert*, ed. David F. Good, Margarete Grandner, and Mary Jo Maynes (Vienna, 1994), 32–47.

45. *Schulvereinskalender für 1884* (Vienna, 1884), 18–22 in AVA, Nachlass Pichl, ct. 27.

(see table 7) of the more than 2,000 executive officers of local branches published in 1883, for example, was meant to illustrate the social diversity in the officers' backgrounds. Its author pointed proudly to the number of different occupations represented on the list, concluding that it offered "convincing proof that the School Association can count active members in every class (*Schicht*) of society." Another observer might note the obvious absence of factory workers, journeymen, and agricultural laborers—all occupations that employed considerable segments of Austrian society. In fact, table 7 confirms the essentially middle-class character of the membership.

One significant development illustrated by this survey was the growing role played by schoolteachers (*Mittelschullehrer*) as the local political activists and organizers of the 1880s. They overtook other professionals such as lawyers and state civil servants, who had dominated local political life earlier in the 1860s and 1870s. And the phenomenon of the teacher-activist was not limited to the School Association. Ernst von Plener wrote with some concern about the increasing numbers of teachers elected to the *Reichsrat* who tended to indulge in a sharply radical nationalist rhetoric. In the words of one historian, teachers had become the new *Honoratioren,* or notables, of Austrian politics in the 1880s and 1890s.[46]

Middle-class women were the most important of the new groups to join the efforts of the School Association. Legally excluded from political organizations and from Austria's legislative bodies, barred from attending most political rallies, and disenfranchised in all but a few provinces, most Austrian women had not participated openly in politics since 1848. Now thousands of middle-class women rushed to join the School Association, where they, in fact, pursued political interests. The organization's nonpolitical status, scrupulously maintained by its leaders, technically allowed women this opportunity.

In his annual speech to the membership in 1883, Chairman Weitlof noted with particular enthusiasm "that our German women and maidens have conquered their natural aversion against asserting themselves in public and are forming a substantial contingent of members in our association . . . and that we have two women who are already chairmen [*sic*] of local groups."[47] Weitlof also welcomed the fifty women who had been elected by their local branches to serve among the 1,250 delegates to the annual meeting. Already in 1883, more than 5,000 women (8.4 percent of the entire membership) had joined the *Schulverein.* In 1884, Nina Kienzl, wife of the liberal mayor of Graz, estab-

46. Cohen, *Politics*, 173–74; Höbelt, *Kornblume*, 72–73; Judson, "German Liberalism," 462–64; Peter Ladinger, "Die soziale Stellung des Volksschullehrers vor und nach dem Reichsvolkschulgesetz (Ph.D. diss., University of Vienna, 1975); Plener, *Erinnerungen*, 2:292, 332. The teachers were the bane of Plener's existence. Their numbers among German liberal deputies in the *Reichsrat* grew from three in 1874 to fourteen in 1885. Of these fourteen, nine belonged to the more radical nationalist *Deutsche Club*.

47. MDS 7 (1883): 3.

TABLE 7. Occupations of German School Association Local Officers, 1882

Occupation	Number
Teachers	532
Lawyer/Notary	207
Commerce	221
Civil Servant	153
Land/House Owner	150
Industry/Merchant	140
Physician	138
Factory Official	103
Artisan	80
Bank Employee	50
Forestry/Agriculture	40
Contractor/Architect	38
Mining	30
Railway Employee	28
Craftsman/Artist	14
Writer/Editor	11
Retired from Military	10
Cleric	5
Unknown	83

Source: Data from MDS 6 (1883): 10. This survey was completed before any of the all-women's branches was founded and before the association would have noted the sex of the officers.

lished a separate women's branch of the association there that mobilized over a thousand members. By 1885, there were eighty-three women's branches with close to 10,000 members in Austria.

The successful mobilization of these women in fewer than five years might have discredited contemporary beliefs that women's very nature prevented them from attaining competence in the conceptually male realm of politics. Yet the language and practices of nationalist politics reinforced these ideas by creating a discrete niche for women's activism. Articles in the *Mittheilungen* drew a connection between ethnic decline in the political sphere and carelessness in the so-called private sphere. For example, using arguments drawn from nature and history, an article in the School Association almanac for 1884 attempted to justify women's mobilization and to allay fears that it might cause a confusion of social roles. "Men alone fight for issues of freedom; these questions are too distant from the concerns of women. But when the enemy threatens the most precious of natural possessions, the holiest legacy of our ancestors, our mother tongue, then a mother's heart is also affected."[48]

48. *Schulvereinskalender für 1884*, 6–7.

Women themselves used this rhetoric to justify the widening scope of their participation, and soon their nationalist activism brought a number of them to public prominence. One of these was Therese Ziegler. The first woman to be elected president of a local branch with both male and female members, Ziegler became a popular favorite at School Association conventions. The organization presented her as a role model for female nationalist activity. Whenever she spoke, Weitlof intentionally introduced Ziegler to the membership as "my colleague," thereby emphasizing her equal public status. And after her first speech, the association began selling her autographed picture.[49] The School Association almanac of 1883 went so far as to compare her favorably to a Norse goddess of wisdom![50] Yet in that first speech to the association, Ziegler carefully reminded her audience that she "considered it no achievement on her part but rather the duty of every German woman to use her abilities to work for the School Association. A woman's major concern [however] should remain her home and family, where she could achieve great successes, by giving her daughters a good example and by raising her sons to be exemplary German men."[51]

As later struggles over anti-Semitism in the School Association would demonstrate, women's participation increased their open politicization, giving them a greater stake in the organization as a whole and an independent role in local organizational procedures. The rapidity of women's politicization, at a time when popular ideology about the sexes stridently denied their ability to function in the public world of men, points again to the importance of the voluntary association as a training ground for political activism. Just as the officially nonpolitical associations of the *Vormärz* had schooled bourgeois men in political and organizational skills, so their experiences in charitable and professional organizations had prepared women for the political conflicts of the 1880s.

Many moderate or traditional liberals also belonged to the School Association, and as might be expected, they exerted their substantial influence on the central committee in Vienna. Well-known liberal politicians soon learned that visible participation in the association could boost their sagging reputations, especially among more nationalist-minded voters. Some reluctant nationalists, like Eduard Herbst and Ernst von Plener, did not actually join but were featured speakers at the group's annual conventions and the accompanying festivities. Others, like former Progressive Club members Joseph Kopp, Johann Ofner, Carl Rechbauer, or the Bohemian party leader Franz Schmeykal took an active role in supporting School Association activities. In St. Pölten, for example, where Ofner also served as mayor, the city council voted to take out a corporate

49. MDS 7 (1883): 25.

50. *Schulvereinskalender für 1884*, 6–7.

51. MDS 7 (1883): 24.

membership in the organization. On the recommendation of men like Kopp and Ofner, the Lower Austrian Diet voted an annual subsidy to the School Association.[52]

The School Association paved the way for other nationalist associations based on similar principles of self-help and designed to appeal to a broad social spectrum. The Union of the Bohemian Woods (*Böhmerwaldbund*), for example, used the nationalist approach of the School Association to influence the economy and demography of an entire region. In particular, this organization in Southern Bohemia focused its attentions on the high rate of emigration among the German-speaking lower classes from the *Böhmerwald* to neighboring areas like Lower Austria or Vienna.

The Bohemian woods region suffered from low agricultural productivity, overcrowded farms, and a generally stagnant economy as well as from the fact that Czech workers apparently accepted lower wages and worse working conditions than their German counterparts.[53] The Union directed its attentions specifically to raising agricultural productivity, founding credit institutions, aiding local manufacture, and encouraging tourism in the region. It sponsored training programs for farmers and handworkers, encouraging local German manufacturers to hire German-speaking journeymen and apprentices and bourgeois women to hire only German-speaking servants. The Union organized craft exhibitions in commercial centers like Budweis, Gablonz, Prague, and Vienna to advertise products made in the *Böhmerwald*. Following the model of popular Alpine resorts in neighboring Austria and Bavaria, the Union even started a tourist bureau, contributed to the building of mountain-climbing huts, and advertised a *Guide through the Bohemian Woods* by a Prague educator.[54]

These measures, designed to combat the Czech demographic infiltration of what was referred to as the German *Besitzstand*, however, also addressed class-based fears shared by local and regional bourgeois nationalists. Publications of organizations like the Union of the Bohemian Woods or the Union of North Moravian Germans constantly stressed that people had to learn certain moral lessons in order to take full advantage of new economic opportunity. In particular, economic self-help required new forms of self-discipline. Repeatedly the consumers of such nationalist publications read that working-class Germans could only survive by adopting German bourgeois values, without which the instruments of self-help would not work.

---

52. AVA, Nachlass Pichl, ct. 27, clippings; Cohen, *Politics*, 160; MDS 7 (1883): 24. These subsidies continued until the liberals lost their majority in the Lower Austrian Diet.

53. HHSA, Nachlass Plener, ct. 33, untitled article published by the *Deutscher Verein* in Budweis gives a German liberal interpretation of 1890 census data regarding the *Böhmerwald* region.

54. Rainer von Reinöhl, "Die Bedrohung des Böhmerwaldes," DW, 1885, 132–34. The league also supported local German-speaking schools and town libraries as well as contributing funds for the erection of local monuments to Emperor Joseph II.

The Union of Germans in North Moravia (*Bund der Deutschen Nordmährens*) emerged some years later, in 1887, to create a greater awareness of their national identity among German speakers in the northern and ethnically mixed borderlands of Moravia. The Olmütz-based Union raised the usual fears about the declining *Nationalbesitzstand*, claiming that formerly German areas were diminishing in size, as greater numbers of German speakers left North Moravia for economic reasons. "The Union wants to make sure that not another square foot from the region that our ancestors inhabited will be lost to our opponents."[55] To accomplish this goal, the association pursued strategies similar to those of the *Böhmerwaldbund*. It proposed to research the economic conditions of this geographic area, create cheap credit opportunities for local businesses, found technical schools to train artisans, find new economic opportunities for the inhabitants, and, wherever needed, provide them with German-speaking apprentices and servants from other parts of Austria. Yet the Union also saw its task as creating among the population a clearer understanding of its own German heritage by distributing pamphlets, starting libraries, and sponsoring lectures on German cultural topics. By 1888, the association claimed over 5,000 members, including several women's branches.[56]

The Union's annual almanac shows us how local activists constructed German identity in terms congenial to traditional liberals. Articles frequently connected authentically German behavior with rational capitalist virtue. Advice columns like the one entitled "Useful Hints for the Home" linked German identity to the technical progress achieved through rational capitalist behavior: "Which farmer today is capable of fulfilling his task? The one who attains a personal and technical proficiency. In the fight for [national] survival, [only] increased technical knowledge and ability can ensure the land will endure."[57] Another column entitled "Golden Rules for Businesspeople" provided valuable information on techniques for conducting a small business. "One should behave in all business situations with careful deliberation; one should always be respectable, punctual, and indefatigable. . . . Everyone should try in an upright and permissible fashion to earn as much money as he can. . . . One should insure all purchases immediately. . . . The best business partner for a middling-sized business will always be a thrifty wife."Still another column described a Moravian German textile factory in terms that linked its attractive exterior and productive interior to its German identity. "The factory buildings themselves are positioned splendidly near a forest and are surrounded by beautiful gar-

55. "Der Bund der Deutschen Nordmährens," in *Deutsche Volkskalender für das Jahr 1889* (Olmütz, 1888), 55.

56. *Deutsche Volkskalender für das Jahr 1889*, 57. The almanac cited the successful example of the *Schulverein* in the hope that more women would join.

57. *Deutsche Volkskalender für das Jahr 1889*, 100.

dens. The internal management is admirable; the treatment of the workers is humane, inspired by well-meaning solicitude. For these reasons, we wish [this factory], created and run by German energy, all the best in the future."[58]

Another Moravian organization, the German Association in Iglau and surroundings, was founded in 1883 to mobilize the German-speaking population of the so-called Iglau *Sprachinsel,* or language island. Claiming that in 1879, "in a brutal denial of all the traditions of the Austrian state, the German majority of the population was thrust aside and the new government declared the reconciliation of the Slavs as its highest goal," the organization called on local Germans to band together in support of a nationalist politics. By 1887 its membership stood at close to 500.[59] During the same period in Brünn, the capital of Moravia, the German Club had over a thousand members.[60]

In 1889 a group of German nationalist activists to the south in Styria founded the *Südmark*. Much like the *Böhmerwaldbund*, this organization hoped to provide economic support for German speakers in the ethnically mixed regions of Styria, Carinthia, and Carniola. Its ambitious organizers advertised for immigrants in crowded rural areas of southern Germany. Promising land and financial aid, they hoped to entice settlers to forge settlement "bridges" literally to connect the various isolated urban *Sprachinseln* of South Styria, where most German speakers could be found. The *Südmark* was the only organization actually to attempt a resettlement program in the hope of winning back or reinforcing parts of the *Nationalbesitzstand*.[61]

The original founders of the *Südmark* were close to Schönerer, and they successfully added a clause to the club statutes that barred Jews from membership. And unlike the other organizations mentioned above, all of which had been founded significantly earlier in the 1880s, the *Südmark* stubbornly retained its anti-Jewish statutes when the issue was raised. This fact caused considerable friction between it and the other organizations when activists attempted to create umbrella coalitions among them or to organize conventions to bring the diverse memberships together in festivals of German unity. Yet despite the Schönerer group's initial influence, even the *Südmark* came to be dominated by more pragmatic Styrian and Carinthian party leaders.

The example of these various self-help organizations suggested to bourgeois activists that a controlled nationalism could work powerfully for their political ends, as long as the liberals adopted the issue wholeheartedly and did not leave it to be defined by pan-German radicals at the universities or to the anti-Semitic artisans in Northern Bohemia. In their early years, many of these

58. *Deutsche Volkskalender für das Jahr 1889*, 54.

59. DVIS, 1887, 7, 181.

60. DVIS, 1887, 167.

61. Friedrich Pock, *Grenzwacht im Südosten. Ein halbes Jahrhundert Südmark* (Graz and Leipzig, 1940).

organizations successfully channeled the potentially disruptive force of nationalism into a manageable form for the German liberals, even as they developed and reproduced new nationalist values and practices. The experience of the School Association in particular proved that nationalism did not have to undermine either the social hegemony or political goals of the bourgeois German liberals. The success of the School Association showed nationalism to be a potent force at the local level for uniting a middle and lower-middle class. This in a time when their disparate economic and social needs made any other political agreement among these groups next to impossible.

The Bohemian wing of the liberal movement under Schmeykal grasped the significance of nationalism for bourgeois politics sooner than its counterparts elsewhere in the monarchy, partly since the liberals here faced stronger challenges to their hegemony than elsewhere. In Bohemia, nationalism had been a significant political Leitmotiv among German speakers for twenty years, and there the effects of rapid industrialization had caused significant demographic change. During the 1880s the Bohemian leadership worked tirelessly to promote the activities of a range of nationalist associations like the School Association or the *Böhmerwaldbund* while holding firm control over political organization. One means to this end involved mobilizing previously ignored occupational groups by founding professional organizations for them.

In 1881, for example, as the Iron Ring government began to woo important social groups away from German liberalism, Bohemian liberal leaders turned their attentions to the problems of the German-speaking farmer in Bohemia. In line with his attempts to diffuse nationalism by stressing economic issues (and just in time to influence the 1881 diet elections), Taaffe organized an anti-German-liberal farmers' party in Bohemia called the *Bauernbündel*. Until the 1880s farmers in Bohemia had no organized interest groups, few interregional connections among themselves, and they did not view their world in terms of nationalist differences.[62] In the words of one recent historian, "nationalism had to be imported," both among Czech and German farmers. If their lack of nationalist identification made their defection to the Iron Ring a possibility, the farmers' regional and social segmentation hampered the success of any provincial organization.[63]

---

62. Bruckmüller, *Landwirtschaftliche Organisationen,* 30–36; 225–34; Peter Heumos, "Interessensolidarität gegen Nationalgemeinschaft. Deutsche und tschechische Bauern in Böhmen 1848–1918," in *Die Chance der Verständigung*, ed. Seibt, 87–99. Bruckmüller argues convincingly that Iron Ring agrarian policy specifically favored the interests of an anticommercial, small-scale sector of the peasantry.

63. Heumos, "Interessensolidarität gegen Nationalgemeinschaft," 91. Heumos cites one German farmer at a Bohemian agrarian congress in 1879 on this issue: "We don't know nationalist hatred. We don't know anything like that. What importance does nationality have for the

Schmeykal reacted to Taaffe's efforts by seeking out farm expert Carl Pickert to help the German liberals develop a closer political relationship with German agricultural organizations in the north. Pickert, a journalist and farmer's son from Leitmeritz, had briefly led the *Jungen* in the early 1870s. After losing a close bid for reelection to the *Reichsrat* in a bitter fight against Eduard Herbst in 1873, Pickert had retired to Leitmeritz, where he edited a newspaper, headed the local industrialists' association, and joined several local agrarian associations. He now began to work with Franz Křepek, the acknowledged spokesman for several farmers' associations, to develop a German liberal nationalist political farm strategy. At a Bohemian farmers' convention held in September 1883 Pickert denounced the anti-German policies of the Iron Ring and persuaded the German Progressive Farmers' Party (*deutsch-fortschrittlich Bauernpartei*) to reject the blandishments of the Taaffe regime. Pickert also founded a newspaper, the *German Farmer* (*Deutscher Landwirt*), to help mobilize agrarian support for the German liberal cause in Bohemia.[64]

With less organizational experience than other property-owning groups in Bohemia, farmers, when they voted at all, still tended in the 1880s to follow the strongly nationalistic arguments of German liberal activists, often with small regard for their own long-term economic interests. These arguments amounted to little more than economic scare tactics designed to relate the individual's own fear of economic decline to the larger issue of the *Nationalbesitzstand*. Many Bohemian farmers in fact came to understand their own economic interests in this highly nationalist context. Unlike their counterparts in Lower or Upper Austria whose organizational tradition predisposed them to vote for clerical, Catholic social, or anti-Semitic parties, the Bohemian farmers could be persuaded to endorse liberal political leadership on the basis of nationalist concerns. The situation only changed after 1900 with the creation of a German Nationalist Agrarian Party.

As with the farmers, liberal leaders in Bohemia tried to attract other groups of formerly unenfranchised petty producers, such as artisans, small manufacturers, and shopkeepers, to gain their support for the bourgeois German liberal movement.[65] These groups were, on the whole, less susceptible

farmer, anyway? The height of freedom for the farmer is when he can say at the end of the year that he has no outstanding debts and look freely toward the future. All the farmers from my region think the way I do, and I am certain that they offer the Czechs their hands in brotherhood." Heumos also cites the particular structures of landownership in Bohemia to explain the relative failure of interest solidarity among Czech and German farmers.

64. Gierschik, *Karl Pickert,* 11–39; Heumos, "Interessensolidarität gegen Nationalgemeinschaft," 91–98. The account of Pickert's bitter loss to Herbst is taken largely from Gierschik, whose sympathies for Pickert led him to exaggerate its importance. Pickert later defeated Herbst in the 1885 *Reichsrat* elections, forcing the leader to run in the safe first district of Vienna.

65. Cohen, *Politics*, 161, 186–92, 201, 207.

to the blandishments of Taaffe's *Wirtschaftspartei*,[66] but they also posed some danger to the liberals. Artisans in Bohemia tended to support the economically more radical constructions of Germanness offered by anti-Semitic nationalists, particularly in Northern Bohemia. In 1884 Schmeykal and the other leaders of the Prague German Association founded the German Handworkers' Society (*Deutscher Handwerker-verein*) in Prague. In the case of a separate association like the Handworkers' Society, some wealthier members of the German Association sat on its board of directors. In many of these cases, national identity was meant to bring people from socially diverse groups together in the context of a political movement, while providing them only a carefully limited forum for their particularist economic demands and social ambitions.[67] In some places, as we will see, this effort failed, and organizations of petty producers and their allies directed their new political energies against local liberal hegemony in municipal politics. This was the case both in Northern Bohemia and in the more homogeneously German-speaking province of Lower Austria, where artisanal organizations opposed the liberals over issues of social policy.[68] While liberals fretted over how to diffuse such attacks, the Taaffe government gained little comfort from the growth of this brand of artisanal radicalism.

The early 1880s witnessed a swift reorientation of liberal political culture away from traditional themes of individual merit and loyalty to the central state to a political vision organized around German national community identity. Particularly at the local and provincial levels, nationalism became, almost overnight, the rallying cry for German Bürger across the monarchy. With the rise of a nationalist politics, and under the threat of a more class-oriented interest politics, bourgeois liberals in provinces with ethnically mixed populations worked, however uneasily, to increase the social diversity of their base of support while maintaining their own social status. The concept of German nationalist identity they propagated resembled the traditional liberal identity in several of its particulars. German virtues, German national characteristics, and German manners looked very much like the bourgeois codes of behavior, developed in opposition to traditional society over the course of the nineteenth century.[69] Control over this implicit understanding of national identity enabled

---

66. HHSA, Nachlass Plener, ct. 24, "Aus dem deutschen Verein in Prag." This publication reproduced the minutes of a meeting in November 1884, at which the organization discussed the failure of the *Wirtschaftspartei* to pose a serious threat in Bohemia.

67. Cohen, *Politics*, 189–91.

68. Höbelt, *Kornblume*, 90–93. In Reichenberg, unlike the situation in Vienna and Lower Austria, petty producers combined their economic demands with a radical nationalist rhetoric.

69. Ulrike Döcker, "Bürgerlichkeit und Kultur-Bürgerlichkeit als Kultur. Eine Einführung" and "'Jeder Mensch gilt in dieser Welt nur so viel, als wozu er sich selbst macht'-Adolph Freiherr von Knigge und die Bürgerliche Höflichkeit im 19. Jahrhundert," in *Bürgertum in der Habsburgermonarchie*, ed. Bruckmüller et al., 95–104, 115–26.

bourgeois Germans to impose a traditionally hierarchic understanding of community on the new, lower-class activists, who joined the broad range of nationalist protective organizations.

This ideological and rhetorical transformation had a profound effect on the liberal parliamentary parties, although in the 1880s this was not yet clear. In particular, the redefinition of the national political community in interest group terms brought provincial and regional political concerns to the fore while downplaying traditional universalist principles. In many parts of Austria this transformation actually helped to rejuvenate the German liberal movement in the 1880s by redefining national politics in a regional and local context. The liberal parties and organizations were able to revive themselves in the 1880s and early 1890s because they appeared to take seriously the local and regional concerns of their constituents. In Styria, for example, the parties actively recalled the autonomist tradition of twenty years before to legitimate their leadership of a new local cross-class, nationalist alliance aimed against Slovenes, the church, and now the central government.[70] In Bohemia, meanwhile, even the traditionalist Ernst von Plener gained surprising public popularity when he led the German liberals in a boycott of the Prague Diet in 1886.

German liberals had far more difficulty maintaining their political hegemony in more homogeneously German provinces like Lower and Upper Austria. In those regions it was harder to tie local fears to nationalist explanations, and the threat of the nationalist "other" was far less immediate than economic concerns. Nationalism was no less virulent in those regions, but it was less important compared to other concerns. When clerical and petty producer opponents of liberalism managed to tie the liberals to the so-called Jewish big business, anti-Catholic, and urban culture of the imperial capital, the liberals were prevented from hiding their association with the social and economic status quo—with big capitalism—behind a rhetoric of nationalist survival. Here politicians might stress nationalist imperatives, but in practical terms nationalism took a back seat to the social, economic, and political ambitions of newly enfranchised petty producers. Increasingly, both agrarian and urban petty producers in those areas organized themselves to challenge liberal party hegemony during the 1880s.[71]

In the 1880s, some regional liberal parties experienced a revitalization, others barely maintained their threatened hegemony, and still others came under successful attacks by lower- middle-class radicals. This incipient regional segmentation and political differentiation within the movement under-

70. Bruckmüller, *Landwirtschaftliche Organisationen*, 213–14.

71. Boyer, *Political Radicalism*; Bruckmüller, *Landwirtschaftliche Organisationen*, 221–24; Johann Prammer, "Konservative und Christlichsoziale Politik im Viertel ob dem Wienerwald" (Ph.D. diss., University of Vienna, 1973), 249–55.

mined the traditional, catch-all United Left Party. The paralysis of the United Left from 1881 to 1885 attests to the increasing inability of the *Reichsrat* liberals and their heirs to find the common ground necessary to unite all German bourgeois groups in one common empirewide organization. It was a considerable irony, but not surprising, that this break-up should have occurred at the very moment when the liberals found a new ideological framework within which they could unite all bourgeois Germans at least locally.

The intense desire to submerge class and regional differences behind a powerful unity caused every activist at least to consider the potential benefits of invoking German nationalism. Yet, as we will see in the following chapter, even as all sought solutions in the same place, their various German nationalisms led them in quite different directions.

CHAPTER 8

National Unity, Anti-Semitism, and Social Fragmentation, 1885–1914

The turn to nationalism within bourgeois German political circles may have revived the bourgeois liberal movement, but it also created opportunities for new kinds of social conflict within that movement. The resulting political battles within associations and parties from 1885 to 1900 constituted a many-sided struggle for the right to speak for the German *Volk* and the power that right would confer on the victor. If the national community was to replace the liberal community as the goal of politics and social life, then the terms on which the nation would be constituted became the most important site of ideological struggle. Which qualities would be valued by Germans, for example, and what kinds of community structures would best nurture those qualities? To most German liberals who tried to control the transformation of public life in the years before 1900 there could be little doubt that the Germans' distinctiveness derived from their superior cultural traditions. The qualities of Germanness were embodied in German cultural achievement and economic contribution to the advancement of civilization in the empire. In this view the national community, like the liberal one before it, was founded on the acceptance of a common German cultural legacy, which was imagined to outweigh all differences of class, occupation, or religion. Nevertheless, within that community, deference and power were due the wealthy, cultivated, and educated members who had through these outward signs achieved the greatest embodiment of Germanness.

Those who challenged the liberals' construction of the German nation, with its internal systems of class deference, did so by offering a new vision of national identity based at least in part on beliefs about biological heritage. According to this latter view, racial identity far outweighed the cultural achievement it may have produced. This racial view by itself was certainly not the only available ideological option with which to challenge the liberal nation. Other potential visions might be organized around democratic, socialist, or religious alternatives. Indeed, an examination of anti-Semitic rhetoric and politics will show that it was effective precisely because of its proponents' ability to exploit its populist potential. But what ultimately made Austrian anti-Semitism politically more central to political discourse than elsewhere in Europe at the turn of the century was its intimate connection to nationalism, a nationalism increasingly defined by reference to several confused racial idioms. And since by 1900 politics in Austria had to be conceived of and expressed with reference to the narrow lens of national interest, anti-Semitic concepts often slipped into nationalist political vocabularies.

From the vantage point of parliamentary politics, the period 1885–95 witnessed a series of struggles within the German liberal nationalist parties, first over the place of nationalism in party policy and then later over its particular construction.[1] The parties did overcome their internal differences sufficiently to replace Taaffe's Iron Ring with a governing coalition of their own in 1893—no mean feat. They accomplished this in part by continuing to appropriate a nationalist rhetoric that proclaimed themselves to be the most effective protectors of a German nationalist interest. Yet once back in office, the liberals failed to convince their own constituents that their government could, in fact, protect that interest, and within a year and a half the coalition collapsed.

By the late 1880s nationalist activists had mobilized unprecedented numbers of people in regional protectionist associations like the German School Association, the Union of the Bohemian Woods, and the *Südmark,* whose focus on themes of national identity created a brief political resurgence for the old liberal movement. It also created new types of internal conflict, as recently mobilized groups soon demanded a more decisive role within the movement. When they were rebuffed, they quickly learned how to manipulate the nationalist agenda to fit their own needs. The rise of competing ideologies of German national identity like racial anti-Semitism mirrored the increasing social divisions that fragmented a supposedly unitary German-speaking middle class. These conflicts over which construction of nationalism was the most authentic undermined the political leaders' authority within their own associations. By 1895 one could no longer speak of a unified German nationalist movement in Austria.

---

1. For a detailed political history of the German Liberal and Nationalist political parties from 1890 until the end of the monarchy, see Höbelt, *Kornblume*. William Jenks's *Austria under the Iron Ring* offers a useful narrative more focused on the internal politics of the Iron Ring parties but attentive to the machinations of the German left. Volume 3 of Plener's *Erinnerungen* gives a detailed summary of the final years of the Iron Ring, mostly as a prelude to his exhaustive account of the short-lived Windischgrätz coalition cabinet in which he served as finance minister.

Any analysis of the emerging conflicts in the German nationalist community is complicated by the common rhetoric, political tactics, and often overlapping memberships shared by the groups that fought to impose competing definitions of Germanness on the larger community. It makes little sense to distinguish ideal categories like *moderate liberal* from *liberal nationalist* or *radical nationalist,* particularly in the early years of the German nationalist movement, since the same people often belonged to more than one group, depending on the political context. A radical nationalist faction that fought a moderate liberal group in municipal politics might ally with moderate nationalists at the level of the provincial diet or *Reichsrat.* And when it came to economic or social policy, *Reichsrat* deputies who considered themselves nationalist radicals frequently had more in common with moderate liberals than they did with anti-Semitic deputies, with whom they nonetheless shared an uncompromising nationalist rhetoric. In this chapter, therefore, terms like *moderate* or *radical nationalist* refer to relative positions taken by individuals or groups in specific contexts and not to fixed ideologies.

Political context determined the content of nationalist ideology in the 1880s partly because of the instrumental value many liberals assigned to nationalism. These liberals viewed nationalist rhetoric as a means to unite disparate social groups, from noble landowners to urban artisans, in a broad political coalition. To accomplish this end, German nationalist ideology had to remain general enough to incorporate different groups of German speakers and just bland enough not to offend any of them. Liberal nationalism aimed above all to strengthen and reproduce the status quo. Its economic and social policy dimensions reveal the degree to which the nationalist politics of the 1880s in fact continued the liberal politics of the 1860s and 1870s.

Populism, Anti-Semites, and the Battle for the Associations

The mobilization of thousands of activist supporters into clubs and parties under the nationalist banner increased opportunities for conflict in a movement whose virtues had never included political flexibility. The more the politicians sounded the trumpet of populist nationalism, the more a small but growing group of radicals challenged them to give specific meaning to their rhetorically vague formulations, just as artisanal and working-class activists had challenged the liberals to fulfill the promise of their democratic rhetoric with specific reforms after 1867. Like the *Jungen* of an earlier decade, some nationalist activists soon grew impatient with the old liberals' tight hold on the leadership of the new movement. A few of them now ventured beyond the example of the *Jungen,* abandoning the unity-at-all-costs arguments of an Ernst von Plener or even a Moritz Weitlof for a new strategy of divide and conquer.

These new activists defined their nationalism more in terms of radical populist reform than broad community unity. They rejected the liberal claim that their nationalist interests necessarily coincided with those of the Austrian state. Instead, they urged German speakers to practice a nationally egotistical interest politics against the state if necessary. Men like Otto Steinwender consciously risked alienating the moderates in the liberal nationalist parties by defining the national community in socially reformist terms. Elected by the urban or rural curias rather than the privileged ones, these men proposed that German nationalism directly represent the specific interests of the urban and rural German-speaking petty bourgeoisie, the true German *Volk.* If this could only be accomplished by a government of bureaucrats ruling above the parties, for example, then the radicals were willing to jettison strict parliamentarism. "It is not important who rules but rather how they rule," claimed Steinwender unapologetically in 1891, rejecting the Liberal Party's strategy of dethroning Taaffe to form its own parliamentary government at all costs.[2]

Radical activists also disparaged the liberal tendency to define Germanness in terms of elite bourgeois cultural values. Instead, they adopted more egalitarian definitions of Germanness to support their demands for leadership positions within the local associations. In particular, anti-Semitism served some of them as a wedge to break the hold of the upper bourgeoisie on those organizations. In its newly politicized form, anti-Semitism promised the German community greater social cohesion while subverting the dominance of the liberal elite. It soon became a mobilizing force similar to nationalism in appeal yet with far more radical implications. German liberals had adopted nationalist rhetoric as a way of maintaining their political and social hegemony within a changing, more socially diverse political community. Anti-Semitism supported the same fiction of community unity, but it replaced the liberal community hierarchy of property and education with an equality based solely on racial identity.

Disagreements over anti-Semitism frequently threatened the unity of the German nationalist movement after 1880. Yet, as we will see, anti-Semitism alone was hardly responsible for the conflicts that engulfed the nationalist organizations. On a political level anti-Semitism could serve as a flexible ideological tool, one that successful politicians like Karl Lueger or Otto Steinwender used to gain strategic advantage. Usually, their political frustration with the liberal nationalist movement, and not racialist obsession alone, motivated their use of anti-Semitism. Others, like Georg von Schönerer, who made radical anti-Semitism the supreme litmus test in his movement, were the exception. Yet no matter what the personal motivation or views of these politicians toward Jews, their public rhetoric produced similar objective results: racialist beliefs about national identity became increasingly popular by 1900, and Jews in Austria came under increased attack by their fellow citizens.

2. Höbelt, *Kornblume*, 35.

From the start, liberal nationalists who fought anti-Semitism underestimated both its power as an explanatory tool and its effectiveness as a political strategy. Instead, they treated anti-Semitism as a reactionary religious legacy of the medieval world, one unbecoming to progressive society in the nineteenth century. Their answer to anti-Semitism was enlightenment through education, not political strategy. Although it had played a role throughout Austrian history as a rural and religious phenomenon, anti-Semitism only became an influential component of populist urban political culture in the 1870s. As such it flourished at first among two largely unconnected and politically marginal groups in Vienna and Graz: urban artisans and university students. Anti-Semitism permeated German nationalist student fraternities especially at the universities in Vienna and Graz, where racial anti-Semitism became an integral part of nationalist, occasionally pro-Prussian, ideology. After the onset of depression in 1873 economic anti-Semitism gained support among artisans in Styria and Northern Bohemia as well.[3]

In the 1870s while German liberal majorities dominated the *Reichsrat* and most provincial diets, anti-Semitism remained an esoteric branch of nationalism, one limited to student radicals. After the Iron Ring coalition ousted the German liberals in 1879, however, Georg von Schönerer brought the two strands of student and artisanal anti-Semitism together, combining his public position as *Reichsrat* deputy with his relation to several anti-Semitic university fraternities.[4] For a time in the 1880s, Schönerer succeeded in fusing the students' racial anti-Semitism with his own interest in the economic plight of rural and urban petty producers. In the long term, however, Schönerer lost mass support precisely because he muted his social and economic concerns for the sake of his anti-Semitic pro-Prussian irredentist obsessions. The more pragmatic and successful anti-Semitic politicians who emerged in the 1880s owed much of their ideological arsenal to the dogmatic Schönerer.[5]

---

3. For a general discussion of German and Austrian anti-Semitism, see Peter Pulzer, *The Rise of Political Anti-Semitism in Germany and Austria* (New York, 1988). Also Steven Beller, *Vienna and the Jews 1867–1938, a Cultural History* (Cambridge, 1989), 188–206; Joseph S. Bloch, *Die nationale Zwist und die Juden in Österreich* (Vienna, 1886); Boyer, *Political Radicalism*, 40–121; Cohen, *Politics*, 151–53, 175–77, 181–82, 210–12; "Jews in German Society: Prague 1860–1914," CEH 10 (1977): 28–54; Robert Hoffman, "Gab es ein 'schönerianisches Milieu'? Versuch einer Kollektivbiographie von Mitgliedern des 'Vereins der Salzburger Studenten in Wien'" in *Bürgertum in der Habsburgermonarchie*, ed. Bruckmüller et al., 275–98; Sigmund Mayer, *Ein jüdischer Kaufman 1831 bis 1911* (Leipzig, 1911) 282–86; McGrath, *Dionysian Art*, 165–207; Paul Molisch, *Politische Geschichte der deutschen Hochschulen in Österreich von 1848 bis 1918* (Vienna, 1939), 136–37; Whiteside, *Socialism of Fools*, 81–106.

4. Hoffmann, "Gab es ein 'schönerianisches Milieu'?"; McGrath, *Dionysian Art*, 176–81. McGrath has suggested that Schönerer's increasing contact with student groups in Vienna in the late 1870s fueled his growing preoccupation with anti-Semitism.

5. McGrath, *Dionysian Art*, 177–78; Schorske, *Politics and Culture*, 120–33.

The new anti-Semites proposed radically different criteria for membership and participation in the political community to replace the socially elitist standards of the liberal nationalists. Since 1848 the liberals had repeatedly justified their political hegemony using a theory of meritocracy that imagined a fundamental equality among all males. The liberals institutionalized this equality in a civic order that guaranteed the vote to men whose talents and abilities had gained for them property and education. Their achievement of property guaranteed their commitment to the health and security of the community. Their education enabled them to see beyond narrow self or corporate interest, to perceive what was good for the entire community. These male property owners would rule until the fledgling liberal school system had educated the rest of society in its political responsibilities and until the self-help institutions had helped the lower classes to achieve economic and moral independence. Other national groups, like the lower classes, could attain a higher political and social status by adopting the culture of the Germans.

For racial anti-Semites, membership and participation within the political community depended on racial identity rather than on education or property or indeed on greater political ability. The liberal values of education, experience (demonstrated mostly by financial success or social status), or even dedication to the community paled before the real issue of racial identity. If liberals clothed their political exclusivity in a language of merit and community service, anti-Semites defined politics as an all-out struggle among different races for mastery of the state. Anti-Semitism also conveyed a social egalitarianism with revolutionary overtones: all racial Germans were equal and had a right, based only on their racial heritage, to participate actively in community affairs. Germans as an embattled national group should have more rights than other so-called nations or races. The words of one German anti-Semitic diet candidate from Reichenberg in 1891, Engelbert Jennel, express this understanding of the German community as a closed interest group, fighting for its very survival: "any truly German nationalist party has to be anti-Semitic by nature." Calling the Jews a "strange element" that had forced its way into the German community, he defended his position from charges of racism or brutality. If Jews were not Germans, then any achievement on their part had to come at the expense of the German community. Asking, "should we let our own *Volk* be worse off by being humane to Jews?" Jennel recommended taking up the fight against the Jewish exploiters out of "pure love for our own *Volk*."

The populist elements in this call to arms are undeniable. The liberals were "upper bourgeois who view the people as a voting machine, who only remember their home districts at election time." Not only that, these so-called representatives who come from the ranks of the large landowners, lawyers, and other learned professions want nothing to do with the little man or his problems. Jennel berated the liberals for having wasted their efforts on abstract constitutional questions at the expense of economic ones. To the socially disadvantaged, liberal freedoms had simply meant "freedom for an exclusive class," and "freedom for Jewish exploiters."[6] Liberal economic policy had allowed "the economy [to] develop free from all state interference," had concentrated capital in the hands of a powerful few, and had contributed to the proletarianization of the Mittelstand. In contrast to this liberal freedom, Jennel called for a "true economic freedom," one that will work for the exclusive benefit of the German Mittelstand. He advocated government economic support for the Mittelstand, the privileging of landownership over capital ownership, social insurance for artisans and small manufacturers, and an end to all forms of indirect taxation.

Anti-Semitism provided hitherto marginalized social groups with a powerful ideological justification for their political demands, serving to level the German middle-class community. These men and women considered themselves to be more German than the elitist bourgeois liberal nationalists who consorted openly with Jews. The former deserved at least equal political status with the latter in the German nationalist community. Such claims disrupted relations within bourgeois nationalist associations in the 1880s, as anti-Semites challenged liberals everywhere for leadership positions.

Not surprisingly, the German School Association provided an early opportunity for just this kind of attack. As the most successful organization for the defense of German nationalist interests, it invited debate over the meaning of Germanness, or just who could share in the benefits of being German. At the 1883 annual convention of the School Association held in Linz, for example, conflict broke out over Schönerer's increasingly public expressions of anti-Semitism. Several delegates challenged his reelection to the central committee. The executive board nevertheless endorsed Schönerer's candidacy, explaining that as a nonpolitical organization, "the School Association has room for representatives of all parties." Calling anti-Semitism a political question, irrelevant in the context of a nonpolitical association, the board sidestepped the question of authentic national identity. Most delegates, however, seem to have realized that the very definition of Germanness was at stake in this election. Either Jews could be Germans, in which case Schönerer's slanderous rhetoric against them divided the German community, or they could not be Germans and should not be admitted. The question allowed no compromise position, and as a result, Schönerer barely won reelection after being forced into a run-off vote.[7]

Contemporary accounts of this incident demonstrate an awareness on both sides of the larger conflict behind the issue of anti-Semitism, one that

6. HHSA, Nachlass Plener, ct. 4, "Wahlrede des von der antisemitischen Partei in Eger Dr. Engelbert Jennel," 22–25.

7. MDS 7 (1883): 20; Wotowa, *Schulverein*, 24.

pitted the more traditional liberal hierarchy against the populist local activists, trying to gain greater status within the associational network. The moderate *Presse* painted a dramatic contrast between the traditional liberals it supported and those people it called "ultraconservatives, who can be recognized by their common characteristic of anti-Semitism." Schönerer, *Die Presse* claimed, was greeted by catcalls, while *Reichsrat* deputy Eduard Herbst met with "demonstrative applause" at the evening festivities. The paper went on pointedly to praise the speech by Joseph Kopp, leader of the United Left Party in the *Reichsrat,* for calling on the membership "not to try to determine whether one is German, another more German, and a third most German." As for the anti-Semites, the paper implied that their lack of popularity prevented any of their leaders from even speaking.[8]

In a scathing account of the same events, however, an anti-Semitic pamphlet described what it considered to be the failure of a desperate liberal conspiracy to unseat the popular Schönerer. "Besides the dear Jews, who naturally played a prominent role in this effort, the United Left [Party] in the person of its leader Dr. Kopp also leapt into action against Schönerer, obviously presuming that no opposition could ever succeed against such an impressive authority [as his own]. Success, however, was against the *Krach* party [and Schönerer was reelected]!"[9] Commentary like this depicted the Liberal Party as an elitist group that lacked anything like the mass following commanded by Schönerer. This same report also accused the liberals of pandering openly to the interests of the Jews, thus connecting antielitism to anti-Semitism. And by calling them the *Krach* party, the anti-Semites raised the question of liberal responsibility for the depression of 1873.

The next time it surfaced, this undercurrent of opposition to the moderate leadership threatened the stability of the association more seriously. At the 1885 School Association convention in Teplitz, Bohemia, the anti-Semites raised another kind of challenge to the leadership. This time, a group of local branches introduced a resolution that challenged the liberals' cultural definition of German nationality.[10] The resolution stated simply that "Jewish community schools may not be supported by the School Association." In their elaboration of the resolution, the anti-Semites cited the indisputable fact that the School Association was an association of Germans for Germans. "The central committee constantly complains that it does not have the means to support all requests for money that it receives. . . . Since the Jews are not Germans, we should not consider supporting any Jewish community schools until the last plea by German parents for German education for their children has been

8. PR, May 16, 1883.
9. AVA, Nachlass Pichl, ct. 24, untitled anti-Semitic pamphlet.
10. MDS 16 (1885): 13.

honored." The resolution complained further that School Association aid to Jewish schools "allowed non-Germans the chance to learn German," implying that German language education for Jews threatened job opportunities for Germans.

Speaking for the central committee, *Reichsrat* Deputy Gustav Gross asked the convention to reject the resolution. Gross pointed to the many German-Jewish members and benefactors of the association and to the fact that in some local branches, Jews accounted for over half the membership. Moreover, Gross claimed that Jewish community schools often represented the only bulwark of German culture in Slavic regions. German Jews in these primarily Slav communities supported the School Association at considerable risk to their personal safety and property. Many German-speaking Christians also relied on Jewish schools to give their children a German education, and it was far more feasible to support such existing schools than to found new ones. Gross also maintained that the central committee gave no support to schools that simply wanted to achieve better employment opportunities for non-Germans by teaching them German but supported only those institutions committed to educating all their students as Germans. He ended by calling on the assembled membership to reject the anti-Semitic proposal by as large a margin as possible, so that the School Association might remain an organization open to "Germans of every kind" in Austria.[11]

Other speakers opposing the resolution were less measured in their response. One Bohemian delegate complained that the central committee had avoided the central question raised by the anti-Semites. "No speaker so far has allowed that Jews are Germans, only that they are useful to the German cause. I ask you whether race or conviction should be the standard. If race, then . . . after the Thirty-Year's War and the French invasions . . . none of you is racially German. [stormy interruptions] . . . Therefore I believe that conviction determines nationality."[12] The central committee had no intention of raising the question of authentic Germanness. Its main concern was to draw as many German speakers as possible into the School Association's sphere of activities and to avert any internal conflict. Accordingly, the delegates voted "with an

11. DW 39 (1884); MDS 16 (1885): 13–14. The journalist Heinrich Friedjung had made a similar point regarding Schönerer's election to the board the previous year. "The man who shouts to every German of the Jewish faith: 'You are no German,' who wounds him so unspeakably deeply in most noble felt national identity, this man cannot be chosen to lead in any nationalist concern, even where the defense of nationalist interests requires the united efforts of all."

12. MDS 16 (1885): 14. The same speaker went on to note that "in today's difficult times, the Germans must all march in closed ranks, and not one person is superfluous . . . . Furthermore, we must consider that if this resolution is adopted, a number of brave fighters will be thrown out, and they will be received [by the Czechs] with open arms. Among the Czechs, a Jew is no longer a Jew but a Czech."

impressive majority" against the anti-Semitic resolution, and Chairman Weitlof expressed the hope that they would return to their work for the national cause "with a renewed spirit of unity."[13]

In the next months, anti-Semitic branches within the School Association continued to challenge the authority of the central committee. Conceding the unlikelihood of mounting a successful challenge at the annual conventions, where moderates made up the majority of delegates, the anti-Semites concentrated their efforts on local branches. Changing their focus from expenditure on schools to local membership policy, they tried to amend individual branch statutes to prohibit Jews from joining the local associations. Hoping thus to make the "*Schulverein Judenrein*" [*sic*] from the bottom up, they tried to diminish the authority of the moderate central committee by giving more power to local branches.

In June 1885 the Vienna University branch of the School Association voted to bar Jews from membership, demanding that the central committee do the same for the entire association. This action cannot have surprised the central committee, given the students' reputation for anti-Semitism and their friendly relations with Schönerer. Nevertheless, the committee demanded a formal retraction from the students, reminding them that the association's statutes made an individual's eligibility for membership contingent only on approval by the central committee and not by the local group. After some unsuccessful attempts at compromise in February of 1886, the central committee dissolved the University of Vienna branch.[14]

The dissolution caused an uproar among anti-Semitic members both in Vienna and in other parts of Austria. The precedent set by the central committee drew angry protests from branches in Bohemia, Lower Austria, Styria, and Vienna, which continued to raise the issue of Jewish membership in the association.[15] In December 1885, the central committee received a complaint from a Jewish woman denied membership by the ninth district Viennese women's branch. Once again the central committee threatened to dissolve the branch in question if it did not comply with the associational statutes. When the local directors refused to comply, Weitlof called a meeting of the entire branch

13. MDS 16 (1885): 15.

14. MDS 18 (1886): 1–2. As a last resort, the students appealed this decision, demanding a hearing with the association's board of arbitration. The board consisted of two parliamentary liberals (Kopp and Rechbauer), a general director of a railway company (Gross), a university professor, and a factory owner. The students protested unsuccessfully against Kopp's participation, since he had recently defended Rabbi J. S. Bloch in the infamous Bloch-Rohling libel case. It came as no surprise when the arbitration board issued a verdict in favor of the central committee. On the Bloch-Rohling case, see Joseph Kopp, *Zur Judenfrage, nach den Akten des Prozesses Rohling-Bloch* (Leipzig, 1886).

15. MDS 18 (1886): 3–4. Protest messages are reproduced in this issue.

membership to discuss the issue. The meeting took place on March 11, only a week after the dissolution of the Vienna University branch.[16]

The evening opened with a bitter harangue by two women against the central committee, the arbitration board, and against Weitlof himself for having dissolved the Vienna University branch. Other members then demanded the immediate dissolution of their own branch, to avoid any similar action by the central committee. When Weitlof tried to defend himself, he was interrupted by shouts and catcalls, in what one Viennese newspaper considered "a regrettably un-German way." The meeting quickly degenerated into chaos. After repeatedly calling for order and warning the women of the legal consequences, the police representative, who by law attended all public meetings of associations, closed down the meeting. The central committee then forcibly dissolved the ninth district women's branch.[17]

Following this incident, anti-Semitic activists in Vienna continued to pursue their localist strategy. The Landstrasse branch of the School Association, which boasted over 600 members, passed a resolution on March 18 calling for a change in statutes to allow individual branches to decide on their own members. Although several prominent democrats in this branch opposed the motion, it nevertheless passed by a wide margin. This event in a strongly democratic district shows the degree to which political anti-Semitism had replaced artisanal democracy as the populist alternative to liberalism in Vienna.[18] In mid-March members of the defunct ninth district women's branch, including Schönerer's wife Philipine, threatened to disrupt the fourth district women's branch at its annual business meeting by applying for membership there. When the women of the fourth district branch informed the central committee of their suspicions regarding these sudden new requests for membership, the committee stalled the membership applications, thereby ensuring that it would be months before any action could be taken on them. The thirty-six lost their opportunity to stage another coup against the central committee. Nevertheless, extreme tension and apprehension surrounded the fourth district's women's annual meeting. The *Deutsche Zeitung* warned its readers on April 8 that women radicals planned to repeat the maneuver that had closed down the ninth district branch and called on members of the fourth district branch to block any takeover attempts by anti-Semites.[19]

During this period the central committee received several messages of support for its stand against anti-Semitic disruption. The majority of School Association members appeared to accept or at least tolerate Jewish partici-

16. MDS 18 (1886): 4.
17. NWT, March 12, 1886.
18. DZ, March 19, 1886.
19. DZ, April 8, 1886.

pation in the association. In one such message that reflected a liberal understanding of nationalism, the women of Währing under Fanny Meissner offered Weitlof their unanimous support. They called for German nationalist unity in the face of members "who would bring dissatisfaction and malice into the association." Refusing to engage in a discourse of race, they criticized such a "pointless and medieval crusade against those of other religions."[20]

The moderates continued to support a more inclusive vision of Germanness and condemned anti-Semitism as a form of religious prejudice that resulted from ignorance. This inclusive vision of the nation presumed the continued social and political hegemony of the more affluent and better educated members. By contrast, the anti-Semitic vision had no room for education, achievement, or parliamentary debate as conditions for status or rank, since none of them derived from so-called racial considerations. Referring to the way in which the central committee had disciplined both the Vienna student branch and the women of the ninth district, the Mödling branch captured this very different view of national community. "Every European nationality, and in particular the Germans, must resolutely reject any temptation to mix with Asiatic elements, [a course] that is [often] presented as beneficial for the strengthening of the race. . . . It is [nothing less than] blind rape to impose parliamentary rules [of procedure] . . . on the strongest and purest representatives of one's own *Volk*."[21]

In mid April 1886 Georg and Philipine von Schönerer resigned from the School Association. In a letter to the central committee, they demanded their "names be removed from the membership list of this judaized (*verjudete*) association." In July 1886 they founded their own anti-Semitic German National School Association (*Deutsch-nationaler Schulverein*). The new association, organized on the same model as the original School Association, attracted a few thousand members but was later disbanded by the government for engaging in openly political activities.[22]

During the mid 1880s, both nonpolitical organizations like the School Association and local liberal political clubs came under attack by anti-Semites who sought to win their considerable resources for the pursuit of a racist and populist reformist agenda. One takeover attempt involved the German Association in Linz. In 1885, during the debate over whether to change the club name from Liberal Political to German Association, one member had argued that "a fading liberalism must give way to nationalist principles." Claiming that economic liberalism had given individual capitalists too much power at the expense of the community, he suggested that it was time to place the good of

20. DZ, March 15, 1886.

21. MDS 18 (1886): 4.

22. MDS 18 (1886): 5; Whiteside, *Socialism of Fools*, 124–27; Wotowa, *Schulverein*, 25.

the German nation ahead of the individual. He asked that, along with its adoption of a new name, the club also revise its statutes to include "the economic welfare of all classes" as one of its main goals.[23] Several club members considered both the name change and statute revision unnecessary, since the club's strong commitment to the German national cause was clearly articulated in its statutes. Nevertheless, local political imperatives swayed most club members to vote in favor of both the name change and the statute revision. The Liberal Party in Upper Austria had recently lost its longstanding majority in the diet, and many party members were anxious to regain their former position by encouraging younger activists to join in revitalizing their movement.

That very night, a group of young activists, followers of Schönerer in their university days, decided to join the club. Praising the association's decision to change its name, these activists promised to work with the liberals for the common cause of nationalist solidarity.[24] The new statutes appeared to set up a compromise between the two groups organized around a shared nationalist identity. The newly articulated support for economic reform in the statutes might be interpreted in a radical sense by the new activists, but it was so vaguely worded that it did not specifically repudiate economic liberalism either.

The new arrangement proceeded with promise. In the next club elections, the new members managed to elect three of their own number to the ten-man executive committee. Older committee members expressed their satisfaction with this infusion of new blood into their declining association.[25] Within a year, however, the new faction made an open bid for more complete control over the association, attempting to radicalize its ideology. The occasion for this bid was a speech to the membership by the social radical and nationalist *Reichsrat* deputy Otto Steinwender in 1886. Following the speech, one of the new radical board members proposed that the club vote a resolution of support for Steinwender's reformist proposals, adding a second resolution that criticized all those who "opposed his efforts in word and deed," including members of Steinwender's own parliamentary party, the German Club.[26]

The second resolution provoked an angry response from moderate club members. At the time, Steinwender was engaged in an intraparty struggle to have Heinrich Friedjung, a Jew, removed from the editorship of the party newspaper, the *Deutsche Zeitung*.[27] Thus, as the embarrassed Steinwender himself

23. OL, Vereinskataster, section 2.

24. Wimmer, *Liberalismus*, 43–44, 105–6.

25. Wimmer, *Liberalismus*, 43–44. The statutes continued to express strong support for both the constitution and the liberal school laws.

26. Wimmer, *Liberalismus*, 46.

27. Heinrich Friedjung, *Ein Stück Zeitungsgeschichte* (Vienna, 1887); Erich Zailler, "Heinrich Friedjung; unter besonderer Berücksichtigung seiner politischen Entwicklung" (Ph.D. diss., University of Vienna, 1949), 71–75.

pointed out, the resolution implicitly required the club to endorse his anti-Semitic position. In addition, the resolution demanded that club members venture well beyond a general expression of support for "social reform" to endorse a specific, and for many liberals overly radical, economic program. Finally, the very use of this aggressive tactic ill accorded with traditional bourgeois attempts to keep conflict out of public view. The resolution struck many club members as a brutal and tactless attempt to force Schönerer's program on them. The liberal nationalists had agreed to join with the radicals for the sake of a common German identity but not to abandon their belief in liberal principles.

As a result of this incident the moderates decided to amend the club statutes again, this time to make it more difficult in the future for the anti-Semites, or any other newcomers, to gain significant influence over the association. Still praising the radicals' devotion to their German heritage, the moderates nevertheless demanded that the club set firm limits on its cooperation with anti-Semites, and they passed a resolution explicitly rejecting Schönerer's anti-Semitic program. After this incident the radicals abandoned the German Association to found their own German National Association in Upper Austria two years later. In this case it was the anti-Semites' aggressive approach to social policy and not simply their ideological differences over authentic Germanness that had prevented an accommodation between the two groups. Although several older club members expressed distaste for anti-Semitism, it alone had not caused the rupture. In other associations, events often took a different course, and sometimes it was the more traditional liberal nationalists who left their organization after a successful anti-Semitic takeover.

Particularly in ethnically mixed regions, nationalist associations similar to the School Association in structure and aims did their best to avoid open confrontation with anti-Semites. A few made a point of rejecting anti-Semitism outright, calling it divisive to the German cause. Most organizations, however, treated anti-Semitism as one of many political directions within a diverse German community. These organizations claimed, at least in theory, to welcome anti-Semites into their ranks, along with Germans of all political persuasions. There was little danger of anti-Semites actually joining, however, since as the above examples suggest, anti-Semitic ideology usually rejected any compromise with rival formulations of German national identity.[28]

Party leaders viewed the growth of political anti-Semitism with some alarm yet proceeded cautiously in their response. "The whole anti-Semitic agitation was extremely unpleasant for our party," recalled Plener, "since we had many dependable supporters among the Jews in the ethnically mixed areas of the Sudetenland . . . supporters who now came into conflict with a part of our Christian electorate. The educated Jews had always stood with the Lib-

28. Cohen, *Politics*, 196–217.

eral Party—only here did they find tolerance and equality." Plener's attitude combined noticeable gentile prejudice with a strong intellectual opposition to racism. He was quite capable of noting on the same page that centuries of oppression had developed some "unpleasant characteristics" among the Jews, and yet, as a group, Jews possessed certain bourgeois virtues "to an unusual degree."

Plener admitted that the strength and brutality of local anti-Semitic movements (especially in Vienna) posed a serious threat to the Jews, "particularly the more sensitive ones." But he feared the tactical complications involved in taking a strong stand against anti-Semitism. "[By] now the anti-Semites identified our entire party completely with the Jews. On the other hand, distinguished Jews took it amiss that we did not open up a general offensive against anti-Semitism, which would have been impossible for those of our deputies whose constituents included petty bourgeois voters. The party could only exercise a general, I would say, theoretical defense [against anti-Semitism] . . . for which we received little thanks from the Jews and at the same time earned [more] abuse from the anti-Semites."[29] The Prague Liberal Party leadership tried to make clear through its actions that it would not tolerate open anti-Semitism within the party. At the same time, Schmeykal took great pains not to alienate any supporters, and this led to Jewish threats to abandon the party.[30] Reporting to Plener on the founding of an Association for Resistance against Anti-Semitism, Schmeykal blamed the success of anti-Semitism on those Jews who organized a response to it. Schmeykal expressed a fervent hope that "German Bohemia will not be dragged into this combination. The last elections [only] proved that such actions can transform anti-Semitism from complete lack of influence to an artificial greatness."[31]

As these examples suggest, despite their radical rhetoric, many German nationalists had inherited their basic understanding of German interests and German identity from liberalism. Their political goal remained a universalist one: to bring as many diverse groups as possible together under their leadership to protect the status of bourgeois Germans in the monarchy. Committed nationalists like Moritz Weitlof of the School Association who tried to mobilize society for the nationalist cause never challenged the fundamental arrangement of the social and economic status quo, as did the anti-Semites. For this reason most of the men elected to the *Reichsrat* in the 1880s as German nationalists had far more in common with the more traditional liberal incumbents they replaced than they did with the anti-Semites, much of whose nationalist rhetoric they nevertheless shared.

---

29. Plener, *Erinnerungen*, 2:233–34.
30. Cohen, *Politics*, 175–83, 196–202.
31. HHSA, Nachlass Plener, ct. 19, letter from Schmeykal dated March 23, 1891.

In the above accounts, liberal nationalists and radical anti-Semites fought each other in the context of Austria's growing network of nationalist associations. Local social conditions and political traditions decided whether anti-Semitic movements would be successful or not. For example, in cities where the urban German-speaking Bürgertum had a long history of division among elitist and populist factions, radicals of all kinds made enormous gains against old-style liberals in the 1880s. This was the case in some industrialized parts of Bohemia, in many urban districts in the Alpine provinces, and above all in Vienna. In provinces like Moravia or the Bukowina with less tradition of popular participation in politics, moderate German liberal elites maintained a firmer control over the definitions of Germanness and the practice of local nationalist politics.

An additional factor frequently gave moderate nationalists an advantage over their radical challengers. In localities where the German-speaking Bürgertum experienced politics as an immediate struggle against a long-established rival ideological bloc, like the Czech nationalists or political Catholicism, moderate liberal elites managed to retain a stronger hold on local politics into the new century. In these regions liberal nationalists often maintained political unity within the German Bürgertum at election time and prevented the kind of internal conflict between elite and populist challenger that so often characterized nineteenth-century municipal politics.

The presence or absence of a hostile, external political bloc at the local level also helps to explain the emerging ideological differences that divided German liberal nationalists in different regions. We have already seen that liberal nationalists from the *Sprachinseln,* figuratively surrounded by a sea of Slavs, clung to a vision of a strongly centralized German state even after the advent of the Iron Ring. Bohemian German speakers, who occupied larger, contiguous areas bordering on Germany or Lower Austria, however, abandoned their earlier identification with the central state and demanded autonomy and administrative separation from the Czechs. In yet a third situation, in Styria and Carinthia, provinces where German-speaking Bürger held a strong numerical majority vis-à-vis both their Slovene nationalist and clerical opponents, the power of a strong central state mattered even less after 1879.

This factor helps to explain why politically moderate liberal nationalists remained strong in a province like Moravia, where the German Bürger minority was constituted largely in *Sprachinseln,* while in Bohemia most German speakers were less immediately threatened and radicalism often flourished. It also explains to some extent the situation in cities like Graz, where the ruling liberal Bürgertum adopted a strongly nationalist rhetoric early on and managed to keep anti-Semitic artisanal challenges at bay. Given the literature on liberal political decline and on the rise of political radicalism in nineteenth-century

Austria, it is striking how rarely the anti-Semites actually gained power and yet how pervasive their ideological tropes became.[32]

The Northern Bohemian city of Reichenberg offers an early example of anti-Semitic success in municipal politics. Here the local balance of power tipped more decisively than usual in favor of the nationalist radicals. Lothar Höbelt has recently shown how a process of industrial rationalization introduced by local textile manufacturers created fertile conditions for a strong anti-Semitic nationalist political faction among this city's enfranchised artisans. As production in smaller workshops declined, municipal politics became polarized between the liberal-nationalist oligarchs of the city's first curia who had traditionally controlled city politics and the anti-Semites who increasingly dominated the city's third curia.[33]

The conflict between the two groups came to a head in the *Reichsrat* election campaign of 1885, which pitted a scion of a local industrial dynasty, Gustav Jantsch, against Heinrich Prade, son of a master joiner. Interestingly, both candidates held identical positions on the question of German nationalism. Both pledged themselves to the creation of a specifically "German nationalist party" in the *Reichsrat.* Prade, however, repeatedly cited his own Mittelstand origins as a guarantee that he would represent the social interests of that group. Despite the fact that Jantsch's nationalist positions actually placed him far to the left of most *Reichsrat* nationalist liberals, his patrician background connoted the traditionally liberal economic approaches of the parliamentary parties.[34]

Prade's victory in 1885 ended the liberal nationalist domination of local politics in Reichenberg. At the same time, a group of radical nationalists staged a successful coup in the local German nationalist association, expelling four prominent liberal nationalist members. Nevertheless, the radicals' local victory did not result in a complete break from liberal nationalist party politics. On the contrary, the successful radicals had to maintain a relationship, however much strained, with Schmeykal, Plener, and the Bohemian party leadership in Prague. Not wishing to be held responsible for destroying German unity, the radicals neither opposed the initiatives of the moderate German liberal nationalist party outright, nor did they join it.[35]

---

32. Höbelt, "Kornblume," 81; Hubbard, *Auf dem Wege zur Grossstadt*, 167–76.

33. Höbelt, *Kornblume*, 90–91.

34. *Reichenberg in der Zeit der Selbstverwaltung vom Jahre 1850 bis 1900* (Reichenberg, 1902), 25–27, 59–61.

35. Höbelt, *Kornblume*, 93; *Reichenberg*, 62–64. Despite his personal antipathies to their brand of nationalist politics, Schmeykal tried repeatedly to bring Prade and followers into the party. In 1892, when the *Statthalter* dissolved the Reichenberg city council for its refusal to implement directives on local language use by officials, Schmeykal supported Prade's decision to

In the late 1890s two unexpected developments actually reunited the liberal nationalists with the radicals in Reichenberg. The Badeni language laws, which drew a vigorous protest from German nationalists across the monarchy in 1897–98, helped reconcile the two erstwhile enemies. They now formed a new German Bürger political alliance. Even more important than the wave of activism surrounding the Badeni crisis was the election of some social democratic deputies by the city's third curia in the 1890s. With the appearance of social democracy, the radicals turned increasingly to the liberal nationalists for support. As in most Austrian cities, franchise privileges accorded to the upper bourgeoisie by the curial system ensured that these liberal oligarchs maintained significant political influence in city government long after universal manhood suffrage was introduced for the *Reichsrat* in 1907.

The Perils of Liberal Nationalism: The Coalition and the Cilli Crisis, 1893–1895

At first, the growing conflicts in local German Bürger politics translated only indirectly into conflict among and within parliamentary parties. The still highly restricted franchise for *Reichsrat* elections and the curial voting system gave moderates a far greater voice in parliament than they enjoyed in local politics. In the early 1880s, liberal nationalists, who were considered moderates in the context of local politics, sounded more like radicals when they reached the *Reichsrat*. However, neither the moderates nor the nationalists in parliament raised the social issues that increasingly drove local politics and made anti-Semites a threat in the municipalities. Only a small group of *Reichsrat* deputies connected their nationalism to socially radical demands, and by the end of the 1880s these men had gradually abandoned the liberal nationalist parties.

Reichsrat party leaders like Ernst von Plener, hoping to topple Taaffe and form a new government, made party unity among German nationalists their highest priority. Forging unity required bringing political groups whose political interests increasingly opposed one another together in one party. The large landowner deputies, who retained a more traditional view, still wanted the party to define German interests as secondary or identical to those of the state as a whole. They opposed, for example, the adoption of the name German

nominate the exact same slate of city council members for election, in order to show the city's determination to fight the *Statthalter*. This placed the Reichenberg liberals in a bind, since the *Statthalter*'s actions offered them the opportunity, with the support of the hated Taaffe government, to regain their majority on the city council. Schmeykal worked hard to prevent the local liberals from becoming the pawns of Taaffe and Thun, but local animosity made it difficult to enforce a strategy of unity.

Club for their organization in 1885 and threatened to form an apolitical center party if the liberals redefined themselves in purely nationalist terms.

By contrast, even the moderates among the German nationalists elected by the urban and rural curias knew that their political fortunes rested on their ability to improve the position of the Germans as an interest group within the monarchy and not simply on toppling a hated minister president. As one nationalist publicist pointed out in 1887, "the desire to overthrow the Taaffe ministry [by itself] is not a goal for which millions of people can pledge themselves." The Germans would have to set aside their age-old preoccupation with the state and "learn to place our own national well-being ruthlessly ahead of all others," for "without national egotism, we will always be at a disadvantage against the other nationalities."[36]

The landowners and the nationalists converged on occasion to protect the constitution, the liberal school laws, or the position of the German language in the internal bureaucracy, but they diverged sharply over the degree to which German nationalist interests could be pursued separate from the state interest. In the early years of Taaffe's rule, party leaders barely held these factions together in the United Left Party, as the more radical members argued for a nationalist name and platform. After the elections of 1885 it proved impossible to hold the two factions together any longer.

The United Left emerged from the 1885 elections having lost some fifteen seats. Some of the losses resulted from Taaffe's continued manipulations of the privileged curia. In the large landowner curia the party lost four seats in Bohemia and another four in the Tirol. In addition, the government ordered a change in the chamber of commerce curia that gave the Czechs another three formerly German liberal seats.[37] Election returns from the urban and rural curias also suggest that a more substantial political realignment was under way in several German-speaking regions. The 1882 enfranchisement of the five-gulden men did not result in the mass rejection of liberal party candidates for progovernment candidates Taaffe had hoped for, but it did play a role in reshaping power relations in formerly safe liberal districts.[38] In Vienna, for example, the liberals lost four seats to populist forces, either Anti-Semites or democrats, hardly a comforting outcome for Taaffe. And in several other

36. *Die Deutschen im Nationalitätenstaat Österreich*, 6.

37. NFP, June 13, 1885; Plener, *Erinnerungen*, 2:290. In the Tirol Taaffe had orchestrated a compromise between the clericals and the Italian nationalists that deprived the liberals of a possible seat. In 1891 the Italians would switch sides and help make a liberal victory possible there. The liberals lost seats in the Prague and Pilsen chambers of commerce.

38. Plener, *Erinnerungen*, 2:291. In some ethnically mixed districts in Bohemia the franchise reform tipped the balance irrevocably in favor of Czech nationalist candidates. Plener himself noted that the statistic of fifteen losses masked a more serious shift in the internal balance of the party toward the nationalists.

traditionally safe liberal districts, candidates who adopted a more decidedly German nationalist rhetoric had far more success mobilizing new voters than did the old-fashioned liberals.

No less a party luminary than Eduard Herbst was ousted from the rural Bohemian district he had represented since 1861 by the nationalist Carl Pickert.[39] Herbst was now forced to seek election in Vienna's safe first district. Plener, who could not have been unhappy about his rival's misfortune, nevertheless referred to this event as the "worst example" of the displacement of old liberals by German nationalist candidates. "The disregard and ingratitude toward a man like Herbst, who had accomplished extraordinary achievements for German Bohemians, was simply shocking."[40] And Pickert, one of the original *Jungen* from 1871, was hardly a radical by 1885 standards. Unlike Schönerer and his anti-Semitic followers, or Steinwender with his social reformism, Pickert could certainly work with Schmeykal and the Prague party leadership. Yet the price for Pickert's cooperation was the destruction of the old, formally supranational, United Left Party. During the election campaign of 1885, Pickert and several other German nationalist candidates pledged themselves to form a specifically German nationalist party in the *Reichsrat*.

Liberal large landowners, led by the capable Moravian Johann Chlumecky, preferred a party organized around supranationalist support for the Austrian state. In 1885 Plener still worried more about alienating these moderates than about keeping the nationalists within the United Left. A large landowners secession to form a centrist party sympathetic to the government would end Plener's fond hopes of toppling Taaffe in the near future. Not all of the moderates in the United Left agreed with Plener that the privileged large landowner curia should in effect dictate the terms of the party's organization. Some considered it strategically preferable to accommodate the thirty to forty energetic nationalists. During the 1885 debate over whether the United Left should adopt the name German Club (*Deutscher Club*), Joseph Neuwirth pointed out that too many issues still prevented the landowners from defecting to Taaffe. He argued that even if the party decided to adopt the more radically nationalist name, the landowners would have no choice but to remain.[41]

Sure enough, when the recently elected German liberal deputies met in September of 1885 before the opening of parliament, they immediately fought over whether to change the party's name to German Club. Forty-seven deputies voted for the change, while seventy-one opposed the new name.[42] Of those

39. Gierschik, *Karl Pickert*, 26–37. Gierschik's account, sympathetic to Pickert, claims that the latter originally had no intention of ousting Herbst but that Herbst had signaled his intention to run in a different district.

40. Plener, *Erinnerungen*, 2:291.

41. HHSA, Nachlass Plener, ct. 32, Neuwirth letter of August 25, 1885.

42. Nachlass Plener, ct. 32, draft invitation to colleagues to found a new party dated June 13, 1885; Plener, *Erinnerungen*, 2:291. Plener had not wanted to invite the nationalists to the Septem-

seventy-one deputies, however, at least thirty belonged to the large landowner curia. Without their votes, the nationalists would certainly have prevailed. The majority now refounded the old United Left, renaming it the German Austrian Party. It soon numbered eighty-four deputies.[43] This club encompassed the centralist moderates from the German *Sprachinseln* in Moravia, Silesia, and the Bukowina, the Viennese liberals, and the deputies from the privileged chamber of commerce and large landowner curias.

Thirty-eight nationalist deputies, however, seceded to form a new party, the German Club. In contrast to the German Austrian Club, the majority of those who founded the German Club represented nationalist districts in Bohemia and the Alpine provinces where regionalism had replaced state centralism.[44] The club program promised to take a more energetic stand in defense of German national rights, although it also reiterated its support for certain liberal accomplishments like the school system. On social and economic policy questions, the German Club seemed to criticize the do-nothing policies of the moderates, who had passively "watched the decline of the agrarian and urban Mittelstand." It was the duty of the state, the program claimed, "not simply to provide its citizens with legal protection but also to fight any obstacles to healthy economic development, using positive measures to encourage those groups in society that work hard and create our values, the farmers and artisans."[45] Significantly, the club did not elaborate on what exactly those measures might entail. This suggests that at least on social and economic policy, the gulf separating the self-consciously nationalist German Club from the moderate German Austrian Club was not as great as some of its members claimed.

Heinrich Friedjung, who had authored much of the Linz Program, now took over the editorship of the *Deutsche Zeitung,* which became the official organ of the German Club in 1886. Friedjung defined the new type of political style that the German Club would pursue as standing somewhere between that of the old-fashioned liberals and that of the demagogic Schönerer. "This is what is meant by the sharper key: the previous hesitation will be

ber meeting but only "those deputies who had been elected on the basis of our [United German Left] program."

43. HHSA, Nachlass Plener, ct. 24, draft program for the German Austrian Club and membership list; Plener, *Erinnerungen*, 2:298. As soon as the long-anticipated split had occurred, Plener changed his tune and began to worry that the absence of the nationalists would tip the party's ideological balance too much in favor of the landowners, who might advocate accommodation of Taaffe.

44. Höbelt, "Kornblume," 17. When deputies of the privileged (chamber of commerce and large landowner) curias are left out of the tally, two-thirds of the Bohemian German liberal deputies and four-fifths of the Styrian deputies joined the new German Club. On the other hand, only one of thirteen Moravians joined the German Club, the rest siding with Plener's German Austrian Club. Höbelt notes the ways in which the political geography of the 1880s continued certain trends already apparent in the 1860s and 1870s.

45. Statement published by the *Deutscher Klub*, "An unsere Wähler" (Vienna, 1885).

replaced by national energy—but in no way by political narrow-mindedness or recklessness."[46]

Only a year and a half later, the German Club itself split over the twin issues of anti-Semitism and socioeconomic reform. In 1887, Steinwender attempted to have Friedjung, a Jew, removed from the editorship of the *Deutsche Zeitung*. At a stormy session in February, the majority of the party supported Friedjung, passing a sharply worded resolution stating the German Club's opposition to "endeavors and factions that elevate class or racial hatred to a principle."[47] Ostensibly as a result of this controversy, sixteen members of the German Club, mostly deputies from Alpine provinces, seceded on February 15, 1887, to form a new party, the German National Union (*Deutsch-nationale Vereinigung*). In an announcement to their constituents the renegades reversed the usual logic of the anti-Semitic position. Instead of insisting on the incompatibility of Germanness and Jewishness, they declared that no one should be forced to adhere to a specific position regarding the Jewish question. "According to the desires of some party leaders, the German Club would have become the first and only parliamentary association that explicitly opposed anti-Semitism in its club program. . . . This strange occurrence, which was designed to force some of us out of the club, is actually consistent with the social and economic policies of the same leaders, who have never been able to overcome their inclination toward old-fashioned economic liberalism."[48]

As in the case of the extraparliamentary liberal associations, the anti-Semites portrayed themselves as populists and their opponents as old-fashioned elitists. And again, as in the nationalist organizations like the School Association, there was clearly more at work here than disagreements over anti-Semitism. Those who seceded from the German Club supported a more vigorously reformist economic program as well as a strong nationalism. In particular, the rebels backed the kind of restrictive economic measures and government intervention that traditional liberals associated with Catholic conservatism.[49] The importance the secessionists attributed to a politics of social reform is also evident from the fact that they did not join Schönerer's tiny League of German Nationalists once they had abandoned the German Club. Schönerer's requirement of absolute personal loyalty and his insistence on a rigid anti-Semitic litmus test for every issue would have restricted the social reform interest of the secessionists too severely.[50]

---

46. *Deutsche Wochenschrift*, May 10, 1885; McGrath, *Dionysian Art*, 204.

47. Friedjung, *Ein Stuck Zeitungsgeschichte*; McGrath, *Dionysian Art*, 206; Plener, *Erinnerungen*, 2:332; Zailler, "Heinrich Friedjung," 70–75. McGrath's otherwise useful account fails to note that despite Ausserer's stated opposition to the politicization of anti-Semitism, he was one of the men who seceded from the *Deutsche Club*, along with Steinwender.

48. HHSA, Nachlass Plener, ct. 24, "An unsere Wähler" in NWT, February 15, 1887.

49. Höbelt, *Kornblume*, 32–39.

50. Some of the members who seceded from the German Club to join the new German Na-

This division in the German Club marked the critical faultline of German bourgeois politics for the next decades. Those who abandoned the German Club moved decisively into the largely uncharted terrain of populist politics through nationalist rhetoric, a move that culminated a decade later in the creation of the German People's Party, destined to become the largest of the German nationalist parties in Austria at the turn of the century. At the same time, Karl Lueger made an equivalent move away from liberalism to populism through Christian social and anti-Semitic ideology in Vienna. Those who remained in the German Club and who opposed anti-Semitism also turned out to share the more traditionally liberal social and economic approaches of those in the German Austrian Club.[51] Not long after the split, the leaders of this rump German Club (among them School Association Chairman Weitlof) approached Plener and the German Austrian Club leadership about possibly forming a new coalition party. The ensuing negotiations produced the 112-member United German Left.[52]

The merger reflected just how quickly circumstances had changed attitudes regarding the thorny question of how much to make nationalism the defining issue of the party. By 1888, the moderate leaders of the German Austrian Club had themselves staked out a surprisingly radical position on the question of German national rights in Bohemia. Starting in 1886, Ernst von Plener had led the Bohemian German deputies in a boycott of the Bohemian Diet. This political tactic, purposely reminiscent of the Czech boycotts of the 1860s and 1870s, grew out of the German liberal frustration with Taaffe's unwillingness to consider legislation to divide Bohemia into separate German and Czech administrative districts. It also reflected a change in Plener's thinking. No longer did he consider the earlier goal of joining a reconstituted Iron Ring even as an option. Instead, he devoted all his energies to bringing about Taaffe's fall.

---

tional Union themselves opposed anti-Semitism but felt strongly enough about the issue of social reform to join the new organization. Interestingly, almost all of the secessionists hailed from the Alpine provinces, while most of the Bohemians remained in the rump German Club. This suggests the greater importance of economic issues to the former, as does the Carinthian Steinwender's increasing distance from the liberal and nationalist blocs.

51. Plener, *Erinnerungen*, 2:332. Plener considered that those responsible for the "shameless and arrogant sundering of the United Left" were now experiencing the same thing in miniature. He too attributed the split completely to the issue of anti-Semitism.

52. HHSA, Nachlass Plener, ct. 24, draft program and statutes for the United German Left; Plener, *Erinnerungen*, 2:362–63. The name change to include the word *German* was partly a victory for the more radical nationalist deputies over the large landowners, as was the stipulation for the first time that party membership would actually be limited to Germans. Plener credited Chlumecky with holding the right wing in line on both these issues. Plener's greater willingness to adopt a sharply nationalist tone reflected changed circumstances since 1885. By the time of the merger, he had himself taken a strongly nationalist position by leading the boycott of the Bohemian Diet by the German deputies.

With the boycott the liberal nationalists appeared to have trumped the radicals on their own issue. Plener, the newly elected leader of the United German Left, now assumed the unaccustomed role of people's tribune among the Germans of Bohemia. For if the boycott was part of a political maneuver designed to regain political influence for the United German Left in Vienna, it was certainly not understood as such by the German bourgeois public. The latter saw Plener striking a blow for German nationalist rights. Public declarations of support for Plener and the party now poured in from local associations and the German nationalist press.

In Bohemia, the boycott created significant political capital for the United German Left. It fired the imagination of German-speaking Bürger and briefly renewed their confidence in the effectiveness of parliamentary party tactics in the fight for national survival. Having created a sense of mass unity, particularly among Germans in Bohemia, the party now appeared to be more effective than Steinwender's German National Unionists. In vain did Schönerer's followers or Steinwender's allies criticize the so-called half measures of the United German Left. That party's strategy seemed to have gained impressive results when late in 1889 the Taaffe government hastily convened a conference in Vienna to negotiate a long-term settlement between the Czechs and Germans in Bohemia.[53]

The preliminary results of the compromise negotiations were announced in January 1890, and both the German and Czech press agreed that the Germans had emerged marginally victorious. This interpretation boosted the political fortunes of the United German Left among German speakers. In Czech circles, however, it discredited the Old Czechs, who appeared to have given away too much, while helping their rivals, the more radical Young Czechs, who had vigorously opposed the very idea of such a conference. In the next elections, the Young Czechs' opposition to the conference helped them to defeat the Old Czechs. This radicalization of Czech politics in turn crippled Taaffe's Iron Ring coalition, which had relied on Old Czech support for its parliamentary majority. Taaffe's fall appeared to be imminent, but it would now come at the expense of the hotly desired Bohemian compromise, which could no longer be implemented.

At first, the United German Left used the public perceptions of its victory in the compromise negotiations successfully to diffuse the attacks made on it by the radical nationalists. A party conference held at Teplitz in February 1890 turned into something of a victory celebration when Plener reported on the outcome of the negotiations to more than 3,000 members. The *Leitmeritzer*

53. HHSA, Nachlass Plener, ct. 33, materials on the Bohemian negotiations; Garver, *Young Czechs*, 148–53; Jenks, *Iron Ring*, 239–70; Max Menger, *Der böhmische Ausgleich* (Stuttgart, 1891); Molisch, *Briefe*, 315–28; Plener, *Erinnerungen*, 2:382–94.

Zeitung commented on Plener's personal transformation, noting that when he had first been appointed party leader, "we did not hide our conviction that the former diplomat lacked the requisite ability to connect with the common people, so necessary to a great leader." Now, however, the newspaper decided that even if Plener's style remained uninspired, the content of his speeches embodied the desires of the people.[54]

Enthusiasm for the United German Left began to wane when it became apparent that the compromise agreement would not be implemented, mostly because of the implacable opposition shown it by the Young Czechs. Nevertheless, in Bohemia, Moravia, and Silesia, the United German Left triumphed in the *Reichsrat* elections of 1891, actually regaining two seats lost in 1885 to radical followers of Steinwender and Schönerer. Overall in Cisleithania, the party entered the campaign with 112 seats and emerged with 107. Its losses were sustained almost exclusively in rural Lower Austria, where both anti-Semitic and clerical candidates took four formerly liberal seats, and in Styria and Carinthia, where Steinwender's nationalists robbed the party of another four seats.[55]

With the Young Czechs in opposition, Taaffe lost his governing majority. He could no longer pursue an openly antiliberal course but had to rule pragmatically, searching for different majorities for each bill in the *Reichsrat.* For a while, Taaffe negotiated with the United German Left, hoping to use its support to pass necessary legislation like the budget and defense bills. The party moved cautiously too. Its leaders wanted to show the emperor their willingness to cooperate for the good of the state, but they did not want to see their party simply replace the Czechs in a reformed Iron Ring coalition under Taaffe.

From 1891 until 1893, liberals like Plener made increasing use of strongly nationalist rhetoric to justify their alternating positions in this delicately balanced relationship with the Taaffe government. During one short period (1891–92), for example, the United German Left authorized Count Gandolf Künberg of Upper Austria to join the Taaffe cabinet as a general minister for German affairs. The party justified this experiment by referring to Künberg as a guarantee that the Iron Ring would no longer ignore German national interests. When they withdrew Künberg from the cabinet, party leaders blamed Taaffe's unwillingness to take German interests into account in the formation of government policy. The danger in this strategy lay in the possibility that it might succeed. The political goals of many deputies in the United German Left,

54. *Leitmeritzer Zeitung*, February 15, 1890. I found this unusual assessment of Plener carefully preserved in HHSA, Nachlass Plener, ct. 33.

55. Lothar Höbelt, "Die Linke und die Wahlen von 1891," MÖSA 40 (1987). Altogether the party gained two seats in Bohemia and two in the Tirol large landowner's curia, while losing five in Lower Austria and two each in Styria and Carinthia.

not simply Plener or Chlumecky, did not accord with their increasingly harsh nationalist rhetoric. Nevertheless, at every opportunity, they raised their nationalist constituents' expectations of how a German government would rule.[56]

By 1893, some in the party hoped to supplant Taaffe by forging a coalition with their old nemesis the Hohenwart conservatives and with the perennially opportunist Poles. The attractiveness of such a coalition to the emperor would be its decidedly centrist nature. Moderates from both right and left would join to protect the monarchy from the political extremes, represented by the obstructionist Young Czechs and German anti-Semites. All sides would agree to a moratorium on divisive issues like school reform, would pledge to maintain *Nationalbesitzstand* as it stood, and concentrate on governing. Yet if the leaderships of the liberals and conservatives could imagine such a combination, many of their followers and constituents could not. This coalition idea could only have been developed by the Bohemian/Moravian wing of the United German Left. It placed liberals from the Alpine provinces in an extremely unpleasant situation, since most of them were engaged in long-term ideological battles directly against the conservatives over school and religious issues in local diets and municipal councils. Many of Hohenwart's clerical followers viewed the idea with equal distaste, preferring mutiny to a coalition with the enemy.

Taaffe finally fell in 1893 over the issue of electoral reform: without warning he had proposed a reform that the Poles and Hohenwart conservatives in his cabinet repudiated as too radical. The two parties then withdrew their support from the government and negotiated a coalition agreement with the United German Left based on the above-mentioned principle of maintaining the national status quo.[57] Believing this to be an opportunity of historic proportions, Plener quickly resigned his leadership of the party to follow in his father's footsteps as finance minister. The Styrian Count Gundackar Wurmbrand joined Plener in the new cabinet as minister of commerce.[58] For the first and last time in Cisleithanian parliamentary history a government was formed from the initiative of the parties themselves and not at the behest of the emperor. The hasty

---

56. Jenks, *Iron Ring*, 283–89; Plener, *Erinnerungen*, 3:24–27, 61–62.

57. Jenks, *Iron Ring*, 272–303; Plener, *Erinnerungen*, 3:86–105. This maneuver was extraordinary for Austrian constitutional history. It was the only occasion during the constitutional monarchy when a parliamentary majority literally dictated a government to the emperor. Francis Joseph did not like having the parties impose on him their choice of a new minister president, nor did he like the prenegotiated division of cabinet seats. He had other plans and hoped eventually to replace Taaffe with Badeni.

58. Plener, *Erinnerungen*, 3:110. Wurmbrand was not the automatic first choice for commerce, but the party's experts on the subject came from Bohemia, while Wurmbrand, a Styrian, gave the Alpine liberals a representative in the cabinet. Wurmbrand was also not congenial to many in the party because of his social-reformist leanings.

negotiations, however, produced a cabinet in which, as one liberal newspaper pointed out, "the Hohenwart Club, with half as many deputies as the United German Left, nevertheless exercises twice as much influence." The conservatives gained a disproportionate number of ministerial portfolios while the United German Left, by far the largest party among the partners, controlled only the ministries of finance and commerce.[59]

Plener severely miscalculated in his choice of ministerial portfolios. By settling on the two economic portfolios for the party, Plener guaranteed that the United German Left would disappoint its nationalist constituents. Had he insisted on the ministries of interior, justice, or even education, the party might have matched its nationalist rhetoric with at least a gesture to German nationalist concerns. Not so in the realm of economic policy. Neither finance nor commerce offered the cabinet ministers much opportunity to strengthen the party's position with its constituents, as Plener soon discovered. In fact, control over the economic ministries only contributed to an increase in party wrangling between free traders and the moderate social reformers, while the mere mention of tax reform, Plener's most ambitious project, set various liberal and nationalist interests against each other as interest groups vied for preferential treatment. Plener's new concerns only confirmed the degree to which his leadership of the party and his recent nationalist conversion had been directed opportunistically to accomplishing the narrow political goal of joining a cabinet. However, the highly nationalist political climate, for which Plener was largely responsible, did not now suddenly disappear.

While he busied himself with the consuming details of Austria's tax code, his party prepared Plener's downfall on a different issue. The Taaffe cabinet had furnished its successor with an awkward legacy: the decision to fund a Slovene language gymnasium in the Styrian town of Cilli. In coalition negotiations with the Poles and the conservatives, the United German Left had agreed in principle to honor the previous government's commitment to the school, which it viewed as a fait accompli. German liberals in the new cabinet had the thankless task of administering a policy that enraged its own German nationalist constituents. According to the 1890 census, 4,452 people in the town of Cilli reported German as their "language of daily use," and 1,577 reported Slovene, while in the surrounding district over 36,000 people reported Slovene as their "language of daily use," as opposed to under 1,000 who reported German. Placing a Slovene-language gymnasium in an "embattled" German town (that is, one perceived to be surrounded by a Slovene hinterland) was an act of expropriation, a gratuitous gift of *Nationalbesitzstand* made to the enemy.[60]

59. *Bohemia*, April 4, 1895.

60. Plener, *Erinnerungen*, 3:144–45; Höbelt, *Kornblume,* 106–15. The Taaffe cabinet had promised the gymnasium to the Slovene deputies, who made up one bloc in Hohenwart's Conser-

Many liberal deputies secretly agreed with Plener that the Cilli issue constituted little more than an annoyance, certainly not worth bringing down the government. This was the case, for example, of Richard Foregger, the Viennese lawyer who represented Cilli in parliament. When Foregger visited his district in the summer of 1894, he was surprised by the degree of anger his constituents expressed over this issue.[61] Yet the attempts by liberals like Foregger or Plener in the 1880s to appropriate nationalist rhetoric and incorporate it into their bourgeois slogans now forced them to oppose the Slovene gymnasium for Cilli or to look like hypocrites. German radicals and anti-Semites, meanwhile, waited eagerly on the sidelines, ready to discredit the moderate liberals if they wavered and to expose them for the reluctant nationalists the radicals knew them to be.

On first inspection the Cilli incident seems to reflect both a growing radicalization of the Austro-German electorate and the inability of bourgeois, "rational" liberals to comprehend, much less to exploit, the changes occurring among their own constituents. This is the view of nineteenth-century contemporaries and later historians for whom *fin de siècle* nationalism appeared to be the irrational enemy of a positivist bourgeois liberalism. However, the very concept of *Nationalbesitzstand* firmly linked German nationalist identity in Austria to a bourgeois liberal ideological heritage.[62] Men like Plener had helped forge this link, the better to create a space for the survival of liberal values in an age of mass mobilization. In particular, they had hoped that their appropriation of nationalist rhetoric would help them to defeat both the divisive localism of radical anti-Semites and the federalist visions propounded by the Czechs, Poles, and Slovenes. Yet in doing so, these liberals made themselves vulnerable to the attacks of radical nationalists outside the government, who could always afford to intensify the level of their nationalist rhetoric far beyond anything the liberals within the coalition might engage in.

The organ of the renegade German nationalist party in Reichenberg, for example, taunted the United German Left continuously throughout the eighteen-month life of the coalition. "The German people no longer expects any good from a 'United Left' that fights shoulder to shoulder with the Poles and the conservatives for progress," sneered its editors in the spring of 1895. Yet it was the Cilli question that raised the most concern in nationalist circles. "We can no longer doubt the [sad] fate of Cilli and other still surviving

vative Party. In 1893 the Slovene deputies threatened to quit the Conservative Party if the cabinet did not carry through on its promise. This incident illustrates the fact that the liberals were not the only large coalition party falling apart at the seams in the 1890s.

61. Molisch, *Briefe*, 335–36. Foregger reported to Liberal Party leader Johann Chlumecky that his constituents were urging him to take radical steps and that they would not be averse to destroying the coalition or the United German Left over this issue.

62. C. B. Macpherson, *The Political Theory of Possessive Individualism: Hobbes to Locke* (Oxford, 1985).

German bulwarks, since the combined weight of the imposing United German Left doesn't carry a fraction of the nationalist influence exercised by a small handful of Hohenwart's Slovenes. . . . Anyone in the United German Left who has the least bit of nationalist sentiment left must bow to party discipline, and in return he gains the higher satisfaction of belonging to a party judged capable of governing [by the emperor]: a truly despicable reward for sacrificing the national honor of the German people!"[63]

By 1895 the tide of German opinion had shifted across the monarchy, and no amount of mundane administrative accomplishment by the government could outweigh the perceived damage to the community caused by locating a single high school in a small South Styrian town. The best that United German Left deputies like Max Menger could argue in their defense was that the coalition still constituted a better alternative for German national interests than had Taaffe's regime, and that the party would only remain a part of this government as long as it could protect the free schools and the German *Nationalbesitzstand.*[64] The nationalist responses called forth by the Cilli crisis demonstrated the degree to which a constituent-based mass politics had come to inform the party system in the Austrian Empire. It confirms the unprecedented degree to which clearly popular movements could influence the course of parliamentary politics. The 1880s had witnessed an increased attentiveness to the rhetoric (if not the actual demands) of new Mittelstand and nationalist organizations. The coalition's failure in 1895 demonstrated that politicians also had to act on that rhetoric.

The Cilli crisis also demonstrated in several ways the degree to which this mass politics had already become an interregional rather than a purely local phenomenon. As I have already suggested, one astonishing result of these events is the degree to which activists in one region of the monarchy identified their own specific regional interests with events in a faraway province. This identification of a large sector of the Bohemian, Moravian, and Silesian German nationalist public with the imagined plight of German speakers in South Styria had little precedent and can only have resulted from a newer understanding of national identity. This new sense of a larger German identity in Austria was anchored in local experience of social conflict, but it remade the larger world of the state in its own image. It had been forged in the years since 1880, largely through the activities of the protectionist associations. As several historians have suggested, the new mass politics developed in cities as diverse as Graz, Reichenberg, and Vienna. It is no accident, for example, that 1895 also saw the breakthrough of Karl Lueger's Christian Socials in Vienna. But what is important is the extent to which nationalist ideologies connected with mass politics transcended their urban origins, offering an increasingly cogent and attractive explanation of events at the level of the empire as a whole.

63. *Deutsche Volkszeitung* (Reichenberg), March 10, 1895.

64. *Bohemia*, March 29, 1895.

The defeat of the liberals by Karl Lueger's anti-Semitic Christian Social Party in Vienna's spring elections became the last straw for many liberals who had remained loyal to Plener. Although the reasons for Lueger's victory had far more to do with the complexities of local politics than with nationalist doubts about the coalition, the combination of municipal and national events finally produced an angry backlash against Plener's absent leadership. In its Easter editorial the *Neue Freie Presse* asked, "When will the leader of the German people in Austria resurrect himself? Is the finance portfolio a political coffin lid that prevents Herr von Plener from leading and protecting the German Bürgertum?"[65] Commenting on this internecine attack by the foremost liberal journal, the radical *Deutsche Volkszeitung* of Reichenberg claimed in its own editorial, entitled "Plener: Where Are You?" that even liberals now admitted that after his elevation to the cabinet Plener had abandoned the German people.[66] Other provincial papers more sympathetic to the United German Left and shocked by Lueger's defeat of the Viennese liberals rushed to defend the former's politics. "The coalition acts as a dam against the extreme parties, whose hands are tied as long as it exists," insisted the antipopulist *Freie schlesische Presse* of Troppau (Silesia).[67] Still other liberal papers like the Prague Germans' *Bohemia* made no mention of the attack at all.

When the Cilli issue finally came before the *Reichsrat* for a vote in June the party deserted Plener to vote against funding for the school. Liberals who represented anticlerical constituents in the Alpine provinces were increasingly uneasy about remaining in a coalition with clerical conservatives. They could not afford to lose their nationalist credentials as well by appearing to support or even tolerate the proposal for a Slovene school in Cilli. And the centrality of German nationalism to the debate forced many Bohemian and Moravian deputies to reexamine their own relationship to the cabinet. Although several opponents of the school admitted that the issue had technically already been decided, and while some did not even believe the school was such a bad idea, their fragile relations with nationalist constituents drove them to adopt a more radical, intransigent position.[68]

---

65. NFP, April 17, 1895; Plener, *Erinnerungen*, 3:242–45.

66. *Deutsche Volkszeitung* (Reichenberg), April 18, 1895. Noting the *Neue Freie Presse*'s disappointment that "Herr von Plener is often sought after but can never be found" in political emergencies, the *Volkszeitung* added gratuitously that it had "never sought his help in national matters, but if [it] had, [it] would have gone straight to whatever banquet was being held in the Hotel Sacher, where we surely would have found him."

67. *Freie Schlesische Presse* (Troppau), April 20, 1895.

68. Richard Foregger, *Zur Cillier Gymnasialfrage* (Vienna, 1894). This was true for deputies elected by the urban and rural curias in Bohemia. Those elected by privileged curias (large landowners and chambers of commerce) could afford to support Plener and the coalition.

With the party's withdrawal from the coalition, Plener exited the cabinet after barely a year and a half in office. Finding himself the object of recrimination and public dishonor, he resigned from the party he had so recently led to victory. Until the last, Plener had not believed that such an insignificant issue could bring down Austria's first truly parliamentary cabinet. In his own defense he later blamed his colleagues, writing that "the party had become more nationalistic and was still filled with the oppositionary spirit of the 1880s," while he, Plener, "had experienced a change toward trying to reach an understanding with the other nationalities."[69] Yet despite such pious disclaimers, Plener was himself largely responsible for the nationalist escalation that led to the Cilli catastrophe. Like many of his colleagues, he could not distance himself from a German nationalism whose growth and particular shape he had himself encouraged by invoking an inflammatory rhetoric organized around *Nationalbesitzstand* in the years since 1885.

By 1895 the question was no longer whether or to what degree nationalism would influence politics, as Plener may have believed it was, but rather which vision of nationalism would determine policy. The battles waged in associations, in the press, and in legislative bodies were not really about questions like a school in Cilli or even the place of anti-Semitism in the German nationalist movement. Rather, they constituted a battle for national legitimacy. The issue at stake was the ability to control the particular content of Germanness. With this ability a party would gain a far greater power to mobilize constituents. This is clear from an event of a far different order that took place simultaneously with the collapse of the coalition and the victory of Lueger's Christian Socials in Vienna.

In May 1895 the German School Association held its fifteenth annual general meeting in Vienna. By now the general meeting had become an annual opportunity for moderates and radicals to argue bitterly in the press about the most effective way to mobilize the German community. A decade after the angry departure of the *Schönerianer* from the association neither side made anti-Semitism itself the issue. Rather, both used the unspoken conflict over anti-Semitism in the association as a means to argue for a particular organizational style, and this in turn represented a particular vision of Germanness. The *Bohemia,* a paper close to the Liberal Party leadership in Prague, used the occasion to express deep regret that the School Association not only had to suffer Czech nationalist attacks but remained a target for radical German troublemakers who refused to work together for the common good of the German community. Citing recent attacks on the association by papers sympathetic to Schönerer, the *Bohemia* noted that the eruption of similar conflicts in

69. Plener, *Erinnerungen,* 3:284.

the Czech camp would be unthinkable. "There all work unselfishly for the whole, without complaint."[70]

At the annual meeting a branch once again petitioned for the right of local groups to determine their own membership, claiming that with such a reform, "a large number of German men and women would not have to remain outside the School Association in the future." Arguing that giving more power to the individual branches—in effect structural democratization—would help revive local activism, the petitioner did not even need to mention the question of anti-Semitism that lay behind the proposal. As in previous years, the School Association leadership had the votes to prevent a discussion of the question, and it was roundly defeated.[71] Papers like the *Deutsche Volkszeitung* (Reichenberg) and the *Ostdeutsche Rundschau* immediately attacked the organization for its dictatorial structure. They agreed that while the organization's goals were laudable, nevertheless its elitist centralized structure discouraged local initiative and prevented the authentic voice of the *Volk* from gaining expression.[72]

Political Legacies, 1895–1914

With the fall of the coalition in 1895, German Bürger politics changed substantially. This event signaled the final collapse of the large interregional liberal parties that had dominated the *Reichsrat* since 1861 and the rise of smaller parties fragmented by special interests. Or did it? True, the United German Left broke up into several regional and ideological component parts. The German liberal nationalists and the centralist large landowners finally created separate parties, while socially reform-minded deputies further to the left founded a party of the enfranchised Mittelstand. Nevertheless, the history of these various groups and their descendants down to 1914 reveals persistent attempts to reconstitute a single German Bürger bloc, one capable of speaking with a unified voice for an imagined German community in Austria. The creation of even more interest-based parties after 1900, from the Agrarians to the parties of small industry, was balanced by their recurring merger in large coalitions designed to protect German nationalist interests.

---

70. *Bohemia*, May 23, 1895. The *Ostdeutsche Rundschau* had written that "ever since the ejection of the true nationalists from the [School] Association, its efforts have become completely ineffective."

71. *Bohemia*, May 24, 1895.

72. *Deutsche Volkszeitung* (Reichenberg), May 23, 1895. The same paper attacked other nationalist organizations like the Bund der Deutschen Nordwestböhmens as do-nothing (April 7, 1895), going so far as to intimate that in Saaz, the local branch could not be officially founded because no one would agree to lead an organization made up of one hundred fifty Jews and only ten Christians (May 23, 1895).

Despite or because of the rise of mass parties organized around particular social and economic interests, the nationalist associations remained the premier site where German identity was most effectively constructed, where Germanness was defined, where differences between Germans and Czechs, or even Germans and Jews, were elaborated and spread. Voluntary associations offered far greater continuity than the individual parties in their ability to reproduce Germanness and its cultural norms. And this continuity largely benefited the bourgeois liberal nationalists. At the parliamentary party level they saw their numbers and influence decline from 1895 to 1914. In the associations, however, they remained the architects of national ideology, the builders and reproducers of a German cultural community. Liberal nationalists continued to wield influence wherever intraclass national unity was perceived as the paramount goal.

After 1895, the "German left" consisted of three interregional movements, each of which retained certain features of the old liberal movement: (1) A constitutionalist large landowner party occupied a position slightly to the left of the political center. (2) A series of German progressive parties carried on liberal nationalist traditions at state and local levels. (3) A more radical German People's Party catered to the social and economic concerns of the Mittelstand. In addition, followers of Georg von Schönerer formed a pro-Prussian and irredentist All German Party, which generally stood apart from the other three but which competed with the Peoples' Party for Mittelstand votes and with the progressives for nationalist votes. Of the three major factions, the progressives constituted the most direct heir of the earlier liberal parties. Their deputies were largely elected from chambers of commerce and urban constituencies in regions where *Mittelstandspolitik* of the populist or Christian Social variety had not developed support and where German nationalism was often identified with state centralism.

In 1897 a new general curia, elected by poorer artisans, white- and blue-collar workers, and peasants, was added to the other four, with the result that the German Peoples' Party now emerged as the strongest of the various German Bürger groups. This party, led by Otto Steinwender in its early years, competed for the support of artisans and peasants against Schönerer's All Germans in the Bohemian lands and against the newer Christian Social movement for similar voters in the western and Alpine lands. Although nationalist, the German People's Party saw its potential strength deriving from its support for social reform. In contrast to the progressive parties, the People's Party worked to create issue-based political alliances with other groups sympathetic to its Mittelstand economic agenda, even those, like clerical conservatives, that more traditional liberal nationalist Germans opposed.[73]

73. Steinwender also continued to propound the view that a nonpolitical cabinet of bureaucrats that functioned beyond the influence of the political parties would be of greater use to his party than a cabinet based on a specific party coalition.

Yet even this most populist of the parties that emerged from the wreckage of the liberal movement remained very much the product of a political process caught in transition. Despite a growing popularization of politics, the system still gave certain groups an inordinately strong political voice through the retention of curial franchises. Not until 1907 did Austrians elect their first *Reichsrat* by universal manhood suffrage, and, even then, provincial diets and municipal councils continued to be elected by curial voting. It is difficult to evaluate the populist potential of an organization like the German People's Party since its strategies and ideological appeals also accorded with the necessities of competing in a hierarchic political system.

Whatever the potential of the German People's Party to become a mass party organized more around economic and social interests than nationality, the Badeni Language Ordinance crisis of 1897–99 put an end to it. The crisis shaped political alternatives in Austria for the next decades by reasserting the fundamental primacy of nationalism in imperial politics. The crisis demanded strict unity among all German Bürger parties, and it effectively relegated social and economic issues to a lower priority. In April 1897 Minister President Badeni's government published a series of language ordinances for Bohemia and Moravia stipulating that all inner bureaucratic correspondence should occur in whatever language a case had first been filed in. Furthermore, Badeni extended the Stremayr ordinances to apply to all Bohemia, not simply to its ethnically mixed regions. This too required that all petitions filed in any district must be answered in the original language of the petition. Badeni set 1901 as the deadline for the relevant officers to be conversant in both Czech and German.[74]

The ordinances called forth protests and later violence by German nationalists on a massive scale across the empire. German Bohemians who still hoped for administrative partition protested the requirement that officials in purely German-speaking districts would nevertheless be required to learn Czech. This stipulation, they claimed, not only favored Czech candidates for administrative jobs, but it also demanded an equality among the two languages even in purely German districts. Why not exempt those districts and limit the ordinance to ethnically mixed ones, demanded German nationalists? For German speakers, the crisis reinforced demands to partition Bohemia into nationally distinct provinces. And as with the Cilli crisis, Germans across the monarchy reacted strongly to the ordinances. In Graz, German nationalists rioted, mindful of the recent Cilli crisis and fearful that the Slovenes might now gain a comparable rule for Styria. In Vienna, violence broke out repeatedly around the parliament as the ordinances were debated.

---

74. Berthold Sutter, *Die Badenischen Sprachenverordnungen*, 2 vols. (Vienna, 1960, 1965); Höbelt, *Kornblume*, 150–66; Molisch, *Geschichte der deutschnationalen Bewegung*, 185–94. This brief account of the Badeni crisis is taken primarily from Sutter.

The progressives and Schönerer's tiny group of All Germans reacted most quickly to the crisis. They devised the brilliantly destructive tactics of obstruction that prevented the *Reichsrat* from legislating for the next two years and that forced the government to retract the ordinances. Some progressives, like Moravian Otto Lecher, who filibustered for fourteen hours, became national heroes. Max Menger, usually known for moderation on most issues, spouted a vituperative rhetoric as a way to strengthen his reputation with constituents. The German People's Party, however, held back at first and joined the obstruction with great reluctance. Steinwender counseled moderation, suggesting that the nationalists practice a "selective obstruction" to enable the *Reichsrat* to take up economic issues of concern to the Mittelstand. Yet his Mittelstand constituents reacted strongly to the nationalist urgency of the situation, and local associations in the Alpine provinces demanded that Steinwender commit himself more fully to the national cause.[75]

So strong was the popular outcry among German speakers in Austria that even the large landowners' party, Lueger's Christian Socials, and some German Catholic conservative deputies found themselves forced to join a so-called *Gemeinbürgschaft,* a loose alliance to coordinate a united front among all German parties with the predictable exception of Schönerer's All Germans. The *Gemeinbürgschaft* operated primarily as a conference of club leaders who met periodically to plan strategy and discuss issues. The arrangement lasted little more than a year in its original form, after which Lueger's Christian Socials withdrew. Still this coalition remained a model for later blocs or fronts meant to unite the German left on nationalist issues.[76]

As this brief discussion suggests, the Badeni crisis ensured the progressives a measure of real popular support, extending their constituencies well beyond their privileged base in the chambers of commerce and urban curias. True, the progressives' *Reichsrat* numbers declined with each franchise reform to the point where, after the introduction of universal manhood suffrage, they elected only twenty to forty seats out of a total of 516. Nevertheless, the progressives acted as the primary organizers of the two important coalitions of German Bürger parties on the left: the German National League (*deutschnationaler Verband*) in 1907 and its successor, the National League of German Progressive Deputies (*Nationalverband der deutschfreiheitlichen Abgeordneten*) in 1908.

This revival of nationalist concern ushered in a process of irreversible decline for the German People's Party. The resignation (or expulsion) of Stein-

75. Höbelt, *Kornblume*, 157–63, 173–77; Sutter, *Sprachenverordnungen*, 2:107.

76. Molisch, *Geschichte der deutschnationalen Bewegung*, 202–6; Höbelt, *Kornblume*, 151, 164–66, 173; John W. Boyer, *Culture and Political Crisis in Vienna: Christian Socialism in Power, 1897–1918* (Chicago, 1995), 40–41. The parties of the coalition produced a Whitsun Program in 1899 setting forth the lingusitic desires of the Germans.

wender and the reassertion of nationalist virtue in that party left it vulnerable to competition from newer parties focused more on specific economic interests, like the Agrarians, and forever suspect, on the other side, to radical nationalists. Several of the radical nationalists from the Peoples' Party now joined with a group of former Schönerer followers to create a German Radical Party. The new party gradually replaced both the German People's Party and Schönerer's All Germans in Bohemia. Despite its rhetorical borrowings from Schönerer, the Radical Party was loyal to Austria and moderate enough eventually to join the bourgeois National League of German Progressive Deputies. The new interest group parties that replaced the People's Party, the Agrarians, the Small Industry, and German Workers' parties, had no more luck combining Mittelstand constituencies than had the People's Party. They too fell back on nationalism as an ideological means to hold their diverse constituencies together, joining the National League as well.[77]

In Austria, German nationalism remained very much the property of what could be called the bourgeois left. All of these Bürger parties, however socially conservative their ideology may appear to have been, nevertheless continued to support several of liberalism's traditional positions, in particular anticlericalism and the need for a free school system. In Germany, nationalism often enabled bourgeois parties to join traditional elites in conservative alliances to repudiate liberal or progressive institutions. In Austria, the importance of nationalism prevented any long-term rapprochement between the populist or *Mittelständisch* parties and the conservative, clerical, or Christian social groupings with whom they might otherwise have had much in common. While the impetus for founding an agrarian party in Bohemia derived from the example of the conservative-led *Bund der Landwirte* across the border in Germany, the pull of nationalism kept the Austrian Agrarians firmly allied with the anticlerical progressives on what was called the "German Left."

Associational Culture: Normalizing Racial Nationalism

The survival of German nationalism as the paramount issue in Austrian politics depended largely on the cultural work and continuity provided by local associations. These organizations continued to mobilize Austrians in public life around the issue of German nationalist survival. The association, far more than the political party, remained the site where German identity was constructed and elaborated for the larger communities. Yet by the mid 1890s, levels of public participation appeared to be declining, and several organizations saw their memberships level off. Nationalists argued that the situation was in fact worse than the public realized, since membership statistics alone

77. Höbelt, *Kornblume*, 187–99; 229–76.

told only part of the story. Critics and activists alike noted that local branches of the larger organizations had often fallen into decline, and some existed only on paper. Observers in organizations like the *Böhmerwaldbund* also noticed that local activists tended to suffer a kind of burn-out after only a few years. These assertions led the leaders of the School Association to devise a structural compromise designed to encourage local initiative without giving in completely to the divisive demands of the anti-Semites. In 1897 the organization voted to allow the creation of more than one branch at the local level, thus implicitly creating a space for anti-Semites to organize themselves separately from the moderates. In 1899, following the retirement of its long-time chair, Moritz Weitlof, the organization finally gave local branches the right to determine membership. According to its own historian, this compromise enabled the School Association to begin rebuilding its membership and to infuse its members with a new degree of nationalist activism.[78]

The Badeni crisis also galvanized German nationalist activists as had no other before it, motivating larger numbers of people to join existing nationalist and protective associations. The more radical League of Germans in Bohemia (*Bund der Deutschen in Böhmen*), founded in 1894 to coordinate nationalist economic activism among several Bohemian protective associations, grew from a membership of 7,000 in 1895 to 60,000 in 1900. The *Südmarck* jumped from 8,500 members in 1896 to 15,000 in 1897. Yet once perceptions of the immediate danger had passed, activism waned again, and associational leaders began once more to warn against apathy. By 1904 the League of Germans in Bohemia had lost two-fifths of its members. Similarly the League of Germans in Eastern Bohemia (*Bund der Deutschen in Ostböhmen*), which had gained close to 8,000 members by 1899, could only report 4,500 in 1904. An analysis of protective associations by Franz Perko published in *Deutsche Arbeit* in 1905 suggested a combination of social and political reasons for the decline, including the possibility that "differences within the German nationalist party have alienated some association members." In addition, Perko concluded that while many activists believed a more decentralized organizational structure might revive local interest, still, "it would [actually] be more advantageous for all the protective associations . . . to work with fewer but stronger, rather than with more but weaker, local branches."[79]

The associational landscape had thus reached a certain level of saturation by 1900, and membership involved less personal commitment to activism; even so, these associations increasingly set the tone for public discourse on the

78. Wotowa, *Schulverein*, 26–27.

79. *Deutsche Arbeit* 10 (1905): 564, 610; Wotowa, *Schulverein*, 72. Membership of the League of Germans in Bohemia fell to 38,000 in 1904. This trend was less drastic for older nationalist associations like the German School Association (over 74,000) or the League of the Bohemian Woods (30,000), whose memberships remained essentially stable during this period.

issue of nationalism. And in this area some notable changes had taken place in the two decades since the founding of the German nationalist movement. The above-mentioned School Association compromise, which enabled local branches to practice a policy of anti-Semitic exclusion, reflects the degree to which anti-Semitic rhetoric had infiltrated the nationalist lexical repertoire by 1900. The compromise reflected a toleration of anti-Semitism that would have been unimaginable in 1885, but it did not result in a wholehearted adoption of an anti-Semitic worldview either. The right of local branches to exclude Jewish members did not lead to any new and overt anti-Semitic practices in the School Association, nor did it result in a reduction of contributions made by the organization to Jewish-run schools. In specific localities it may have contributed to a reconsideration by Jews of their national loyalties and options, but viewed from a distance, it did not mark a break in the association's development. The fact that this association positioned itself within the liberal nationalist tradition, although tolerating anti-Semites at the local level, suggests that by 1900 anti-Semitism had somehow become normalized. Neither support for it nor opposition to it any longer constituted the critical division between liberals and *völkisch* radicals that it once had. Ironically, the more radical nationalist associations understood this best. They continued to boycott meetings that included the still suspect School Association. The *Südmarck*'s own historian noted forty years later that the internal reform of 1899 had not amounted to a true refounding of the School Association "on the basis of national purity (*Volksreinheit*)," and this made any serious collaboration with it quite impossible.[80]

German nationalist discourse grew increasingly racialist after 1900. In the 1880s, activists had worked to awaken an awareness of national identity among those Germans who were ignorant of it. Nationalists had focused on defining Germanness for the individual as a means of bringing him or her into a larger community. Now nationalist publications and organizations in Bohemia underscored the need to maintain stricter boundaries between Germans and Czechs in the ethnically mixed regions. This new concern for separation resulted in part from the German strategy of defining a purely German-speaking Bohemian territory that might someday achieve administrative autonomy from the rest of the province. Every Czech incursion in ethnically mixed borderlands diminished the degree to which a national delineation could reasonably be made. But at least in part, the heightened concern about national mixing reflected the degree to which racial anti-Semitism had come to influence beliefs about nationality. The figure of the racially "other" Jew did differ significantly from the figure of the nationally "other" Czech in radical nationalist rhetoric. The former had no legitimate home, no authentic *Nationalbesitzstand* (except what

80. Pock, *Grenzwacht*, 21.

he could steal), while the latter had a legitimate *Nationalbesitzstand* of his own, which he aggressively sought to increase at the expense of his German neighbors.

Such differences in individual stereotyping paled beside the growing tendency to understand national differences in biologically racialist terms. Nationalist rhetoric about the Czechs borrowed increasingly from racialist, and from British and French colonialist, discourse, in its growing insistence on the virtues of cultural and physical separation. In popular almanacs and magazines authors continued to use both fiction and statistics to warn their readers about the often subversive attacks made by the Czechs on German communities. They had worried publicly about how to keep German property in German hands for some twenty years; now with a newly racialized understanding of national differences they warned against the dangers of intermarriage.[81] "To prevent our enemies from making further progress we must practice a personal national separation to the extreme," explained one moderate leader, "starting from the endeavor to encourage and support everything that helps us to maintain every possible opposition between the German population and the Czech."[82]

The "Ten Commandments of the German Farmer," published in the 1880s, were recast and rewritten as the "Ten Commandments of the German People" in 1898. Where the former had stressed self-help, independence, and capitalist virtue, the latter now warned against "social contact with strangers" or "succumbing to alien customs and beliefs," while commanding pride in "German descent."[83] And where publications of the 1880s had occasionally encouraged their readers to buy from German vendors wherever possible, almanacs and magazines around 1900 urged people to buy products that, through their very consumption, would demonstrate the individual's nationalist loyalty. The organization *Nordmarck,* the Silesian version of the *Südmarck,* marketed matches, soap, decorative buttons, and pins in the late 1890s. The matchboxes and soap wrappers carried the symbols and colors of the organization, along with the motto "Remember that you are a German."[84]

---

81. *Deutscher Volks-Kalender für Schlesien 1898* (Troppau, 1898), 92–96; "Szenen aus der Tragödie Ferdinand Bernts '*Zwischen zwei Sprachen*'" *Deutsche Arbeit* 8 (1905): 505–14; "Von unseren Gegnern," *Deutsche Volkszeitung* (Reichenberg), October 4, 1895. The latter article warned against the dangers for German men of marrying Czech women. In "Eine Mischheirat" by radical nationalist *Reichsrat* deputy Karl Türk, a young man ignores the warnings of his parents and, taking the advice of a local Jew, he marries a Czech woman from another village. The result is catastrophic. He loses his fortune, his national identity, and eventually his life.

82. "Die Aufgaben der nationalen Schutzvereinen," *Deutsche Rundschau* 1 (1895): 5.

83. "Die zehn Gebote des deutschen Volkes," *Deutscher Volks-Kalender für Schlesien 1898*, 115.

84. *Deutscher Volks-Kalender für Schlesien 1898*; Pock, *Grenzwacht*, 22. The sale of these products was not simply geared toward profit-making although in the case of the *Südmarck,* which

Although extremely at odds with earlier liberal concepts of national identity, these newer beliefs carried with them important legacies of liberalism. Where they differed was in the way they made visible the kinds of hierarchy that for liberals had remained hidden and subject to potential change only in the distant future. Liberals had denied the rights of citizenship to racial inferiors or women since both groups were deemed dependents who were incapable of using reason. Liberal rhetoric had lingered far more on the promise of universal citizenship and progress than on the specifics of who remained unenfranchised, but as we have seen, its revolutionary potential was matched by its hierarchic elements. Radical nationalist rhetoric focused far more pessimistically on the hidden categories of "others," seeing them often as biologically different and using them, just as the liberals had, to distinguish one population from another.

The Survival of Bourgeois Politics

German liberals and their ideological descendants managed to maintain political influence wherever nationalist unity was understood as outweighing the particular demands of interest group politics. In the period down to 1914, the liberal nationalists exercised a far more influential political role in the *Reichsrat* than one would expect, given their small numbers. They also maintained a strong voice in municipal and provincial institutions, thanks also to the survival of curial voting systems, which guaranteed them an extremely influential role in regulating local and regional affairs. Here the German Bürger parties often managed effectively to postpone franchise reform by forging compromises with nationalist opponents. The successful attempt at a national compromise (*Ausgleich*) between Czechs and Germans in Moravia (1905), and the subsequent willingness of both parties to negotiate at the municipal level in a city like Budweis, suggests that nationalist compromise offered the best means of maintaining class privilege. Moderates maintained their political influence by deploying a harsh nationalist rhetoric, but they occasionally found in national compromise an equally effective way of retaining local hegemony.

In Moravia, the proportion of German to Czech speakers was actually much smaller than in Bohemia. Nevertheless, the Germans exercised far more political power in the Moravian Diet than did their counterparts in Bohemia, largely because they dominated provincial industry more completely. Far less industry was in the hands of the Czechs in Moravia, and the national groups were divided more clearly along urban and rural lines than in Bohemia. Given an electoral system that assigned comparable numbers of deputies to urban and

marketed nationalist postcards, matchboxes decorated with mottos, and election slogans, the organization earned 38,000 krone from 1897 to 1904.

rural constituencies, the Germans, who always dominated the urban and chamber of commerce curias, gained equal political representation with the Czechs, who only controlled the rural one. The balance was held by the Moravian large landowners who, unlike their politicized counterparts in Bohemia, had formed a neutral *Mittelpartei* in the 1880s.[85]

German nationalists in Moravia also did not demand the kind of territorial division sought by the Bohemian Germans. With some exceptions, these city and town dwellers did not occupy a large contiguous area of territory, as did their Bohemian counterparts. They were far more concerned with the maintenance of their local *Nationalbesitzstand* than with complete physical separation, and they were satisfied with guarantees of control over tax expenditures and the school system. In return, the Moravian Germans did not object to bilingualism among officials or to ceding the Czechs a majority of deputies to the Moravian Diet. The Moravian Compromise guaranteed that in the future, the diet would consist of three curias: the Czech, the German, and the large landowner. Since any alteration of the system would require a 75 percent majority vote, no franchise reform could pass that did not take into account the interests of all three groups, and universal manhood suffrage for the diet was thus effectively and indefinitely postponed.

How did the compromise determine membership in the Czech or German curias, since no territorial division was to take place? The Moravian Germans agreed to a novel division of voting districts requiring that every eligible voter be assigned to a provincial cataster based on national identity, to be determined by local officials and according to the wishes of the individual. Germans voted separately from Czechs for their own diet and *Reichsrat* candidates, even when they lived in the same political district. This reform did diffuse nationality conflict as a factor in electoral politics. The only time national conflict flared up was over the administrative question of determining how to register certain individuals in the national catasters. A serious cultural effect of the Moravian Compromise, however, was the way it forced citizens to choose a national identity. Declaring one's allegiance to a German or Czech nationality in order to gain the right to vote did far more to diminish traditional Moravian bilingualism and the popular concept of a specifically Moravian identity than had, for example, the Austrian census questions about language of daily use.

The compromise should be understood not simply in nationalist terms, since its greatest accomplishment was arguably to maintain the social status quo by preventing further electoral reform. Other attempts at national compromise, including ongoing work to achieve some agreement in Bohemia, resembled the Moravian one in their efforts to maintain the social hegemony

85. Brix, *Umgangsprachen*, 269, 322–23. According to the census of 1900, Germans constituted 37.27 percent of the Bohemian population and 27.91percent of the Moravian population.

of the Bürger of both nationalities. In Budweis Czech and German leaders devised a municipal compromise similar to the Moravian one in its general outline. Budweis was the only city in the majority Czech region of Bohemia with a substantial German population and a German-dominated city council. In the census of 1910, 27,000 people reported Czech as their language of daily use and 17,000 reported German. Given the curial voting system and the concentration of German speakers in the higher tax brackets, it was not until 1906 that the Czechs even gained a majority in the city's third curia. In negotiations between 1906 and 1914 the two sides agreed to divide voter, tax, and school lists by nationality, to assure the Germans minority representation in the local chamber of commerce, to assign one deputy each for representation to the Bohemian Diet, and to attach the German voters to a predominantly German district for the *Reichsrat* elections. The city and district governments approved the reform, and it only required approval by the diet, which, in 1914, was suspended due to German obstruction. Not surprisingly, the social democrats in Budweis opposed this compromise vigorously, since it diminished Czech support for franchise reform. In both the Moravian and Budweis examples, bourgeois Czechs, who might have supported franchise reform as the only way to gain a political majority, were effectively turned away from this strategy by compromises that gave them a nationalist majority while leaving most Czechs without a vote.[86]

In other cities German bourgeois nationalists used different strategies to maintain their power against potential challenges. Often they tried to revive popular anticlericalism as a tool against the growing threat of Christian social movements that appealed to the Mittelstand. In the year following the Badeni crisis this became a particularly potent issue once again in parts of Austria where German nationalists linked Catholic priests to the rise of Slavic nationalism and accused clerical politicians of abandoning the German nationalist cause. The periodic resort to nationalism, to anticlericalism, and the continued reliance on suffrage privilege also eroded certain liberal traditions even as they created new spaces for the survival of others. At the parliamentary level the German Bürger parties pursued a far different relationship to the state in the early twentieth century than had their nineteenth-century ancestors. Parties no longer sought direct participation in governments, and the most skilled minister presidents avoided the appearance of governing in the interests of a particular majority. After the Badeni crisis, any government associated too closely with a specific majority, left or right, Slavic or German, risked obstruction by the minority. And any moderate party that associated too closely

86. Emil Brix, "Der Böhmische Ausgleich in Budweis," *Österreichische Osthefte* 24 (1982): 225–48; Jiří Kořalká, *Tschechen im Habsburgerreich und im Europa, 1815–1914* (Munich, 1991), 164–65.

with the cabinet risked being outflanked by nationalist radicals, since no cabinet could grant any party its complete desires. A skilled minister president like Ernest von Koerber (1899–1904) even put pressure on radicals by offering them places in his cabinet, clearly hoping either to domesticate them or to revive the popularity of the moderates.

Still, if the new system of governing appears to have ceded parliamentary power to the state and to the bureaucracy in particular, it did not result in a complete collapse of parliament's prerogatives. The system required that every cabinet build a strong consensus in the *Reichsrat* for all legislation, particularly since the former needed to find close to a 90 percent majority to pass any legislation without danger of obstruction. And if cabinets invoked paragraph fourteen more routinely now than ever before, they did so to maintain the status quo and not to impose drastic change. As some historians have recently pointed out by way of contrast to imperial Germany's Kaiser Wilhelm, Francis Joseph may have manipulated the constitution in these years, but he never considered invoking paragraph fourteen to carry out a *Staatsstreich*.[87]

At the local level German liberal traditions appear to have suffered less erosion in their basic structures than in the parliament. The gradual and ongoing integration of new social groups into the Bürger polity was bound to weaken the tight hold that the liberal elites had traditionally exercised over local social and political life through their positions in the voluntary associations. Yet the persistence of the association as a model for public participation in an age of nationalist political mobilization guaranteed the survival of much of the liberal tradition, its modes of community decision-making, and its distinctive internal hierarchies, well into the age of mass politics.

---

87. Höbelt, *Kornblume*, 180–86. Francis Joseph may have been willing to manipulate the constitution but not to carry out a *Staatstreich*. At the level of the state, the coalition regime of 1893–95 had represented both the highpoint and also the endpoint of a particular ideal of liberal parliamentary life. This, after all, was the only time in the history of the monarchy when parliamentary parties had themselves chosen a government. If the 1893–95 coalition represented the first and last government literally constructed from below by the majority parties, after 1895 German nationalists, progressives, and liberals rejected the majority rule idea, preferring instead cabinets that ruled in combination with loose coalitions or blocs. This reflected their perception that the interests of the German community would more likely be hurt by hostile political majorities, while an apolitical cabinet would best be able to maintain a status quo that inevitably favored the Germans. Although most historians have viewed this development as heralding a revival of bureaucratic absolutism, the inevitable result of a parliamentary system fatally weakened by nationalist conflict, in fact this system suited the new kinds of political parties quite well. It gave moderates a way to engage in the kind of radically nationalist rhetorical flourishes demanded by the new constituent politics while retaining a moderating voice on social and economic issues. By remaining outside the cabinet itself, politicians managed to avoid the accusations of nationalist weakness and compromise that had undermined the coalition.

CHAPTER 9

Conclusion: The Limits of Bourgeois Politics

In his three-volume memoir published between 1911 and 1921, Ernst von Plener meticulously detailed the history of the German liberal parties in Bohemia and Austria starting with his first election to the *Reichsrat* in 1873 and ending with the collapse of the monarchy. Plener's narrative is filled with commentary on the characters, political capacities, and personal foibles of the men he met during his long political career. When he reached the year 1879, Plener stopped to pay a kind of tribute to Liberal Party stalwart Carl Giskra, the former student activist and one-time minister of the interior who died in that year. After remarking on Giskra's vanity, his exaggerated rhetoric of pathos, and his highly questionable financial dealings, Plener nevertheless conceded that "his figure will always stand above the rest in the history of parliamentary speech-making in Austria, and few will ever match his power and energy." Never one to exaggerate the accomplishments of others, the sober Plener had rendered a judgment with which few who had known Giskra could disagree.[1]

Contrary to Plener's expectations, neither Giskra nor in fact any nineteenth-century German liberal retains a place in the collective memory of Central European political culture. The personalities and urgent legislative dramas that dominate the pages of Plener's densely packed memoir have left no trace. The liberal movements that once dominated constitutional life in Cisleithania have been all but forgotten. Their early defeat in the lands that comprise contemporary Austria, and their strength in the German and ethnically mixed regions of Bohemia, Moravia, and Silesia, mean that they have left no tangible legacies on which modern Austrians might build anew. When the representatives of the Sudeten Germans had to depart the German Austrian National Assembly in 1919, Austrian liberalism lost its popular and its organizational foundations.

1. Plener, *Erinnerungen*, 2:154.

The basic tenets of nineteenth-century liberalism, however, survived to inform the political programs and rhetoric of several parties on both the right and left of the political spectrum in the twentieth-century successor states. Both the radical class rule on which Dolfuss founded his extraordinary dictatorship in 1934 and the nationalist, often racialist hierarchy around which society in the Third Reich was organized have several roots in nineteenth-century liberalism's response to political crises of the 1880s. Different, if related, liberal values emerged to structure postwar Austria's social and political system in the 1950s. And while no liberal parties rule either in Austria or anywhere in Europe, there may be no need for them either, so pervasive and unquestioned are the key rhetorical legacies of nineteenth-century liberalism.

Both in 1848 and again in the 1860s, Austrian liberals maintained that as soon as their own forces, allied with objective standards of science and progress, had demolished their feudal opponents, political parties and interest groups would diminish in importance. An efficient and impartial state would enforce civil equality among individuals, while mass education would ensure the eventual integration and participation of all social and ethnic groups in a harmonious community. There would be no need for interest groups to compete for power in a world where individuals had as much freedom to develop their varied potentials as possible. This utter disavowal of politics was one of the most telling and problematic attributes of nineteenth- century liberal rhetoric. It presumed that educated people who disagreed over some aspect of public policy could settle their differences in everyone's best interest without resorting to the naked exercise of power. It presumed that a disinterested balance among interests could be achieved. And it did so because it assumed that everyone worth listening to shared a similar social experience.

And yet, as the history of Austrian liberalism repeatedly demonstrated, this fundamental belief in equality itself rested on an invisible, elaborately stratified understanding of social experience. If liberals believed in equality of citizenship, this equality rested on the disingenuous presumption that all individuals in the community in fact shared the same narrow interests, the same form of subjectivity. Liberals promoted a pluralist vision in which individuals gained increasing freedom to develop their varied potentials, yet they limited the individual's possible choices to a range of German bourgeois cultural possibilities. In fact, the liberal rhetoric of freedom of choice often translated into policies that constrained those citizens who clearly did not share the same basic experiences, beliefs, goals, or interests as liberals themselves. The latter paid a high political price (their loss of predominance in state politics) for failing to address this enormous, yet rhetorically invisible, contradiction. It is not that liberals didn't continue in their own way to extend freedoms to new groups of people, but rather that they made too many demands for homogeneity on these groups. "Be free, but be like us," they demanded. Other groups preferred to fight for freedoms on their own terms, using the basic political structure that the liberals bequeathed to Austria.

Nowhere is this contradiction more apparent than in the liberals' changing views of the nationality issue in the Habsburg monarchy. Nationalism in mid-century Austria had been largely an ideological component of liberalism. Early nationalists had stressed the links that connected liberal values of education and humanism to membership in the German nation. They had argued that educated members of all ethnic or religious communities could commit themselves to a German identity by adopting liberal values. According to traditional liberal rhetoric in Austria, German identity corresponded to the cultivation of middle-class cultural values like education, enlightenment, self-control, and freedom. In theory at least, individuals from any background, from Jews to Slavs, could attain a German identity through education and acculturation.

These early German liberal nationalists did not seek to justify their influential position in terms of their numbers but rather in terms of their role in creating a civilized public culture in Central Europe. Neither geographic location nor sheer quantity (the number of people who spoke a given language) was as decisive in determining a group's relative status or power as was quality, defined by cultural and financial achievement. Other peoples might gain greater status for themselves as they adopted this German culture. Austro-German nationalists did not even demand what we would call complete ethnic assimilation from those who aspired to this German identity. In theory they encouraged the local preservation of non-German languages and traditions. After all, what language one spoke in the private sphere or at the local level was hardly a matter of political concern. Nationalists did, however, expect a strict assimilation to cosmopolitan German values in the context of one's public or institutional life. For these German speakers, nationalism served as an ideology of public integration in Central and Eastern Europe.

Most historians believe that this attitude changed in 1866 when Prussia defeated Austria and ejected the monarchy from the Germanic Confederation. With the benefit of hindsight, German Austrians should perhaps have treated this moment as critical to their national future. But they did not do so. As I have shown in chapter 5, liberals saw the military defeat primarily in moral and not nationalist terms. To them it suggested that the emperor's suspension of constitutional rule had weakened the moral character of Austrian society by undermining the very ability of its citizens to exercise constitutional rights in a responsible fashion. In fact, within Austria, the power and cultural hegemony of the German middle classes was still on the rise. Only a year later in 1867 the German liberals in Austria celebrated their greatest political triumph as the emperor conceded to their demands for a real constitution.

Only when the German Liberal Party fell from power in 1879, to be replaced by an aggressively antiliberal coalition of conservative, clerical, and

Slavic nationalist parties, only then did the German liberal public witness the unimaginable: an Austrian state that no longer endorsed the privileged position of the German language. These changed circumstances promoted a different understanding of politics among the German liberal activists of the 1880s. Both the unsettling experience of economic turmoil in the 1870s and now the hostile rule of the Iron Ring convinced many liberals that their harmonious, apolitical vision of community was unattainable. The liberal political system they had fought so hard to establish simply gave whichever social groups controlled it the freedom to exploit the resources of the state for their own purposes. From a discrete activity designed to establish the *Rechtsstaat* for the pursuit of a universal community good, politics became viewed increasingly as a tool for achieving a better social, economic, and even civic status relative to other social groups in the monarchy.

Far from the opinions of contemporaries and later historians who saw these events as disastrous for the German-speaking Bürgertum, my approach suggests that this process of fragmentation strengthened the long-term ability of the local German-speaking middle classes to maintain their considerable political influence and privilege. By translating their traditional principles into a universalist rhetoric of German nationalism, liberals found a way to restate the visions of 1848 and 1867 in more effective political terms for the Austria of the 1880s. German speakers increasingly defined themselves in opposition to other perceived groups rather than encouraging others to join them. That German national identity, which had previously been understood as something contingent and at least potentially universally applicable, was increasingly imagined by many German liberal nationalists in the 1880s as something fixed, inborn, transhistorical, and limited.

I have emphasized the ways in which the basic tenets of both liberalism and German nationalism clearly derived from specific social experience in Austrian society, above all from the experience of the voluntary association and not from misunderstood or misapplied ideas imported from a "liberal West." The Austrian liberal vision of a pluralist yet homogenous bourgeois world emerged from the culture of bourgeois association in the early nineteenth century. Its rules of group behavior and the assumptions about people that structured its social practice were understood as natural and universally applicable. Thus the rights and responsibilities of citizenship modeled on club membership could only be extended to those people who implicitly accepted or fit those rules and assumptions. In the same way the experience of and tensions within the voluntary associations shaped the ideological conflicts that divided the nationalist community in the 1880s and 1890s.

If the liberals lost the early battles to preserve their own narrow political predominance, they may have won the war in their efforts to maintain a political system based on their particular worldview. For example, almost all the groups that challenged the liberal parties in the nineteenth century did so using the new rules of politics established by the liberals themselves. Yet the liberal victory goes much deeper than the general acceptance of a set of political principles. Liberal freedoms like the fundamental right to own property, the right to produce commodities and to commodify the labor of others, the right to bring progress through domestic or foreign acts of colonization—all of these have become understood at specific historical moments as the natural rights of human beings. Their realization in particular contexts is cause for some debate and discussion, but their role as ideal standards remains beyond question.

Other legacies of liberalism such as the rhetorical link connecting the individual citizen to the state through exclusivist ideas of cultural, national, or even racial identity also remain largely unquestioned. Liberal community visions, however pluralist, have required at least a modicum of assimilation before they can tolerate limited forms of individual difference. The threshold for acceptance into a liberal community has always demanded a prior respect for various forms of individual and group property ownership. Throughout the history recounted here, groups that did not respect such requirements (and even some that did) could not attain the liberal promise of freedom for individual development. Nineteenth-century Austrian liberals, for example, never extended full citizenship to even the most circumspect and respectable of wage laborers since these employed arguments organized around class conflict and collective ownership, a rhetoric that ill suited the liberal vision of social harmony based on individual property ownership. Nor could the same liberals grant even the minimal linguistic demands of the non-German-identified bourgeois groups in the monarchy. Their increasing adoption of nationalist principles in turn blinded the liberals to the demands for citizenship made by their own wives, sisters, and daughters, even though these women accepted most of the cultural and economic assumptions underlying liberal principles. The liberal tendency to find justifications for such exclusionary principles in a rhetoric of nature, calling on an emerging positivist natural science for proof, has so far succeeded in placing these very principles outside the realm of critical discussion to such an extent that neither contemporaries nor current scholars have called them into question. Their relatively recent invention is thereby more easily ignored. It is one more ambiguous achievement of nineteenth-century liberalism that we take these underpinnings for granted, even if our own political systems are no longer dominated by formally liberal parties.

A century later we see that in contemporary Austria the political system encourages the very management of conflict and depoliticization originally envisioned by the nineteenth-century Austrian liberals. And ironically, given the pluralist claims of liberal visions, oppressive assumptions of shared interests make innovation or the open expression of different social identities in today's Austria a highly risky business, as the recent controversy over "outing" in Austria attests.[2] This suggests that the implicit hierarchy within which forms of difference are understood by liberal thought is at least as important, if not more so, than the liberal insistence on diversification and pluralism. It is perhaps unfair for the modern observer to criticize the nineteenth-century liberals for not seeing the obvious contradictions and paradoxes in their thought, for not fighting to extend twentieth-century freedoms to nineteenth-century peoples. One could even argue that European liberals remained true to their principles to the extent possible, given the challenging historical context they faced. This has not, however, been my purpose. I have tried instead to examine two subjects, liberalism and nationalism, which are overly familiar to twentieth-century observers, to make them less familiar and therefore more available to a critical, historicizing assessment. In my examination of liberal political culture I have tried to show how popular ideas emerge from particular kinds of social interactions, why some ideas gain currency while others do not, and most of all, how apparently transhistorical ideas, like those about nationalist identity, serve as grounds for the contestation and revision of power relations within a larger community.

2. See Matti Bunzl, "Unerträglich Salonfähig," *Profil*, (1995) 33:70–71; Robert Buchacher and Christian Seiler, "Gestehe, dass du Schwul bist" *Profil*, (1995) 31:26–29.

Abbreviations

AVA	Österreichisches Staatsarchiv: Allgemeines Verwaltungsarchiv
CEH	*Central European History*
DW	*Deutsche Worte*
DVIS	*Deutsche Volkskalender für die Iglauer Sprachinsel*
DZ	*Deutsche Zeitung*
FA	Familienarchiv Auersperg
GT	*Grazer Telegraf*
HHSA	Haus-, Hof-, und Staatsarchiv
JMH	*Journal of Modern History*
KVZ	*Konstitutionelle Vorstadt-Zeitung*
MDB	*Mittheilungen des deutschen Böhmerwaldbundes*
MDS	*Mittheilungen des deutschen Schulvereins*
MGH	*Mittheilungen für Gewerbe und Handel*
MIÖG	*Mitteilungen des Instituts für österreichische Geschichtsforschung*
MÖSA	*Mitteilungen des österreichischen Staatsarchivs*
NÖLA	Niederösterreichisches Landesarchiv
NBF	Österreichische Nationalbibliothek: Flugblätter- und Plakate- Sammlung
NFP	*Neue Freie Presse*
NWT	*Neues Wiener Tagblatt*
OL	Oberösterreichisches Landesarchiv
PA	Parlamentsarchiv
PR	*Die Presse*
SLA	Steiermärkisches Landesarchiv
SPHA	*Stenographische Protokolle über die Sitzungen des Hauses der Abgeordneten*
SPNÖ	*Stenographische Protokolle des Landtages für das Erzherzogthum Österreich unter der Enns*
SRG	*Schwarz-Roth-Gold*
WZ	*Wiener Zeitung*

Bibliography

Archival and Library Collections

Haus,- Hof,- und Staatsarchiv
Familienarchiv Auersperg
Ministerkonferenz und Ministerratsprotokolle 1860–1865
Nachlass Plener
Nachlass Anton Ritter von Schmerling

Niederösterreichisches Landesarchiv
Vereinskataster 19 politische Vereine

Oberösterreichisches Landesarchiv
Flugschriftenversammlung
Vereinskataster politische Vereine

Österreichische Nationalbibliothek
Flugblätter- und Plakate- Sammlung

Österreichisches Staatsarchiv, Allgemeines Verwaltungsarchiv
Ministerium des Innern, Allgemeine Registratur 15: Politische Vereine
Nachlass Pichl

Steiermärkisches Landesarchiv
Vereinskataster politische Vereine
Familienarchiv Kaiserfeld

Wiener Stadt und Landesarchiv
Politische Vereine

Newspapers and Periodicals

Bohemia
Demokratische Zeitung
Die Constitution
Deutsche Arbeit

Deutsche Rundschau
Deutsche Volkszeitung Reichenberg
Deutsche Wochenschrift
Deutsche Worte
Deutsche Zeitung
Deutsche Zeitung aus Böhmen
Freie Schlesische Presse
Für das Volk
Grazer Telegraf
Die Grenzboten
Der Herold
Konstitutionelle Vorstadt-Zeitung
Leitmeritzer Zeitung
Mittheilungen für Gewerbe und Handel
Morgenpost
Neue Freie Presse
Neue politische Strassenzeitung
Neues Wiener Tagblatt
Ostdeutsche Rundschau
Politische Frauenzeitung
Politisch-ökonomische Rundschau
Die Presse
Die Rundschau
St. Pöltner Wochenblatt
Tagesbote aus Böhmen
Unverfälschte deutsche Worte
Vaterland
Wiener Zeitschrift für Kunst, Literatur, Theater und Mode
Wiener Zeitung

Published Documents and Collections

Ämtliche Verhandlungs-Protokolle des Gemeindeausschusses der Stadt Wien von 25. Mai bis 5. Oktober, 1848. Vienna, 1848.

Artarias Karte der österreichischen Reichsrathswahlen. Vienna, 1891.

Bericht über die bisherige Thätigkeit (Allgemeine nieder-österreichischer Volksbildung Verein). Vienna, 1889.

Czörnig, Karl von. *Ethnographie der österreichischen Monarchie*. Vienna, 1857.

———. *Österreichs Neugestaltung*. Stuttgart, 1858.

Dunder, Wenzel. *Denkschrift über die Wiener Oktober-Revolution. Ausführliche Darstellung aller Ereignisse aus ämtlichen Quellen geschöpft, mit zahlreichen Urkunden begleitet*. Vienna, 1849.

Freytag, G. and E. Kindermann. *Die Gruppierungen der Mitglieder des österreichischen Abgeordnetenhauses in der Wahlperiode 1885-1891*. Vienna, 1886.

Grazer Geschäfts und Adress-Kalender für das Jahr 1885. Graz, 1885.

Grazer Geschäfts- und Adressen Kalender für das Jahr 1891. Graz, 1891.

Hahn, Sigmund. *Reichsrathsalmanac für das Jahr 1867.* Vienna, 1867.

———. *Reichsrathsalmanach für das Jahr 1879.* Vienna, 1879.

———. *Reichsrathsalmanach für das Jahr 1885.* Vienna, 1885.

———. *Reichsrathsalmanach für die Session 1891–1892.* Vienna,1891.

Handbuch der Vereine für die im Reichsrath vertretenen Königreiche und Länder nach dem Stand am Schlusse des Jahres 1890, Bureau der k.k. staatliche Central-Commission. Vienna, 1892.

Knauer, Oswald. *Das österreichische Parlament von 1848-1966.* Vienna, 1969.

Molisch, Paul. *Briefe zur deutschen Politik in Österreich von 1848 bis 1918.* Vienna, 1934.

Neues Adress- und Geschäfts- Handbuch der Landeshauptstadt Graz. Graz, 1877.

Neumann-Spallart, F. X., and G. A. Schirmer. *Die Reichsraths-Wahlen vom Jahre 1879 in Österreich.* Stuttgart, 1880.

Niederösterreichischer Amtskalender. Vienna, 1875, 1880, 1886.

Der Oberösterreichische Geschäfts- Haus- und Amtskalender. Linz, 1870, 1875, 1880, 1885.

Peyer, F. *Wiener Chronik für das Jahr 1848.* Vienna, 1850.

Protokolle der öffentlichen Sitzungen des Gemeinderathes der k.k. Reichshauptstadt- und Residenzstadt Wien. Vienna, 1866

Der Reichsrat. Biographische Skizzen, Programmen der Parteien, 1861. Vienna, 1861.

Reichsrathsalmanach. Vienna, 1864.

Richter, Karl. "Statistische Übersichten zur Entwicklung der böhmischen Länder und ihrer Bedeutung in Zisleithanien 1848-1914." *Handbuch der Geschichte der böhmischen Länder.* vol. 3. Edited by Karl Bösl. Stuttgart, 1968.

Rutkowski, Ernst von. *Briefe und Dokumente zur Geschichte der österreichisch-ungarischen Monarchie unter besonderer Berücksichtigung des böhmisch-mährischen Raumes. Teil 1, Der Verfassungstreue Grossgrundbesitz, 1880–1893.* Munich, 1983.

Springer, Anton, ed. *Protokolle des Verfassungsausschusses im österreichischen Reichstag, 1848–1849.* Leipzig, 1885.

Statistische Karten der österreichischen Reichsraths-Wahlen. Vienna, 1891.

Stenographische Protokolle des Landtages für das Erzherzogthum Österreich unter der Enns. Vienna, 1861, 1888, 1889.

Stenographische Protokolle über die Sitzungen des Hauses der Abgeordneten. Vienna,1861–95.

Stenographische Protokolle über die Sitzungen des Herrenhauses. Vienna, 1861–95.

Stubenrauch, M. von. *Statistische Darstellung des Vereinswesen im Kaiserthume Österreich.* Vienna, 1857

Verhandlungen des provisorischen Landtages des Herzogthumes Steiermark. Graz, 1848.

Vodnarik, Eduard. *Landesvertretung der Markgrafschaft Mähren vom Inslebentreten der Verfassung vom 26. Februar 1861 bis zum Jahre 1884.* Brünn, 1884.

Wurzbach, Constant von. *Biographisches Lexikon des Kaisertums Österreich.* 60 vols. Vienna, 1856–1923

Zeitungsausschnitte und Vereinspublikationen des allgemeinen österreichischen Frauenvereins. vol. 1. Vienna, 1889-1899.

Publications by and about Liberal Political and Nationalist Associations

Die allgemeine deutsche Lehrerversammlung zu Wien. Vienna, 1870.

Bericht des consititutionellen Vereines in Laibach. Laibach, 1871, 1874, 1878, 1881.

Bericht der Vereinsleitung des politischen Vereins "Fortschritt" für den Wahlbezirk Vöcklabruck über die abgelaufene Landtagssession 1869. Wels, 1869/70.

Bericht über die Thätogkeit des Bundes der Deutschen in Böhmen im zweiten Vereinsjahr. Prague, 1896.

Bericht über die Thätigkeit des Deutschen Schulvereins in Krain. Laibach, 1884.

Bericht über die Thätigkeit des liberalen politischen Vereines für Oberösterreich in Linz. Linz, 1870–71.

Bericht über die Thätigkeit des politischen Vereines der Liberalen in Znaim. Znaim, 1873–75.

Bericht über die zehnjährige Thätigkeit des znaimer deutschen Bürgervereins anlässlich dessen am 11. Juli Stattfindenen Gründungsfeier. Znaim, 1880.

Bilger, Ferdinand. *Die Wiener Burschenschaft Silesia.* Heidelberg, 1911.

Chaises, Adolf, ed. *Vorträge des Dr. Schütte und politische Debatten der Gesellschaft der Volksfreunde.* Vienna, 1848.

Deutsche Klub, "An unsere Wähler." Vienna, 1885

Deutscher Volkskalender für 1876. Prague, 1875

Deutscher Volkskalender für das Jahr 1889. Herausgegeben vom Bund der Deutschen Nordmährens. Olmütz, 1888.

Deutscher Volkskalender für die Iglauer Sprachinsel. Iglau, 1886, 1887, 1893, and 1899.

Deutscher Volks-Kalender für Schlesien. Troppau, 1989.

Deutscher Volkskalender herausgegeben vom Deutschen Verein zur Verbreitung gemeinnütziger Kenntnisse in Prag. Prague, 1876–84.

Göllerich, August. *Der deutsche Parteitag vom 26. Februar 1871 und seine Beschlüsse.* Vienna, 1871.

Hainisch, Michael. *Die Zukunft der Deutsch-Österreicher. Eine statistisch-vokswirtschaftliche Studie.* Vienna, 1892.

Hohenblum, J. S. *Statuten zur Bildung des Vereines der Freunde der constitutionellen Ordnung und wahren Freiheit.* Vienna, 1848.

Keldorfer, J. *Der Vereinswesen in Salzburg.* Salzburg, 1881.

Kiemann, Anton. *Die ersten vierzig Jahre des Vereines Deutschen Kasino in Prag, 1862–1902.* Prague, 1902.

Lehrer Calender des deutschen Landeslehrer Vereins in Böhmen. Reichenberg, 1882–83.

Mittheilungen der Wiener demokratischen Gesellschaft Vienna, 1873

Mittheilungen des Bundes der Deutschen Ost-Böhmens. 1895.

Mittheilungen des deutschen Böhmerwaldbundes. Budweis, 1885–1901.

Mittheilungen des Vereines der Deutschen aus Gottschee. Vienna, 1891–93.

Mittheilungen des Vereines der Lehrerinnen und Erzieherinnen in Österreich. Vienna, 1886–93.

Mittheilungen des Vereins für Geschichte der Deutschen in Böhmen. Prague, 1862–85.

Nationales Erbauungs-Buch für das deutsche Volk in Österreich. Brünn, 1882.

Politischer Volks-Kalender für 1878. Klagenfurt and Villach, 1877.

Politischer Volkskalender für das Jahr 1871. Linz, 1870.
Politischer Volkskalender für das Jahr 1872. Linz, 1871.
Schwarz-Roth-Gold; Vereinsblatt der Deutschen in Österreich. Vienna, 1848.
Statuten des ersten Wiener demokratischen Frauen-vereins. Vienna, 1848.
Der Südmark-Calender auf das Jahr 1898. Ein Jahrbuch für Stadt und Land. Graz, 1898.
Tuma, Josef. *Jahresbericht des liberalen Vereines in Wels üeber das I. Vereinsjahr vom 11.2.1868 bis 12.2.1869*. Wels, 1869.
Die Vereine in Mähren, nach dem ämtlichen Zusammenstellung geordnet. Brünn, 1885.

Memoirs and Contemporary Writings

Andrian-Werburg, Victor von. *Österreich und dessen Zukunft*. 2 vols. Hamburg, 1843–47.
Angerstein, Wilhelm. *Bilder aus Österreich*. Leipzig, 1873.
———. *Die Korruption in Österreich*. Leipzig, 1872.
———. *Österreich's parlamentarische Grössen*. Leipzig, 1872.
———. *Volkswirtschaftliche Zustände in Österreich*. Leipzig, 1871.
Arneth, Alfred von. *Anton, Ritter von Schmerling*. Vienna, 1894.
Auersperg, Carl. *Wofür kämpft Ungarn*. Vienna, 1865.
[Bauernfeld, Eduard von.] *Pia Desideria eines österreichischen Schriftstellers*. Leipzig, 1843.
Beidtel, Karl. *Die Geldangelegenheiten Österreichs*. Leipzig, 1847.
Berger, J. N. *Die Pressefreiheit und das Pressegesetz*. Vienna, 1848.
———.*Zur Lösung der österreichischen Verfassungsfrage*. Vienna, 1861.
Beust, Franz Ferdinand von. *Aus drei Vierteljahrhunderten*. 2 vols. Stuttgart, 1887.
Bloch, Joseph S. *Der nationale Zwist und die Juden in Österreich*. Vienna, 1886.
Czörnig, Carl von. *Die deutschen Sprachinseln im Süden des geschlossenen deutschen Sprachgebietes in ihrem gegenwärtigen Zustande*. Klagenfurt, 1889.
Die Deutschen im Nationalitätenstaat Österreich. Meran, 1887.
Die Deutschen in Österreich. Ihre nationale Stellung und ihre politische Aufgabe. Leipzig, 1879.
Das Deutschtum in Krain. Ein Wort zur Aufklärung. Graz, 1862.
Das Deutschtum in Österreich. Leipzig, 1871.
Dumreicher, Armand, Freiherr von. *Südostdeutsche Betrachtungen*. Leipzig, 1893.
Das Ende der Vefassungspartei. Vienna, 1882.
Exner, Wilhelm. *Erlebnisse*. Vienna, 1929.
Foregger, Richard. *Zur Cillier Gymnasialfrage*. Vienna, 1894.
Frankl, Ludwig A. *Erinnerungen Ludwig August Frankl*. Prague, 1910.
Friedmann, Bernhard. *Die Wohnungsnot in Wien*. Vienna, 1857.
Fröbel, Julius. *Ein Lebenslauf*. 2 vols. Stuttgart, 1890–91.
Friedjung, Heinrich. *Ein Stuck Zeitungsgeschichte*. Vienna, 1887.
———. *Julius Freiherr von Horst*. Vienna, 1906.
Gierschik, Julius. *Dr. Karl Pickert. Ein Beitrag zur Geschichte der deutschnationalen Bewegung in Böhmen*. Leitmeritz, 1913.
Giskra, Carl, "Wahlrede des Dr. C. Giskra für die Landtags-Candidaten des II. Bezirks in Brünn." Brünn, 1861.

Hasner, Leopold von. *Denkwürdigkeiten. Autobiographisches und Aphorismen.* Stuttgart, 1892.
Hainisch, Michael. *Die Zukunft der Deutch-Österreicher.* Vienna, 1892.
Hruschka, Ella. *Der Wirkungskreis des Weibes. Ein Beitrag zur Lösung der Frauenfrage.* Vienna, 1892.
Hugelman, Karl. *Studien zum österreichischen Vereins- und Versammlungsrechte.* Graz, 1879
———. "Beiträge zur Geschichte und Statistik der politischen Vereine in Österreich." *Österreichische Zeitschrift für Verwaltung* 13 (1880)
[Klaar, Alfred]. *Franz Schmeykal. Eine Gedenkschrift.* Prague, 1894.
Knoll, Philipp. *Beiträge zur heimischen Zeitgeschichte.* Prague, 1900.
Kopp, Joseph. *Zur Judenfrage, nach den Akten des Prozesses Rohling-Bloch.* Leipzig, 1886.
Krones, Franz von. *Moritz von Kaiserfeld. Sein Leben und Wirken.* Leipzig, 1888.
Kudlich, Hans. *Rückblicke und Erinnerungen.* Vienna, 1873.
Kuefstein, Franz von. *Die Grundsätze der bedeutendsten politischen Parteien.* Vienna, 1880.
Kummer, C. G. *Deutsch-nationale Politik in Österreich.* Graz, 1885.
Lippert, Julius. *Der Antisemitismus.* Prague, 1883.
———. *Die Erziehung auf nationaler Grundlage.* Prague, 1882.
———. *Die Geschichte der Familie.* Stuttgart, 1884.
Menger, Max. *Der böhmische Ausgleich.* Stuttgart, 1891.
———. *Die auf Selbsthilfe gestützten Genossenschaften im Handwerker- und Arbeiterstande.* Vienna, 1866.
———. *Die Wahlreform in Österreich.* Vienna, 1873.
Mauthner, Fritz. *Prager Jugendjahre.* Frankfurt/M, 1969.
Mayer, Sigmund. *Die soziale Frage in Wien.* Vienna, 1871.
———. *Ein jüdischer Kaufmann 1831 bis 1911.* Leipzig, 1911.
Plener, Ernst von. *Erinnerungen.* 3 vols. Stuttgart and Leipzig, 1911–21.
———. *Die englische Fabriksgesetzgebung.* Vienna, 1871.
———. "Ignaz von Plener." *Biographisches Jahrbuch und deutscher Nekrolog* 16 Berlin, 1914.
———. *Reden, 1873–1911.* Leipzig, 1911.
Pollak, Heinrich. *Dreissig Jahre aus dem Leben eines Journalisten.* 3 vols. Vienna, 1898.
———. *Die Stellung der Deutschmährer in Vergangenheit und Gegenwart.* Neutitschein, 1872.
Rauchberg, Heinrich. *Die nationale Besitzstand.* 3 vols. Leipzig, 1905.
Reinöhl, R. von. *Die Hut der Sudetenländer durch den deutschen Schulverein.* Vienna, 1886.
Reschauer, Heinrich. *Die Aufgaben Deutschösterreichs nach dem 26. Februar.* Vienna, 1861.
———. *Der Juridisch-politisch Leseverein im Monat März, 1848.* Vienna, 1888.
Reschauer, Heinrich and Moritz Smets. *Das Jahr 1848, Geschichte der Wiener Revolution.* 2 vols. Vienna, 1872.
Reichenberg in der Zeit der Selbstverwaltung vom Jahre 1850 bis 1900. Reichenberg, 1902.

Rogge, Walter. *Österreich seit der Katastrophe Hohenwart-Beust*. 2 vols. Leipzig and Vienna, 1879.
———. *Österreich von Villagos bis zur Gegenwart*. 3 vols. Vienna and Leipzig, 1873.
Schmerling, Anton Ritter von and Gottfried, Freiherr von Buschmann, *Die niederösterreichischen Landstände und die Genesis der Revolution in Österreich im Jahre 1848*. Vienna, 1850.
Schusselka, Franz. *Österreich über Alles wenn es nur will*. Vienna, 1848.
Schwarzer, Ernst von. *Geld und Gut in Neuösterreich*. Vienna, 1857.
Singer, Bernhard. *Unsere Orientspolitik*. Vienna, 1878.
Springer, Anton. *Geschichte Österreichs seit dem Wiener Frieden 1809*. Leipzig, 1863–65.
Steinwender, Otto. *Die ethischen Ideen und die politischen Parteien*. Vienna, 1883.
———. *Die nationalen Aufgaben der Deutschen in Österreich*. Vienna, 1885.
Stingl, Hans. *Die Nationalvereine der deutschen Bürger und Bauern*. Krems, 1881.
———. *Verdeutschungsmerke für Gemeinden*. Krems, 1892.
Stoerk, Felix. *Das verfassungsmässige Verhältnis des Abgeordneten zur Wählerschaft*. Vienna, 1881.
Stremayr, Carl von. *Erinnerungen aus dem Leben*. Vienna, 1899.
Suess, Eduard. *Erinnerungen*. Leipzig, 1916.
Unger, Josef. *Bunte Betrachtungen*. Vienna, 1911.
Violand, Ernst. *Die soziale Geschichte der Revolution*. Vienna, 1850.
Weitlof, Moritz. *Unsere heutige Volksschule*. Krems, 1875.
Wiesner, Alois. *Die österreichische Revolution und die Provinzen*. Zürich, 1849.
Wotowa, August, *Der deutsche Schulverein 1880–1905*. Vienna, 1905.

Secondary Literature

Abraham, David. *The Collapse of the Weimar Republic: Political Economy and Crisis*. Princeton, 1981.
Albrecht, Catherine. "National Economy or Economic Nationalism in the Bohemian Crownlands 1848–1914." In *Labyrinth of Nationalism Complexities of Diplomacy: Essays in Honor of Charles and Barbara Jelavich* Edited by Richard Frucht. Columbus, 1992.
———. "Pride in Production: The Jubilee Exhibition of 1891 and Economic Competition between Czechs and Germans in Bohemia." *Austrian History Yearbook* 24 (1993).
Amann, Peter. *Revolution and Mass Democracy: The Paris Club Movement in 1848*. Princeton, 1975.
Anderson, Benedict. *Imagined Communities*. Revised edition. New York, 1991.
Anderson, R. D. *France 1870–1914: Politics and Society*. London, 1977.
Bahm, Karl. "Beyond the Bourgeoisie: Rethinking Nation, Culture, and Modernity in Fin-de- siècle Central Europe," unpublished paper presented to the Center for Austrian Studies, October, 1995.
Baier, Dietmar. *Sprache und Recht im alten Österreich. Artikel 19 des Staatsgrundgesetzes vom 21. Dezember 1867, seine Stellung im System der Grundrechte und seine Ausgestaltung durch die oberstgerichtliche Rechtsprechung*. Munich, 1983.

Baltzarek, Franz, *Die Geschichte der Wiener Börse*. Vienna, 1973.
Banik-Schweitzer, Renate et al., ed. *Wien im Vormärz*. Vienna, 1980.
Beller, Steven. *Vienna and the Jews 1867–1938, a Cultural History*. Cambridge, 1989.
Benedikt, Heinrich, ed. *Geschichte der Republik Österreich*. Vienna, 1954.
Berend, Istvan and György Ranki. *Economic Development in East-Central Europe in the Nineteenth and Twentieth Centuries*. New York, 1974 .
Berger, Peter, ed. *Der österreichische-ungarische Ausgleich von 1867, Vorgeschichte und Wirkungen*. Vienna, 1967.
Berghahn, Volker R. *Imperial Germany 1871–1914: Economy, Society, Culture and Politics*. Providence RI, 1994.
Berner, Peter, Emil Brix, and Wolfgang Mantl, ed. *Wien um 1900. Aufbruch in die Moderne*. Vienna, 1986.
Bibl, Viktor. *Die niederösterreichischen Stände im Vormärz. Ein Beitrag zur Vorgeschichte der Revolution des Jahres 1848*. Vienna, 1911.
Blackbourn, David. *Class, Religion and Local Politics in Wilhelmine Germany*. New Haven, 1980.
———. *Populists and Patricians: Essays in Modern German History*. London, 1987.
——— and Geoff Eley. *The Peculiarities of German History: Bourgeois Society and Politics in Nineteenth Century Germany*. Oxford, 1984.
——— and Richard Evans, eds. *The German Bourgeoisie: Essays on the Social History of the German Middle Classes from the Late Eighteenth to the Early Twentieth Century*. London and New York, 1991.
Bograd, Peter. "Beyond Nation, Confession, and Party: The Politicization of Professional Identity in Late Imperial Austria." In *Austrian History Yearbook* 27 (1996).
Bowman, William. "Religious Associations and the formation of Political Catholicism in Vienna, 1848 to the 1870s." In *Austrian History Yearbook* 27 (1996).
Boyer, John. "Catholic Priests in Lower Austria, Anti-Liberalism, Occupational Anxiety and Radical Political Action in Late Nineteenth Century Vienna." *Proceedings of the American Philosophical Society* 118 (1974).
———. *Culture and Political Crisis in Vienna: Christian Socialism in Power, 1897–1918*. Chicago, 1995.
———. "The End of an Old Regime: Visions of Political Reform in Late Imperial Austria." JMH 58 (1986).
———. "Freud, Marriage and Late Viennese Liberalism: A Commentary from 1905." JMH 50 (1978).
———. *Political Radicalism in Late Imperial Vienna: Origins of the Christian Social Movement, 1848–1897*. Chicago, 1981.
———. "Religion and Political Development in Central Europe around 1900: A View from Vienna." *Austrian History Yearbook* 25 (1994).
Brandt, Harm-Hinrich. *Der österreichische Neoabsolutismus. Staatsfinanzen und Politik, 1848–1860*. 2 vols. Göttingen, 1978.
Breuilly, John. *Labor and Liberalism in Nineteenth-Century Europe. Essays in comparative history*. Manchester and New York, 1992.
Brix, Emil. "Der böhmische Ausgleich in Budweis." *Österreichische Osthefte* 24 (1982).
———. "Die Erhebung der Umgangssprache im zisleithanischen Österreich (1880–1910). Nationale und sozio-ökonomische Ursachen der Sprachenkonflikte." MIÖG 87 (1979).

———. *Die Umgangssprachen in Altösterreich zwischen Agitation und Assimilation. Die Sprachenstatistik in den zisleithanischen Volkszählungen 1880 bis 1910.* Vienna, 1982.

Brown, Karen. *Karl Lueger, The Liberal Years: Democracy, Municipal Reform, and the Struggle for Power in the Vienna City Council, 1875–1882.* New York and London, 1987

Bruckmüller, Ernst. *Landwirtschaftliche Organisationen und gesellschaftliche Modernisierung. Vereine, Genossenschaften und politische Mobilisierung der Landwirtschaft Österreichs vom Vormärz bis 1914.* Salzburg, 1977.

———, Ulrike Döcker, Hannes Stekl, and Peter Urbanitsch, eds. *Bürgertum in der Habsburgermonarchie.* Vienna, 1990.

Brügel, Ludwig. *Soziale Gesetzgebung in Österreich 1848–1918.* Vienna, 1919.

Bruschek-Klein, Brigitte. "Ernst von Pleners Weg in die Politik." MIÖG 89 (1982).

Buchacher, Robert and Christian Seiler. "Gestehe, dass du Schwul bist." *Profil* 31 (1995)

Bunzl, Matti. "Unerträglich Salonfähig." *Profil* 33 (1995)

Burkert, Günther R. "Deutschnationale Beeinflussungsversuche steirischer Bauern 1880–1914." *Österreich in Geschichte und Literatur* 30 (1986).

Burns, Michael. *Rural Society and French Politics: Boulangism and the Dreyfus Affair 1886–1900.* Princeton, 1984.

Charmatz, Richard. *Deutsch-Österreichische Politik: Studien über den Liberalismus und über die Auswärtige Politik Österreichs.* Leipzig,1907.

———. *Österreichs innere Geschichte.* 2 vols. Leipzig, 1909.

Chickering, Roger. *We Men Who Feel Most German.* London, 1984.

Cohen, Gary B. "Jews in German Society, Prague, 1867–1914." CEH 10 (1977).

———. *The Politics of Ethnic Survival: Germans in Prague, 1861–1914.* Princeton, 1981.

———. "Recent Research on Czech Nationbuilding." JMH 51 (1977).

Crew, David. *Town in the Ruhr: A Social History of Bochum, 1860–1914.* New York, 1979.

Czedik, Alois von. *Zur Geschichte der k.k. österreichischen Ministerien 1861–1916.* 4 vols. Leipzig, Teschen, Vienna, 1917–20.

Czeike, Felix. *Cajetan Felder. Erinnerungen eines Wiener Bürgermeisters.* Vienna, 1964.

———. *Liberale, christlichsoziale, und sozial-demokratische Kommunalpolitik 1861–1934.* Vienna, 1962.

———. *Wien und seine Bürgermeister.* Vienna, 1974.

———, ed. *Wien in der liberalen Ära.* Vienna, 1978.

Dahrendorf, Ralf. *Society and Democracy in Germany.* London, 1968.

Dann, Otto, ed. *Lesegesellschaften und bürgerliche Emanzipation. Ein europäischer Vergleich.* Munich, 1981.

Davidoff, Lenore and Catherine Hall. *Family Fortunes. Men and Women of the English Middle Class 1780–1850.* Chicago, 1987.

Deak, Istvan. *Beyond Nationalism: A Social and Political History of the Habsburg Officer Corps 1848–1918.* New York and Oxford, 1990.

———. "Comments," *Austrian History Yearbook* 3 (1967).

———. *The Lawful Revolution: Louis Kossuth and the Hungarians.* New York, 1979.

Doblinger, Max. *Studententum. Burschenschaft und deutsche Einheitsbewegung in Graz bis 1880*. Graz, 1921.

Dopsch, Heinz, ed. *Vom Stadtrecht zur Bürgerbeteiligung. Festschrift 700 Jahre Stadtrecht von Salzburg*. Salzburg, 1987.

Düding, Dieter. *Organisierter gesellschaftliche Nationalismus in Deutschland (1808–1847). Bedeutung und Funktion der Turner- und Sängervereine für die deutsche Nationalbewegung*. Munich, 1984

Ebert, Kurt. *Die Anfänge der modernen Sozialpolitik in Österreich. Die Taaffesche Sozialgesetzgebung für die Arbeiter im Rahmen der Gewerbeordnungsreform 1879–1885*. Vienna, 1975.

Eder, Karl. *Der Liberalismus in Altösterreich: Geisteshaltung, Politik, und Kultur*. Munich, 1955.

Eley, Geoff. *From Unification to Nazism: Reinterpreting the German Past*. Boston, 1986.

———. *Reshaping the German Right*. New Haven, 1980.

Elwit, Sanford. *The Making of the Third French Republic: Class and Politics in France, 1868–1884*. Baton Rouge, 1975.

———. *The Third Republic Defended. Bourgeois Reform in France, 1880–1914*. Baton Rouge, 1986.

Engel-Janosi, Friedrich. “Der Wiener juridisch-politische Leseverein; seine Geschichte bis zur Märzrevolution.” *Mitteilungen des Vereines für Geschichte der Stadt Wien* 4 (1923).

Epstein, Klaus. *The Genesis of German Conservatism*. Princeton, 1966.

Erdödy, Gabor, ed. *Das Parteienwesen Österreich-Ungarns*. Budapest, 1987.

Evans, Richard J. *Rethinking German History: Nineteenth-Century Germany and the Origins of the Third Reich*. London, 1987

Fellner, Fritz. “Das Februarpatent von 1861. Entstehung und Bedeutung.” MIÖG 63 (1955).

———. “Kaiser Franz Josefs Haltung in der Krise des Bürger-ministeriums. Nach Aufzeichnungen und Briefen Ignaz von Pleners.” MÖSA 6 (1953).

———. “Kaiser Franz Josef und das Parlament. Materialien zur Geschichte der Innenpolitik Österreichs in den Jahren 1867–1873.” MÖSA 9 (1956).

———, ed. *Schicksaljahre Österreichs, 1908–1919. Das politische Tagebuch Josef Redlichs*. 2 vols. Graz, 1954.

Fenske, Hans. “Der deutsche Liberalismus bis zum Ausgang des 19. Jahrhunderts. Literatur aus den Jahren 1987–1991.” *Historisches Jahrbuch* 112 (1992).

Franz, Georg. *Liberalismus. Die deutschliberale Bewegung in der habsburgischen Monarchie*. Munich, 1955.

Freudenberger, Hermann. “Industrialization in Bohemia and Moravia in the Eighteenth Century.” *Journal of Central European Affairs* 19 (1960)

Freudenberger, Hermann and Gerhard Mensch. *Von der Provinzstadt zur Industrieregion*. Göttingen, 1975

Frevert, Ute, ed. *Bürgerinnen und Bürger. Geschlechtsverhältnisse im 19. Jahrhundert*. Göttingen, 1988

Friedjung, Heinrich. *Der Kampf um die Vorherrschaft in Deutschland, 1859–1866*. 2 vols. Stuttgart and Berlin, 1912.

Garver, Bruce. *The Young Czech Party 1874–1901 and the Emergence of a Multiparty System*. New Haven, 1978.
Gerschenkron, Alexander. *Economic Backwardness in Historical Perspective*. New York, 1965.
———. *An Economic Spurt That Failed*. Princeton, 1977.
Glatz, Ferenc and Ralph Melville eds. *Gesellschaft, Politik und Verwaltung in der Habsburgermonarchie 1830–1918*. Budapest, 1987
Good, David F. *The Economic Rise of the Habsburg Empire, 1750–1914*. Berkeley and Los Angeles, 1984.
———. "Stagnation and Take-Off in Austria, 1873–1913." *Economic History Review* 27 (1974).
Grandner, Margarete. "Conservative Social Politics in Austria, 1880-1890." In *Austrian History Yearbook* 27 (1996).
Haas, Hanns. "Von liberal zu national. Salzburgs Bürgertum im ausgehenden 19. Jahrhundert." In *Politik und Gesellschaft im alten Österreich* 1 (1981).
———. "Salzburger Vereinskultur im Hochliberalismus (1860–1870)." In *Vom Stadtrecht zur Bürgerbeteiligung Ausstellungskatalog 700 Jahre Stadtrecht*. Edited by Rainer Wilflinger and Peter Michael Lipburger. Salzburg, 1987.
Hagwood, J. A. "Liberalism and Constitutional Developments." *The New Cambridge Modern History*. Edited by J. P. T. Bury. Cambridge, 1971.
Hanák, Peter. "The Bourgeoisification of the Hungarian Nobility-Reality and Utopia in the Nineteenth Century." *Études historiques hongroises*. Budapest, 1985.
Handler, Richard. *Nationalism and the Politics of Culture in Quebec*. Madison, 1988.
Hanke, Alfred. *Die nationale Bewegung in Aussig von 1848–1914*. Prague, 1943.
Harrington-Müller, Diethild. *Studien zur Geschichte des Fortschrittsklubs im Abgeordnetenhaus des österreichischen Reichsrats,1873–1910*. Vienna, 1972.
Hauch, Gabriella. *Frau Biedermeier auf den Barrikaden. Frauen Leben in der Wiener Revolution 1848*. Vienna, 1990.
Häusler, Wolfgang."'Noch sind nicht alle Märzen vorbei . . . ' Zur politischen Tradition der Wiener Revolution von 1848." In *Politik und Gesellschaft im alten Österreich*. Edited by Isabella Ackerl, Walter Hummelberger, and Hans Mommsen. Vol. I. Vienna, 1981.
———. *Von der Massenarmut zur Arbeiterbewegung; Demokratie und soziale Frage in der Wiener Revolution von 1848*. Vienna, 1979.
Heindl, Waltraud. *Gehorsame Rebellen. Bürokratie und Beamte in Österreich 1780 bis 1848*. Vienna, 1990.
Höbelt, Lothar. "Ausgleich und Ausstellung, Politik und Wirtschaft in Böhmen um 1890." *Bohemia. Zeitschrift für die Geschichte und Kultur der böhmischen Länder* 29 (1988).
———. "The Great Landowners Curia and the Reichsrat Elections during the Formative Years of Austrian Constitutionalism 1867–1873." *Parliaments, Estates and Representation* 5 (1985).
———. "Iustitia und der Paragraph 19." *Bohemia. Zeitschrift für die Geschichte und Kultur der böhmischen Länder* 28 (1987).
———. *Kornblume und Kaiseradler. Die deutschfreiheitlichen Parteien Altösterreichs 1882–1918*. Vienna, 1993.

———. "Die Linke und die Wahlen von 1891." MÖSA 40 (1987).

Höbelt, Lothar, ed. *Der Vater der Verfassung. Aus den Denkwürdigkeiten Anton Ritters von Schmerling*. Vienna, 1993.

Hooks, bell. *Black Looks: Race and Representation*. Boston, 1992.

Hubbard, William H. *Auf dem Weg zur Grossstadt. Eine Sozialgeschichte der Stadt Graz 1850–1914*. Munich, 1984.

———. "Politics and Society in the Central European City, Graz, Austria, 1861–1918." *Canadian Journal of History* 5 (1970).

Hugelmann, Karl. *Die österreichischen Landtage im Jahre 1848*. Vienna, 1928.

———. *Das Nationalitätenrecht des alten Altösterreich*. Vienna and Leipzig, 1934.

Jarausch, Konrad and Larry Eugene Jones, ed. *In Search of a Liberal Germany*. New York, 1990.

Jászi, Oscar. *The Dissolution of the Habsburg Monarchy*. 3rd edition Chicago, 1964.

Jenks, William. *Austria under the Iron Ring, 1879–1893*. Charlottesville, VA., 1965.

Johnston, William. *The Austrian Mind: An Intellectual and Social History, 1848–1938*. Berkeley and Los Angeles, 1972.

Judson, Pieter M. "Die unpolitische Bürgerin im politisierenden Verein. Zu einigen Paradoxa des bürgerlichen Weltbildes im19. Jahrhundert" In "*Durch Arbeit, Besitz, Wissen und Gerechtigkeit," Bürgertum in der Habsburgermonarchie II*. Edited by Hannes Stekl et al. Vienna, 1992.

———. "Deutschnationale Politik und Geschlecht in Österreich 1880–1900." *In Frauen in Österreich*. Edited by David F. Good, Margarete Grandner, and Mary Jo Maynes. Vienna, 1994.

———. "Frontiers, Islands, Forests, Stones: Mapping the Geography of a German Identity in the Habsburg Monarchy, 1848–1900." In *The Geography of Identity*. Edited by Patricia Yeager. Ann Arbor, 1996.

———. "Inventing Germans: Class, Nationality and Colonial Fantasy at the Margins of the Hapsburg Monarchy." In *Nations, Colonies and Metropoles*. Edited by Daniel A. Segal and Richard Handler. *Social Analysis* 33 (1993).

———. "Whether Race or Conviction Should Be the Standard": National Identity and Liberal Politics in Nineteenth-Century Austria" *Austrian History Yearbook* 22 (1991).

———. " 'Not Another Square Foot!' German Liberalism and the Rhetoric of National Ownership in Nineteenth-Century Austria." *Austrian History Yearbook* 26 (1995).

Kammerhofer, Leopold, ed. *Studien zum Deutschliberalismus in Zisleithanien 1873–1879*. Vienna, 1992.

Kann, Robert. *The Multinational Empire*. 2 vols. New York, 1950.

Kaplan, Marion. *The Making of the Jewish Middle Class: Women, Family and Identity in Imperial Germany*. New York, 1991.

Kennedy, Hubert. *Ulrichs: The Life and Times of Karl Heinrich Ulrichs, Pioneer of the Modern Gay Movement*. Boston, 1988.

Klabouch, Jiri. *Die Gemeindeselbstverwaltung in Österreich, 1848–1918*. Vienna, 1968.

Klemperer, Klemens von. *Ignaz Seipel*. Princeton, 1972.

Kocka, Jürgen. *Bürgertum im 19. Jahrhundert*. 3 vols. Munich, 1988.

——— and Allan Mitchell, ed. *Bourgeois Society in Nineteenth-Century Europe*. Oxford, 1993.

Kolmer, Gustav. *Parlament und Verfassung in Österreich*. 5 vols. Vienna and Leipzig, 1902–5.

Komlos, John, ed. *Economic Development in the Habsburg Monarchy in the Nineteenth Century*. Boulder, 1983.

König, Bruno. "Von der Nationalgarde 1848–1851." *Zeitschrift für die Geschichte und Kulturgeschichte österreichisch-Schlesiens*. Troppau, 1906.

Kořalka, Jiří. *Tschechen im Habsburgerreich und im Europa 1815–1914*. Munich, 1991.

Koshar, Rudy. *Social Life, Local Politics, and Nazism, Marburg, 1880–1935*. Chapel Hill and London, 1986.

Kren, Jan. "Die böhmischen Länder in der Krise 1870/71." *Bohemia. Zeitschrift für die Geschichte und Kultur der böhmischen Länder* 28 (1987).

Krieger, Leonard. *The German Idea of Freedom*. Chicago, 1972.

Kuess-Scheichelbauer. *200 Jahre Freimauerei in Österreich*. Vienna, 1959

Kuhnigk, Armin. *Die 1848er Revolution in der Provinz. Am Beispiel des Kreises Limburg-Weilburg*. Camberg, 1980.

Lammich, Maria. *Das deutsche Osteuropabild in der Zeit der Reichsgründung*. Boppard am Rhein, 1976.

Langewiesche, Dieter, ed. *Liberalismus im 19. Jahrhundert. Deutschland im europäischen Vergleich*. Göttingen, 1988.

Lebovics, Herman. *True France: The Wars Over Cultural Identity, 1900–1945*. Ithaca NY, 1992.

———. *The Alliance of Iron and Wheat: Origins of the New Conservatism of the Third Republic,1860–1914*. Baton Rouge, 1988.

———. *Social Conservatism and the Middle Classes in Germany, 1914–1933*. Princeton, 1969.

Locke, John. *Two Treatises of Government*. New York, 1965.

Macartney, C. A. *The Habsburg Empire, 1790–1918*. London, 1969.

Macpherson, C. B. *The Political Theory of Possessive Individualism: Hobbes to Locke*. Oxford, 1985

März, Eduard. *Österreichische Industrie- und Bankpolitik in der Zeit Kaiser Franz Josephs I. am Beispiel der k.k. priviligierten österreichischen Credit-Anstalt für Handel und Gewerbe*. Vienna, 1968.

Maier, Charles. *Recasting Bourgeois Europe: Stabilization in France, Germany and Italy in the Decade after World War I*. Princeton, 1975.

Matis, Herbert. *Österreichs Wirtschaft 1848–1913. Konjunkturelle Dynamik und gesellschaftlicher Wandel im Zeitalter FranzJosefs I*. Berlin, 1972.

———. "Sozioökonomische Aspekte des Liberalismus in Österreich 1848–1918." In *Sozialgeschichte heute. Festschrift für Hans Rosenberg zum 70. Geburtstag*. Edited by Hans-Ulrich Wehler. Göttingen, 1974.

——— and Herbert Bachinger, "Österreichs industrielle Entwicklung," in *Die Habsburgermonarchie 1848–1918*. Vol. 1, *Die wirtschaftliche Entwicklung*. Ed. Adam Wandruszka and Peter Urbanitsch. Vienna, 1973.

Mayer, Arno. *The Persistence of the Old Regime: Europe to the Great War*. New York, 1981.

McGrath, William. *Dionysian Art and Populist Politics in Austria*. New Haven and London, 1974.

Mechtler, Paul. "Sozialgeschichtliche Notizen über die österreichischen Minister von 1848 bis 1920." *Politik und Gesellschaft im alten Österreich* 1 (1981).
Mill, John Stuart. *On Liberty*. New York, 1973.
Moeller, Robert G. "The Kaiserreich Recast?" *Journal of Social History* (1984).
Molisch, Paul. *Geschichte der deutschnationalen Bewegung in Österreich*. Jena, 1926.
———. *Die deutschen Hochschulen in Österreich*. Munich, 1922.
———. *Politische Geschichte der deutschen Hochschulen in Österreich von 1848 bis 1918*. Vienna, 1939.
———. "Anton von Schmerling und der Liberalismus in Österreich." *Archiv für österreichische Geschichte* 116 (1943).
Mommsen, Wolfgang. "Der deutschen Liberalismus zwischen 'Klassenloser Bürgergesellschaft' und 'organisiertem Kapitalismus.' Zu einigen neueren Liberalismusinterpretationen." *Geschichte und Gesellschaft* 4 (1978).
Moore, Barrington. *The Social Origins of Dictatorship and Democracy*. London, 1967.
Nipperdey, Thomas. *Deutsche Geschichte, 1800–1866: Bürgerwelt und starker Staat*. Munich, 1983.
———, ed. *Gesellschaft, Kultur, Theorie. Gesammelte Aufsätze zur neueren Geschichte*. Göttingen, 1976.
Nödl, Carl, ed. *Das unromantische Biedermeier, eine Chronik in Zeitdokumenten, 1795–1857*. Vienna, 1987.
Noltenius, Rainer. *Dichterfeier in Deutschland. Rezeptionsgeschichte als Sozialgeschichte am Beispiel der Schiller—und Freiligrath—Feiern*. Munich, 1984.
Nord, Philip G. *Paris Shopkeepers and the Politics of Resentment*. Princeton, 1986.
Obermann, Karl. "Die österreichischen Reichstagswahlen 1848. Eine Studie zur Fragen des sozialen Struktur und der Wahlbeteiligung auf der Grundlage der Wahlakten." MÖSA 26 (1973).
Pech, Stanley. *The Czech Revolution of 1848*. Chapel Hill, 1969.
Pichl, Eduard. *Georg Schönerer*. 6 volumes. Oldenburg i. O., 1938.
Pirchegger, Hans. *Geschichte der Steiermark 1740–1919*. Graz, Vienna, Leipzig, 1934.
Pock, Friedrich. *Grenzwacht im Südosten. Ein halbes Jahrhundert Südmarck*. Graz and Leipzig, 1940.
Polišenský, Josef. *Aristocrats and the Crowd in the Revolutionary Year 1848, a Contribution to the History of Revolution and Counterrevolution in Austria*. Translated from the Czech by Frederick Snider. Albany, 1980.
Pulzer, Peter. *The Rise of Political Anti-Semitism in Germany and Austria*. New York, 1988.
Rath, R. John. *The Viennese Revolution of 1848*. Austin, 1958.
Redlich, Josef. "Lasser und Schmerling nach ihren Briefen." *Österreichische Rundschau* 19 (1909).
———. *Das österreichische Staats- und Reichsproblem*. 2 vols. Leipzig, 1920–26.
———. *Das Wesen der österreichischen Kommunalverfassung*. Leipzig, 1910.
Reinalter, Helmut ed., *Jakobiner in Mitteleuropa*. Innsbruck, 1977.
———. "Der Nationsbegriff der österreichischen Jakobiner." MIÖG 91 (1983).
Retallack, James N. *Notables of the Right: The Conservative Party and Political Mobilization in Germany 1876–1918*. Boston, 1988.

Ritter, Harry. "Austro-German Liberalism and the Modern Liberal Tradition." *German Studies Review* 7 (1984).

———. "Austria and the Struggle for German Identity." *German Studies Review* 15 (1992).

———. "Autobiography as *Zeitgeschichte*: The Memoirs of Ernst von Plener (1841–1923)." Unpublished manuscript, 1987.

Rosenberg, Hans. *Grosse Depression und Bismarckzeit. Wirtschaftsablauf, Gesellschaft und Politik*. Berlin, 1967.

Rossbacher, Karlheinz. *Literatur und Liberalismus*. Vienna, 1992.

Rostow, Walter. *The Stages of Economic Growth*. Cambridge, MA, 1965.

Rozenblit, Marsha. *The Jews of Vienna, 1867–1914: Assimilation and Identity*. Albany, 1983.

Rudolph, Richard. "The Pattern of Austrian Industrial Growth from the Eighteenth to the Early Twentieth Century." *Austrian History Yearbook* 11 (1975).

Rudolf, Wolfgang. "Karl Fürst Auersperg als Ministerpräsident 1868." MIÖG 85 (1977).

Rumpler, Helmut. "Der Kampf um die Kontrolle der österreichischen Staatsfinanzen 1859/60. Ein Beitrag zur Geschichte des parlamentarischen Budgetrechtes." In *Gesellschaft, Parlament und Regierung. Zur Geschichte des Parlamentarismus in Deutschland*. Edited by Gerhard A. Ritter. Düsseldorf, 1974.

———, ed. *Die Protokolle des oesterreichischen Ministerrates*. Vol. I. Vienna, 1970.

——— and Arnold Suppan, eds. *Geschichte der Deutschen im Bereich des heutigen Slowenien 1848–1941*. Vienna, 1988.

Schorske, Carl. *Fin de siècle Vienna: Politics and Culture*. New York, 1980.

Schütz, Friedrich. *Werden und Wirken des Bürgerministeriums*. Leipzig, 1909.

Segal, Daniel A. "'The European.' Allegories of Racial Purity." *Anthropology Today* 7 (1991).

———. "Nationalism: Comparatively Speaking." *Journal of Historical Sociology* 1 (1988).

——— and Richard Handler. "How European is Nationalism?" *Social Analysis* 32 (1992).

——— and Richard Handler. "U.S. Multiculturalism and the Concept of Culture." *Identities* 1 (1995).

Seibt, Ferdinand, ed. *Die Chance der Verständigung. Ansichten und Absätze zu übernationaler Zusammenarbeit in den böhmischen Ländern 1848–1918*. Munich, 1987.

———, ed. *Vereinswesen und Geschichtspflege in den böhmischen Ländern. Vorträge der Tagungen des Collegiums Carolinum in Bad Wiessee vom 25. bis 27. November, 1983, und vom 23. bis 25. November 1984*. Munich, 1986.

Seliger, Maren and Karl Ucakar. *Wahlrecht und Wahlverhalten in Wien 1848–1932*. Vienna, 1984.

Sheehan, James. *German History 1770–1866*. Oxford, 1989.

———. *German Liberalism in the Nineteenth Century*. Chicago, 1978.

———. "Liberalism in the City in Nineteenth-century Germany." *Past and Present* 51 (1971).

———. "Liberalism and Society in Germany, 1815–1848." JMH 45 (1973).

Sieber, Ernst K. *Ludwig von Löhner: Ein Vorkämpfer des Deutschtums in Böhmen, Mähren und Schlesien im Jahre 1848/1849.* Munich, 1965.

Slapnicka, Harry. "Oberösterreich. Die politische Führungsschicht 1861 bis 1918." *Beiträge zur Zeitgeschichte Oberösterreichs* 9 (1983).

Somogyi, Eva. *Vom Zentralismus zum Dualismus. Der Weg der deutschösterreichischen Liberalen zum Ausgleich von 1867.* Wiesbaden, 1983.

———. "Die Reichsauffassung der deutschösterreichischen Liberalen in den siebziger Jahren des 19. Jahrhunderts" *Gesellschaft, Politik und Verwaltung in der Habsburgermonarchie 1830–1918.* ed., Ferenc Latz and Ralph Melville. Budapest, 1987.

Sperber, Jonathan. "Festivals of National Unity in the German Revolution of 1848–1849" *Past and Present* 136 (1992).

———. *Rhineland Radicals: The Democratic Movement and the Revolution of 1848–1849.* Princeton, 1991.

Srbik, Heinrich Ritter von. *Deutsche Einheit.* 4 vols. Munich, 1935–42.

———. *Quellen zur deutschen Politik Österreichs 1859–66.* 5 vols. Berlin and Leipzig, 1934–38.

Steinberg, Michael. *The Meaning of the Salzburg Festival.* Ithaca, 1990.

Stekl, Hannes, Peter Urbanitsch, Ernst Bruckmüller, and Hans Heiss, eds. *"Durch Arbeit, Besitz, Wissen und Gerechtigkeit," Bürgertum in der Habsburgermonarchie II.* Vienna, 1992.

Stoler, Ann. "Rethinking Colonial Categories, European Communities and the Boundaries of Rule." *Comparative Studies in Society and History* 31 (1989).

Stourzh, Gerald. "Die österreichische Dezemberverfassung von 1867." *Österreich in Geschichte und Literatur* 12 (1968).

———. *Die Gleichberechtigung der Nationalitäten in der Verfassung und Verwaltung Österreichs 1848–1918.* Vienna, 1985.

———. "Galten die Juden als Nationalität Altösterreichs?" *Studia Judaica Austriaca* 10 (1984).

Strakosch-Grassmann, Gustav. *Geschichte des österreichischen Unterrichtswesen.* Vienna, 1905.

Sutter, Berthold. *Die Badenischen Sprachenverordnungen.* 2 vols. Vienna, 1960, 1965.

Talos, Emmerich and Wolfgang Neugebauer, ed. *"Austrofaschismus." Beiträge über Politik, Ökonomie und Kultur 1934–38.* Vienna, 1984

Taylor, A. J. P. *The Course of German History: A Survey of the Development of German History since 1815.* New York, 1946.

Tenfelde, Klaus. "Adventus. Zur historischen Ikonologie des Festzugs." *Historische Zeitschrift* 235 (1982).

Till, Rudolf. "Die Mitglieder der ersten Wiener Gemeinde-Vertretung im Jahre 1848." *Wiener Geschichtsblätter* 5 (1950).

Ucakar, Karl. *Demokratie und Wahlrecht in Österreich.* Vienna, 1985.

Verdery, Katherine. *Transylvanian Villagers: Three Centuries of Political, Economic and Ethnic Change.* Berkeley, 1983.

Vocelka, Karl. *Verfassung oder Konkordat? Der publizistische und politische Kampf der österreichischen Liberalen um die Religionsgesetze des Jahres 1868.* Vienna, 1978.

Wadl, Wilhelm. "Die demokratischen Bewegung in Kärnten im Jahre1848." *Österreich in Geschichte und Literatur* 28 (1984).

———. *Liberalismus und soziale Frage in Österreich. Deutschliberale Reaktionen und Einflüsse auf die frühe österreichische Arbeiterbewegung 1867–1879.* Vienna, 1987.

Wahrman, Dror. *Imagining the Middle Class: The Political Representation of Class in Britain, c. 1780–1840.* Cambridge, 1995.

Walker, Mack. *German Home Towns. Community, State and General Estate, 1648–1871.* Ithaca, NY, 1971.

Wandruszka, Adam. *Geschichte einer Zeitung. Das Schiksal der "Presse" und der "Neuen Freien Presse" von 1848 zur zweiten Republik.* Vienna, 1958.

Wandruszka, Adam and Peter Urbanitsch, ed. *Die Habsburgermonarchie 1848–1918.* Vols. 1-3. Vienna, 1973–80.

Wank, Solomon. "Some Reflections on Aristocrats and Nationalism in Bohemia, 1861–1899." *Canadian Review of Studies in Nationalism* 20 (1993).

Weiland, Daniela, ed. *Geschichte der Frauenemanzipation in Deutschland und Österreich.* Düsseldorf, 1983.

Weinzierl-Fischer, Erika. *Die österreichische Konkordate von 1855 und 1933.* Vienna, 1960.

Weitensfelder, Hubert. *Interessen und Konflikte in der Frühindustrialisierung: Dornbirn als Beispiel.* Frankfurt/M, 1991.

White, Dan. *The Splintered Party: National Liberalism in Hessen and the Reich.* Cambridge, MA, 1976.

Whiteside, Andrew. *The Socialism of Fools: Georg Ritter von Schönerer and Austrian Pan-Germanism.* Berkeley and Los Angeles, 1975.

Wilflinger, Rainer and Peter Michael Lipburger, eds. *Vom Stadtrecht zur Bürgerbeteiligung. Ausstellungskatalog 700 Jahre Stadtrecht.* Salzburg, 1987.

Wimmer, Kurt. *Liberalismus in Oberösterreich. Am Beispiel des liberal-politischen Vereins für Oberösterreich in Linz 1869-1909.* Linz, 1979.

Winter, Eduard. *Revolution, Neoabsolutismus und Liberalismus in der Donaumonarchie.* Vienna, 1969.

Wiskemann, Elizabeth. *Czechs and Germans.* Oxford, 1967.

Wolf, Mechtild. *Ignaz von Plener. Vom Schicksal eines Ministers unter Kaiser Franz-Joseph.* Munich. 1975.

Zöllner, Erich. *Der Österreichsbegriff. Formen und Wandlungen in der Geschichte.* Vienna, 1988.

Zontar, Jozef, ed. *Handbücher und Karten zur Verwaltungsstruktur bis 1918, Kärnten, Krain, Küstenland, Steiermark.* Graz, Klagenfurt, Ljubliana, Gorizia, Trieste, 1988.

Exhibition Catalogs

*Aufbruch in das Jahrhundert der Frau? Rosa Mayreder und der Feminismus in Wien um 1900.*Vienna, 1990.

Bürgersinn und Aufbegehren. Biedermeier und Vormärz in Wien 1815–1848. Vienna, 1988.

Die Frau im Korsett, Wiener Frauenalltag zwischen Klischee und Wirklichkeit; 1848–1920. Vienna, 1984.

Freiheit, Gleichheit, Brüderlichkeit auch in Österreich? Auswirkungen der französischen Revolution auf Wien und Tirol. Vienna, 1989.

Vom Stadtrecht zur Bürgerbeteiligung. Ausstellungskatalog 700 Jahre Stadtrecht. Edited by Rainer Wilflinger and Peter Michael Lipburger. Salzburg, 1987.

Unpublished Ph.D. Dissertations and, where noted, Habilitationsschriften

Bittner, Georg. "Dr. Gustav Marchet." Ph.D. diss., University of Vienna, 1950.

Bowman, William. "Priests, Parish, and Religious Practice: A Social History of Catholicism in the Archdiocese of Vienna, 1800-1870." Ph.D. diss., Johns Hopkins University, 1989.

Deschka, Brigitte. "Dr. Gustav Gross." Ph.D. diss., University of Vienna, 1966.

Enöckl, Rheinhold. "Der Einfluss der revolutionären Wiener Journalistik auf die Politik des Jahres 1848." Ph.D. diss., University of Vienna, 1967.

Fischer, Freya. "Victor von Krauss 1845–1905." Ph.D. diss., University of Vienna, 1973.

Ghelardoni, Paul. "Die feudalen Elemente in der österreichischen bürgerlichen Gesellschaft von 1803 bis 1914." Ph.D. diss., University of Vienna, 1961.

Gruber, Walter. "Der Politiker Josef Kopp. Ein Beitrag zur Geschichte der Verfassungspartei." Ph.D. diss., University of Vienna, 1949

Haintz, Dieter. "Dr. Carl Giskra, 1820–1879." Ph.D. diss., University of Vienna, 1963.

Hartmeyer, Hans. "Die führenden Abgeordneten des Liberalismus in Österreich." Ph.D. diss., University of Vienna, 1949.

Höbelt, Lothar. "Kornblume und Kaiseradler. Die deutschfreiheitlichen Parteien Altösterreichs 1882–1918." Habilitationsschrift, University of Vienna, 1990.

Hubbard, William. "A Social History of Graz, Austria, 1861–1914." Ph.D. diss., Columbia University, 1973.

Judson, Pieter M. "German Liberalism in Nineteenth-Century Austria: Clubs, Parties, and the Rise of Bourgeois Politics." Ph.D. diss., Columbia University, 1987.

Kammerhofer, Leopold. "Das politische Vereinswesen und der deutsch-österreichische Liberalismus in Zisleithanien von 1867 bis 1879." Ph.D. diss., University of Vienna, 1986.

Klebl, Irmgard. "Fürst Adolf Auersperg (1821–1885); seine politische Karriere und seine Persönlichkeit." Ph.D. diss., University of Vienna, 1971.

Ladinger, Peter. "Die soziale Stellung der Volksschullehrer vor und nach dem Reichsvolksschulgesetz." Ph.D. diss., University of Vienna, 1975.

Loibl, Alfred. "Die Stellung der Konstitutionellen Vorstadt-Zeitung zur sozialen Frage, 1855–1878." Ph.D. diss., University of Vienna, 1950.

Lukas, Herbert. "Der Welser Stadtsekretär August Göllerich (1819–1883). Ein oberösterreichischer Liberaler." Ph.D. diss., University of Salzburg, 1981.

Maier, Helga. "Börsenkrach und Weltausstellung in Wien. Ein Beitrag zur Geschichte der bürgerlichen-liberalen Gesellschaft um das Jahr 1873." Ph.D. diss., University of Graz, 1973.

Martinek, Jutta. "Materialien zur Wahlrechtsgeschichte der Grossgrundbesitzerkurie in den österreichischen Landtagen seit 1861." Ph.D. diss., University of Vienna, 1977.

Müllner, Karl. "Freiherr Josef Lasser von Zollheim, eine Biographie." Ph.D. diss., University of Vienna, 1962.

Obrovski, H. "Die Entwicklung des Vereinswesens im Vormärz." Ph.D. diss., University of Vienna, 1970.

Ortner, Heidemarie. "Das Eindringen des wiener Bürgertums in den landtäflichen Grundbesitz Niederösterreichs, 1815–1895. Ph.D. diss., University of Vienna, 1968.

Pfeisinger, Gerhard. "Die Revolution von 1848 in Graz." Ph.D. diss., University of Salzburg, 1985.

Prammer, Johann. "Konservative und christlichsoziale Politik im Viertel ob dem Wienerwald." Ph.D. diss., University of Vienna, 1973.

Rudolf, Wolfgang. "Fürst Karl Auersperg 1814–1890. Ein liberaler österreichischer Staatsman und Politiker." Ph.D. diss., University of Vienna, 1974.

Sandler, Samuel. "Das Bürgerministerium, 1867–1870." Ph.D. diss., University of Vienna, 1930.

Ucakar, Karl. "Demokratie und Wahlrecht in Österreich. Zur Entwicklung von politischer Partizipation und staatliche Legitimationspolitik." Habilitationsschrift, University of Vienna, 1984.

Unterberger, Erhard. "Der Liberalismus in St. Pölten (1870–1918)." Ph.D. diss., University of Vienna, 1966.

Wadl, Wilhelm, "Liberalismus und soziale Frage in Österreich." Ph.D. diss., University of Vienna, 1978.

Wymetal, Elizabeth. "Eduard Herbst, sein Werdegang und seine Persönlichkeit vornehmlich auf Grund seiner selbstbiographischen Aufzeichnungen." Ph.D. diss., University of Vienna, 1944.

Zailler, Erich. "Heinrich Friedjung; unter besonderer Berücksichtigung seiner politischen Entwicklung." Ph.D. diss., Univeristy of Vienna, 1949.

Index